Escaping Bondage

Escaping Bondage

*A Documentary History of Runaway Slaves
in Eighteenth-Century New England, 1700–1789*

Antonio T. Bly

LEXINGTON BOOKS
Lanham • Boulder • New York • Toronto • Plymouth, UK

Published by Lexington Books
A wholly owned subsidary of The Rowman & Littlefield Publishing Group, Inc.
4501 Forbes Boulevard, Suite 200, Lanham, Maryland 20706
www.rowman.com

10 Thornbury Road, Plymouth PL6 7PP, United Kingdom

British Library Cataloguing in Publication Information Available

Library of Congress Cataloging-in-Publication Data

Escaping bondage : a documentary history of runaway slaves in eighteenth-century New England,
1700–1789 / [edited by] Antonio T. Bly.
  p. cm.
Includes index.
ISBN 978-0-7391-7032-8 (cloth : alk. paper) — ISBN 978-0-7391-7033-5 (pbk. : alk. paper) —
ISBN 978-0-7391-7034-2 (electronic)
1. Fugitive slaves—New England—History—18th century—Sources. 2. Slavery—New England—
History—18th century—Sources. I. Bly, Antonio T.
 E445.N5E74 2012
 306.3'62097409033—dc23
 2012018315

Printed in the United States of America

For my parents and for my ancestors.

Contents

List of Images

Acknowledgments

I would like to extend my appreciation to the many individuals who encouraged and assisted me throughout the course of this work.

First, I am indebted to Drs. Robert A. Gross, Rhys Isaac, Grey Gundaker, and James P. Whittenburg who motivated me, sometimes in very subtle and not so subtle ways, in the development of this project that originated out of my doctoral thesis at the College of William and Mary.

I am also indebted to Jamie Hagar and Robert Rennie whose help with transcribing the notices proved invaluable. Reading the short hand notes I compiled during the year I spent in the Library of Congress could not have been easy. Sometimes I did not understand my own handwriting. For painstakingly proof-reading each notice, I owe another enormous debt to Tamia Haygood. I thank you all for your assistance and also offer you my heartfelt apology.

I owe a debt of gratitude to Terri Lockwood as well. Without your help, particularly in helping me secure the needed funds for this project, this book would probably remain on my list of things to do. I thank you, the Office of the Vice Provost for Faculty Affairs, and the Faculty Fellows Program at Appalachian State University for your support.

Finally, to my wife, to whom I can only express my deepest thanks for sharing not only this work, in its various stages, but also my life.

Introduction: "When He Went Away"

*Reading Runaway Slave Notices
as History and Biography*

Without question, runaway slave advertisements are a staple of African American Studies. Because few slaves left any written records behind, scholars from varying disciplines have mined advertisements for fugitives to discern various aspects of slave behavior and culture. Indeed, given the sparse nature of most eighteenth and nineteenth-century slave sources, one historian, David Waldstreicher, recently interpreted the advertisements for absconded slaves as a type of proto-slave narrative.[1] Long before Olaudah Equiano, Frederick Douglass, and Harriet Jacobs published their life stories, the short vignettes hidden in the advertisements revealed the tales of courageous slaves who dreamt of freedom and ran away to realize those very dreams. Long before the celebrated slave-poets Phillis Wheatley and Jupiter Hammon penned their first lines in the eighteenth century, slave notices filled newspapers, inscribing in print the efforts of numerous African Americans and their struggle to live life on their own terms.

For almost a century, advertisements for fugitive slaves have provided scholars a rich source about black life in the past. For Gerald W. Mullin and Lathan A. Windley, they demonstrated that African Americans were far from being the happy and dutiful servants U. B. Philips portrayed in his *American Negro Slavery*.[2] Just the opposite. In 1774, Virginia runaway Isaac Bee, "a likely Mulatto Lad . . . [and] formerly the Property of the late President Blair" of the College of William and Mary, left his master because "his Father was a Freeman" and "he thinks he has a Right to his Freedom." In that distinction, Bee was not alone. Quite the contrary, he had been one out of many. Eight years earlier in the tobacco colony, for example, "SAM HOW-

1

EL, 23 years old, about 5 feet 9 inches high, well made for strength, [and] has a remarkable good set of teeth," left his "Cumberland county" owner, "WADE NETHERLAND." Like Bee, he too was a mulatto. His mother was a white indentured servant, his father a free black. Like Bee, Howell also believed that the circumstances of his birth entitled him his freedom. "His pretence for going away," Netherland explained to the public at large, "was to apply to some lawyer at Williamsburg to try to get his freedom."[3]

(Incidentally, Howell did have his day in court. In April of 1770, a young lawyer by the name of Thomas Jefferson argued on the mulatto's behalf. [See Appendix for a copy of Jefferson's argument] But despite Jefferson's best efforts, the die had been cast and not in the slave's favor. As a matter of colonial custom and law, racially mixed Virginians, particularly those born of "Negro" fathers, slave or free, were bound to an artisan until they reached the unlikely age of thirty-one. Howell, however, disagreed with the court's decision. Like a number of other enslaved Virginians of mixed racial stock, he refused to wait for his freedom. Three months after he had his day before the esteemed panel of adjudicators, he ran away again. But on that occasion, he did not go alone. With only the clothes on his back, the "sensible fellow and a good sawyer," left with his brother, Simon, "about 25 years of age, 5 feet 8 or 9 inches high, has a thin visage, and sharp chin."[4])

Of course, slaves' discontent did not end there. In 1775, after part, if not all, of Mann Page's estate in "*King William* county" had been sold, Ned, "a negro man. . . about 19 or 20 years of age," disappeared. Presumably, he left to return to "those parts, or to his mother, who lives with mr. *Thomas Booth*, in *Richmond* town." A "Negro man named TEMPLE" absconded for similar reasons. In 1766, he "took a gun with him" and set off for "Bull Run, in Fauquier county, where he formerly lived." Like Ned, Temple's flight was one of reunion as well. According to his owner's notice, he was purchased recently "with his mother and sister" from one Mr. Barradall of Williamsburg.[5]

Other historians have used runaway advertisements to document something more than just acts of the enslaved taking matters into their own hands. During the American Revolution, several notices demonstrated that slaves were quite aware of the political times in which they lived. Some in fact adopted the revolutionary rhetoric of the day. In both their studies of African Americans in the era of the American Revolution, Benjamin Quarles and Sylvia Frey observed that slaves who were inspired by the revolutionary spirit of the Declaration of Independence claimed their own freedom and ran away to realize their natural rights. Indeed, property they had already possessed in themselves. Life and liberty they had been denied. That is apparently what "4 negro men," three identified as being "Virginia born," had in mind when they ran and joined "Dunmore's service" in 1776. That was also what "Charles," a "negro man" of Stafford County, intended when he decided to disappear. Just one day after Dunmore issued his inflammatory Proclamation, Charles "who is a very shrewd [and] sensible fellow" fled to the British side. As his owner claimed, Charles had no "cause of complaint, or dread of whipping for he has always been remarkably indulged." Still, despite that favorable treatment, or perhaps because of it, the slave ran. In Purdie's *Virginia Gazette*, Robert Brent lamented the loss of the prized bondservant who once "waited upon" him. Unwittingly, he might have also betrayed something of his true relationship with Charles when he observed that his "design of going off was long premeditated."[6]

Simply put, Charles did not need the burgeoning crisis between Great Britain and her North American subjects to take matters into his own hands. Far from it, he had a crisis of his very own to deal with and perhaps long before colonials complained of taxes and tea. As he waited upon his master and his guests, one can only image what he made of their discussions of the fast changing times. In private he balked at their declarations for freedom and independence. Inwardly he might have thought their protest humorous. On occasion, he may have even mocked them in their cries that they were in fact slaves. That is to say, in secret, among Brent's other house servants, Charles might have assumed the center within that sable party as he mimicked for their entertainment his master and those he had observed. By November of 1775, he had clearly had more than his fair share of his master's kind graces. Judging himself free man, he left and on his own volition.[7]

One historian has suggested that runaways were central actors in the larger movement towards Revolution. Many were patriots in their own right. Like the Sons of Liberty, they too answered freedom's call. In *Forced Founders*, Woody Holton noted the role slaves, Native Americans, and "middling sort" whites played in forcing the founding fathers to choose independence. By his account, these sable sons of the Virginia colony seized the moment and prompted not only a Royal Governor to declare "all able bodied Negroes" free but also forced an otherwise reluctant lot of tobacco planters and Burgesses into declaring independence from Great Britain. Increasingly, as another study of Virginia runaways reveals, slaves there protested with their feet, instilling (albeit unwittingly) within their masters a renewed spirit for liberty.[8]

Runaway slave advertisements also reveal other insights. Both Luther P. Jackson and W. Jeffrey Bolster used them to portray a thriving maritime culture in which black slaves worked as sailors and pilots before and during the American Revolution. A notice for a "Negro Boy" named Pompey offers one example in that regard. Months before the Sons of Liberty, disguised as Native Americans, boarded East India tea company ships in the Boston harbor, broke open the cargo, and tossed the tea into the sea, Pompey, who was "about eighteen Years old [and] five Feet three Inches high," worked as a seaman along the James River in Virginia. According to the notice, the young lad had been "bred to the Sea." Not surprisingly, when Pompey decided to make his bold gesture of defiance, John Goodrich, Jr. informed the readers of Purdie & Dixon's *Virginia Gazette* that the said slave "may endeavour to get on Board a Ship, and make his Escape out of the Colony."[9]

Similarly, in their recent studies of early African American culture, Michael A. Gomez and Shane White and Graham White drew on runaway advertisements to show how the memory of African homelands informed slave hair styles, ideas about clothing, gestures, and body language. Eighteenth-century slaves, they explained, used dyes to achieve an African sense of fashion with respect to choices of colors for clothing. When "Dick," for instance, a "Shoemaker by Trade" who belonged to James Walker ran away in 1772, he carried with him "a Negro cotton short coat double breasted, dyed purple breeches of the same, a red frize waistcoat." By examining absconded slaves' fashion choices, White and White showed how enslaved American Americans expressed an African-oriented sense of style. Such was the case of another Virginia runaway named "JACOB," who left his owner, Isaac Younghusband, in 1774. As Younghusband told it, the slave carried with him "a cotton jacket, dyed with maple bark and copperas, a brown cloth coat, a pair of buckskin breeches, a big coat, of an ash colour, yarn stockings, country shoes."[10] Through dyes, slaves like Jacob and Dick not only resisted their master's efforts to demean them by making them wear inferior "Negro" clothing but also expressed their own "polyrhythmic" African style with respect to apparel. Put another way, jazz, that is the ability to spontaneously create something out of nothing, borrowing from everything from without and within, survived the horrific Middle Passage.[11] Absconded slaves' clothes affords us but one of many examples of their cultural dynamism.

For Herbert G. Gutman and Philip D. Morgan, runaway notices registered a record of an enduring black family. As many of the advertisements themselves show, slaves often ran away to be with loved ones. Others ran to protect their families. That was certainly true of Roger, a Negro man, "born of Angola," and his "18 years old, Virginia born," wife Moll. In 1739, the two ran away together. According to the account given in the newspaper, Moll had been "very big with Child." Perhaps the fear of sale encouraged the couple to take flight.[12]

More recently, in a study of slave consumption in the eighteenth-century, another historian observed that runaways participated in a consumer revolution that began to crisscross the Anglo-Atlantic world during the latter part of the colonial era. Increasingly, like their owners, slaves realized that clothing communicated status. So as to dress the part of a free man, many runaways took with them additional clothes. In a society where race was not the sole symbol for slavery, clothes did more than just make the man, they told the fashion savvy colonial world that he may in fact own himself.[13] In that manner, Nick left his owner, Benjamin Harrison, in 1770. As Harrison reported, the mulatto man "took with him a pair of leather breeches, a blue surtout coat, and many other good clothes" which he supposed the slave would use "to pass for a freeman." In 1768, William Porter also believed his runaway slave Tom would "change his clothing" in his "endeavour to pass for a freeman."[14]

In her study of patriarchy in early America, Kirsten Denise Sword used runaway notices both for slaves and for wayward wives to illustrate different ways in which slaves and women challenged the authority of their masters and husbands–often one and same person. By their actions, Sword maintained, slaves and wayward wives dissented from the "natural" patriarchal order, forcing otherwise reluctant masters, husbands, and, by extension, the larger male community first to take notice of their slaves and their women folk's discontent and then to reassert their power over those they considered unfree.[15] Though true of most fugitives in a general sense; that was particularly evident in the case of Peter, John Custis' house slave. As the notice for his safe return demonstrates, the "Virginia born" man was an unruly domestic. Outlawed by the locals of Williamsburg, Peter appears to have run away several times. On one occasion after he had been returned, the thirty-year-old was forced to wear chains underneath his garments. As a matter of etiquette, his shackles were disguised in an effort to conceal from polite, genteel eyes the brute facts of power and patriarchy in his master's household.[16]

Whether challenging the boundaries of patriarchy, demonstrating slaves' awareness of the politics of their day, recording aspects of their African past, or documenting efforts to preserve family ties, advertisements for fugitive slaves represent not only an invaluable resource of African American Studies, but also an invaluable resource of American history as well. For as much as they tell us about their subjects, they also reveal just as much about those who paid to have such notices for *their* property printed in colonial newspapers. "Although the slaves advertised as running away," Lathan Windley noted, "constituted a relatively small part of the total slave population, they [nonetheless] . . . represent a cross-section of the different types within these colonies." Peter Wood concurred, observing that notices for absconded slaves represented "little more than the top of an ill-defined iceberg."[17]

And yet, however "ill-defined," even less known is the story of New England fugitives. Indeed, many of those short vignettes, those colonial WPA documents, have been overlooked for Southern ones. If not for fugitives of colonial Virginia or South Carolina, the New England runaway has been overlooked for those who absconded in the expanding Southern section of the new United States. Although overlooked, Massachusetts runaway slaves objected to their plight. Like absconded slaves elsewhere, they too protested with their feet. And as a result, they too left behind an enduring record of black culture and resistance.

Accordingly, the contribution *Escaping Bondage* makes to scholarship is threefold. Highlighting at once runaways in New England and slavery during the colonial era, this collection of slave runaway notices that appeared in eighteenth-century newspapers in Massachusetts, Connecticut, Rhode Island, and New Hampshire between 1700 and 1789 complements similar collections in print, namely, Lathan A. Windley's exhaustive four-volume collection of runaway and captured notices in the Chesapeake (Maryland and Virginia) and the low country (the Carolinas and Georgia), Billy G. Smith and Richard Wojtowicz's *Blacks Who Stole Themselves: Advertisements for Runaways in the Pennsylvania Gazette, 1728–1790*, Graham Russell Hodges and Alan Edward Brown's *"Pretends to Be Free": Runaway Slave Advertisements from Colonial and Revolutionary New York and New Jersey*, and, most recently, John Hope Franklin and Loren Schweninger's *Runaway Slaves: Rebels on the Plantation.*[18]

Secondly, *Escaping Bondage* offers both students and scholars who explore early America an accessible and useful resource to examine different aspects of black and white life in New England during the colonial and revolutionary eras. Indeed, such a reference tool is invaluable for those who would like to delve into the subjects of slave resistance and culture, early African American material life and black agency, as well as the evolution of racial ideologies in eighteenth-century America. Third, *Escaping Bondage* affords scholars and students of history and of British North America a fuller portrait of the black experience during the colonial era. For like runaways in other colonies, Massachusetts slaves objected to their plight. More than that, many registered their displeasure with slavery in multiple ways, ways enshrined in several notices that appeared in print. Judging from New England newspaper advertisements, slave names, body markings, and clothing (among other things) suggest that they fought against their masters in both subtle and not-so subtle ways, succeeding ultimately in keeping for themselves a sense of dignity, humanity, and, in some instances, something of their African past. In that regard, Mingo, a "middle sized negro Man" who ran away from his Massachusetts owner in 1721 offers us one such example. "About 25 Years of Age" and blacksmith "by Trade," Richard Brown considered the bondsman a highly prized member of his household. But besides that fact and of course his mastery of the hammer and anvil, the runaway notice Brown posted for Mingo's safe return reveals that either he or his perhaps parents were successful in their effort to hold fast to their memory of their African homeland. Because Mingo is an African name—much like Sambo, Quash, or Juba. A diminutive of Domingo, Mingo is Spanish and Portuguese for Sunday. An African day name, Mingo reveals not only a West African tradition in which children were named for the day of the week they were born, but also the complex relationship between masters and slaves where the two negotiated daily the terms of power. For Mingo and his parents, slavery was not an absolute institute. Far from it, it was a struggle, where neither party (masters nor their slaves), could claim at any given moment a compete victory. Furthermore, like runaways in the South and in the Northwest, enslaved New Englanders also came from all walks of life. Mingo, for example, was an artisan. Others, however, were not. While some were simple farm hands, many more had mastered one, if not several trades.

Lastly, *Escaping Bondage* challenges the current scholarly emphasis on slavery in the South by demonstrating that there were numerous enslaved African Americans in New England who also resisted their enslavement. Despite the fact that they lived in "societies with slaves," communities in which slavery represented a marginal part of life, slaves in Massachusetts, Connecticut, Rhode Island, and New Hampshire were no less content with their status. Although many were probably better fed, clad and arguably better treated, enslaved African Americans in the Puritan colonies were far from being happy and dutiful subjects. Disproportionately, compared to the number of runaways in the Virginia colony, New England proved to be a hotbed of discord. In other words, while New England had a much smaller slave population compared to its southern counterpart, its newspapers reported almost twice as many runaways between the 1730s and 1750s. Between 1700 and 1789, over 800 runaway slave notices would appear in New England newspapers. This volume reveals their unheralded story—the story of "when [they] went away."

NOTES

*Portions of this introduction have been previously published in "'Pretends he can read': Runaways and Literacy in Colonial America, 1730-1776," *Early American Studies* no. 6, vol. 2 (Fall 2008): 261–94, and in "A Prince among Pretending Free Men: Runaway Slaves in Colonial New England Revisited," *Massachusetts Historical Review* 13(2012), both written by the author.

1. David Waldstreicher, "Reading the Runaways: Self-Fashioning, Print Culture, and Confidence in Slavery in the Eighteenth-Century Mid-Atlantic" *William and Mary Quarterly* 56. 2 (April 1999): 247.

2. U. B. Philips, *American Negro Slavery* (New York: D. Appleton-Century Company, Inc., 1918), 342. For a reaction to Philip's dutiful slave thesis, see Windley, *Profile*, xiii–xix; Mullin, *Flight and Rebellion*, chaps. 3–5. For fuller account, see Lorenzo J. Greene, "The New England Negro as Seen in Advertisement for Runaway Slaves" *Journal of Negro History* 29. 2 (April 1944): 125–146; Daniel E. Meaders, "South Carolina Fugitives as Viewed through Local Colonial Newspapers with Emphasis on Runaway Notices, 1732–1801" *Journal of Negro History* 60 (1975): 288–319; Michael P. Johnson, "Runaway Slaves and the Slave Communities in South Carolina, 1799 to 1830" *William and Mary Quarterly* 3rd Series 38 (1981): 418–441; Billy G. Smith and Richard Wojtowicz, *Blacks Who Stole Themselves* (Philadelphia: University of Pennsylvania Press, 1989).

3. *Virginia Gazette* (Purdie & Dixon), September 8, 1774, 3; Ibid, May 2, 1766, 3.

4.   William W. Hening, ed., *The Statutes at Large Being a Collection of all the Law of Virginia . . .* (Richmond, Virginia: Samuel Pleasants, Jr., 1819–1823), 3: 452–453; *Virginia Gazette* (Purdie & Dixon), August 16, 1770, 3; Paul Leicester Ford, comp. and ed., *The Writing of Thomas Jefferson* (New York: G. P. Putman's Sons, 1892): 1: 373–382.

5.   Virginia (Purdie), May 26, 1775, 4; *Virginia Gazette* (Purdie & Co.), June 6, 1766, 3.

6.   Benjamin Quarles, "Lord Dunmore as Liberator" *William and Mary Quarterly* 3rd Series, 15. 4 (October 1958): 494–507; Quarles, *The Negro in the American Revolution* (Chapel Hill: University of North Carolina Press, 1961), chap. 3, esp. 42–50; Sylvia R. Frey, "Between Slavery and Freedom: Virginia Blacks in the American Revolution" *Journal of Southern History* 49. 3 (August 1983): 375–398; Frey, *Water From the Rock: Black Resistance in a Revolutionary Age* (Princeton: Princeton University Press, 1991), chaps 2 and 5. For quotes concerning the revolutionary slaves from the newspaper see, *Virginia Gazette* (Pinkey), January 6, 1776, 3; *Virginia Gazette* (Purdie), November 17, 1775, 1 Supplement. Incidentally, the four men's names were identified: Harry, Aaron, Lewis, and Matthew.

7.   For a fuller account of how colonial Americans appropriated slavery during the American Revolution, see F. Nwabueze Okoye, "Chattel Slavery as the Nightmare of the American Revolutionaries," *William and Mary Quarterly* 37. 1 (January 1980): 3–28. Also, for an interesting account of how servants mocked their masters, see James Townley's *High Life Below Stairs. A Farce in Two Acts*. This popular play of the era captures various aspects of the master servant/slaves relationship. As it reveals, slaves mocked masters routinely and vice versa.

8.   Dunmore, *Proclamation*, November 7, 1775 [broadside]; Woody Holton, "Rebel Against Rebel: Enslaved Virginians and the Coming of the American Revolution" *Virginia Magazine of History and Biography* 105, no. 3 (Spring 1997): 157–192. For a fuller account of Holton's thesis concerning African Americans and their role in Virginia declaring Independence, see his *Forced Founders*, chap 5; for the other study see Philip D. Morgan and Michael L. Nicholls, "Slave Flight: Mount Vernon, Virginia, and the Wider Atlantic World" in *George Washington's South*, eds. Tamara Harvey and Greg O'Brien (Gainsville: University Press of Florida, 2004), 199–222. Also, for a fuller account about how slavery engendered notions of liberty see Edmund Morgan, "Slavery and Freedom: The American Paradox" *Journal of American History* 59.1 (June 1972): 5–29.

9.   L. P. Jackson, "Virginia Negro Soldiers and Seamen in the American Revolution" *Journal of Negro History* 27.3 (July 1942), pp. 247–287; Bolster, *Black Jacks: African American Seamen in the Age of Sail*; for Pompey's account, see *Virginia Gazette* (Purdie & Dixon), April 8, 1773, 4.

10.   Gomez, *Exchanging Our Country Marks: The Transformation of African Identities in the Colonial and Antebellum South* (Chapel Hill: University of North Carolina Press, 1998); White and White, *Stylin': African American Expressive Culture: from Its Beginnings to the Zoot Suit* (New York: Cornell University Press, 1998), chaps. 1–4; for Dick's account, see *Virginia Gazette* (Rind), March 12, 1772, 4; for Jacob's account, see Ibid., March 17, 1774, 3.

11.   White and White, *Stylin'*, 36.

12.   Gutman, *The Black Family in Slavery and Freedom, 1750–1925* (New York: Vintage Books, 1976), 262–269; Philip D. Morgan, "Colonial South Carolina Runaway: Their Significance for Slave Culture" *Slavery & Abolition* 6.3 (December 1985): 57–78; Morgan, *Slave Counterpoint: Black Culture in the Eighteenth-Century Chesapeake & Lowcountry* (Chapell Hill: University of North Carolina, 1998), 87–90; for Roger and Moll's story, see *Virginia Gazette* (Parks), October 26 to November 2, 1739, 4.

13.   Waldstreicher, "Reading the Runaways," 252–254; 257. Waldstreicher also addresses the subject of slaves and the consumer revolution in his *Runaway America: Benjamin Franklin, Slavery and the American Revolution* (New York: Hill and Wang, 2004), chap 1, esp. 7–8.

14.   *Virginia Gazette* (Purdie & Dixon), October 18,1770, Supplement; Ibid., January 28, 1768.

15.   Kirsten Denise Sword, "Wayward Wives, Runaway Slaves and the Limits of Patriarchal Authority in Early America" (Ph.D. Diss.: Harvard University, 2002), chap. 1.

16. Virginia Gazette (Park), May 9, 1745, 4. For a fuller biography of Peter, see my "'Pretends he can read': Runaways and Literacy in Colonial America, 1730–1776" *Early American Studies* 6.2 (Fall 2008): 261–294; esp. 288–293.

17. Windley, *A Profile of Runaway Slaves in Virginia and South Carolina, 1730–1787* (New York: Garland Publishing, Inc., 1995), xviii; Wood, *Black Majority: Negroes in Colonial South Carolina From 1670 Through the Stone Rebellion* (New York: W.W. Norton & Company, 1974), 240.

18. Smith, Billy G. and Richard Wotowitcz, *Blacks Who Stole Themselves: Advertisement for Runaways in the Pennsylvania Gazette, 1728–1790* (Philadelphia: University of Pennsylvania Press, 1989); Hodges, Graham Russell and Alan Edward Brown, *Pretends to Be Free: Runaway Slave Advertisements from Colonial and Revolutionary New York and New Jersey* (New York: Garland Publishing, Inc., 1994); Franklin, John Hope and Loren Schweninger, *Runaway Slaves: Rebels on the Plantation* (New York: Oxford University Press, 1999).

A Note on the Notices

In most instances I have followed the original wording of the advertisements. The original spelling, punctuation, and capitalization were retained. I have made modest alterations to spacing. Illegible words or text are indicated by bracket, as are letters added for clarity. Reprints and variant copies are noted at the bottom of each advertisement. The glossary defines many contemporary terms in the notices. Notices are printed alphabetically in accordance with the newspaper's name and chronologically. While I have tried to be both thorough and diligent in documenting all of the notices in the New England newspapers examined, I must acknowledge here that there might have been some that went unnoticed.

A Note on the Newspapers

Below is a list of the New England newspapers I examined at the Library of Congress. Included in that list are the variant titles for each newspaper. This list is not a comprehensive one. Instead it reflects those newspapers for which there were copies for at least five years.

MASSACHUSETTS

Boston Evening Post, 1735–1775
  Boston Gazette, 1719–1789

Variant Titles:

- The Boston Gazette (December 21, 1719 to October 19, 1741)
- The Boston Gazette, or New England Weekly Journal (October 20, 1741 to October 20, 1741)
- The Boston Gazette, or Weekly Journal (October 27, 1741 to December 26, 1752)
- The Boston Gazette, or Weekly Advertiser (January 03, 1753 to April 01, 1755)
- The Boston Gazette, or Country Journal (April 07, 1755 to March 29, 1756)
- The Boston-Gazette, or Country Journal (April 05, 1756 to April 05, 1756)
- The Boston-Gazette, and Country Journal (April 12, 1756 to April 17, 1775)

- The Boston-Gazette, and Country Journal (June 05, 1775 to April 05, 1779)
- The Boston Gazette, and the Country Journal (April 12, 1779 to December 30, 1793)

Boston News-Letter, 1704–1776

Variant Titles:

- The Boston News-Letter (April 17, 1704 to December 22, 1726)
- The Weekly News-Letter (January 05, 1727 to October 22, 1730)
- The Boston Weekly News-Letter (October 29, 1730 to August 25, 1757)
- The Boston News-Letter (September 01, 1757 to March 18, 1762)
- The Boston News-Letter, and New-England Chronicle (March 25, 1762 to December 30, 1762)
- The Boston News-Letter, and New-England Chronicle (January 06, 1763 to March 31, 1763)
- The Massachusetts Gazette, and Boston News-Letter (April 07, 1763 to October 31, 1765)
- The Massachusetts Gazette (November 07, 1765 to May 15, 1766)
- The Massachusetts Gazette, and Boston News-Letter (May 22, 1766 to April 21, 1768)
- The Boston Weekly News-Letter (May 28, 1768 to September 21, 1769)
- The Massachusetts Gazette, and the Boston Weekly News-Letter (September 28, 1769 to November 17, 1769)

Boston Post Boy, 1735–1775

Variant Titles:

- The Boston Weekly Post-Boy (April 21, 1735 to June 10, 1750)
- The Boston Post-Boy (June 11, 1750 to December 30, 1754)
- The Boston Weekly Advertiser (August 22, 1757 to December 31, 1758)
- Green & Russell's Boston Post-Boy and Advertiser (January 01, 1759 to May 29, 1763)
- The Boston Post-Boy and Advertiser (May 30, 1763 to October 01, 1769)
- The Massachusetts Gazette, and the Boston Post-Boy and Advertiser (October 02, 1769 to April 25, 1773)
- The Massachusetts Gazette, and the Boston Post-Boy and Advertiser (April 26, 1773 to April 17, 1775)

Continental Journal, 1776–1787

Variant Titles:

- The Continental Journal, and Weekly Advertiser (May 30, 1776 to April 27, 1785)
- The Continental Journal, and Weekly Advertiser (April 28, 1785 to June 21, 1787)

Independent Chronicle, 1776–1789
    Variant Titles:

- The Independent Chronicle (September 19, 1776 to November 06, 1776)
- The Independent Chronicle, and the Universal Advertiser (November 07, 1776 to January 28, 1789)
- Independent Chronicle, and the Universal Advertiser (January 29, 1789 to February 16, 1791)

Independent Ledge, 1778–1786
    Variant Titles:

- The Independent Ledger, and American Advertiser (June 15, 1778 to July 19, 1778)
- The Independent Ledger, and American Advertiser (July 20, 1778 to October 16, 1786)

Massachusetts Spy, 1770–1775

Variant Titles:

- The Massachusetts Spy (July 17, 1770 to October 07, 1772)
- The Massachusetts Spy, or Thomas's Boston Journal (October 08, 1772 to November 02, 1774)
- The Massachusetts Spy, or Thomas's Boston Journal (November 03, 1774 to April 06, 1775)

Massachusetts Spy, 1775–1789

Variant Titles:

- Thomas's Massachusetts Spy, or American Oracle of Liberty (August 16, 1775 to May 31, 1776)
- Haswell's Massachusetts Spy, or American Oracle of Liberty (August 14, 1777 to December 04, 1777)

- Thomas's Massachusetts Spy, or Worcester Gazette (May 24, 1781 to March 30, 1786)
- The Worcester Magazine (April 01, 1786 to April 01, 1788)

New England Chronicle, or Essex Gazette, 1768–1775
 New England Weekly Journal, 1727–1741

Variant Titles:

- The New-England Weekly Journal (March 20, 1727 to August 25, 1735)
- The New England Weekly Journal (August 26, 1735 to October 13, 1741)

CONNECTICUT

Connecticut Courant, 1764–1789

Variant Titles:

- The Connecticut Courant (October 29, 1764 to November 03, 1766)
- The Connecticut Courant, and the Weekly Advertiser (November 10, 1766 to April 04, 1767)
- The Connecticut Courant (April 11, 1767 to May 31, 1774)
- The Connecticut Courant, and Hartford Weekly Intelligencer (June 07, 1774 to February 10, 1778)
- The Connecticut Courant (February 17, 1778 to February 17, 1778)
- The Connecticut Courant, and the Weekly Intelligencer (February 24, 1778 to April 28, 1778)
- The Connecticut Courant (May 05, 1778 to May 12, 1778)
- The Connecticut Courant, and the Weekly Intelligencer (May 19, 1778 to January 02, 1781)
- The Connecticut Courant and Weekly Intelligencer (January 09, 1781 to September 02, 1783)
- The Connecticut Courant, and Weekly Intelligencer (September 09, 1783 to September 09, 1783)

Connecticut Gazette, 1755–1789

Connecticut Journal, 1767–1789
 Variant Titles:

- The Connecticut Journal, and New-Haven Post-Boy (October 23, 1767 to December 25, 1767)

- The Connecticut Journal, and New-Haven Post-Boy (January 01, 1768 to April 10, 1772)
- The Connecticut Journal, and New-Haven Post-Boy (April 17, 1775 to August 23, 1775)
- The Connecticut Journal, and New-Haven Post-Boy (August 30, 1775 to September 06, 1775)
- The Connecticut Journal (September 13, 1775 to December 26, 1792)

RHODE ISLAND

The American Journal and General Advertiser, 1779–1781
    Exeter Journal, 1778–1779
    Freeman's Journal, 1776–1778
    Newport Mercury, 1758–1789

NEW HAMPSHIRE

Variant Titles:

- The Newport Mercury, or the Weekly Advertiser (June 17, 1758 to January 23, 1795)
- The Newport Mercury (March 20, 1759 to October 30, 1775)
- An Occasional Paper (November 06, 1775 to November 06, 1775)
- Freshest Advices (November 13, 1775 to November 27, 1775)
- The Newport Mercury (December 04, 1775 to December 02, 1776)
- The Newport Mercury (January 05, 1780 to December 31, 1799)

New Hampshire Gazette, 1756–1789

Variant Titles:

- The New Hampshire Gazette (October 07, 1756 to March 04, 1763)
- The New-Hampshire Gazette, and Historical Chronicle (March 11, 1763 to January 09, 1776)
- Freeman's Journal, or New-Hampshire Gazette (May 25, 1776 to June 09, 1778)
- New-Hampshire Gazette, or State Journal and General Advertiser (June 16, 1778 to September 03, 1781)
- New-Hampshire Gazette, and General Advertiser (September 08, 1781 to December 17, 1784)

- Fowle's New-Hampshire Gazette, and General Advertiser (December 24, 1784 to June 02, 1787)
- The New-Hampshire Gazette, and General Advertiser (June 09, 1787 to April 09, 1793)

Providence Gazette, 1762–1789

Variant Titles:

- The Providence Gazette, and Country Journal (August 31, 1762 to March 11, 1765)
- Vox Populi, Vox Dei. A Providence Gazette Extraordinary (August 24, 1765 to August 24, 1765)
- Providence Gazette (March 12, 1766 to March 12, 1766)
- The Providence Gazette, and Country Journal (August 09, 1766 to December 28, 1781)
- The Providence Gazette, and Country Journal (January 05, 1782 to December 26, 1789)

United States Chronicle, 1784–1789

Massachusetts Notices 1700–1789

New-England. (PUBLIC LIBRARY)   Numb. 1578

The *Boston* Weekly News-Letter.

From **Thursday** April 25, to **Thursday** May 2. 1734.

On Tuesday last arrived Capt. Shepherdson from Lon-
don, by whom we have the following Advices from
the publick Prints:

L O N D O N, *February* 21, 22, 23. 1 7 3 4.

HIS Majesty has been pleased to appoint Sir
John Norris to be Commander in Chief of
the Fleet that will sail for the Mediterranean
this Spring, who will hoist the Union Flag at the
Main Topmast Head on board the Britannia, a first Rate
of 110 Guns & 1000 Men; to be assisted by Sir George
Walton, who will hoist the Red Flag at the Fore Top;
mast Head on board the Namure, a second Rate of 90
Guns and 700 Men; and Admiral Stewart, who will
hoist his Flag at the Mizen Topmast Head on board
the Torbay, a Third Rate of 80 Guns and 550 Men;
The whole Fleet will consist of 30 Ships of the Line,
two BombKetches, twoFireships, and twoHospitalShips.
Yesterday at Noon, Sir John Norris, Knt. Admiral
of the Blue, waited on their Majesty's at St. James's,
and was most graciously received. At the same Time
he had the honour to kiss their Majesties Hands; on his
being appointed Commander in Chief of his Majesty's
Fleet in the Mediterranean.
The same Day Orders were sent to hoist the Union
Flag on board the Britannia at Chatham.
The Lords of the Admiralty have appointed Capt.
Thomas Whitney, a brave and experienced Officer of
the Navy, who served as first Lieutenant of the Cumberland, a Third Rate of 80 Guns, for many Years in
the Baltick under Sir John Norris, and has since been
promoted to the Command of several of his Majesty's
Ships of War, to be now Captain of the Britannia;
and at the same Time their Lordships appointed six
Lieutenants to the said Ship.
Thursday last his Majesty went with the usual State
to the House of Peers, and gave the Royal Assent to
the Bill for continuing the Duty on Malt, Mum, Mead,
Cyder, Perry, &c. and to four private Bills.
Wednesday the Hon. House of Commons granted 2 s.
in the Pound for the Land-Tax for the Year 1734.
On Saturday last JohnTalbot, Esq; eldest Son to the
Right Hon. the Lord High Chancellor, was married
to Mrs. Sarah Cardonnel, only Child of the late Adam
Cardonnel, Esq; Secretary to the late Duke of Marlborough during all his glorious Successes in Flanders,
a Lady of 70,000 l. Fortune.
The Settlement lately made and agreed to by all
the Commission and Warrant Officers belonging to the
Navy, for the Provision made for their Widows and
Family after their Demise, by the Fund that has been
agreed on, by the Payment of Three-Pence in the Pound
out of each Officers Wages, is now entirely established-
ed, a Clause having been lately added thereto, that
theWidow of noOfficer, either Commission orWarrant,
in hisMajesty'sService, shall be capable of receiving any
Benefit therefrom, whose Husband was seventy Years
before she was married to him; and likewise all such
Widows, as shall think proper to marry again, will
be excluded the Benefit thereof.
In the high Wind on Sunday Morning last, several
Boats were lost in the River, and the Passengers
drowned; a House in Jews-Row Chelsea, was blown
down, whereby a Woman was kill'd, and several other
Persons very much hurt; a great many Trees were
blown up by the Roots, and a Stack of Chimnies be-
longing to his Highness the Duke's Apartment in St.
James's blown down.
The Tallies have been struck at the Exchequer for
the Payment of the 80,000 l. being the Prince's Royal's
Marriage-Portion, as allowed by Act of Parliament.
Our last Letters from Bath inform us, that the
Prince of Orange is so well recovered, that he has
left off the Waters.

Bath, Feb. 18. The Prince of Orange's Rout from
the Bath, by the way of Oxford, &c. is now laid aside
and his Highness will set out on Monday next th
direct Road, and be in London on Thursday,
Paris, February 14.
BEsides the 35 Ships of War and three Frigates that
are fitting out in the several Ports of this Kingdom
'tis said 15 more will be equipped.
Warsaw, Feb. 12. The Russian Troops have taken
the important Fortress of Bialacerkiow, which is the
Key of Polish Ukrania. We have received from Li-
thuania a Confirmation of the Action between the
Russians and Poles, which latter not being supported
by the Troops of M. Pociey, were entirely defeated.
Copenhagen, Feb. 13. Some days ago, an Officer,
a Saxon by Birth, was seized by the King's Order,
and conducted to the Citadel, the Cause of his Con-
finement not being then known; but we have since
learnt, that he had form'd a most detestable Scheme
to poison King Augustus, Elector of Saxony, and that
to effect his abominable Design, he had address'd
himself to the Count de Plelo, Ambassador of France;
but that his Excellency shock'd with the Motion, and
detesting so black an Attempt, had immediately im-
parted the same to the King, who after having con-
victed him of the intended Design, condemned him
to perpetual Imprisonment.
Dantzick, Feb. 16. The Russian General Leslie is arrived at Prest, a Village situate about a League from
this Place; and several Cossacks have already appeared under the Cannon of this City. At the Ap-
proach of the Russians, the Sluices on the Side of the
Fields have been open'd, which puts the Place in a
State of Security on that Side; but 'tis however much
fear'd that they will make themselves Masters of
the Fort of Wechselmund, which would not fail of
cutting off the Communication between the Sea and
this Town, to the great Prejudice of the Inhabitants;
but as that Fort is well provided with Artillery and
all Sorts of Ammunition, we flatter ourselves, that it
may hold out till the Arrival of the expected Succours
as 'tis given out, from more than one Place; and we
are the more induced to give Credit to it, since 'tis
judg'd that the King and so many Lords would not
expose themselves to stay in a Town surrounded with
Enemies, without certain Hopes of Relief.
Paris Feb. 22. The Affairs of King Stanislaus,
however they stand in Poland, go well in Rome.
The Count Zalosky, that King's Minister, has had a
long Audience of Cardinal Firau, Secretary of State,
on that Subject. His Eminence gives the Count Hopes,
that, as soon as a proper Occasion offers, the Holy
See will take up Arms in that Prince's Favour: Not
by raising of Troops or fitting out Squadrons, nor by
using any sort of Ammunition but the Powder and
Shot of the Vatican, which have been found of so
great Proof, that Countries have been made desolate,
Armies disarmed, and Princes dethroned by it. It is
true, the Bulls that do all this Execution, have lost a
little of their Force since the Reformation; but if the
Elector of Saxony is as good a Catholick as he pretends to, he will sit still, and suffer the Pope's cano-
nical Thunder to do him all possible Mischief, and
thank his Holiness afterwards for his fatherly Correction. They have received at Rome an Express
from Ferrara, with Advice that a Body of 4000 Men
of French Troops, have seized Massola, and other
Towns on the Po, dependent on the Ecclesiastical State,
tho' without any Prejudice to the Holy See, because
it is to hinder the Debarkation of Imperialists that
may come from Trieste; and also with a charitable
Design of starving the Garrison of Mantua, which is
now very numerous. They really acquaint us that
there

Figure 0.1. **Cover page: Boston News-Letter, published as The Boston Weekly News-Letter, Thursday April 25, to Thursday May 2, 1734.**

Chapter One

Massachusetts Notices

Boston News-Letter, Monday June 19, to Monday June 26, 1704.

Ran-away from Capt. Nathanael Cary, of Charlston, on Saturday the 17th Currant, a well set middle sized Maddagascar Negro Woman, called Penelope, about 35 years of Age: With several Sorts of Apparel; one whereof is a flowered damask Gown; she speaks English well. Whoever shall take up said Negro Servant, and her convey to her above-said Master, shall have sufficient Reward.

Boston News-Letter, Monday July 10, to Monday July 17, 1704.

There is a Negro man taken up, supposed to be a Runaway from his Master; he said he was a free Negro, and lived at Bristol, but upon being sent to Prison, he owned he was a Servant and made his escape from his Master Matthew Howard at Seaconet, about 5 Weeks ago; he is a Lusty Fellow, says his name is George; upon paying the Post-master for this Advertisment the owner may be informed where he is, and also upon paying the charge and reward for taking him up, may have said Negro again.

Boston News-Letter, Monday September 25, to Monday October 2, 1704.

There is a Negro man taken up, supposed to be a Runaway from his Master, he is small boned, middle stature, small beard, gray Jacket, gray homespun kersey breeches, a Souldier's cap, no stockings, an old pair of shoes, calls himself Sambo, for paying the Postmaster for this Advertisment, the Owner may be informed where he is, and also upon paying the charge and reward for taking him up, may have said Negro again.

Boston News-Letter, Monday December 3, to Monday December 10, 1705.

Ran-away from his Master William Pepperil Esqr. at Kittery, in the Province of Maine, a Negro Man-Slave named Peter, aged about 20, speaks good English, of pretty brown Complexion, middle Stature, has on a mixt gray home-spun Coat, white home spun Jacket and Breeches, French fall Shoes, fad coloured Stockings, or a mixt worsted pair, and a black Hat. Whosoever shall take up said Negro, and bring or convey him safe to his said master, or secure him and send notice of him either to his Master, or to Andrew Belcher Esqr. at Boston, shall be well rewarded for his pains, and all reasonable charges paid besides.

Reprint: Boston News-Letter, Monday December 24, to Monday December 31, 1705.

Boston News-Letter, Monday July 15, to Monday July 22, 1706.

Ran-away from his Master George Robinson Carver of Boston, on Tuesday last the 16th Currant, a Negro Man-Slave Named Jo, of middle Stature, well-set, Speaks good English, aged about 32 years, has on a fad coloured Jacket, white Shirt, and Leather Breeches. Whosoever shall apprehend and take up the said Runaway so that he may be delivered unto his said Master, or give any true Intelligence of him, shall have a Sufficient reward.

Boston News-Letter, Monday November 8, to Monday November 15, 1708.

Ran-away from his Master Col. Nicholas Paige of Rumley March, on Tuesday the 2d of this Instant November, a Negro Man-Servant, aged about 45 years, call'd Jack Bill, of middle Stature, a comely Fellow, speaks good English: He has on a black Hat, black Coat, blew Jacket, a broad cloth pair of Breeches with Livery Lace, and a pair a white Stockings. Whoever shall apprehend the said Runaway, and him safely Convey to his said Master, or unto Mr. John Geerish, Gunsmith, at Upper-End of King-Street in Boston; or give any true Intelligence of the said Negro Man-servant to either of them, so as that his Master may have him again, shall be sufficiently Rewarded, besides all necessary Charges paid.

Boston News-Letter, Monday April 9, to Monday April 16, 1711.

Ran-away from his Master Robert Rumsey at Fairfield in Connecticut Colony, on the 27th of March last, a negro man call'd Jack, a tall thin fac'd Fellow, exceeding black, a considerable scar in his face, can play on a Violin, he hath carried his Fiddle with him, and a considerable bundle of Cloaths.

Whoever shall apprehend the said Runaway Negro man, and him safely Convey to his said Master, or give any true Intelligence of him, so as his Master may have him again, shall be sufficiently Rewarded, besides all necessary Charges paid.

Boston News-Letter, Monday December 24, to Monday December 31, 1711.

Ran-away from his Master John Oulton, Merchant, in Marlborough-street, Boston, a Negro Man named Harry, of a middle Stature and well sett, with a Leather Jacket. Whoever shall apprehend the said Runaway, and him safely Convey to his said Master, or give any true Intelligence of him, so as his Master may have him again, shall be well Rewarded, besides all necessary charges paid.

Reprint: Boston News-Letter, Monday June 22, to Monday June 29, 1713.

Boston News-Letter, Monday August 11, to Monday August 18, 1712.

Ran-away from their Masters in Connecticut Colony the following Negro's and a Spanish Indian, viz from Mr. George Phillips in Middle-town Two Negro Men one Named Trankilo aged about Thirty years, of a middle stature, speaks good English, well Apparelled, one finger of one hand Stump'd. The other Negro Named Harry aged about 20 years, straight Lim'd, has on a blew Shirt, Red Jacket, Castor Hat, Speaks broken English, and well Apparelled.

Ran-away also from Mr. Jehiel Hauley of Durham, A Spanish Indian Man, Named Peter aged about Twenty years, of a Middle Stature, a Cheridary Wastcoat, a Soldiers blew Coat fac'd with red, the Cape taken off, he speaks very good English.

And on the 18th of July, Ran-away from Mr. Ebenezer Hubbard of said Middletown, a Negro Man nam'd Peter, aged about 18 years, a Slim Fellow, thin fac'd, having a Skare on the back of one of his hands near the Nuckles, with a Slit on one of his Ears, speaks good English.

Whoever shall apprehend said Run-away or any of them, and him or them safely convey to his or their said Masters, or give any true Intelligence, of them or either of them, so as their Masters may have them again shall have Fourty Shillings reward, for each Servant, besides all necessary Charges paid.

Boston News-Letter, Monday June 22, to Monday June 29, 1713.

Addington Davenport, Register.

Ran-away from his Master, Thomas Palmer Esqr. at Boston on Tuesday last the 23d of this Instant June, a Negro man named Lester, aged about 25 years, of a full round face, having on a light coloured Broad-cloth Coat, and a yellow Broad-cloth Jacket, with Gold Buttons, and a pair of old blue and white linen Breeches, a pair of dark coloured homespun yarn Stockings, round to'd Shoes.

Whoever shall apprehend the said Run-away, and him safely convey to his said Master, or give any true Intelligence of him so as his Master may have him again shall be sufficiently rewarded besides all necessary Charge paid.

Boston News-Letter, Monday May 17, to Monday May 24, 1714.

Ran-away from his master John Scott of Newport Rhode-Island, a Molatto Man named Daniel, born in New England, and by Trade a Ship Carpenter, formerly belonging to Edward Wanton of Situate, he is about 20 years of Age, indifferent tall, and slender bushy hair, carried with him white and speckled Shirts, Sea cloaths and Bedding, and other good Cloaths as a Cinnamon coloured Broad-Cloath Coat trim'd with Froggs, Ticking breeches, Worsted Stockings &c. Whoever shall apprehend the said Runaway and bring him to his said Master, or secure him and give notice to his Master aforesaid that he may him again shall have reasonable Satisfaction and Charges paid.

Reprint: Boston News-Letter, Monday September 22, to Monday September 29, 1712. In that notice, Edward Wanton is noted as being Daniel's master.

Boston News-Letter, Monday August 29, to Monday September 5, 1715.

Ran-away at Portsmouth, New Hampshire from his Master Jonathan Studley, on Saturday the 27th of August past, a Portuguise Molatto Servant Man, aged about 22 Years, a short thick fellow, black Curl'd hair, has on a out-side Jacket fad coloured, old and broken, he speaks but little English: Whoever shall apprehend the said Run-away and him safely convey to his said Master, or give any true Intelligence of him so as his Master may have him again shall be sufficiently rewarded to Content, besides all necessary Charges paid.

Boston News-Letter, Monday April 9, to Monday April 16, 1711.

Ran-away from his Master Peter Burr Esq; at Fairfield in Connecticut Colony, on the 27th of March last, a Malatto Servant Man, call'd John More, a young well sett smooth fac'd Fellow, of a middle Stature; having on a blewish mix coloured home made flannel Coat, an old gray Kersey Vest, & a new reddish coloured cloth searge Vest Leather Breeches, a good Castor Hat; he speaks & reads English well. Whoever shall apprehend the said runaway servant, and him safely convey to his said Master, or give any true Intelligence of him, so as his Master may have again, shall be sufficiently Rewarded, besides all necessary Charges paid.

Boston News-Letter, Monday June 7, to Monday June 14, 1714.

Ran-away on Wednesday the 26th Day of May last at Beverly, from his Master Joseph Tuck, a Negro Man-Servant, Named Peter, a slim Fellow not very Tall, goes a little Lame, lost his Fore-upper Teeth, has on a close-bodied Coat, and Pale Copper-coloured Jacket, Coat and Jacket tarr'd in some Places, white Worsted Stockings, Leather Breeches, and French fall Shoe, the heels goes much back: He was formerly Servant to Mr. Pepperel of Kittery, Mr. Boreman Tanner in Cambridge. Mr. Morecock in Boston, and Mr. Hubbard of Middleton.

Whoever shall apprehend the said Run-away, and him safely Convey to his said Master, or to Mr. Nathan Howell Merchant in Boston, or give any true Intelligence of him so as his Master may have him again, shall be Sufficiently Rewarded, besides all necessary Charges paid.

*Peter Ran away from his previous owner, Mr. Pepperel. See Boston News-Letter, Monday December 3, to Monday December 10, 1705.

Boston Gazette, Monday January 11, to Monday January 18, 1720.

Run away on Wednesday night last, from John Jekyll Esq; his Negro Servant named Caesar, aged about 17 Years, having on a Pea Jacket, and a Child's new Hatt. Whoever brings him to his said Master at the Custom House in Boston, shall have all reasonable Satisfaction.

Boston Gazette, Monday June 12, to Monday June 19, 1721.

Ran-away from his Master Mr. Edward Watts of Winnesimit, on the Third Instant, a Negro Man Servant named Quacco, about 25 Years of Age, of a middle Statue, his Legs are crook'd, one of his upper fore-Teeth out; He had on when he went away, dark colour'd Drugget Coat, a double-breasted Kersey Jacket, wash Leather Breeches, square to'd Shoes. He is supposed to have parted with some of his Cloathes.

Whoever will take up the abovesaid Run-away, and him safely convey to his abovesaid Master at Winnesimit shall have Twenty Shillings Reward, and all necessary Charges paid.

Boston, June 13th, 1721.

Boston Gazette, Monday June 12, to Monday June 19, 1721.

Ran-away from his master Capt. Richard Brown of Newtown, a middle sized Negro Man named Mingo, about 25 Years of Age, having on a Homespun Quakers Coat, with a pair of Square to'd Shoes, with Leather strings, a Blacksmith by Trade.

Whoever secures the said Negro and brings him to Mr. Philip Musgrave Post-Master of Boston shall have Twenty Shillings Reward and reasonable Charges.

The Boston Gazette, Monday October 28, to Monday November 4, 1728.

Whereas Caesar Swift a Negro Man deserted from Capt. Marwood, commander of His Majesty's Ship Lyme, who lately belonged to Capt. Carnwal, about five Foot seven Inches high, has 3 Scars on each Cheek, had on when he went away, a Blew Coat, with white Mettle Buttons; Whoever shall apprehend and bring the said Run-away to the aforesaid Capt. Marwood, shall have all due Reward.

Boston News-Letter, Thursday July 30, to Thursday August 6, 1724.

Ran-away from Master Capt. Richard Trevett of Marblehead, a Negro Named Pompey, about Twenty-two Years of Age, a Lusty, Tall Fellow: He had on when he went away, a striped homespun Jacket, Cotton & Linen Shirt, dark coloured Kersey Breeches, grey yarn Stockings, round To'd leather heel Shoes, and Felt Hat. Note, he deserted his Master Service in the Shallop Ann, at Plymouth. Whoever shall apprehend the said Run away, and him safely convey to his said Master at Marblehead, or to Mr. Francis Miller in Boston, near the Green Dragon, shall have Fifty Shillings Reward and all necessary Charges paid.

Boston Evening-Post, 10-20-1735.

Ran away from Mr. Thomas Salter of Boston, Cordwainer, about the beginning of September last, a Negro Man-Servant named George, a sturdy well set Fellow, aged about 26 or 27 Years, with thick Lips, a flat Nose, large Legs, is very Black, and much Pock broken. He speaks good English, and is a Shoe-maker by Trade. He had on when he went away, a Woollen Jacket, Leather Breeches, and a Cap, but no Coat or Hat, Stocking or Shoes.

Ran away at the same Time, from Mr. John Billings of Boston, a Negro Woman Dinah, about 24 Years old, a handsome likely Wench, of middle Stature, with a Callico Jacket, a blue Bays Petticoat, blue Stocking with white Clocks, and high heel'd Shoes.

Whoever shall take up the above said Servants, and bring them to their respective Masters in Boston, shall have Three Pounds Reward, or Thirty Shillings for either of them, besides all necessary Charges paid.

Reprints: Boston Evening-Post, 10-27-35; 11-3-35. Reprints of this notice were also printed in the Boston Gazette, 10-27, to 11-03-35. Thomas Salter would have a separate notice printed in the Gazette, 10-06 to 10-13-35 and in the Weekly Rehearsal, 08-20-1733; 08-27-1733. Similarly, John Billings would do the same for Dinah in the Boston Gazette, 01-03, to 10, 1735.

Boston Evening-Post, 10-04-1736.

Ran away from Mr. Bejamin Astills, now of Boston, on Friday the 17th of September Instant, a Negro Man named Cajo, about 11 Years old, with an Iron Collar about his Neck, with the Name of his Master engraven upon it in Capital Letters. He had on a double breasted Jacket of a greenish Colour, an Oznabrigs Frock and Trouzers, but not a Hat or Cap, Shoes or Stockings. Whoever shall take up the said Negro, and bring him to Mr. James Gordon, Merchant, living in Cornhill in Boston, shall have Twenty Shillings Reward, besides all necessary Charge paid.

Reprints: Boston Evening Post, 09-27-1736; 10-04-1736.

Boston Evening-Post, 08-08-1737.

LAST Night went away from Major Mascarene's House, a Negro Lad aged about Sixteen Years, pretty tall and slim; he had on a dark homespun Kersey Coat, with red Buttons and Button holes, a light Drugget pair of Breeches with Metal Buttons, and a light pair of Worsted Stockings. Whoever shall take up the said Run-away, and safely convey him to his said Master, Major Mascarene, shall have all necessary Charges paid, and be rewarded for his

Pains, and all Masters of Vessels and others are hereby caution'd not to entertain or convey away the said Negro, as they will avoid the Penalty of the Law.

N.B. The said Negro's Name is Harry.

Monday, August 8th. 1737.

Reprint: Boston Evening-Post, 08-15-1737.

Boston Evening-Post, 10-03-1737.

Ran away from his Master, Mr. John Belden of Norwalk, a lusty Negro Fellow named Jack, about 18 Years old, full faced, speaks good English, but stammers or stutters in his Talk. He had on a Linsey Woolsey Coat with flat Pewter Buttons, a white Fustian Jacket, Leather Breeches with Brass Buttons, a Tow Shirt, Yarn Stockings & Shoes with large Pewter Buckles. Has also taken with an Olive coloured Broad Cloth Coat, turn'd and something worn, and a good New Holland Shirt. Suppos'd to be seduced by an Irish Fellow named John Davission, alias William Mackgee, an Indentured Servant of Mr. Samuel Belden of said Norwalk, who is also run away, and taken said Negro with him. Davission alias Mackgee is a lusty Fellow, full faced, of a pale Complexion, wears his own Hair of a brownish Colour, is something Pock broken, suppos'd to be about thirty five Years of Age, and a Weaver by Trade. His Cloathing was a new Duroy Coat, of a light Gray Colour, and old brown Cloth Coat, a striped Holland Jacket, Camblet Breeches, Tow Trousers, a speckled Holland Shirt, and homespun Linen Shirt, Worsted Stockings, Shoes with white Mettal Buckles, and a new Castor Hat. Whoever shall take up the said Run-aways, or secure them so that their said master may have them again, shall have a Reward of Ten Pounds, for both, or Five Pounds for either of them, with necessary Charges, paid by

John Belden

Norwalk, Sept. 15, 1737

Boston Evening-Post, 07-17-1738.

Ran away from his master, William Browne, Esq; of Salem, on the Tenth of this Instant July, a short Negro Fellow named Maximus, dress'd in Black, who can play well upon a violin. Whoever shall take up the said Negro, and bring him to his said Master in Salem, or secure him so that may be had again, shall have Five Pounds Reward, and all necessary Charge paid.

N.B. The said Negro went away in Company with a tall strait Lim'd Negro Fellow named Will, belonging to Mr. Cockrell Reeves of said Salem. They stole and took with them a large Bay Horse with a large Scar in his Forehead, and a Bay Mare that has been wrenched behind. They are cunning crafty Fellows, and are suppos'd to be gone towards New York.

Reprints: 07-24-1738; 07-31-38.

Boston Evening-Post, 07-24-1738.

Ran away the 4th Instant from Mr. George Tilley of Boston, a negro Fellow, named Bristol, aged about 35 Years, he is tall and slim, walks very upright, speaks broken English, he had on when he went away, a Felt Hat, a homespun striped Jacket, and striped Linen Breeches, a Cotton and Linen Shirt, no Stockings, a pair of old Shoes. N.B. He has lately been seen with a Frock and Trouzers on. Whoever shall take up the said Runaway and him safely convey to his abovesaid Master in Boston aforesaid, shall have Twenty Shillings Reward, and all necessary Charges. And all Masters of Vessels are hereby cautioned against concealing or carrying off said Servant on Penalty of the Law in that Case made and provided.

Boston Evening-Post, 10-23-1738.

Ran away from his Master, Capt. Samuel Carlton of Salem, Mariner, on Tuesday the 10th of this Instant October, a tall lusty Negro Fellow named Millet, but call himself Tom Brown, about six Foot high, with the Letters L D branded on his Breast, and talks good English. He had on or took with him when he went away, a dark coloured double breasted Jacket of Homespun, a striped homespun under Jacket, and an old thick Jacket of a Purple Colour, but faded , and mended with the same at both Elbows; a white Shirt, and an old Ozenbrigs Shirt, homespun dark coloured Breeches, and a pair of Purl Yarn Stockings, with old Shoes. He is a Shoemaker by Trade, and carries his Tools in a Bag. N.B. All Masters of Vessels and other Persons are hereby cautioned against harbouring, concealing, or carrying off the said Servant, as they will avoid the Penalty of the Law in that Case made and provided.

Whoever shall take up the said Servant, and bring him to his abovesaid Master in Salem, shall have Three Pounds Reward, and all necessary Charged paid.

Reprints: Boston Evening-Post, 12-17-1738; 12-24-1739.

Boston Evening-Post, 07-09-1739.

Ran away from Mr. James Jeffs of Boston, Printer, on the 22d of this Instant June, a Negro Boy Scipio, aged above 16 Years, pretty short for his Age, but very well set. He has three Scars on the middle of his Forehead, and a Sore on one of his Shins. He had on when he went away, a Cotton Shirt, and a Frock and Trouzers, pretty much painted. All Masters of Vessels and other are hereby cautioned against harbouring, concealing or carrying off the said Negro, as they avoid the Penalty of the Law. And whoever shall take up the said Negro, and bring him to his abovesaid Master, living near Clark's Ship Yard, at the North End, shall have Forty Shillings Reward and all necessary Charges paid.

Reprints: Boston Evening-Post, 07-16-1739; 07-23-1739; 07-30-1739.

Boston Evening-Post, 07-09-1739.

Ran away from his Master, Mr. Nathanael Brown of Salem, on Wednesday the 4th of this Instant July, a Negro Fellow named Cuffe, about 20 Years of Age, a strait limb'd handsome Fellow of a middle Stature, plays upon a violin, and dances pretty well. He carried away with him a Gray Woollen Coat, a brown Holland Coat a striped Jacket and Breeches, a pair of white Trouzers, sundry pair of Stockings, one of which is Blue and a new Felt Hat. All Master of Vessels and other Persons are hereby cautioned against harbouring, concealing, or carrying off the said Servant as they will avoid the Penalty of the Law in that Case made and provided. Whoever shall take up the said Servant, and bring him to his abovesaid Master in Salem, shall have Five Pounds Reward and all necessary Charged paid.

Reprints: Boston Evening-Post, 07-16-39; 07-23-39.

Boston Evening-Post, 07-16-1739.

Ran away from his Master, Mr. John Woods of Groton, on Thursday, the 12th of this Instant July, a Negro Man Servant named Caesar, about 22 Years of Age, a pretty short well sett Fellow. He carried with him a Blue Coat and Jacket, a pair of Tow Breaches, a Castor Hat, Stockings and Shoes of his own, and a Blue Cloth Coat with flower'd Metal Buttons a white flower'd Jacket, a good Bever Hat, a Gray Wigg, and a pair of new Shoes of his Master's, with some other Things. It is suspected there is some white Person that may be with him or design to make Use of his Master's Apparel above described.

Whoever shall take up the said Servant, and bring him to his abovesaid Master in Groton, or be a Means of convicting any Person or Confederate with said Servant as above suspected, shall have Five Pounds Reward for each of them and all necessary Charges paid.

Reprints: Boston Evening-Post, 07.23.39; 07.30.39.

The Boston Gazette, Monday March 9, to Monday March 16, 1730.

Ran-away on the 10th of February last from his Master, Maj. James Brown of Newport, a Negro Man, Named Robin, but sometimes call'd Christmas, about 22 years of Age, of middle Stature, and pretty slim: He had with him a Silk Jacket and Breeches, and dark colour'd Callicoe Jacket and Breeches.

Whoever will apprehend the said Run-away, and him safely conveys to his said Master, shall have Three Pounds Reward, and all necessary charges paid.

Reprint: The Boston Gazette, 3-23 to 30-1730.

The Boston Gazette, Monday October 19, to Monday October 26, 1730.

Ran-away from Col. Samuel Browne, of Salem, two Negro Men, the one Named Juba, a tall lusty well set Fellow, with great Lips, formerly belonging to Judge Lynde: the other of midling Stature, Named Ceasar, liv'd formerly with Major Merrit of New-London, they both speak good English; and went away on Monday Octo. 19, 1730. If any Person will take up said Negros and convey them to their abovesaid master, shall be well rewarded for Charge and Trouble.

Reprint: The Boston Gazette, 10-26 to 11-02-1730.

The Boston Gazette, Monday October 19, to Monday October 26, 1730.

Ran-away the 23d, of this Instant, at Night, from his Master Mr. William Wilson, a Negro man Servant Named Boston, a Lusty Strong Fellow, about 27 Years of Age, formerly belonged to Mr. Daniel Henshaw of Boston: Whoever shall take up the abovesaid Servant and him safely convey to Mr. George Monk, near the Crown Coffee-House in Boston, shall have Forty Shillings Reward, and all necessary Charges paid.

The Boston Gazette, Monday July 26, to Monday August 2, 1731.

Ran-away from Bond and Blowers, on Thursday last a Negro Man named Tom, about 22 Years old, he is a tall well shap'd Fellow, he had on a Swanskin Jacket, speckled Shirt and Ozenbrigs Trowzers. Whoever will take up said Negro and bring him to said Bond and Blowers, shall be satisfied to content.

The Boston Gazette, Monday February 7, to Monday February 14, 1732.

Ran away from his Master Mr. Edward Langdon of Boston, Wigmaker, living near the Salutation Tavern, early this Morning it being the 12th of February, a young Negro Man-Servant, Named Jack, about 18 Years of Age, of a Middling Stature, well set, something Pock-broken, his upper Teeth are artificially made sharp, speaks English. He had on when he went away, an old Felt Hat, an old Kersey Coat with close Slieves of a lightish Colour, an old Cloath Jacket something lighter than his Coat, a Leather pair of Breeches, grey Yarn Stockings, and an old pair of Shoes. He has a hole in one of his Ears.

Whoever shall take up the abovesaid Negro Servant, and him convey to his abovesaid Master, shall have Five Pounds Reward, and all necessary Charges paid.

N.B. 'Tis suppos'd he was entic'd by some ill minded Person in order to be carry'd out of the Country.

This is to desire all Masters of Vessels to take Notice that there is a great Penalty in the Law for carrying away any such Servant.

Reprints: The Boston Gazette, 02-21 to 02-28-1732. This notice was also printed in the New England Weekly Journal, 02-14-1732; 02-21-1732; and, 02-28-32.

The Boston Gazette, Monday May 21, to Monday May 29, 1733.

ON the 18th Instant Run-away from his Master Mr. Richard Long, of Salisbury, a Negro Man, about 24 Years of Age, a lusty thick set Fellow, had on a brown homespun Coat & Waistcoat, and a new pair of Shoes. Whoever secures the said Negro, so that his said Master may have him again shall receive as a Reward Three Pounds, besides being paid all necessary Charges.

The Boston Gazette, Monday June 4, to Monday June 11, 1733.

Ran away on the 20th of May last from his Master James Brown, Esq; of Providence, a Negro Man servant, named Cuffe, about 30 Years of Age, a thick well sett Fellow, a pretty large Stature, his left Leg is above twice as large as his right, and is attended with running Sores: He had on when he went away, a new dark homespun Jacket, an Ozenbrigs Shirt and a pair of Linnen Breeches. Whosoever shall apprehend the above Run-away and him convey to his said Master in Providence, shall have Twenty shillings reward, and all necessary Charges paid.

Providence, June 14, 1733.

Reprint: The Boston Gazette, 06-18 to 06-25-1732.

The Boston Gazette, Monday July 23, to Monday July 30, 1733.

Ran-away from the Rev. Mr. Pigot of Marblehead, a Negro Man Servant, Named Cuffy, who had on a broadcloth Jacket lined with black, a pair of black Leather Breeches lined with shamy, an Ozenbrigs Shirt, a bouble worsted Cap, and a silk Handkerchief. He is distinguished by an oblong Wen over his left Eye. Whosoever shall secure said Negro shall receive Forty Shillings reward, with reward, with reasonable Charges.

The Boston Gazette, Monday October 15, to Monday October 22, 1733.

Ran away from his Master Mr. William Spikeman of Boston, Baker, on Saturday the 6th of this Instant October, a Negro Man servant named Caesar, of a middle Stature but well set, between 30 and 40 years old, is splaw Footed, has thick Lip, and speaks good English. He had on when he went away, a thick blue Jacket, and a thin blue Jacket under it, a pair of Leather Breeches, and has with him a suit of Black with other Cloathing. Note, the said Negro formerly lived with the later Rev. Mr. Thayer of Roxbury. Whoever will take up the abovesaid Run away and bring him to his said Master in Boston, shall have Five Pounds Reward, and all necessary Charges paid.

Newport, October 17, 1733.

Reprints: The Boston Gazette, 10-22 to 10-29-1733. This notice was also printed in the Boston News Letter, 12-06 to 12-13-1733.

The Boston Gazette, Monday October 22, to Monday October 29, 1733.

Ran-away on the 17th of this Inst. October, a Negro Man Named Harry, about 40 Years of Age, belonging to Mr. John Gooch, Sugar Baker, he is a very lusty Fellow and had on an old pair of Leather Breeches, Oznabrigs Frock and Trousers, a great duffel Coat. Also a Negro Girl Named Phillis, about 14 Years old, belonging to Capt. Roger Denon. She is a short well set Girl, having on a dark coloured serge Jacket, a blew and white checks cotton Coat, she carried away with her several other things as Shoes and Coats, &c. Whoever shall apprehend said Runaways and bring them to Mr. John Gooch, shall be well satisfied for their Trouble and have all necessary charges paid.

The Boston Gazette, Monday July 22, to Monday July 29, 1734.

Ran-away from Timothy Keeler of Ridgefield in the County of Fairfield in Connecticut, about the last of June, a Negro Man Named Mingo, a likely well grown Fellow, thick set, speaks good English, can read and write, one of his little Toes is wanting, he is about 28 Years of Age. He had on a good duroy Coat of a lightish colour, a striped Calimineo Vest and Breeches, good Shoes and Stockings, a plain cloth Home-made great Coat with brass Buttons. He had (as I am inform'd) a false Pass, a Pocket Compass, and several Books. Whoever shall take up said Fellow and convey him to Capt. Samuel Keeler at Norwalk in Connecticut, shall have Seven Pounds Reward and all necessary charges paid,

by me Timothy Keeler

Reprints: The Boston Gazette, 07-29 to 08-5-34; 08-5 to 08-12-1734; 08-12 to 08-19-1734.

The Boston Gazette, Monday September 9, to Monday September 16, 1734.

Ran-away from their Master Mr. William Wall of Prudence Island, the beginning of this Month, a Welsh Man Servant Named William Jones, a well set Fellow, a short thick Neck, great Head, bushy brown hair, about 25 or 30 years old, he had on a homespun mixcoloured blue druget Coat, grayish camblet Breeches, long linen ditto, 2 cotton Shirts and one linen, a castor Hat. He carried away several things of value. Also Ran-away a Negro Man named Cuffee, about 24 Years of Age, middle Stature, speaks pretty good English, slim bodied, had on a beaver Hat, Ozenbrigs Waistcoat, he carried away several Shirts both of linen and woolen, a cinamon coloured Coat flat pewter Buttons long linen Breeches, shoes and Stockings. Whoever shall take up said Runaways and conveys them to their Master shall, have Six Pounds for the white Man, and Four for the Negro, with all necessary Charged paid by William Wall.

All Masters of Vessels are warn'd not to carry off the above said Servants, at their Pearl.

The Boston Gazette, Monday October 14, to Monday October 21, 1734.

Ran-away from his Master Mr. John Hood of Boston Shipwright, on the 11th Instant at Night, a Negro Servant Lad named Ben, about 18 Years of Age: He had on when he went away, a white Coat with brass Buttons, dark colour'd Breeches, a speckl'd shirt, a pair of new Shoes, but no Stockings. Whoever shall take up said Run away and him convey to his said Master near the Sign of the Bull, shall have Three Pounds Reward and all necessary Charges paid.

The Boston Gazette, Monday September 15, to Monday September 22, 1735.

A Negro Boy about 15 years of Age, who speaks good English, and by his Apparrel, &c. appears as if bred to the Sea, has lately been taken up at Noddles-Island by Capt. Temple. The Master or Owner of said Negro may have him again by applying to John Boydell, and paying the reasonable Charges on him.

Reprint: The Boston Gazette, 10-06 to 10-13-1735.

The Boston Gazette, Monday June 14, to Monday June 21, 1736.

Ran away from his Master Mr. James Halsey of Boston, the 16th of this Instant June, a lusty well set Negro Lad, about 18 Years old, with a very full Face: He had on when he went away, a blue Jacket trim'd with red and Brass Buttons, a Cotton and Linnen Shirt, a pair of Leather Breeches, a good narrow-brimb'd Hat.

Whoever shall take up the said Servant, and him safely convey to his said Master, living near the Draw-Bridge in Boston, shall have Forty Shillings Reward, and all necessary Charges paid.

The Boston Gazette, Monday October 18, to Monday October 25, 1736.

Ran-away from his master Jableel Brenton of Newport on Rhode Island, the 10th Instant, a Negro Man named Melech: He had on when he went away a grey Kersey Coat with flat metal Buttons, a pair of linen Trousers, a white Shirt made of tow Cloth; he is about six feet high, of a yellow Complection, of about 23 Years of Age, he was born and bred in the Jerseys near New-York. Whoever shall apprehend said Servant and bring or safely convey him to his said Master at Newport aforesaid, shall receive for his trouble Ten Pounds Reward, and all necessary Charges paid by me.

Jableel Brenton

Newport, October 15th, 1736.
Reprint: The Boston Gazette, 10-18 to 10-25-1736.

The Boston Gazette, Monday November 1, to Monday November 8, 1736.

ON Tuesday the 12th of October, Runaway from his Master Ebenezer Brenton of South Kingston, on the Colony of Rhode Island, a Mustee Man servant, named Abel, aged about 23 Years, a short thick set Fellow, something stooping in his shoulders, bare Leg'd, short Hair a little Brown, he shews something of white in his Complection ('tis supposed that his Father was a Dutch man, his Mother a Spanish Indian). He had on when he went away, a Grey Kersey Great Coat & Jacket, Linnen Frock & Trousers, New Felt Hat, and New Shoes; he took with him a Gun. Whoever shall apprehend said Runaway, and convey him safe to his Master shall have Ten Pounds reward & all necessary Charges paid by

Ebenezer Brenton

Reprints: The Boston Gazette, 11-08 to 11-15-1736; 11-15 to 11-22-1736.

The Boston Gazette, Monday January 17, to Monday January 24, 1737.

Ran-away from Mrs. Pullen on Saturday Morning last, the 22d Instant, a Negro Woman of middling Stature named Cuber, about five & thirty Years of Age, with a Scar over her right Eye, a pair of Gold Ear Kings in her Ears, and had on when she went away a light coloured Riding Hood and a striped homespun Jacket & Petticoat, having with her a large Bundle of wearing Cloaths. Whoever will apprehend & take up the abovesaid Runaway, and her safely convey to the Town Dock Market in Boston, or to the Publisher hereof shall be well rewarded for their Trouble.

This is likewise to forewarn all Persons whatsoever to Harbour the above-said Runaway, and Masters of Vessels to carry her off on Penalty of the Law.

Boston, January 24th, 1736,7.

The Boston Gazette, Monday June 6, to Monday June 13, 1737.

Ran away from her Master Isaac White of Boston, Shipwright, a Negro Wench named Juno.

Whoever shall bring the said Negro to her Master, or give any Intelligence of her shall be very well satisfied for their Trouble.

The Boston Gazette, Monday July 4, to Monday July 11, 1737.

These are to give Notice that Capt. Job Almy of Newport, took up a Runaway Negro Boy, about 18 or 19 Years old, on the 8th of July 1737, who on Examination confessed that he belonged to Lieu Hopkins of the Scarborough Man of War, he the said Negro told his Name was Emanuel before he said he belonged to the said Hopkins & afterwards he was named Charles. Whoever shall make a lawful Right and Title to the abovesaid Negro, shall have him again, paying all necessary Charges, who is now secured in Goal till a true Owner appear.

The Boston Gazette, Monday August 22, to Monday August 29, 1737.

A Negro Man Named Caesar belonging to Mr. Thomas Pearson, Gingerbread Baker, in this Town, is Runaway from his Master; he formerly belong'd to Mr. Lee, Lime Burner; a well set Fellow, Middle Stature: Having on an Ozenbrigs Jacket and Trousers, and blew Worsted stockings; Aged about Twenty Eight Years, speaks but Ordinary English. Whoever secures said Negro, and brings or give Notice to said Master, so that he may be had again, shall have Forty Shillings Reward. All Masters of Vessels are hereby forbid carrying him off at their Peril.

Reprint: The Boston Gazette, 08-29 to 09-05-1737.

The Boston Gazette, Monday September 19, to Monday September 26, 1737.

Ran-away from Peter Weare of North-Yarmouth, a stout Negro Man, about 26 years of Age: he had on a Cotton and Wool Shirt, a brownish Fustion Coat: a light colour'd Cloth Jacket, an old pair Trousers and a pair of strip'd Cotton & Wool Breeches under them, an old Felt hat, gray Stockings, and a new pair of Shoes: Note, he speaks good English. Whoever shall take up said Negro and him convey to his said Master, shall have Five Pounds reward and all necessary Charges paid him by

Peter Weare.

The Boston Gazette, Monday September 26, to Monday October 3, 1737.

Ran away from their Master Capt. William Mirick of Boston, on Tuesday the 27th of September last, Two Servant Men, one a Negro Man named Peter, about 27 Years old, of a middle Stature, but rather short. Had on when he went away, a blue Jacket, two pair of old Trouzers, and a hat painted of several Colours.

N.B. His Hair is longer than Negro's hair commonly is, and he talks good French and Spanish, and pretty good English. The other is an English Man named Daniel Davis, about 19 Years old, of a middle Stature, with smooth Face and large Eyes, and is pretty slow of Speech. He has short light Hair, and had on when he went away, a light coloured Kersey Jacket, spotted with Tar, leather Breeches, speckled Shirt, a pair of rib'd Yarn Stockings, old Shoes and a very good Bever hat, and has with him a short light colour'd natural Wigg.

N.B. All Masters of Vessels and other Persons are hereby cautioned against harbouring, concealing and carrying off the said Servants, as they will avoid the penalty of the Law in that Case made and provided.

Whoever shall take up the said Servants, or either of them, and bring them to their abovesaid master, living at the North End of Boston, shall have Five Pounds Reward for each, and all necessary Charges paid.

Boston, September 28th, 1737.

Reprint: The Boston Gazette, 10-03 to 10-10-1737.

The Boston Gazette, Monday October 3, to Monday October 10, 1737.

Ran-away on the 26th of this Instant September, from Mr. John Smibert of Boston, Painter, a Negro man Servant named Cuffee, who formerly belong'd to Capt. Prince, and understands something of the business of a Sailor, he is about 22 Years of Age and speaks good English, a pretty tall well shap'd Negro with bushy Hair, has on a large dark colour'd Jacket, a pair of Leather Breeches stain'd with divers sorts of Paints, and a pair of blue Stockings. Whoever shall take up said Runaway and him safely convey to his abovesaid Master in Boston, shall have Three Pounds Reward, and all necessary Charges paid. All Masters of Vessels are hereby warned against carrying off said Servant on penalty of the Law in that Case made and provided.

Boston, Sept. 30th, 1737.

Reprints: Boston Gazette, 10-10 to 10-17-1737. This notice was also printed in the New England Weekly Journal, 10-11-1737; 10-18-1737; and 10-25-1737.

The Boston Gazette, Monday July 24, to Monday July 31, 1738.

Ran-away on the third Instant, from his Mistress Mrs. Margaret Payne, a Negro Man named Jack, between 40 & 50 Years of Age. He had on when he went away a strip'd homespun Jacket, a pair of dark colour'd cloth Breeches, with brass Buttons, blue worsted or yarn Stockings: He speaks very broken English, and has a Felm in one Eye. Whoever shall secure said Negro and bring him to his Mistress at her House at the South End near the Fortifications shall have Forty Shillings Reward, and all necessary Charges paid.

Boston, July 29th, 1738.

The Boston Gazette, Monday October 2, to Monday October 9, 1738.

Ran-away from John Ledyard, Esq; of Groton, a Negro called Pompey, about 25 Years old, a well made Fellow, has a Sore on one of his Legs, and has with him a Fiddle and a Bundle of Cloaths. Whoever brings him to his Master, or secures him, and advises where he may be had shall be well rewarded and paid all necessary Charges.

N.B. He had been secured in South Kingston Goal, and made his Escape from the Person who was bringing him Home the 30th of September last.

Reprints: The Boston Gazette, 10-09 to 10-16-1738; 10-16 to 10-23-1738.

The Boston Gazette, Monday March 5, to Monday March 12, 1739.

Monday 5th of this Instant, Ran away from his Master William Fountain of Norwich, then in Boston, a Likely Negro Man commonly called Tom the Fidler, about 20 Years of Age speaks Good English, he had on when he went away a Light Colour'd great Coat no Buttons nor Button holes to it and a Dark Colour'd Close Body'd Coat with Mettle Buttons, and a Green Cloath Westcoat a Worsted Cap and a very narrow Brim'd Hatt. Whoever takes up said Negro and carrys him to Mr. Clear's at the sign of the White Horse at the South End of Boston shall have Three Pounds Reward, if any ways in the Country shall have Five Pound Reward and necessary charges paid.

Reprint: The Boston Gazette, 03-19 to 03-26-1739.

The Boston Gazette, Monday March 26, to Monday April 2, 1739.

Absconded from her Master John Wass of Boston, a Negro Girl, named Letitia former bought of Mr. James Gordon. Whoever will take up the said Negro, and bring her to said Wass at the South End of Boston, shall be satisfied for their Trouble.

Reprint: the Boston Gazette, 04-2 to 04-09-1739.

The Boston Gazette, Monday June 11, to Monday June 18, 1739.

Boston, June 11, 1739, Ranaway from the Bunch of Grapes & Three Sugar Loaves in King Street, a Mulatto Wench, called Mercy, she had on when she went away, a white Jacket with a variety of Petticoats, some Silk, some Callico; she is well set, of a middle Stature. Whoever secures the said Runaway and conveys her to the above place, shall be rewarded to their satisfaction.

The Boston Gazette, Monday July 9 to Monday July 16, 1739.

Two Negro Fellows belonging to Capt. French (formerly Capt. Warren's) Jack & Robin are Runaway from their Master, whoever secures them shall Receive Forty Shillings Reward each & all necessary Charges paid.
    Reprint: The Boston Gazette, 07-16 to 07-23-1739.

Boston News-Letter, Thursday November 26, to Thursday December 3, 1730.

Whereas a Sloop belonging to Mr. George Lucas of Antigua, and sent by him to St. Christophers the 18th August last, is supposed to be Run-away with by the Master & Men, which may be come into some Parts of the Continent: the Sloop is Connecticut Built, about Forty feet by the Keel, and about Seven Years old, she is called the Endeavour; the Master's Name is John Cades, a short black haired well looking Man, but Snuffles much in his Speech; the Sloop was Navigated with two White Men besides the Master, and three Negros (also belonging to said Lucas) whose Names are Lingo, Mingo & London, all Short, Black, Squat Fellows and they speak pretty good English. Whosoever shall give true Intelligence of the said Sloop & Negroes so that the said Lucas may have them again; or to Mr. Samuel Royall of Boston shall Receive the Sum of One Hundred Pounds Reward.

Boston News-Letter, Thursday October 9, to Thursday October 16, 1735.

Ran-away on the 8th Instant from his Master, Capt. Thomas Lawton of Bristol, a Molatto Slave named Caesar, about 32 Years of Age: Had on when he went away, a double breasted Jacket of greyish Colour, and Breeches of the same, a white Flannel Shirt, and Castor Hat. N.B. He is thick and well set, with bushy Hair, a down Look and surly Countenance. Whoever shall apprehend the said Run-away, and him convey to his said Master, shall have Five Pounds Reward, and all necessary Charges paid.

Boston News-Letter, Thursday April 21, to Thursday April 28, 1737.

Ran-away early on Sunday Morning the 24th of this Instant, from her Master Mr. Benjamin Astill now residing at the South End of Boston near the great Elm Trees, (but lately from Jamaica) a negro Woman called Mimbo, aged about 26 Years, she is likely Wench of a middle Size, and had on when she went away, a dark colour'd Bays Gown, and over that a blue and white strip'd Holland Petticoat with a red one under it; She also took with her a strip'd Callimanco Jacket with a blue Ferret round the Bottom, a pair of low heel'd old Shoes, and generally wears an Handkerchief on her Head, she is mark'd on one of her Shoulders with the Letters K.S. but pretty well worn out. Whoever shall take up the said Run-away, and Convey her to her above-said Master at Boston aforesaid, shall have Forty Shilling Reward, and all necessary Charges paid. This is also to caution all Masters of Vessels and others from carrying off said Servant, upon the Penalty of the Law in that Case provided. Boston, April 8, 1737.

New England Weekly Journal, 08-03-1730.

Ranaway on the 26th Instant July, from Mr. Christopher Phillips of North-Kingstown, a Spanish Indian Man named Warmick, about 24 years of Age, of a middle Stature, and Slim, Short Hair, a Tanner by Trade.

And a Mallagasco Negro Man, Named Cato, about 21 Years of Age, a Thick Short Fellow of a Tawney Complection, long Bushy Hair if he has not since cut it off, a Currier by Trade; They both Speak good English. Whoever shall take up the abovesaid Servants and them convey to their abovesaid Masters, shall have Five Pounds Reward, besides all necessary Charges paid by Christopher Phillips,

North-Kingstown, July 31, 1730.

New England Weekly Journal, 08-24-1730.

Whereas a New Negro Fellow was this Morning taken up, and understand by him he has been from his Master a Week, but can't know by him who his Master is, nor where he Lives, but up in the Country: he has on a striped Jacket open at the Sleeves without Risbands, a Cotton & Linnen Shirt, a pair of Trousers, a white Silk Hankerchief and a torn Hat. Whoever shall claim said Negro, may be farther Inform'd by Capt. Ebenezer Breed of Charles-town.

Charlestown, August 23, 1730.

New England Weekly Journal, 05-03-1731.

Ran-away from Mr. Joseph Knowlton of Newport on Rhode-Island, House-wright, on the 1st of April last, a Negro Man Servant, named Cuffee, about 28 Years of Age, a pretty tall Fellow, speaks broken English, is of a very black colour, & has several marks in his Face, wears a Cap & a good Hat, he took with him a large Bundle of Clothing, a broad Cloth Coat lin'd with blue a dark colour'd Duroy Fly, a light colour'd Duffle great Coat white Flannel Jacket, a Seersucker one, a Silk one &c. Whoever shall take up said Run-away, & him safely convey to his said Master at Newport or to Mr. Joseph Brown Distiller, near Mr. Waldo's Stillhouse in Boston, shall have Forty Shillings Reward & all necessary Charges paid. Tis suppos'd the said Negro has a forg'd Pass & designs to get off to Sea.
   Reprint: New England Weekly Journal, 05-17-1731.

New England Weekly Journal, 05-10-1731.

Ran-away from his Master Capt. John Wildman, on Saturday the 24th of April last, from on board the Sloop Endeavour, then lying at the Town Dock, a Negro Man servant, named Jack, about 30 Years of Age, Speaks pretty good English, a short thick fellow. He had on when he went away, a Woollen Jacket, Leather Breeches, a homespun Linnen Shirt, a strip'd Woolen Cap, Old Yarn Stockings, he has neither Shoes nor Hat.
   Whosoever shall take up the abovesaid Negro, and him convey to his abovesaid Master at Norwalk, or to Mr. Richard Rogers of Stratford, or to Mr. Samuel Edwards of Boston, shall have Forty Shillings Reward and all necessary Charges paid.
   Reprint: New England Weekly Journal, 05-17-1731.

New England Weekly Journal, 08-02-1731.

Tuesday Evening last a lusty new Negro Fellow that can speak little or no English was missing and has not been since heard of, and 'tis tho't he has lost himself by his going without the least provocation. He had on a dark drugget Jacket, Cotton & Linnen Shirt Ozenbrigs Breeches, he has three long Cuts from his Temple downwards on each side his Face. Any Person that can give any account of him to the Printer hereof shall have Thirty Shillings Reward, and all necessary Charges paid.
   Reprints: New England Weekly Journal, 08-09-1731; 08-16-1731.

New England Weekly Journal, 08-16-1731.

Ranaway from his Master Capt. John Bulkley of Boston, on the Ninth of this Instant August, a Negro Man Servant, Named Will, about 30 Years of Age, a well set Fellow, Pock broken, Speaks good English. He had on when he went away, a striped Worsted Cap, Cotton & Linnen Shirt, a striped Flannen Wastecoat, Linnen Breeches, and Yarn Stockings. Whoever shall take up the abovesaid Run-away, and him convey to his abovesaid master living in Queen Street, near the Town House, shall have Forty Shillings Reward and all necessary Charges Paid.

New England Weekly Journal, 10-11-1731.

Stray'd away from Mr. Matthew Ellis of Medford on the 26th of Sept. last, Two new Negro Men, one about 40, the other about 30 years of Age; the oldest had on a light colour'd broad Cloth Coat, the youngest had on a blue broad Cloth Coat, his little Finger on one hand cut off, they both had new checker'd Shirt. Neither of them can speak English. Whoever shall take up the abovesaid Negro's, and bring or convey to the abovesaid Ellis at Medford, or Mr. John Foy Merchant in Boston, shall have Reasonable Satisfaction, & necessary Charges paid.

New England Weekly Journal, 06-12-1732.

Ran-away from Mr. Nathan Cheever of Rumney Marsh, in the Township of Boston, on Monday the 5th Instant, a Negro Man Servant named Portsmouth, about 24 or 25 Years old, a pretty short well set Fellow, speaks good English, and can Write pretty well. He had on when he went away, an old Hat or Cap, a grayish homespun Coat, with Mettle Buttons, a homespun Jacket, a speckled homespun woollen Shirt, a pair of Ozenbrigs Trouzers, yarn Stockings, and old round toed Shoes. Note, said Negro has been used to go in a Boat, and 'tis tho't will endeavour to get off to Sea; therefore all Masters of Vessels and others are forbid entertaining him, as they will answer it in the Law. He plays upon a Violin & is suppos'd to have one with him. Whoever shall take up the abovesaid Negro, & bring him to his abovesaid Master, or to Mr. Joshua Cheever at the North End of Boston, shall have Three Pounds Reward, & all necessary Charges paid.

Boston, June 10th, 1732

New England Weekly Journal, 08-14-1732.

Broke out of Bridewell on Monday the 7th Currant, a Negro Man named Tom. He is about Twenty-five years of Age, a tall, comely well shap'd Fellow, he had a strip'd Swan skin Jacket, and is suspected to have taken some other Cloaths with him: He was seen on a Horse the 9th Instant riding towards Braintree. Whoever shall take up said Negro, & bring him to Pyam Blowers Merchant in Boston, shall have Three Pounds Reward, and all necessary Charges paid.

New England Weekly Journal, 07-15-1734.

Ran-away on the second of this Instant July, from his master Mr. George Tilley, Shop-keeper in Kingstreet Boston, a Negro Man-Servant named Cuffee, about 35 Years of Age, of middling Stature. He had on when he went away, a Cotton and Linnen Shirt, Oznabrigs Frock & Trouzers, Old Shoes, a pretty good Hat, Speaks good English, and has had the Small Pox. Whoever shall take up the abovesaid Runaway, and him convey to his abovesaid Master, shall be well rewarded for their Pains and Trouble, & all necessary Charges.

New England Weekly Journal, 08-04-1735.

Ranaway from the Sloop Martha and Elizabeth, lying at Clark's Wharfe, Nathanael Owen Commander, on the 30th of July last, a Negro Man Servant, Named Sam, about 28 Years of Age, a lusty well set Fellow; he had on when he went away, a Frock & Trowsers, and a Worsted Cap. Whoever shall take up said Runaway and him convey to the abovesaid Sloop, or to the House of Mrs. Barnsdale at the North End of Boston, shall have Three Pounds Reward, and all reasonable Charges paid by

Nathanael Owen

New England Weekly Journal, 10-28-1735.

Ranaway on Monday the 13th Instant from Mr. John D'Cosler of Boston, Mason, living in Milkstreet, a Negro Woman named Binah, she is lusty and well set with a round full Face pretty much Pock broken, her Nose somewhat Flat, and her Lips thick; speaks tolerable good English; she had on when she went away, a Cinamon colour'd Camblet Cloak, and yellow colour'd Head, a strip'd red and green Stuff Robe, a red and white quilted Callico Petticoat, and under blue and Linsey Woolsey Petticoat, with others, Cotton and Linnen Shist, blue yarn Stockings, and red Shoes. Whoever shall apprehend said Negro and her convey to her said Master, shall have Forty Shilling Reward, and all necessary Charges paid.

N.B. All Persons are hereby forbid Entertaining said Negro under the Penalties of the Law in that Case made and provided.

Reprints: New England Weekly Journal, 11-04-1735; 11-11-1735.

New England Weekly Journal, 08-24-1736.

Ran-away from his Master John Horsewel of Little Compton, on the 17th of July last, a Molatto Fellow named Isaac, thick, well set and full Fac'd, about twenty-one Years of Age, who was advertis'd in July last, and taken up on the Advertisement the 12th of this Instant August and made his Escape from the Person that took him up, was pinioned on the 15th following at Stoughton, and was cloath'd with a light colour'd short Coat, almost worn out, and patch'd up the Back, long Breeches, strip'd Worsted Cap, Linen Shirt, and Shoes with Brass Buckles. Whoever shall apprehend the said Molatto Fellow, and convey him to his said Master in Little-Compton aforesaid, or to any of his Majesty's Goals, or to Mr. Benj Williams in Boston, or Mr. Samuel Atherton at Rehoboth, shall have Five Pounds Reward, and necessary Charges paid by

John Horsewel

Reprint: New England Weekly Journal, 09-07-1736.

New England Weekly Journal, 10-26-1736.

Ran-away from Mrs. Margaret Steel of Boston, on Saturday the 23 Instant, a Negro Man named Tom, alias Tom Scipio, aged 36 Years, is of a middle Stature, much pitted with the Small Pox, his Eyes are small, and much sunk in his Head, he speaks good English, born in this Country, has been used to the Sea: He had on when he went away a speckled Shirt, a Kersey Jacket lined with white Woollen, an Ozenbrigs Frock, a Woollen Cap, a pair of square to'd Shoes with Wooden Heels. Whoever shall take up said Negro, and deliver him to his abovesaid Mistress at her House in Hanover Street, shall have Five Pounds Reward, & all necessary Charges paid. All Persons are hereby forbidden entertaining, or imploying said Negro & from carrying him off to Sea.

New England Weekly Journal, 12-14-1736.

Ran-away from Mr. David Snoden of Boston, Chair maker, on Monday the 6th of this Instant December, a Negro Man, named George, about 20 Years of Age, a tall lusty wellset Fellow, in a Chimney Sweeper's Dress. Whoever will take up said Negro and bring him to his said Master near Dr. Cutler's Church shall be well rewarded for their Trouble.

New England Weekly Journal, 01-31-1738.

Ran away from Master, Mr. Samuel Capen of Dorchester, on Friday the 23d Day of December, last, a Negro Man named Jo, upwards of Forty Years old, of a middle Stature, but well set, was born in Boston, and speaks very good English. He had on when he went away, a brownish coloured Drugget Coat, a blue Jacket, a speckled Woollen Shirt, old Yarn Stockings, and a pretty good Hat.

N. B. All Masters of Vessels and other Persons are hereby cautioned against harbouring, concealing, or carrying off the said Servant, as they will avoid the Penalty of the Law in that Case made and provided.

Whoever shall take up the said Servant and bring him to his abovesaid Master, living in Dorchester, shall have Forty Shillings Reward, and all necessary Charges paid.

Reprints: New England Weekly Journal, 02-07-1738; 02-14-1738; 02-27-1738.

New England Weekly Journal, 09-26-1738.

BROKE out of His Majesty's Goal in Boston, the last Night, nine Persons, as follows, viz. Thomas Dwyer an Irish Man, being a lusty full fac'd Fellow, of a pale Complection, having long strait black Hair; he had on when he went away, a dark blue Coat, about 25 Years of Age.

John Maccarty, a tall slim pock broken Fellow with a Scar upon his right Temple, about 30 Years of Age, he had on a green double breasted Jacket with Mettal Buttons.

Michael Hair, about 25 Years of Age, of middle Stature, short black Hair, down look, he had on a dark colour'd Coat; a Turner by Trade.

Alexander Maccarty, about 20 Years of Age, a likely Fellow, wears a light Wig, and a Cloth colour'd Coat.

One —— Hambleton, about 30 Years of Age, wears his own Hair, his fore locks are White, and is a short Fellow small Face, he had on a dark colour'd Coat; This fellow together with the aforegoing are Irish Men.

Thomas Mayby alias Thomas Manning, an English Man, a lusty well set Fellow, about 40 Years of Age, he had on a dark colour'd Coat & Great Coat.

And one Elizabeth Decoster about 30 Years of Age, a very likely Woman, she had on a strip'd Callimanco Gown.

An Indian Fellow named John Baker, a short Fellow, and who has but one Arm.

A Negro Fellow Named Jocco, about twenty Years of Age, a well set Fellow, speaks very good English, and is Servant to Capt. Sigourney.

Whoever shall apprehend the said Absconded Prisoners, and bring them to the said Prison, shall have Three Pounds Reward for each or either of them, paid by me, William Young.

Reprints: New England Weekly Journal, 12-19-1738; 12-20-1738; and 01-02-1739.

New England Weekly Journal, 10-10-1738.

Ran away from the Rev. Mr. Samuel Allis of Somars in the County of Hampshire, a Negro Man about 34 or 5 Years of Age, named Coffe, well built, of a middling Stature, talks very good English. He took away with him all his wearing Apparel consisting of sundry good Cloaths, viz a plain Cloth Coat of a brownish Colour with brass Buttons, another Coat of plain Cloth being black and white with large pewter Buttons, a Jacket of blue Camblet, with two pair of Linnen Breeches, two pair of Stockings, the one of black Worsted, and another of white Cotton, with a pair of Yarn Leggins, a pair of round to'd Shoes, the Heels of them being filled with Horse Nails, he had two Hatts, the one a Felt, and another of Leather, he took away with him his Master's Gun of several Pounds Value, being neatly zigg'd with Brass, the top of which Gun hath had its Stock broken off about four or five Inches, and it is splic'd with Brass, he had with him several Pounds of Money. Whoever shall take up the said Runaway and convey him to his Master in Somars aforesaid, or to Mr. Jonathan Dwight at the Sign of the Lamb in Boston, shall have Three Pounds Reward, and all necessary Charges paid. All Masters of Vessels and others, are hereby caution'd against concealing or carrying off the laid Servant on Penalty of the Law in that Case made and provided.

Somars, October 4, 1738.

Reprints: New England Weekly Journal, 10-17-1738; 01-09-1739.

New England Weekly Journal, 04-24-1739.

Ran-away from Mr. Pierson Richardson of Woburn, on the 30th of March past, a Negro Man Servant, named Jim about 29 Years of Age, middling Stature, ready to talk, and speaks good English, had on when he went away a grey colour'd homespun Coat, flat Pewter Buttons, a Cape on the Coat, strip'd Wastecoat, Breeches strip'd blue and white, old Shoes, Felt Hat.

Whoever shall take up the said Runaway, and him safely convey to his said Master at Woburn, shall have Forty Shillings and all necessary Charges paid. Boston, April 19th, 1739.

New England Weekly Journal, 10-30-1739.

Broke out of His Majesty's Goal in Boston, the 28th Instant at Night, Seven Prisoners, Named and Described as follows, Viz.

Gideon Braydon, about 26 Years of Age; He had on a dark Fustian checkered Coat, a Green Jacket, and a light Wigg.

John Call, about 21 Years of Age, of middling Stature, a stammering Speech; He had on a Great Coat, a Green Jacket, a pair of Trousers, and an old Hat.

John Rullo, about 20 Years of Age, a lusty young Fellow; He had on a yellowish colour'd Coat, and a white Cap.

Thomas Manuel, a free Negro Man, about 50 Years of Age, Gray-Headed; He had on dark colour'd Great Coat, a strip'd Jacket, and worsted Cap.

Lawrence Hoar, about 30 Years of Age, a lusty well set Fellow, has sore Eyes, short black Hair; He had on a Red Jacket, and a pair of Trowsers.

Thomas Weeks, about 23 years of Age, a short thick set Fellow; He had on a dark colour'd Great Coat, strip'd homespun Jacket, and a woolen Cap.

Carter McCarty, about 23 Years of Age, a short thick well set Fellow; He had on a Red Jacket, Wash-Leather Breeches, yarn Stockings, an old pair of Shoes, and a Leather Apron.

At the same Time, Ranaway from his Master John German, of Boston, Locksmith, an Irish Man Servant, named William Lenox, of middling Stature, pale thin Face, about 21 Years of Age; He had on a light colour'd Coat with a Cape, and Mettal Buttons, a dark colour'd Jacket, red Cloth Breeches with white Mettal Buttons, speckled Shirt, Felt Hat, gray worsted Stockings; tho' 'tis thought he has chang'd his Cloaths.

Whoever shall take up the abovesaid Runaways, and them safely convey or bring to His Majesty's Goal in Boston aforesaid, shall have Five Pounds Reward for each or either of the four first named Persons, and Three Pounds to each or either of the other Persons Named and Described as above, paid by

William Young

Boston, October 29th, 1739

Boston Evening Post, 10-11-1742.

Ran away from his Master, Capt. John Aves of Boston, on the 5th of this Instant August, a Negro named Phillip, about 28 Years old, much pitted with the Small Pox, and speaks pretty good English and Portuguise. He is use to the Sea, and 'tis supposed will endeavour to get off in some Vessel, having carried away his Sea Bedding and all his other Cloathes; therefore all Masters of Vessels and other Persons are hereby cautioned against concealing or carrying him off, as they will avoid the Penalty of the Law. And whoever shall take up the said Negro, and bring him to his abovesaid Master, living near Dr. Culter's Church at the North End of the Town, shall have Five Pounds Reward (Old Tenor) and all necessary Charges paid.

Reprint: Boston Evening Post, 10-25-1742.

Boston Evening Post, 10-18-1742.

Ran away from his Master, Shadrach Keen of Bristol, a Negro Man named Ben, about 29 Years old, small of Stature, and very full faced. He had on when he went away, a red Cloth double breasted Jacket, with a few Brass Buttons, but without Lining, and an old striped Flannel Shirt, a pair of old Shoes, and a Felt Hat with the Brim cut, and carried with him a Fiddle. He Ran away on the 9th Day of this Instant October. Whoever shall take up the said Servant, and bring him to his abovesaid Master in Bristol, shall have Five Pounds Reward in Old Tenor. October 14, 1742.

Reprints: Boston Evening Post, 10-25-1742; 11-15-1742.

Boston Evening Post, 11-08-1742.

Ran away from his Master, Mr. Joseph Callender of Boston the 13th of June past, a Negro Man named Coffy. He had when he went away, a check'd woolen Shirt, a Cloth Jacket, the Sleeves pretty long. He pretends he was freed by the Rev. M. Waldron of Boston, with whom he formerly lived. He has changed his Name when he Ran away before, to Sambo. Whoever shall take up the said Negro, and bring him to his said Master, shall have Three Pound (Old Tenor) Reward, and all necessary Charges paid, by

Boston, Oct. 21, 1742.

Joseph Callender, Jun.

Boston Evening Post, 12-06-1742.

Ran-away from his Master Mr. James Adams of Boston, Blockmaker, on the 26th Instant, a Negro Boy named Cicero, about 17 Years of Age, spare and thin, of a tawney Complection, and has a Scar in his under Lip, speaks good English; had on a double breasted Jacket with white mettal Buttons, a Cotton and Linnen Shirt, Leather Breeches, short Trousers, yarn Stockings, old Shoes.

Whoever shall take up said Runaway, and him safely convey to his said Master in Boston, shall have Five Pounds Reward old Tenor, and all necessary Charges paid.

All Masters of Vessels are caution'd against carrying off said Servant on Penalty of the Law. Boston, November 30, 1742.

Reprints: Boston Evening Post, 12-13-1742; 01-03-1742; 01-17-1743. This notice was also printed in The Boston Gazette, 11-30-1742; 01-04-1743; 01-11-1743.

Boston Evening Post, 01-03-1743.

Ran away from his Master, Mr. Lewis Vassall of Brantrey, a Negro Man named Cuffy, a short thick well set Fellow. Whoever shall take up the said Negro, and him safely convey to his aforesaid Master, shall have Three Pounds Reward, Old Tenor.

Reprint: Boston Evening Post, 01-17-43.

Boston Evening Post, 04-11-1743.

Ran away from Mr. Benjamin Hallowell of Boston, Shipwright, on Tuesday the 5th Instant, a Negro Boy about 19 Years old, named Paul, (who formerly belong'd to Major Lockman) well set, with a Scar in his Face. He had on when he went away, a blue jacket, Breeches and Stockings, a striped Cap, and had Brass Buckles in his Shoes. Whoever shall take up the said Negro, and bring him to his abovesaid Master, shall have Five Pounds Reward, Old Tonor, and all necessary Charges paid.

Reprints: Boston Evening Post, 08-1-1748; 08-8-1748. This notice was also printed The Boston Gazette, 04-12-1743; 04-19-1743.

Boston Evening Post, 06-06-1743.

Ran away from Capt. John Henderson of Boston, on the first Instant, a Negro Man named Charles, a tall well shap'd Fellow, with a Scar from the lower Part of his Nose through his upper Lip. He had on when he went away, speckled Shirt, a pair of Trouzers and a Cloth Jacket. Whoever shall take him up, and convey him to his said Master in Boston, shall have Forty Shillings Reward, Old Tenor, and all necessary Charges paid. All Master of Vessels and other are cautioned against entertaining or carrying off said Negro, as they would avoid the Penalty of the Law.

Reprint: Boston Evening Post, 06-13-1743.

Boston Evening Post, 08-01-1743.

Broke out of Bridewell Yesterday, and made his Escape, a lusty, stout and comely Negrow Fellow, named Dorus, belonging to Mr. James Griffin, Merchant in Boston. He had on a Leather Cap, a blue Sailor's Jacket, with Canvas Seams, a pair of Trouzers, and a pair of Shoes. Whoever shall take up the said Negro, and bring him to his abovesaid Master, living in Summer-Street, shall have Ten Pounds Reward, Old Tenor, and all necessary Charges paid. N.B. He is suppos'd to be gone towards Braintree.

Boston Evening Post, 09-19-1743.

Ran away from Mr. James Clark of Biddiford, at the Eastward, about two Months ago, a Negro Man named Quambe, about 40 Years old. He has a Hurt on two of his Fingers, and his Face is a little on one side. Whoever shall take up said Negro, and bring him to Mr. Benjamin Mathes or Joseph Sias at Durham in New-Hampshire, shall have Five Pounds Reward, Old Tenor, (or secure him and send them Word) and all necessary Charges paid.
      Reprint: Boston Evening Post, 09-26-1743.

Boston Evening Post, 01-09-1744.

Ran away from Capt. James Oliver of Boston, a Negro Man named Cambridge, about 27 Years old and Pockbroken, that has been used to work at the Baker's Trade. He had on a new double breasted light coloured Cloth Jacket, with flat Metal Buttons, lined with blue Bays, and a great Coat and Breeches of the same Cloth, or else a pair of blue Cloth Breeches, and a Seal-skin Cap. Whoever takes him up, and brings him to his abovesaid Master shall have 40s. Reward, old Tenor, and all necessary Charges. And all Masters of Vessels are forbid carrying him off, at their Peril. N.B. He is to be sold.
      Reprint: Boston Evening Post, 01-16-1744.

Boston Evening Post, 06-04-1744.

Newport, May 21st, 1744.
      Ran away on the 16th of this Instant May in the Night, from his Master Evan Mallbone of Newport, a Negro Man named Cuff, who formerly belonged to Thomas Borden of Portsmouth, and used to tend said Borden's Ferry; he is a stout lusty Fellow, aged about thirty Years; had on when he run away, a speckled Shirt and an Ozenbrig Frock and Trowzers, pretty much tarred, and Leather Breechesl and took with him a blue great Coat. He has but one Testicle.

Whoever shall apprehend said Negro and convey him to his abovesaid Master, shall have five Pounds old Tenor Reward, and all necessary Charges paid. Evan Mallbone.

Reprint: Boston Evening Post, 06-11-1744.

Boston Evening Post.; Date: 12-03-1744; Issue: 487; Page: [3].

Ran away from Samuel Morgareidge of Newbury, Shipwright, a Negro Fellow called Primus, alias Isaac, near 6 Feet high, well set, strait lim'd, speaks good English; had on when he went away, a scarlet Waistcoat with white metal Buttons, a blew out-side Jacket pretty much worn, and Leather Breeches, new Shoes and Hose, and a check'd wollen Shirt, no Hat nor Cap. Whosoever shall safely convey him to his abovesaid Master, shall have Five Pounds, old Tenor. Reward, and all necessary Charges paid them by me,

Newbury, Nov. 21st, 1744.

Samuel Morgareidge.

Reprints: Boston Evening Post, 10-09-1749. This notice was also printed in The Boston Gazette, 10-03-1749.

Boston Evening Post, 12-17-1744.

Ran away from the Hon. Benjamin Lynde, Jun. of Salem, Esq. on the 15th of this Instant December, a Negro Man named Cicero, about 22 Years old, pretty slim but tall. He had on when he went away, a blue great Coat, and an Olive-coloured Cloth Coat under it, a striped homespun Jacket, dark coloured Cloth Breeches, a speckled Shirt, gray Yarn Stockings, double soled Shoes, a Worsted Cap, and a Castor Hat. Whoever shall take up the said Negro, and him safely convey to his abovesaid Master in Salem, shall have Five Pounds, Old Tenor, Reward, and necessary Charges paid.

Boston Evening Post, 07-15-1745 (Supplement).

Ran away from John Martin of Jamestown, near Newport, Rhode-Island, on the 19th of June, a Negro named Glasgow, about 27 Years of Age. Had on a brown full'd Cloth Jacket, and a white one under it, a pair of Buckskin Breeches, a Bever Hat, and a Flannel Shirt. Whosoever shall apprehend said Runaway, and bring him to his Master, shall have Ten Pounds, old Tenor, Reward, and all necessary Charges paid by me, John Martin.

Reprint: Boston Evening Post, 07-22-1745.

Boston Evening Post, 07-22-1745 (Supplement).

Ran away from Thomas Fleet of Boston, Printer, last Night, the 18th Instant, a Negro Fellow named Newport, about 20 Years old. He is a sly cunning Rogue, of middle Stature, but pretty slim and spry, and has a large Scar over his right Eye, occasion'd by the Kick of a Horse. He had on a Cotton and Linen Shirt, and striped homespun Jacket and Breeches.

Whoever shall take him up, and bring him to his Master, at the Heart and Crown in Cornhill, shall be satisfied for their Trouble, and have all reasonable Charge paid.

N.B. he will endeavour to get of by Sea, therefore all Masters of Vessels and others are cautioned against harbouring, concealing or carrying him off on any Pretence whatever, as they would avoid the Penalty of the Law.

Boston, July 19, 1745.

Reprints: Boston Evening Post, 07-29-1745; 04-28-1746; 05-05-1746; 05-12-1746.

Boston Evening Post, 08-26-1745.

Ran away from Deacon Thomas Waite of Boston, about a Fortnight ago, a Negro Man named Cuffee, about 36 Years old, a stout well set Fellow, that speaks very good English, and has lost two of his upper Fore-Teeth. He had on when he went away, a blue Jacket and a striped Jacket, a pair of square toed Shoes, a pair of black Stockings, and a pair of tanned Trouzers. Whoever shall take up the said Run-away, and give Notice to his Master, shall have Five Pounds old Tenor, Reward, and necessary Charges paid. All Masters of Vessels and others are forewarned of carrying off the said Servant, on the Penalty of the Law in that Case made and provided.

Boston, Aug. 24, 1744.

Reprints: Boston Evening Post, 09-02-1745; 09-09-1745.

Boston Evening Post, 09-30-1745.

RUN away from Deacon Thomas Wilson of Exeter, on the 24th Instant, a Negro Slave named Cato, about Forty Years of Age, pretty slender body'd about five Foot and eight Inches high, walks with his Toes standing outward, has lost some of his upper fore Teeth; he carry'd away with him a brown Camblet Coat and Jacket, a white half thick Coat trim'd with black, a greyish colour'd Duroy Coat cuffed with black, a greenish homespun Coat with large flat Buttons, a blue Ratteen Jacket with wash'd Buttons, and Ratteen Briches with flat Buttons, and a good pair of Boots; a black Callimanco Jacket and Briches, and a greenish colour'd great Coat with large flat Buttons; five linnen Shirts and two check'd Cotton and Wool Shirts, with sundry pair of Stockings of diverse Colours, and a good Bever Hat, Silver lac'd, and a good Felt Hat, with sundry other Things.

Whoever shall take up said Negro, and bring him to his said Master in Exeter, shall have Five Pounds old Tenor as a Reward, and all necessary Charges paid, by me

Thomas Wilson.

Reprint: Boston Evening Post, 10-14-1745.

Boston Evening Post, 10-14-1745.

Ran away from his Master, Mr. Daniel Rea, of Boston, Tailor, some Weeks ago, a Negro Boy named Prince, about 16 Years of Age. He had on when he went away, a dark Cloth Jacket, Leather Breeches, and a check'd Shirt, but no Stockings or Shoes. Whoever shall take up the said Negro, and bring him to his said Master, shall have Forty Shillings Reward, Old Tenor, and all necessary Charges paid. N.B. All Masters of Vessels and others are cautioned against harbouring, concealing or carrying off said Negro, as they would avoid the Penalty of the Law. Boston, October 14, 1745.

Reprints: Boston Evening Post, 10-21-1745; 10-28-1745.

Boston Evening Post, 01-27-1746.

Ran away from Capt. Thomas Homans of Watertown, a Negro Man named Constant, about Twenty Seven Years old, of this Visage, and middling Stature, has a Scar under his Right Eye, and speaks good English. He had on when he went away, a blue Coat, with flat Brass Buttons, and a Leather Jacket, double breasted, with round Metal Buttons, and a Leather Apron. Whoever takes up the said Negro, and secures him so that his Master may have him again, shall have Three Pounds Reward, Old Tenor, and all reasonable Charges paid.

N.B. All Masters of Vessels and other Persons are hereby cautioned against harbouring, concealing, or carrying off the said Negro, as they would avoid the Penalty of the Law in that Case made and provided.

Boston, Jan. 23, 1745, 6.

Boston Evening Post, 02-03-1746.

Ran away from John Craister of Boston, a Negro Man named Will, about Thirty Years old, a thick short Fellow, speaks bad English: He had on when he went away, a Frock over a Cloth Jacket, and a red pair of Breeches. Whoever takes up the said Negro, and brings him to his said Master, at the South End, shall have Forty Shillings Reward, Old Tenor. N.B. All Masters of Vessels and other Persons, are hereby cautioned against harbouring, concealing or carrying of the said Negro, as they would avoid the Penalty of the Law in that Case made and provided. Boston, February the 1st, 1745,6.

Boston Evening Post, 02-24-1746.

Run away from his Master, Capt. John Steel, at the North End of Boston, the 17th Instant, a young Negro Fellow named Pompey, speaks pretty good English, is about 19 or 20 Years of Age, is short in Stature and pretty long Visaged, has been used to change his Name; he had on a green Ratteen Coat, Waistcoat and Breeches, the Coat pretty old with white Metal Buttons, a cotton and linen Shirt, an ordinary worsted Cap, and grey yarn Stockings; he took with him an old Hat, and a Leather Jocky-Cap, a pair of old black Stocking, and a new Ozenbrig Frock, and an old pair of Boots. He has made several Attempts to get off in some Vessel, therefore all Masters of Vessels are caution'd not to entertain him. Whoever shall apprehend the said Negro, and convey him to said master shall have Five Pounds, old Tenor, Reward, and all necessary Charges paid by, John Steel.

Boston, Feb. 19, 1745,6.

Reprints: Boston Evening Post, 03-10-1746. This notice was also printed in the Boston Weekly News Letter, 02-2-1746; 02-27-1746; 03-14-46. Notice was also printed in the Boston Gazette, 02-25-46; 03-04-1746; 03-11-1746.

Boston Evening Post, 08-25-1746.

Ran away from his Master, John Horsewell of Little Compton, on the 8th of this Instant August, a Negro Man named Prince, about 30 Years old, of a midling Stature, and some Words he cannot speak plain. He had on a new Castor Hat, Linen check'd Shirt, a double breasted Linen striped Jacket, a gray Jacket with Pewter Buttons, one pair of check'd Trouzers, and another pair of white, two pair of Stockings, one of Yarn and the other Worstead, of a bluish Colour, and a pair of single soled Calf skin Shoes. Whoever shall take up said Negro, and bring him to his said Master, shall have Five Pounds Reward, Old Tenor, and all necessary Charges paid. Aug. 15, 1746.

Reprints: Boston Evening Post, 09-01-1746; 09-08-1746.

Boston Evening Post, 09-29-1746.

Ran away from his Master, Col. William Williams, a lusty well set Negro named Caesar, (sometimes calls himself Archalus) near six Feet tall, speaks pretty good English; had on when he went away, a grey Jacket, Buff

Breeches and a rusty Hat, the Brims cut narrow. Whoever shall apprehend said Negro, and bring him to his said Master in Boston, shall have Five Pounds, Old Tenor, Reward, paid by

WILLIAM WILLIAMS.

Note, all Masters of Vessels and others are hereby cautioned against concealing, harbouring or carrying off said Negro, as they will answer the same.

Boston Evening Post, 03-16-1747.

Ran away from Col. Joseph Stafford of Warwick, the 1st of January last, a Molatto Man Servant named Ben Peg, alias Ben Austin, a lusty well set Fellow, who had on a light coloured Pea Jacket, old Shoes and Stockings, with a Scar on his Nose, and a large Scar on one of his Legs. Whoever shall take up said Servant, and send him Home, or secure him that he may be had, shall have Five Pounds Reward, Old Tenor, and all necessary Charges paid by Martin Howard of Newport, or Joseph Stafford.

Reprints: Boston Evening Post, 03-23-1747; 03-30-1747.

Boston Evening Post, 04-06-1747.

A Negro Fellow named Moses, about 24 Years of Age, Servant to the Rev. Mr. Welsted, left his Master's House last Friday Evening, and is suppos'd to be conceal'd on board some Vessel. He had on a blue Coat and a Leather Jockey Cap, but is suspected to have furnish'd himself with Seamen's Cloaths. All Masters of Vessels and others are cautioned against carrying him off, and if any Person will give Information where he may be found, they shall receive Five Pounds, Old Tenor, Reward.

Reprint: Boston Evening Post, 04-13-1747.

Boston Evening Post, 05-04-1747.

Run away from me the Subscriber, about three Weeks past, a likely Negro Man called Robin about 22 Years of Age, and had on when he went away, a short blue Jacket, and blue Breeches. Whoever takes up said Negro, and conveys him safely to me at Cambridge, shall have Ten Pounds (old Tenor) Reward, and all necessary Charges paid them. And all Persons are hereby forbid to harbour or carry off said Negro, as they would being prosecuted with the utmost Rigour of the Law. HENRY VASSALL.

Reprint: Boston Evening Post, 05-11-1747.

Boston Evening Post, 10-05-1747.

Ran away from the Rev. Mr. Samuel Brown of Abington, on the 26 of this Instant September, a Mulatto Fellow named Cuffy, about 20 Years of Age, of a short Stature, pretty well set, and has a Scar or two upon his Neck, under his Shirt Collar, which was occasioned by the King's Evil. He had on when he went away, a short brown double breasted Jacket, with a greenish Cast, and Pewter Buttons, and an under Jacket o striped Linnen and Wool, also Linnen Trowsers.

Whoever shall take up said Servant, and bring him to his said Master, or secure him so that his said Master may have him again, shall have Three Pounds Reward, old Tenor, and all necessary Charges paid.

Note, his Hair is cut off.

N.B. That all Masters of Vessels and other Persons are hereby forbidden concealing or carrying off said Servant, as they would avoid the Penalty of the Law in that Case made and provided.

Boston Evening Post, 07-04-1748.

Ran away from his Master, a Negro Boy named Cato, the 30th June, lately belonging to Dr. Stevens of Roxbury, now of Boston. Had on when he went away, a white Cloth Coat, a white Flannel Waistcoat, without Sleeves, a white Shirt, a Bever Hat, about 16 Years old, speaks good English, and stutters a little. Whoever will bring said Negro to the Printer, shall have Five Pounds, Old Tenor, Reward, and all necessary Charges paid; and all Masters of Vessels and others are desired not to conceal or harbour him, upon Penalty of the Law.

Reprints: Boston Evening Post, 07-11-1748. This notice was also printed in The Boston Gazette, 07-05-1748.

Boston Evening Post, 08-01-1748.

Ran away from his Master, John Allen, Merchant of Newton, a Negro Man named Quomino, about 21 Years of Age, a likely Fellow, of a midling Stature, his Head shav'd half over, and speaks good English, carried away with him, an Olive coloured Cloth Coat with Buttons of the same Colour, a new Jacket and Breeches, dark Cloth Colour, homespun, with Pewter Buttons on, two pair of Trowsers, two Tow Shirts, two Linnen Shirts, an old Bever Hat, and large Brass Buckles in his Shoes, &c. He also carried with him a Scythe.

Whoever shall take him up and return him to his said Master, shall receive of him the Sum of Five Pounds, and all necessary Charges, in Old Tenor Money: And all Masters of Vessels are upon their Peril, forbid concealing or carrying off said Servant.

Newton, July 26, 1748.

Reprint: Boston Evening Post, 08-08-1748.

Boston Evening Post, 09-26-1748.

Ran away on the 19th of this Instant September, from his Master John Johnson of Boston, Jack-maker, a Negro Man Servant named Jo, about 23 Years of Age, a likely Fellow, who had on when he went away, a dark coloured Fly Coat, with flat white Metal Buttons, a Swan Skin double breasted Jacket, Leather Dear-Skin Breeches, a pair of high heel'd thick soled Shoes. He can play on the Flute, has a Scar on his upper Lip, and speaks good English. Whoever shall take him up, and deliver him to his said Master, shall have Ten Pounds Reward, Old Tenor, and all reasonable Charges paid.—All Masters of Vessels and others, are hereby cautioned against harbouring, concealing or carrying off said Negro, as they will avoid the Penalty of the Law.

Reprints: Boston Evening Post, 10-03-1748 and 10-10-1748. This notice was also printed in the Boston Weekly News Letter, 09-22-1748; 10-06-1748; and, 10-13-1748.

Boston Evening Post, 10-10-1748.

Ran away from his Master, Mr. John Wakefield of Boston, a Negro Man Servant named Bonney, about 23 Years of Age, who had on when he went away, a Bengall Coat, the Buttons of the same, lined with Blue, a striped homespun Jacket, with Pewter Buttons, a pair of blue Kersey Breeches, with Pewter Buttons, a pair of blue worsted Stockings, and a check'd Shirt. Whoever shall take him up and bring him to his said Master, near the Rev. Mr. Mather's Meeting House, shall be satisfied for their Trouble, and have all necessary Charges paid,

by John Wakefield

Boston, October 10, 1748.

Reprints: Boston Evening Post, 10-17-1748; 10-24-1748. This notice was also printed in the Boston Gazette, 11-20-1753 and 11-27-53.

Boston Evening Post, 05-22-1749.

Ran away from his Master, Mr. Matthew Hopkins of Boston, Sawyer, on the 13th of this Instant May, a stout well set Negro Man named Herculus, about 30 or 35 Years of Age, and speaks good English. He has a large Bump on his left Shin, and had on when he went away, a blue Cloth Jacket, stitch'd up the Seams with Canvas, and an under Jacket laced up the Breast, a woollen check'd Shirt, a pair of Buck skin Breeches, with plain metal Buttons, a pair of Shoes and blue Yarn Stockings, but no Hat. Whoever shall take up the said Negro, and bring him to his said Master, shall have Five Pounds Reward, old Tenor, and all necessary Charges paid. N.B. All Masters of Vessels are cautioned against concealing or carrying off said Negro, as they would avoid the Penalty of the Law.

Reprints: Boston Evening Post, 05-29-1749; 06-05-1749.

Boston Evening Post, 06-26-1749.

Ran away the 17th of June from John Hunt of Watertown, a Negro Servant named Caesar, about 17 Years old, middling Stature for his Age, speaks English, but has a hoarse Voice constantly, understands Farming Business, and lived with Mr. Nath. Battle of Dirham, and is suppos'd his Intention was to go to a Township call'd Narragansett No. 4. Had on when he went away a dark striped Homespun Jacket and Breeches, a pair of light Worsted Stockings, and new Pumps. Whoever shall take up said Runaway, and him convey to said Hunt, shall have Ten Pounds, old Tenor, paid him by said Hunt, and all necessary Charges, and all Masters of Vessels and others are hereby caution'd against concealing, or carrying off said Servant, as they would avoid the Penalty of the Law.

Reprints: Boston Evening Post, 07-03-1749; 07-10-1749. This notice was also printed in the Boston Gazette, 06-27-1749.

Boston Evening Post, 07-31-1749.

Whereas a French Negro named Francis, Ran away from his Master James Smith of Boston, Sugar Baker, on the twelfth Instant: Whoever will bring the said Negro to his Master, or secure him in any of his Majesty's Goals, shall have Five Pounds, old Tenor, Reward, and necessary Charges. The said Negro is of middle Stature, well featured, very black, smooth skin'd, flat nosed, and speaks with a low Voice. Had on when he Ran away, a white Cap and Frock, blue Jacket and Breeches, with Brass Buttons, Shoes and Stockings, and sometimes wears a Gold Ring in his Ear. N.B. He was taken from Martinico, carried to Louisbourg, and brought to Boston by Sir Peter Warren.

James Smith.

Reprint: Boston Gazette, 07-18-1749.

Boston Evening Post, 08-07-1749.

Ran away from his Master, Mr. John Read of Norwich, on the 31st of July, a Mulatto Man Servant, a stout lusty Fellow, speaks good English; he hath been branded in the Forehead with the Letter B, and hath his right Ear cut. Whoever will secure said Servant, and him safely convey to his said Master, shall have Ten Pounds, old Tenor, Reward, and all necessary Charges paid.
    Reprint: Boston Evening Post, 08-21-1749.

Boston Evening Post, 09-11-1749.

Ran away from Master, William Bucknam, of Falmouth in Casco Bay, in the Month of July last, a Negro Man named Cuffe, aged about 40 Years, a pretty tall spare Fellow, who had on a blue Broad Cloth Coat, a black Jacket and striped Breeches and Trowsers, gray Stockings, and thick Shoes, a Worsted Cap and a Fe't Hat, He has Scares on each Cheek, and I hear he has with him a forged Pass, which he got with the Help of some evil minded Person, which protects him from being taken up. Whoever shall take up said Fellow, and convey him to his said Master in Falmouth, or to Capt. Benjamin Blany in Malden, shall have Twenty Pounds, Old Tenor, Reward, and all necessary Charged paid by me, William Bucknam.
    N.B. He has been something used to the Sea, and will endeavour to get off; therefore all Masters of Vessels and other Persons are hereby cautioned against harbouring, concealing or carrying him off, as they will avoid the Penalty of the Law. Sept. 3, 1749.
    Reprints: Boston Evening Post, 09-18-1749; 09-25-1749; 04-07-1755; 05-26-1755; 06-30-1755; 07-05-1755; 07-14-1755. This notice was also printed in the Boston Weekly News Letter, 09-14-1749; 09-28-1749; the Boston Gazette, 08-15-1749.

Boston Evening Post, 09-25-1749.

Ran away from his Masters, John Salmon and Company, the 15th Instant, a Spanish Negro Man named Andrew, (but calls himself Andress) between 30 and 40 Years of Age, a thick square set Fellow, with a Scar on his Chin, talks broken English, had on when he went away, a strip'd Worsted Cap, a Lead coloured outside thick Kersey Jacket, with thick Metal Buttons on it, a strip'd homespun blue and white under Jacket, with the Stripes made the cross Way, a speckled Linen Shirt, a pair of Buckskin Breeches, (almost new) with Leather Buttons, a pair of gray Yarn or blue Worsted Stockings, and a pair of half worn Shoes, with a pair of large broad Buckles. Whoever shall take up said Runaway, and him convey to his Masters in Boston, shall have Ten Pounds Old Tenor, and all necessary Charges paid.

Reprints: Boston Evening Post, 10-02-1749; 10-09-1749. This notice was also printed in the Boston Gazette, 09-26-1749.

Boston Evening Post, 10-23-1749.

Ran away from his Master Dr. William Clark, of Boston, on the 14th Instant, a likely strait lim'd Negro Boy, about 16 or 17 Years of Age, and speaks very good English. He had on a blue grey Broad Cloth Jacket, and a blue and white striped Swanskin Jacket under it, a Cotton and Linen Shirt, and a greasy pair of Leather Breeches. Whoever shall take up the said Runaway, and bring him to his said Master, shall have Ten Pounds, old Tenor, Reward, and all necessary Charges paid.

Boston Gazette, Monday August 10, to Monday August 17, 1741.

Ran-away from his master Mr. John Pinder, of North Kingstown, in the Colony of Rh. Island, on June 22d 1740, a Negro Man Servant named Plumb, about 25 Years of Age, a thick well set Fellow, middling Stature, full fac'd, has a bump on the inside of his right Thumb; and he can play on a Fiddle.

Whoever shall take up the abovesaid Runaway, and him safely convery to his said Master, shall have Ten Pounds Reward, and all necessary Charges paid by me.

John Pinder.

Boston Gazette, Monday October 5, to Monday October 12, 1741.

Broke out of Bridewell the last Week a Negro Fellow named Pompey, belonging to Mrs. Margaret Jeykll of Boston; he is about 22 Years of Age middling Stature, had on a black Lambskin Wigg, black Cloth Jacket, blue Cloth Breeches, gray Rib'd Stockings and new Shoes. Whoever apprehends him and convey to his Mistress, shall have Three Pounds Reward, and all necessary Charges.

Boston Gazette, 03-15-1743.

Newport, Rh Island, March 10, 1743.
Ran away from his Master the 6th or 7th Inst a tall, well set Spanish Negro Man, about 26 Years of Age, is something of a yellowish Complexion, and bow leg'd, talks little or no English, and had on when he Ran away, a Castor Hat, a grey homespun double breasted short Jacket, with Metal Buttons, old Breeches and Stockings. All Persons are cautioned against harbouring or entertaining the said Fellow, and whoever takes him up, and brings

him to the Subscriber, or conveys Intelligence so as he may come at him, shall have Three Pounds Reward, old Tenor, and all necessary Charges paid by

Patrick Grant.

Boston Gazette, 06-07-1743.

Ran-away from Capt. John Bulkley of Boston on the 25th of last Month, a Negro Girl named Billah, about 18 Years of Age, short of Stature, and well dress'd. Whoever takes her up and brings her to her said Master, shall be satisfied to Content. And all Persons are hereby caution'd against entertaining, concealing or carrying off said Servant on Penalty of the Law.
    Reprints: Boston Gazette, 11-03-1747; 09-27-1748; 10-11-1748; 10-18-1748.

Boston Gazette, 07-12-1743.

Ran-away from on Board the Snow Katherine John Pharour Master, a lusty Negro Fellow named Robin; he had on when he went away a speckled Shirt, and a pair of Ozenbrigs Trousers. Whoever shall take up said Runaway and bring him to his Master on Board said Snow lying at Hutchingson's Wharffe, shall have Six Pounds old Tenor Reward, and all necessary Charges paid.

Boston Gazette, 08-02-1743.

Taken away from Mr. James Dolebeare of Boston, Braslet, some few Days ago, a Negro Female Child called Rose, aged about five Years, had on a green Petticoat, and a white Wastcoat, and has a large Scar on one of her Breast. If any Person can give information to said Dolbeare, where said Negro may be found; it being apprehended that she is concealed by some ill minded and malicious Persons, the Person that makes the Discovery shall be suitably rewarded. And all Persons are hereby forewarned from entertaining said Negro on any Pretense whatever at their Peril, even Mr. Benjamin Babbidge himself.

Boston Gazette, 09-13-1743.

Ranaway from Capt. Thomas Frankland, Commander of His Majesty's Ship Rose, a Negro Man Servant named Joseph Green, about 5 Feet 6 Inches high, speaks good English, had on a light coloured Cloth Jacket and a pair of Trowsers, is about 22 Years old.

Whoever takes up said Negro and brings him to the Collector Henry Frankland, Esq; in Boston, shall have five Pounds Reward, old Tenor, and all necessary Charges.

And all Masters of Vessels are forbid carrying off said Servant on Penalty of the Law.

Boston Gazette, 06-12-1744.

Ran-away from Mr. John Hunt of Watertown, a Negro Man nam'd Ben, about 30 Years of Age, (he says 27) yellow Complection, round Face, speaks good English, a pleasant Countenance, middle Stature, treads light, understands Farming; he had on when he went away, a Drabb Cloth colour'd Jacket, near the Colour of his Complection, a Pair of black Sheep Skin Breeches, his Wool was just cut off, he plays on a Violin. Whoever shall take up the abovesaid Run-away, and him convey to his said Master, shall have Five Pounds (old Tenor) Reward, and all necessary Charges. All Masters of Vessels are hereby caution'd against carrying off said Servant, on Penalty of the Law.

Boston Gazette, 09-25-1744.

Ran-away from her Master George Tibbits of North Kingstown, a Mustee Servant Woman named Phelice, of a short Stature, fat of Body, very crooked Legs, about 30 Years of Age; she hath taken away with her two Gowns, one a striped Cotton, the other a striped black and white Drugget, a quilted Coat, and a striped Flannel Coat, three Shifts two old Tow and one a Flannel; she went away the 13th of this Instant in the Night in Company with a Mustee Man named Benjamin: They have taken sundry Things from said Tibbits.

Whoever shall take up said Servant Woman, shall have Three Pounds old Tenor and five Pounds for both of said Runaways, and all necessary Charges paid, they conveying them or either of them to said Tibbits, or securing them so that said Runaways may be had again.

Septemb. 14th 1744.

George Tibbits.

Boston Gazette, 03-12-1745.

Ran-away from Mr. David Snoden of Boston, on the 25th ult, a Negro man named Peter, about 30 Years of Age, speaks good English, in a Chimney-Sweeper's Dress, and generally employed in that Business. Whoever shall take up said Negro, and bring him to his said Master, shall be well rewarded. And all Masters of Vessels and others are hereby warn'd against carrying off said Servant.

Reprint: Boston Gazette, 03-19-1745.

Boston Gazette, 06-18-1745.

Ran-away from Master David Wallis of Woodstock, on the 22d of last May, a Negro Man named Jammey, speaks good English, but stutters something, he is of a middling Stature and well set; had on when he went away, a good beaver Hat, a blue strait bodied Coat, with brass Buttons, duroy Jacket and Breeches of a light blue, trim'd with Mohair of the same Colour, blue Stockings and new Shoes; carried with him five Shirts, two Woollen and three Linnen, and two pair of Leather Breeches, and a Hanger, a blue great Coat. Whoever shall take up said Runaway and bring him to his said Master, or secure him in any Jail, so that his Master may have him again, shall have five Pounds Reward, old Tenor, and all reasonable Charges paid

by David Wallis

And all Masters of Vessels and others are hereby caution'd against concealing or carrying off said Servant, on Penalty of Law.

Reprints: Boston Gazette, 09-24-1745; 10-08-1745.

Boston Gazette, 07-09-1745.

Ran-away from Capt. Joseph Hale of Newbury, a Negro Man named Cato the 6th Instant, about 22 Years of Age, short and small, speaks good English, and can read and write, understands farming Work, carry'd with him a striped homespun Jacket & Breeches, and Trousers, and an outer Coat & Jacket of home-made Cloth, two pair of Shoes, sometimes wears a black Wigg, has a smooth Face, a sly Look, took with him a Violin, and can play well thereon. Had with him three Linnen Shirts home-made pretty fine yarn Stockings. Whoever shall bring said Negro to his said Master, or secure him so that he may have him again, shall have five Pounds Reward, and all necessary Charges paid by me

Newbury July 8th 1745.

Joseph Hale.

Reprint: Boston Gazette, 07-16-1745.

Boston Gazette, 08-20-1745.

Ran-away from Mr. Daniel Lyon of Woodstock, a Negro Man named Cuffey, aged about 35 Years, middle Stature, had on a double breasted light colour'd broad Cloth Jacket, &c. speaks good English, a sensible understanding Fellow, and can tell a fair Story. Whoever takes up said Negro, and shall bring or send him to his Master, shall have five Pounds, old Tenor Reward, and all necessary Charges.

And all Persons are hereby warned against concealing or carrying off said Servant. Woodstock, July 25, 1745.

Reprints: Boston Gazette, 08-27-1745; 09-03-1745; 09-17-1745.

Boston Gazette, 09-24-1745.

Ran-away from her master Thadeus Mason of Charlestown, on the 22d Instant at Night or the next Morning, a Negro Woman named Jenny, about thirty Years of Age, middle Stature, well set, and speaks good English, she carry'd away with her a black Crape Gown, a strip'd Holland and flower'd Callico, and a Cotton and Linnen ditto, also a homespun Gown much worn, with sundry other Cloaths in a wooden Box, and Pillow Case.

Whoever shall take up said Run-away, and convey her to her said Master, shall have Three Pounds, old Tenor, Reward, and necessary Charges paid.

And all Persons are caution'd against harbouring, concealing or carrying off said Negro.

Charlestown, Sept. 23d 1745.

Boston Gazette, 10-08-1745.

Ran-away from Thomas Disbrow of Fairfield in Connecticut, on the 27th of last Month, a Negro Man named Newport, aged about forty Years, a tall slim Fellow, talks very good English: Had on when he went away, a homespun brown Jacket and Linnen Trousers; he also had with him a Leather Jacket and Breeches, two Coats, the one a blue Duroy fly Coat, and the other a Flannel one with brass Buttons, four Jackets one of them streaked, three Shirts two of them chequer'd and one new tow Frock, two pair of woolen Stockings. Whoever shall take up said Run-away, and bring or secure him, so that I may have him again, shall have five Pounds Reward, old Tenor, and all necessary Charges paid, by me

Thomas Disbrow.

And all Persons are caution'd against harbouring, concealing, or carrying off said Negro. Fairfield, Sept. 20th 1745.

Reprint: Boston Gazette, 10-15-1745.

Boston Gazette, 02-04-1746.

On the ninth Day of January Instant, one Jonathan Black broke out and Ran away from his Majesty's Goal in York, in the Province of the Massachusetts Bay, who stood committed upon a Conviction of Theif, and upon an Action of Debt. He is a Molatto Fellow of a middle Stature, pretty thin and spare in his make, of a swarthy Complection, black Eyes and Beard, about twenty eight Years of Age: He had on when he went away an old red duffle Great

Coat. Whoever shall apprehend said Fellow and secure him, so that he may be retaken, shall ten Pounds old Tenor Reward, and all reasonable Charges paid. York, January 10, 1745.

Joseph Plaisted.

Boston Gazette, 06-10-1746.

Ran-away on the 6th Instant, from his Master John Barrell, of Boston, a Negro Man named Pompey, about 20 Years old, well-shap'd, of a midling Stature, had on when he went away a blue Jacket, white Shirt, Leather Breeches, white worsted Stockings. Whosoever shall apprehend the said Run-away, and bring him to said Barrell's House in Sudbury Street: shall have Three Pounds old Tenor, Reward, and all necessary Charges paid.

And all Masters of Vessels are hereby caution'd not to entertain or carry off the said Negro, upon Penalty of the Law, in that Case made and provided.

Reprint: Boston Gazette, 06-17-1746.

Boston Gazette, 07-15-1746.

Ran-away from his Master Capt. John Leppington of Charlestown, on Tuesday Evening the 8th Instant, a Negro Man named York, a tall stout Fellow, about twenty Years of Age, he had on when he went away a strip'd homespun Jacket, a blue Cloth Breeches, and Cotton and Linnen Shirt, wor[faded] Cap, no Hat Shoes nor Stockings. Whoever shall take up the abovesaid Runaway and him safely convey to his said Master in Charlestown, shall have Five Pounds old Tenor Reward, and all necessary Charges paid.

And all Masters of Vessels are hereby warned against carrying off said Servant, on Penalty of the Law in that Case made and provided.

Boston July 12, 1746.

Boston Gazette, 07-15-1746.

Ran away on the 3d instant, a Negro Man named Portsmouth, aged about 40 Years, of middle Stature, walks Limping and Sp'a-footed, talks good English, and plays on the Fiddle, he carried with him an Orange coloured Coat with yellow mettal Buttons, a Wast Coat of thin Stuff, and Cloath Breeches.

Whoever takes up said Fellow is dressed to convey him to Robert Temple at his House in Charlestown, and they shall have Five Pounds Reward old Tenor, and all necessary Charges paid.

Boston Gazette, 10-28-1746.

Ran away from his Master Philip Caverly of Colchester in Connecticut, on the 24th of April last, a negro Man named Japhet, about 21 Years old, his Toes on one Foot froze off, and Part of the other: He had on when he went away a Great Coat of a brown Colour, and a close bodied Coat of the same colour, Linnen Breeches, gray Stockings; but I suppose that in this length of Time he may have chang'd his Cloaths: He passes himself for a Freeman. Whoever shall take up said Runaway, and convey him to his Master, shall have twenty Pounds old Tenor Reward, and all necessary Charges paid: And if taken up forty Miles from Home, commit him to the next Goal, and sent me Word.

Boston Gazette, 05-05-1747.

Ran away from Samuel White of Haverhill the 27th ult, a thick well set Negro Man, named Boston, 25 Years of Age, with a lightish colour'd Home-spun Coat with Jacket Sleves, with a dark green Jacket, a striped Jacket and Breeches, large brass shoe Buckels. Whosoever shall take up said Negro, and return him to the Subscriber shall have five Pounds old Tenor Reward, and all necessary Charges defrayed by me

Samuel White.

N. B. The Fellow above described has also a light colour'd great Coat a red Cap with a black Wig, and will doubtless, as is usual for Runaways, change and vary his Dress, as often as possible, that he may the more effectually compleat his Design.

Boston Gazette, 06-30-1747.

Broke from His Majesty's Goal in Boston, on Tuesday the 23d of June Instant, a Negro Man named George, belonging to Robert Oliver, Esq; of Dorchester, committed for Theft: He is a pretty tall likely Fellow, very black, speaks good English; he had nothing on when he went away but a check'd Shirt, & a pair of Trousers.

Whoever shall apprehend the said Negro, and bring him to the said Prison in Boston, shall have ten Pounds old Tenor, Reward, and all necessary Charges paid, by

Wm. Young.

And all masters of Vessels and others are hereby caution'd against concealing or carrying off said Negro, on penalty of the Law.

Boston, June 24th, 1747.

Reprints: Boston Gazette, 07-07-1747; 07-14-1747; 09-15-1747; 09-22-1747; 09-29-1747.

Boston Gazette, 11-17-1747.

Ran away from Messieurs Dean and Mason of Boston, about the 10th Currant, a Negro Man Servant, named Ned, about 30 Years of Age, speaks good English and French, a tall slender well set Fellow, about 5 Foot 10 Inches high, had on a blew Jacket, and Breeches of the same, speckled Shirt, and appears as a Sailor.

Whoever shall take up said Run-away, and him safely convey to the said Dean and Mason, living in New Boston, shall have five Pounds old Tenor Reward, and all necessary Charges paid:

And all Masters of Vessels and others, are hereby forbid concealing or carrying off said Servant on Penalty of the Law.

Reprint: Boston Gazette, 11-24-1747.

Boston Gazette, 02-02-1748.

Ran-away on the 26th of January from his Master, Joseph Procter of Boston, a Negro Man named Brislo, about 26 or 7 Years of age, a well set likely Fellow somewhat Pock broken in his Face, speaks good English, he had on and carried away, a good blew great Coat, a light kersey Jacket and a black Jacket, and a red under Jacket, grey Yarn Stockings, and a pair of large Shoe Buckles. Whoever shall take up the abovesaid Negro, and safely convey him to his abovesaid Master, shall have ten Pounds old Tenor Reward, and all necessary Charges paid.

N.B. And all Masters of Vessels and others, are hereby caution'd against concealing or carrying off said Negro on Penalty of the Law.

Reprint: Boston Gazette, 02-16-1748.

Boston Gazette, 03-22-1748.

Ran-away the 20th Instant from his Mistress Ruth Clark of Boston, a Negro Man named Cambridge, who formerly belonging to Mr. Newhall of Roxbury, had on when went away a strip'd Homespun Jacket, blue Coat, with Pewter Buttons, and a blue Great Coat, Leather Breeches and Trowsers, yarn Stockings, round to'd Shoes and large buckles, white Shirt, check'd Hankerchief, bever Hat, strip'd worsted Cap, and took with him a drab cloth Jacket, a blue ditto, fine Garlix shirt and a woollen check one: Whoever shall take up said Negro and bring to the Printer hereof, shall have three Pounds old Tenor, and all necessary Charges paid.

And all Masters of Vessels are hereby caution'd against carrying off said Negro on Penalty of the Law. Boston March 22, 1748.

Reprint: Boston Gazette, 04-26-1748.

Boston Gazette, 09-20-1748.

Ran-away from his Master Chadwallader Ford of Wilmington, on the 16th Instant, a Negro Man named Cyrus, a lusty well set Negro, about 29 Years of Age, stammers in his Speech, full fac'd, had on when he went away a homespun Jacket with hard metal Buttons, Garlix and a tow Shirt, and rock with him dithers or her Cloaths. Viz a Coat & Jacket of red Cambler, a homespun Coat lin'd with red, and an old black Wigg, which he sometimes wears, a lac'd Hat something worn, blue rib Stockings, and other worsted & yarn Stockings. The said Negro formerly liv'd with Mr. Hubbard of Runland, after that with Mr. Ward of said Worcester, and then with Col. Chandler of Worcester, then with Mr. Hunt of Watertown. 'Tis suppos'd he has taken Worcester or Rhode-Island Road.

Whoever shall take up said Servant and him convey to his aforesaid Master at Wilmington, shall have ten Pounds old Tenor Reward and all necessary Charge paid.

The said Negro has been us'd to lie by a Days and travel in the Night; he took a Halter with him with a Design 'tis probable to steal a Horse.

And all masters of Vessels & others, are hereby caution'd against concealing or carrying off said Negro on Penalty of the Law. Sept. 20. 1748.

Boston Gazette, 11-15-1748.

Ran-away from his Master Mr. Samuel Miller of Boston, Gunsmith, on the 28th Day of May last, a Negro Man named Caesar, aged about 30 Years, a pretty sensible Fellow, well set, of midling Stature has a Scar under his Throat, speaks very good English, had on when he went away, a grey broad Cloth Coat, and a blue Cloth double breasted Jacket, all trim'd, and blue Breeches, has since his cunning away been Privateering out of Rhode Island, and is lately retun'd, and calls himself Jo Adams, and may probably now appear in a Sailor's Habit.

Whoever shall take up the abovesaid Runaway, and convey him to his Master abovesaid, shall have thirty Pounds, old Tenor Reward, and all necessary Charges paid, by Samuel Miller.

Reprint: Boston Gazette, 11-22-1748.

Boston Gazette, 12-06-1748.

Ran-away on the 24th of November last from their master Timothy Stevens of Boston, two Negro Men [Slaves,] both aged about 24 Years, one named Cato, a tall well set Fellow, speaks English pretty well, had on when he went away, a dark Great Coat something patch'd, a new Felt Hat, a pair of short Trowsers, blue rib'd Stockings, woollen check'd Shirt. The other named

London a middle siz'd well set Fellow, speaks but little English, had on a dark Great Coat much worn, new Felt Hat, Waistcoat, black Leather Breeches, blue ribb'd Stockings, double Channel'd Pumps, steel Buckles, woollen check Shirt. Whoever shall take up said Runaways, and convey them to their Master, shall have five Pounds old Tenor Reward for each or either of them, and all necessary Charges paid by me

Timothy Stevens.

Reprint: Boston Gazette, 04-04-1749.

Boston Gazette, 03-07-1749.

Ran-away from her master Richard Smith of Boston, Inholder, on Sunday the nineteenth of February Instant, a Negro Woman named Diana, about twenty five Years of Age; she had on when she went away a homespun Gown, with a Patch on the Corner of another Sort; she carried away sundry other Cloaths with her. She formerly belong'd to Mr. Billings.

Whoever shall take up said Negro, and bring her to her said Master at Admiral Vernon's Head in King's Street, or secure her in any of his Majesty's Goals, shall have five Pounds old Tenor Reward, and all necessary Charges paid.

And all Masters of Vessels and others are hereby caution'd against carrying off or concealing the said Negro, as they would avoid the Penalty of the Law, in that case made and provided.

Boston, Feb. 27. 1748,9.

Reprint: Boston Gazette, 03-21-1749.

Boston Gazette, 05-02-1749.

Ran-away from his Master William Ellery of Cape Ann, on the 14th Instant at Night, a Negro Man named Caesar, is a very likely Fellow, speaks good English has lost his left Hand little Finger, and the next to it is a little crooked; is about 30 Years of Age, had on when he went away, a Cloth colour'd Kersey Jacket, lin'd with blew Bays, and flat Pewter Buttons, an old Pair of red Cloth Breeches, a Pair of Trousers, black Stockings, and a Pair of large Brass Shoe-Buckels.

Whoever shall take up said Negro, and bring him to his Master at Cape Ann aforesaid, or secure him so that his Master may have him again, shall have seven Pounds old Tenor Reward, and all necessary Charges paid.

And all Masters of Vessels and others, are hereby warned against concealing or carrying off said Servant on Penalty of the Law.

Boston, April 27th 1749.

Boston Gazette, 05-09-1749.

Ran-away on the 27th of April past, from his master Jonathan White of Weymouth, a Negro Man Servant named Scipio about 27 Years of Age, of middling Stature, had on a double breasted Jacket, gray colour, with flat Metal Buttons, and a blue under one, a new check Shirt, small Bever Hat, a Pair of Trousers, and round to'd Shoes. Whoever shall take up said Runaway, and bring him to his abovesaid Master, shall have ten Pounds, old Tenor Reward, and all necessary Charges paid. And all Masters of Vessels and others, are hereby caution'd against concealing or carrying off said Servant on Penalty of the Law.

Boston. May 5th 1749.

Boston Gazette, 06-20-1749.

Ran-away from his Master, John White of Boston, Baker, on the 15th Instant a Negro Man Servant; named Quaco, about 22 Years of Age, speaks good English, well set Fellow, had on a striped homespun Jacket, Leather Breeches, check Shirt, white cotton Stockings, good pair of Shoes brass Buckles, new worsted Cap new yellow Silk Handkerchief, Caster Hatt about half worn.

Whoever shall take up said Negro, and safely convey to his abovesaid master in Boston, shall have five Pounds old Tenor Reward, and all necessary Charges paid.

All Masters of Vessels and others, are hereby caution'd against concealing or carrying off said Negro, on penalty of the Law.

Boston Gazette, 07-25-1749.

Ran-away on the 13th Instant from his Master Mr. Albert Dennle of Boston, Negro Boy named Cato, about Seventeen Year of Age, a slim likely Fellow, stammers something in his Speech, had on when he went away a light-short Broadcloth Jacket, without Sleeves, broad Linnen Shirt brown coarse Kersey Breeches, no Stockings nor Shoes.

Whoever shall take up said Runaway, and him safely convey to his said Master, in Boston, aforesaid, shall have five Pounds old Tenor Reward, and all necessary Charges paid.

And all Masters of Vessels and others, are hereby caution'd against concealing or carrying off said Servant on Penalty of the Law. Boston, July 17th 1749.

Boston Gazette, 09-26-1749.

Ran-away from his Master Hezekiah Blanchard in Boston, on the 19th Instant, a small Negro Man named Bedford, had on when he went away, a new worsted Cap, red Jacket, Leather Breeches. Whoever shall take up said Negro and him safely convey to his abovesaid Master, shall be well rewarded, and all necessary Charges paid.

Boston Gazette, 10-17-1749.

Ran-away from their Master Edward Gray of Boston, Ropemaker, two likely streight limb'd Negro men of about twenty five Years of Age, both talk good English, as they were brought up in the Country; they had on when they went away, strip'd cotton Caps, pea Jacket of redish colour, with Mettle Buttons, Leather Breeches, Trowsers, &c. Whoever shall take up said Negroes, or either of them, and safely convey them to their said Master, shall have ten Pounds old Tenor reward for each of them, & all necessary Charges paid. And all Masters of Vessels and others, are hereby caution'd against concealing or carrying off said Servant on Penalty of Law.
Reprint: Boston Gazette, 10-24-1749.

Boston News-Letter, Thursday March 6, to Thursday March 13, 1740.

Ran-away from his Master Mr. Isaac Brewer, of Springfield, sometime in May last past, a certain Negro Man Servant Named Anser, aged about 30 Years; he was a slim Fellow, midling for height, speaks good English, and is very handy and ingenious about almost any sort of Husbandry work, as also he is well acquainted with work within Doors, especially about Cooking and Dressing of Victuals: He had on when he went away, a grey drugget Coat something faded, a striped Callaminco Waistcoat, a good pair of Leather Breeches, a fine Shirt, a fine pair of Yarn Stockings, a Felt Hat, and a good pair of Shoes, but it is suppos'd his Cloathes are most of them worn out. Whosoever can find said Negro, and safely convey him to his said Master, shall have Ten Pounds Reward, and all necessary Charges paid.
Springfield, Feb. 29, 1739, 40.
Isaac Brewer.
Reprints: Boston Evening Post, 03-13 to 03-20.1740; 03-20 to 03-28-1740.

Boston News-Letter, Thursday May 1, to Thursday May 8, 1740.

Ran-away seven Days since from her Master, Andrew Signourney, jun. a likely Negro Wench Named Janto purchas'd of Mr. Edmund Quincy; she had on her Head a speckled Handerchief; a striped Woollen Jacket, a white Oznabrigs Petticoat. Whoever shall apprehend and safely convey her to her Master shall have Twenty Shillings Reward, and all necessary Charges paid.

Reprints: Boston Weekly News-Letter, 05-8 to 05-15-1740; 05-15 to 05-22-1740.

Boston News-Letter, Thursday July 17, to Thursday July 24, 1740.

Ran-away from his Master Mr. Benjamin Hallowell, of Boston, Shipwright, a Spanish Negro Man Servant, Named JACK, speaks pretty good English, has a short Neck and is Pock broken, he had on when he went away, a blew Cloth Jacket with red Button Holes and Brass Buttons, and a Homespun Jacket, a checkt woollen Shirt, and a pair of black Breeches, light blue yarn Stockings, and a pair of double Channel Pumps with large Brass Buckles, and a Beaver Hat. Whoever shall take up the abovesaid Runaway and him safely convey to his abovesaid Master, shall have Forty Shillings Reward, and all necessary Charges paid.

Boston Weekly News-Letter, Thursday August 14, to Thursday August 21, 1740.

Ran-away from his Master Mr. Arthur Noble of Boston, Trader, on Sabbath Day, the 1st Instant, a Negro Woman, named Mary, about 30 Years old of a middle Stature, but straight, slim and well shap'd of a Pale Complexion can speak good English; she formerly belong'd to Mr. John Do [faded]are, deceas'd, who purchas'd her of a West India Gentleman at [faded]om, She carried with her, a strip'd Homespun Jacket and a White Holland one; a blue and white Holland Gown, and a paned Calico one, Two Linnen and Two Cotton and Linnen Shifts. One pair of Blue Stockings; several Caps and sundry other Things yet unknown. Whoever shall take up the said Negro and convey her to her abovesaid Master, living near the Red Lion, shall have Five Pounds Reward, and all necessary Charges paid.

N. B. All Masters of Vessels and other Persons are hereby cautioned against harbouring, concealing or carrying off the said Negro, as they would avoid the Penalty of the Law.

Reprint: Boston Weekly News-Letter, 08-28 to 09-04-1740.

Boston Weekly News-Letter, Thursday October 30, to Thursday November 6, 1740.

The Governours Negro Man JUBA having broke Goal: This is to forewarn all Persons from harbouring him, and to desire he may be return'd by any Person that may find him. He as on a Grey Coat, and a Linnen Wastcoat and Breeches.

Reprints: Boston Weekly News-Letter, 11-06 to 11-14-1740; 11-14 to 11-20-1740.

Boston Weekly News-Letter, Thursday August 20, to Thursday August 27, 1741.

TEN POUNDS to be Received.

On the 24th of July last, Ran-away from his Master, Mr. Richard Billings of Boston, Taylor, a Negro Man Servant, named Exeter, of a short Stature, yellow Complection; had on when he went away a colour'd Canvas Coat pretty long a blue Jacket not lin'd, with Brass Buttons, and a Cloth colour'd pair of breeches: he has likewise a Mould on the right Side of his Face: He formerly liv'd with Mr. John Hill at Narraganset. He works well at the Taylor Trade; is suppos'd to be at Work in some Country Town, and to have chang'd his Cloathes.

Whoever shall apprehend said Runaway, and convey him to his said Master in Boston, shall have Ten Pounds Reward and all necessary Charges paid by

Richard Billings.

All Masters of Vessels and other are caution'd against concealing or carrying off said Servant, as they would avoid the Penalty of the Law.

Reprint: Boston Gazette, 08-24 to 08-31-1741.

Boston Weekly News-Letter, Thursday November 19, to Thursday November 26, 1741.

A Negro Fellow who calls himself Cato, was taken up at Brooklin, last Week, and his Master not being known, was committed to Bridewell in Boston, where the Owner may have him; Upon his discharge the said Owner is desire to repair to the Printer hereof, in order to pay such Charges as shall be thought reasonable.

Boston Weekly News-Letter, Friday April 9, to Thursday April 15, 1742.

Ran-away on Saturday Night last the 11th Inst. from Mr. Gershom Flagg of Woburn, a Negro Man Servant, Indented for 7 Years, named Pompey York, about 35 Years of Age, speaks good English, of middle Stature; He had with him, two old cotton & linen Shirts, much patch'd a grey Broad Cloth great Coat fac'd with Yellow, a blew Camblet Coat full trim'd, a blew Jacket made up of divers Pieces, light Cloth Breeches patch'd with a brown Cloth in the Seat, two Pair of grey Yarn Stockings, one Pair New, a Pair of old Shoes which had a Patch upon each Side, an old Hat patch'd on the Crown. He had also a Spoon and Dial Mould and other Tinker's Tools. Whoever shall take up the said Negro and bring him to his Master shall have Twenty Shillings Old Tenor, if he is found within Twenty Miles, if above, then Forty Shillings Reward, and all necessary Charges. All Persons are caution'd not to conceal or harbour the said Negro, as 'tis suspected some do, as they would avoid the Penalty of the Law.

N.B. The said Negro can read and write well, and is very deceitful, pretending to be a new Convert, and is very forward to mimick some of the Strangers that have of late been preaching about among us.

Reprints: Boston Weekly News-Letter, 04-22 to 04-29-1742; 04-29 to 05-06-1742; 03-31-1743. This notice was also printed in the Boston Gazette, 11-08-1748; 11-15-1748.

Boston Weekly News-Letter, Thursday June 17, to Thursday June 24, 1742.

Ran-away from his Master Hugh Scott of Cambridge, on the 19th Instant, a Negro Man named Nevis, he formerly belong'd to Mr. Brewster the Chocolate-Maker: Whoever shall take up the said Negro, and bring him to Capt James Williams in Common-Street, shall be handsomely Rewarded, and all Charges paid.

Boston Weekly News-Letter, Thursday August 26, to Thursday September 2, 1742.

Broke out of Bridewell last Lord's Day was sev'nnight a Negro Man Servant belonging to the Rev. Mr. Gee of Boston, named Tom, suppos'd to be about 29 Years of Age, he is of a lively and active Disposition, and is well known in Boston: Whoever shall take up the said Servant, and bring him to his said Master shall have 3£ . as a Reward, and all necessary Charges paid.

Boston Weekly News-Letter; Date: 06-23-1743.

RUN-away from Josiah Browne of Sudbury, on the 6th Day of June Instant, A Negro Man named Sampson, about 23 Years of Age; middling Stature; has a pretty large Leg, walks light & spritely on the Ground: Had on when he went away, a Castor Hat, a Cap, a dark coloured Coat all Wool, with plain white Metal Buttons, blue Cloth Jacket, with brass Buttons filled with Wood & Catgut Eyes, a Cotton & Linnen Shirt, Leather Breeches, white cotton

Stockings, a Pair of double-sol'd turn'd Pumps; and took with him a Pair of large Silver Buckles, a dark colour'd Silk Handkerchief. Whoever shall take up said Run-away and him safely convey to his abovesaid Master at Sudbury shall have Five Pounds old Tenor Reward.

Reprint: Boston Weekly Newsletter, 06-30-1743.

Boston Weekly News-Letter, 08-04-1743.

Taken up and taken Care of by James Foster of Dorchester, a small Yawl; it was left there the 3d Instant by three Negro's which were Runaways as I have since been inform'd: This is to give Information that the Owners may have her again paying Charges. Dorchester, July 21.

James Foster.

Reprints: Boston Weekly Newsletter, 08-11-1743; 08-18-1743.

Boston Weekly News-Letter, 09-01-1743.

WHEREAS a Negro Fellow about 40 Years of Age, who calls his Name Quan, a stout well set Fellow, large Eyes, speaks broken English, who says, he was formerly a Servant to Mr. James at Casco but is now free, and goes about seeking Employ at Farming; and for that purpose came to Mr. Wm Cheney of Roxbury, on the 25th of last Month, where he now is; but it being suspected he might be a Runaway Servant, Tis publick Notice is given, that his Master or Owner (if he has any) may repair to said Cheney, and take him away paying Charges.

Reprints: Boston Weekly Newsletter, 09-15-1743; 09-22-1743.

Boston Weekly News-Letter, 10-20-1743.

Ran away on the 12th Instant, from the Widow Sarah White of Havehill a Negro Man named Scipio, about 30 Years of Age, a well set Fellow, of middle Stature, had on when he went away, a new felt Hat, a dark woollen Coat with Pewter Buttons, light colour'd woollen Jacket, brown Breeches, and grey yarn Stockings: He limps a little as he goes.

Whoever shall take up the said Negro, and convey him to his said Mistress in Haverhill aforesaid, shall have Five Pounds, old Tenor, Reward, and necessary Charges paid.

Reprints: Boston Weekly News-Letter, 10-27-1743; 11-03-1743. This notice was also printed in the Boston Gazette, 10-18-1743.

Boston Weekly News-Letter, 08-02-1744.

Boston, Wednesday, August 1, 1744.

Last Night Ran away from her Master Thomas Drowne, a very spritely Negro Girl, named Violet, of middle Stature, 20 Years old, speaks good English: Whoever shall take up the said Runaway, and convey her to her said Master, shall have Five Pounds, Old Tenor, Reward, and all necessary Charges paid by

Thomas Drowne.

N.B. As she has been lately enquiring for a Passage to go off all Masters of Vessels are more especially caution'd against concealing or carrying off the said Negro, as they would avoid the Penalty of the Law.

Boston Weekly News-Letter, 12-13-1744.

Ran-away on Tuesday the 11th Instant, from Mrs. Ann Philips, living near the Orange Tree in Boston, a Negro Girl about 14 Years of Age, named Violet, pretty lusty; she had on when she went away a black Linsey woolsey Coat and Jacket, a strip'd Callimancoe Petticoat under it; and had also with her a new blew Bays Jacket, and a Callico Petticoat, lin'd with a seersucker. Whosoever shall bring the said Girl to her Mistress, shall be well Rewarded, and have all necessary Charges paid.

Boston Weekly News-Letter, 05-16-1745.

Ran-away from his Master Mr. James Howell of Boston, an Indian Molatto Man, aged about 20 Years, he had on when he went away a green Jacket, and yellow Leather Breeches, he left his Hat behind him, but I am inform'd he has got two Hats since. Whoever shall take up said Runaway, and bring him to Mr. Alexander Thorpe's near the Common shall receive Three Pounds Reward, Old Tenor, and all necessary Charges paid by me. James Howell.

Reprint: Boston Weekly News-Letter, 05-23-1745.

Boston Weekly News-Letter, 07-11-1745.

Ran-away from Ebenezer Gray of Lebanon in Connecticut, on the 28th Day of June last, at Night, a Negro Man named Hector, about 24 Years of Age, speaks pretty good English, he is a lusty, stout, well sett, square-shoulder'd, well-featur'd Fellow, of middle Size for Stature, and has a well-proportioned Leg, about 4 Years ago he was Servant to one Mr. Swift of Sandwich, and sold by him to Zebulon West, Esq; of Tolland: He had on when he went away a dark-colour'd homespun Coat, a lightish colour'd fustian Jacket, with the Sleeves cut off, a tow Cloth Shirt and Trowsers, yarn Stockings, and a good Pair of Shoes, a yellow and white strip'd muslin Handkerchief, he carried away with him also a blew and white homespun checker'd flannel Shirt, and a Pair of very good cloth colour'd Buckskin Breeches, with a

Watch Pocket in them, and the Buttons covered with Leather. Whosoever shall take up said Negro and him convey to said Gray in Lebanon aforesaid, shall have a Reward of Three Pounds, old Tenor, and all necessary Charges paid them by

Ebenezer Gray

Reprints: Boston Weekly News-Letter, 07-19-1745; 07-25-1745.

Boston Weekly News-Letter, 08-08-1745.

Ran-away from her Mistress Margaret Robinson, on the 2d Inst. Nancy, a Negro Girl of a middling Stature, mark'd in her Face with the Small-Pox: She had on when she went away a white Linnen Jacket, and a large check'd Petticoat: Whoever shall take up said Runaway and convey her to her Mistress at Mr. Joseph Marion's opposite to the North Door of the Town House, Boston, shall be well rewarded and have all necessary Charges paid.—All Masters of Vessels and others are hereby forbid harbouring or carrying off said Negro.

Reprints: Boston Weekly News-Letter, 08-15-1745; 08-22-1745.

Boston Weekly News-Letter, 03-06-1746.

Ran-away from his Master Richard Smith of Boston, Inn-holder, on Saturday the 25th of February past, a Negro Man Servant, named Cato; about 23 Years of Age. He had on when he went away a light colour'd Cloth Coat with Mohair Buttons, a pair of homespun Breeches, two homespun Jackets, a pair of yarn Stockings, and round to'd Shoes; he speaks pretty good English, but shows his Tongue pretty much when he speaks: He is a Shoemaker by Trade, and can read and write. Whoever shall take up the said Servant, and bring him to his said Master at the Sign of Admiral Vernon in King-street, or secure him in any of his Majesty's Goals, shall have Five Pounds Reward, old Tenor, and all necessary Charges paid, by Richard Smith.

And all Masters of Vessels and others, are hereby caution'd against concealing or carrying off said Servant, on Penalty o the Law.

Reprints: Boston Gazette, 03-04-1746; 03-11-1746.

Boston Weekly News-Letter, 04-17-1746.

Ran-away from his Master Dr. Nathaniel Ames of Dedham, a Negro Man Servant named Cato, a lusty Fellow, aged about 21 Years, speaks good English, had on a pale dy'd Cloth colour'd Great Coat and small Coat of the same, sheep skin Breeches, &c. He has endeavour'd to enlist to go to Cape-Breton. Whosoever shall take up said Negro and commit him to his Majesty's Goal in Boston, or convey him to his said Master in Dedham, or give

Intelligence of him so this he may be had, shall have Five Pound, old Tenor, Reward, and all necessary Charges paid. All Persons are desired not to harbor said Negro; and all Masters of Vessels are caution'd not to take said Negro on board their Vessels upon the pain and penalties of the Law.

Dedham, April 15, 1746.

Nathaniel Ames

Boston Weekly News-Letter, 06-19-1746.

Ran-away from his Master Jonathan Dwight, of Boston, Innholder, on the 15th Instant at Night, a Negro Man named Newham, lately owned by Mr. Luke Vardy, had on a blue Coat, red Lining, and blue ribb'd Stockings: Whoever will inform of, or bring him to his said Master, shall be well Rewarded therefor; and all Persons are hereby caution'd against entertaining or concealing him.

Boston Weekly News-Letter, 07-17-1746.

Ran-away from his Master Col. Joseph Buckminster, of Framingham, on the 22d Day of June last past, a Negro Man Servant, named Cobbo, alias Pompey, about 15 Years of Age, speaks very broken English, of middling Stature, well-set, full-fac'd, something Pock fretten. He had on a Cap, an old Hat, a good Tow Cloth Shirt, woolen cloth colour'd Jacket, Camblet Breeches, yarn Stockings the Feet newly stock'd. Whosoever shall take up the said Negro and convey him to his said Master at Framingham, or to Mr. William Cowell, Goldsmith in Boston, shall have Five Pounds old Tenor Reward, and all necessary Charges paid.

Reprints: Boston Weekly News-Letter, 07-24-1746; 07-31-1746.

Boston Weekly News-Letter, 01-29-1748.

Ran-away from Mr. Bananael Bower's Ship Yard in Swanzey, the 2d Instant, a Negro Man named Caesar, about 35 Years of Age; he is a tall well-set Fellow, had on when he went away, a double-breasted dark colour'd Kersey Pea Jacket, with yellow metal Buttons, a blue Devonshire Kersey Fly Coat, with large Copper Buttons, double breasted, without Lining, he carried with him a Variety of other Cloathing; he speaks indifferent English, is a cunning artful Fellow (a Negro of Mr. Bower't went off with him.) Whoever shall take him up, and bring him to his Master John Banister at Newport, shall have ten Pounds old Tenor Reward, and all necessary Charges paid, by John Banister.

Reprints: Boston Weekly News-Letter, 02-04-1748; 02-11-1748. This notice was also printed in the Boston Gazette, 01-26-1748; 02-02-1748; 02-16-1748.

Boston Weekly News-Letter, 10-20-1748.

Ran-away from his Master Joseph Clap of Scituate, on the 29th of this Instant September, a Negro Man named Primus, being about Forty Years of Age; speaks good English, had a goof Set of Teeth, he looks up glaring with his Eyes, has a Wen on the Joint of one of his great Toes, which makes his Shoe stick out a little: He had on when he went away, a good Kersey Coat and Breeches, a Tow Shirt and Trowsers, a good Felt Hat, Stockings and Shoes: Whosoever shall take up said Negro and bring him to his said Master, or secure him so as he may have him again, shall have Four Pounds old Tenor Reward, and all necessary Charges paid. Joseph Clap.

Reprints: Boston Weekly News-Letter, 10-27-1748; 11-10-1748.

Boston Weekly News-Letter, 07-20-1749.

Ran away from his Master, on the 18th Instant, a Negro Man named Cato, who formerly belong'd to Dr. Stevens of Boston, aged 25 Years; a tall well-set Fellow, speaks pretty good English, hath lost all his Toes by the Frost; He had on a Shirt and Trowsers of check'd Linnen, (carried away with him a Bundle of the same) a red great Coat, and a pair of Leather Breeches. N.B. He is us'd to this Practice, and hath been often guilty of stealing Poultry, Shoats, Lambs, &c. hides in the Day Time and Travels in the Night.

Whosoever shall secure the said Negro, and inform the Printer hereof, so as his Master may have him again, shall have Five Pounds Old Tenor Reward, and all necessary Charges paid.

Reprints: Boston Weekly News-Letter, 07-07-1749; 08-03-1749.

Boston Weekly News-Letter, 08-10-1749.

Ran away from his Master Capt. John Payson, of Woodstock, a Servant Man named Byrant Macdormant, about 17 Years of Age, of small Stature, had on when he went away a Brown all woollen Coat, a white Fustian Jacket, a Speckled Shirt and Trowsers, has a sore Head. Whosoever shall take up said Runaway, and bring him to his said Master in Woodstock aforesaid, or secure him, so that his Master may have him again, shall have Five Pounds old Tenor Reward, and all necessary Charged paid by me. John Payson.

Dated in Woodstock, August 8, 1749.

Also Ran away at the same Time from Mr. David Wallis of Woodstock, a Negro Man Servant, named Christmas alias Quosbe, a short Fellow, about 30 Years of Age, who formerly belonged to Mr. Samuel Jackson in Boston; Whoever shall bring him to his Master, shall have Five Pounds old Tenor Reward.

All Persons are caution'd not carry off either of the said Servants as they would avoid the Penalty of the Law.

Reprints: Boston Weekly News-Letter, 08-17-1749; 08-25-1749.

Boston Weekly News-Letter, 08-31-1749.

Ran-away on the 29th of August, from his Master John Williams of Roxbury, a Negro Man Servant, named Sharper, a lusty Fellow about 25 Years of Age, speaks good English, and is something [stammered]: He had on when he went away, a check'd Woolen Shirt, a pair of white Trowsers, a pair of grey yarn Stockings, a pair of calk skin Shoes, with large pewter Buckles, a striped blue and white Jacket, a small bever Hatt, and the Wool on the Top of his Head newly shaved; he also carried away with him a dark blue Jacket trimm'd with black, one fine shirt, a Jocky-cap, a pair of dark blue worsted Stockings, and a pair of yarn Stockings, black and white, stock'd with grey a little above his Shoes. Whoever takes up said Servant, and conveys him to said master at Roxbury, shall have Five Pounds old Tenor Reward, and all necessary Charges paid by me John Williams.

Reprint: Boston Weekly News-Letter, 09-07-1749.

Boston Weekly News-Letter, 09-28-1749.

Ran-away from his master, Joseph Barnard of Deerfield, a Negro Man named Prince, of middling Stature, his Complection not the darkest or lightest for a Negro, slow of Speech, but speaks good English; He had with him when he went away, an old brown Coat, with Pewter Buttons, a double-breasted blue Coat with a Cape, and flat metal Buttons, a brown great Coat with red Cuffs and Cape, a new brown Jacket with Pewter Buttons, a Pair of new Leather Breeches, check'd linnen Shirt and Trowsers, tow shirt and Trousers, a red Cap, two Castor Hats, several Pair of Stockings, a Pair of Pumps, a Gun and Violin. Whoever shall apprehend said Fellow and convey him to his Master, shall have Ten Pounds old Tenor, and all necessary Charge paid by

Deerfield, Sept. 18, 1749. Joseph Barnard.

All Masters of Vessels and others are caution'd not to conceal or carry off the said Negro, as they would avoid the Penalty of the Law.

Reprints: Boston Weekly News-Letter, 10-05-1749; 10-12-1749.

Boston Weekly News-Letter, 11-02-1749.

Ran away from her Master Joseph Kidder of Boston, on the 17th of October past, a tall slim likely Negro Girl, about 16 or 17 Years of Age, named Cloe, of a very black Complection, she has been about four Years in the Country, and talks English very well: She had on when she went away a blue and white homespun Petticoat, and an Oznabrigs jacket. Whoever shall take up said Runaway and will bring her to her Master or the Printer hereof, shall have Four Pounds, old Tenor, Reward, and all necessary Charges paid.

Boston, November 2d, 1749.

Reprints: Boston Weekly News-Letter, 11-09-1749; 11-17-1749.

Boston Weekly News-Letter, 11-02-1749.

Ran-away from his Master, on Monday Night last, A Negro Man named Jack, of a middling Stature, much Pock-broken: He had on when he went away, a cloth Colour Drugget Coat, with a Patch on the left Shoulder, of a different Colour, a strip'd Jacket, a worsted Cap and Leather Breeches. Whosoever shall take up said Negro and bring him to his Master shall be paid Five Pounds old Tenor, and other necessary Charges by me,

Hopestill Foster.

Boston, November 2, 1749.

Boston Evening Post, 07-23-1750.

Ran away on Monday the 9th Instant, a Negro Man named Achelles, alias Hercules, a short squat Fellow, about 24 Years old; hath a pretty broad Face, and has had his Head shaved since he Ran away. He had on when he went away, only a white Shirt and Trowzers, and a Handkerchief about his Head, no Shoes, Stockings or Hat. Whoever secures said Negro, and brings him to his Master James Forbes, of Boston, shall have Twenty Pounds, old Tenor, Reward, and reasonable Charges. All Masters of Vessels and others, are hereby cautioned not to conceal, entertain or carry off said Negro, as they would avoid the Penalty of the Law.

N.B. He speaks very good English, and chews Tobacco.

Boston, July 12, 1750.

Reprints: Boston News-Letter, 07-12-1750; 07-19-1750.

Boston Evening Post, 08-27-1750.

Ran away from his master Mr. Benjamin Hallowell, of Boston, the 10th Instant, a new Negro Man named Cuffey, has been in the Country about Ten Weeks. He had on when he went away, a dark colour'd stript Homespun Jacket and a mixt Jacket, a speckled Shirt, a new double Cap, a Bever Hatt, new dress, a pair of Shoes with Brass Buckles, has no Stockings on, a pair of Oznabrigs Trousers, a large Scar on his left Leg, is pockfreckled. Whoever will take up said Negro, so that his Master may have him again, shall have Ten Pounds, Old Tenor, Reward, and all necessary Charges paid.

Reprints: Boston Evening Post, 09-03-1750. This notice was also printed in the Boston Post Boy, 08-27-1750; 09-03-1750; and 09-10-1750.

Boston Evening Post, 10-08-1750.

Ran away from his Master, Thomas Hodson, of Boston, on Friday the sixth of this Instant October, a Negro Man named Scipio, with a Frock and Trouzers, and a Leather Jocky Cap. Whoever shall take up the said Negro, and bring him to his said Master, shall be well rewarded for their Trouble, and have all necessary Charges paid.

N.B. The Fellow has been used to the Sea, and will probably attempt to get off. He had a Dog with him when he went away, which is very fond of him.

Reprints: Boston Evening Post, 10-15-1750; 10-22-1750.

Boston Evening Post, 05-06-1751.

Ran away the 17th of this Instant April, from her Master Daniel Marquand of Newbury, a Molatto Servant Woman named Peach, aged about 30 Years. Whoever will take up said Runaway, and bring her to her Master, shall have Four Dollars Reward, and all necessary Charges paid them; and all Persons are warned against concealing or entertaining the said Servant; and all Masters of Vessels or others that carry the said Servant away, may expect to be prosecuted according to Law.

Boston Evening Post, 07-15-1751.

Lately Ran away from his Master, Richard Hunt of Boston, a Negro Man named Bristol, very tall, and goes lame of his right Knee. He had on when he went way, a stone grey Duroy Coat, a scarlet Jacket, double breasted, a pair of light coloured Kersey Breeches, a pair of Yarn Stockings, and carried with him a black Callimanco Jacket, and sundry other Things. Whoever shall take up the said Negro, and bring him to his said Master, shall have Four Dollars Reward, and necessary Charges paid.

Reprint: Boston Evening Post, 07-29-1751.

Boston Evening Post, 09-16-1751.

Ran away from his Master, Elisha Jones of Weston, near Boston, on the 2d of this Instant, a Negro Man named Caesar, about 30 Years old, a tall stout Fellow, and speaks good English: He had on a mix'd homespun Coat, with Brass Buttons, one Garlix and two Tow Shirts, a pair of Leather Breeches, bluish mill'd Stockings, a pair of double Channel Pumps, and an old Bever Hat.

Whoever shall take up said Servant, and convey him to his said Master, shall have a Reward of Four Dollars, paid by

Elisha Jones.

N.B. He is supposed to be gone towards Connecticut or New-York.
Reprint: Boston Gazette, 09-10-1751.

Boston Evening Post, 10-07-1751.

Run away on Sabbath-Day the 29th of September last, from Ebenezer Ellinwood of Beverly Ferry, a Negro Man named Caesar, who has gone in the Ferry-Boat there for about two Years past: He is about thirty two Years old, is near Six Feet high, speaks good English, goes something stooping, and one of his Legs is much larger than the other. He had on when he went away, a whitish Cloth Coat, a Castor Hat, Worstead Cap, and black Yarn Stockings.

Whoever shall take him up, and convey him to his said Master, shall have SIX DOLLARS reward, and all necessary Charges paid by me
Beverly, October 3, 1751.

Ebenezer Ellinwood.

Reprints: Boston Evening Post, 10-14-1751; 10-21-1751.

Boston Evening Post, 07-06-1752.

On the 7th Instant, Ran away from his Master Timothy Perkins of Middleton, a Negro Man named Pompey, aged about 30 Years, of midling Stature and strait lim'd: He speaks good English, has had the Small Pox, and hath lost one of his little Fingers by means of a Sore; he carried away with him a homespun light coloured Drugget Fly Coat, a white Linen Jacket, a black homespun Jacket, 2 Woollen Shirts, 1 Linen Shirt and a pair of all Wooll homespun Breeches. Whoever will stop and secure the said Negro, so that his said Master may have him again, shall receive a Reward of Six Pounds, old Tenor, and all Charges paid by
Middleton, June 18, 1752.

Timothy Perkins.

Reprints: Boston Evening Post, 07-13-1752. This notice was also printed in the Boston Gazette, 11-06-1758; 11-13-1758; 11-13-1758 (Supplement).

Boston Evening Post, 07-27-1752.

Run away last Night from Thomas Brownell, of Portsmouth, a Mustee Fellow named Jack, about 23 Years of Age, is a short thick Fellow, and had on when he went away, a half worn Bever Hat, a Linen Cap, a dark coloured Fly Coat, chequer'd like Diamonds, with Metal Buttons, a striped Flannel Jacket, a white Tow Shirt, striped Tow Trowsers, a pair of dark colour'd Yarn, and a pair pale blue Worsted Stockings, and a pair of Pumps.

Whoever takes up the said Fellow, and delivers him to his Master, or secures him, so that he may be had again, shall have THIRTY POUNDS, old Tenor, Reward, and all necessary Charges paid, by

Thomas Brownell.

All Masters of Vessels and others, are hereby forbid carrying of or concealing said Fellow, as they would avoid the Penalty of the Law.

Reprint: Boston Evening Post, 08-03-1752.

Boston Evening Post, 12-04-1752.

Ran away from his master Mr. Joseph Reynolds, of Bristol, on the 20th Instant, a Molatto Boy, about 15 Years of Age, he had had on when he went away, a homespun Jacket of a light Colour, with a mixture of black, a pair of Linen Breeches, a Felt Hat, a Linen Shirt and a pair of dark grey Stockings. Whoever shall take up said Runaway, and bring him to Mr. Jeremiah Belknap, of Boston, or to his said Master in Bristol, shall have Five Pounds, old Tenor Reward, and all necessary Charges paid.

Bristol, November 26, 1752.

Reprints: Boston Evening Post, 12-11-1752; 12-18-1752.

Boston Evening Post, 12-25-1752.

Ran away from his Master William Downe of Boston, Esq; on the 18th Instant, a Negro Man Servant named London, about Thirty five Years of Age; he had on when he went away, a dark colour'd Bearskin Coat, a strip'd homespun Jacket, he wears a Cap, but went off without a Hat. Whoever shall take up the said Runaway, and convey him to his said master, shall have Two Dollars Reward, and all necessary Charges paid, by William Downe.

All Masters of Vessels and others are hereby cautioned against concealing or carrying off said Servant on Penalty of the Law.

Boston, 25th December 1752.

Reprint: Boston Evening Post, 01-01-1753.

Boston Evening Post, 06-04-1753.

Ran away from his Master, Capt. Timothy McDaniel of Boston, a Negro Man named Homer, aged about thirty Years, a slim Fellow about five feet eight Inches high, speaks very broken English; had on when he went away a blue Sailors Jacket, red Breeches and a white Waistcoat, two old Buckles in his Shoes, grey Yarn Stockings, and a red & blue Cap. The said Negro is very much pitted with the Small Pox. Whoever shall take up said Negro and bring him to his said Master's House at New Boston, shall be well rewarded for their Trouble by one

    Boston, May 28, 1753.

Elizabeth McDaniel.

Boston Evening Post, 07-30-1753.

Ran away the 14th Instant, from his Master Eleazer Tyng, esq; of Dunstable, a Negro Man named Pompey, about 40 Years of Age, midling Stature, heavy eyed, one of his Fingers is reckoned to be so crooked that he cannot hold it out straight; he carried away with him a Homspun grey Coat with yellow Metal Buttons, 2 Jackets, one a scarlet Cloth with a pink coloured Lining, and white Metal Buttons, the other blue German Serge, Buttons of the same Colour, red Shalloon Lining, light blue German Serge Breeches, white Metal Buttons, a white Linen and a Woollen Shirt, grey Yarn Stockings, a pair of Pumps, one Felt and one Bever Hat, and a white Linen Cap. He can play on a Violin. Whoever shall take up said Runaway, and convey him to his said Master at Dunstable, or to Mess. Alford and Tyng, Merchants at Boston, shall receive Five Dollars as a Reward, and all necessary Charges paid. Eleazer Tyng.

    Reprints: Boston Evening Post, 08-06-1753; 08-13-1753.

Boston Evening Post, 02-11-1754.

RUN away, on September 2d, 1753, from his Master Channcey Graham, of Rumbout, in Dutchess County, and Province of New-York, a likely lusty Negro Man, named Cuff, about 30 Years old, well sett, has had the Small Pox, is very black, speaks English pretty well, and very flippant; he is a plausible smooth Tongue Fellow: Had with him a pair of greenish Plush Breeches about two thirds worn, and a pair of Russel ditto, flowered green and yellow, two white Shirts, two Pair of middling short Tow Trowsers, one Pair of Thread Stockings knit in Squares, one Pair of fine blue Wool ditto flower'd, one Diaper Cap, one white Cotton ditto, one blue Broad Cloth Jacket with red Lining, one blue homespun Coat lined with streaked Linsey Woolsey, or Woolen, &c. He is a strong smoker, and supposed to have a sham Pass—Whoever shall take up and secure said Servant, so that his Master may have him again, shall have a PISTOLE Reward, and all reasonable Charges, paid by Chauncey Graham.

N.B. All Masters of Vessels are forbid to carry off said Servant, as they would not incur the utmost Rigour of the Law in that Case made and provided.

Reprint: Boston Evening Post, 02-18-1754.

Boston Evening Post, 10-07-1754.

Ran away from Henry Sherburne Jun. of Portsmouth, Merchant, a Negro Man named Cromwell, about forty five Years of Age, of midling Stature, small Eyes, a running Sore in one Leg, almost if not quite dried up, talks good English, can read and write, and understands Husbandry Work. Had on and carried away with him, a blue Cloth Coat and Breeches, a Scarlet Cloth Jacket with Metal Buttons, and one pair of dark coloured Plush Breeches, also some white Oznabrigs Jacket and Breeches, Linen and Cotton Shirts, white Cotton and some Yarn Stockings, good Worsted Caps, &c. Whosoever will take up said Runaway, and him safely convey to his said Master in Portsmouth, shall have Eight Dollars for their Trouble, and all necessary Charges paid.

Portsmouth, October 3, 1754. Henry Sherburne.

Reprints: Boston Evening Post, 10-14-1754; 10-21-1754. This notice was also printed in the Boston Gazette, 10-22-1754.

Boston Evening Post, 01-27-1755.

Ran away from Capt. John Ewing at Newport, Rhode Island, a Negro Fellow named Bristol, is Lame, his Right Knee bending inward, aged about 40 Years, had on when he went away, a blue Shag Great Coat, pretends he is free. Whoever will secure him and give Notice to Mr. Andrew Heatly at Newport, shall have Two Dollars Reward, and all reasonable Charges paid.

Reprints: Boston Evening Post, 02-03-1755; 02-10-1755; 02-17-1755.

Boston Evening Post, 04-07-1755.

Ran away from Jeremiah Niles of South-Kingston, on the 30th past, a pale Negro or Mustee Man called Toney, with bushy hair. Had on a light Mill coloured Kersey Fly Coat, a white and grey Kersey Wastcoat, a pair of white Kersey Breeches, and an old Felt Hat, pair of thick double soled Shoes, with Nails in the Soles, and white y[arn] Stockings. He is a short Fellow. Whoever takes him up and returns him to said Niles, shall have Ten Pounds, old Tenor, Reward, and all necessary Charges paid by Jeremiah Niles.

South Kingston, April 1st, 1755.

Boston Evening Post, 06-23-1755.

East Chester, April 18th 1755.

Ran away the 16th of this Instant April, from John Hunt and Israel Honeywell, jun. Executors of William Pinkney, sen. Late of East Chester, deceased, a very likely Negro Man of a yellow Complexion, aged about 30 Years, a tall slender long leg'd Fellow, born at East Chester named Methias, a streight limb'd Fellow: Had on a good pair of leather Breeches, and very well cloathed; he carried away with him a small Bay Horse well set, about 14 Hands high, went a small pace, which he stole, likewise a good hunting Saddle, with a blue plush Housing, bound with russet Leather: It is suppos'd some evil minded Person has given him a pass to Travel, as a free Man. He is a very handsome Fellow, speaks good English. Whoever shall take up the said Negro and Horse, and bring them either to said Hunt or Honeywell, living in West Chester, or secure him in any of his Majesty's Goal, shall have Five Pounds New York Money Reward, and all reasonable Charges paid by us,

John Hunt.
Israel Honeywell, jun.

Reprints: Boston Evening Post, 06-30-1755; 07-05-1755.

Boston Evening Post, 08-04-1755.

Ran away from his Master William Pattin of Boston, last Week, a Negro Boy named Caesar, about 18 Years of Age, a spry Fellow: He had on when he went away, a Homespun Jacket, blue Breeches, and black Stockings. Whoever shall take up said Runaway, and bring him to his said Master, or put him in Goal, and give Notice thereof, shall have TWO DOLLARS Reward, and all necessary Charges paid by

Boston, August 2, 1755. William Pattin.

Reprints: Boston Evening Post, 08-11-1755; 07-05-1755.

Boston Evening Post 01-26-1756.

Ran away from his Master, Mr. Nathan Brown of Ipswich, on the 16th Instant, a Mulatto Man Servant, named Warreson, about Twenty Years of Age, and speaks good English. He had on when he went away, a light brown double breasted Robbin, a check'd Linen Shirt, a striped Jacket, Leather Breeches, with a pair of Trousers over them, Yarn Stockings, round toed

Pumps, a Castor Hat, and sometimes wears a brown Wig. Whoever shall take up the said Run-away, and convey him to his said Master, shall have TWO DOLLARS Reward, and all necessary Charges paid, by Nathan Brown.

All Master of Vessels and others, are hereby cautioned not to conceal, entertain or carry off said Servant, as they would avoid the Penalty of the Law. December 24, 1755.

Reprint: Boston Evening Post, 02-02-1756.

Boston Evening Post, 04-05-1756.

Ran away from Amos Seavey, a likely, lusty Negro Fellow, about twenty three Years old, born in New England: He has large long Feet, and is about five Feet ten Inches high, has a good Set of white Teeth, and a light Complection. He carried away with him a dark coloured homespun Coat, lined with blue Bays, with Brass Buttons, one Pair of Leather Breeches, and one Pair of old blue Breeches, a blewish mixt homespun great Coat, a light coloured Kersey Jacket, one light coloured Camblet Coat, lined with Pink coloured Tammey, it is of a long Waist, a Pair of light blue Stockings, and one Pair of grey Stockings. If any Person will take him up, and bring him to said Seavey, so that may get him again, he shall have Five Dollars Reward, and all necessary Charges paid, by Amos Seavey.

Reprints: Boston Evening Post, 04-12-1756; 04-19-1756; 04-26-1756.

Boston Evening Post, 05-17-1756.

Ran away from the Subscriber at Newbury, about the 15th of April last, a Negro Fellow named Daniel, about 20 Years old, of a middle Size. He had on when he Ran away, a brown Kersey Jacket, check'd woollen Shirt, a pair of red broad Cloth Breeches, and a mill'd Cap. He formerly belong'd to Capt. Edward Sheaf of Charlestown. Whoever will secure said Runaway, so that his Master may have him again, shall have TWO DOLLARS Reward, and all necessary Charges paid. All Masters of Vessels, &c. are caution'd against concealing or carrying off said Negro, as they would avoid the Penalty of the Law. Joseph Cottle.

Newbury, May 10th, 1756.

Reprints: Boston Evening Post, 05-24-1756; 05-31-1756. This notice was also printed in the Boston Gazette, 05-24-1756; 05-31-1756; the Boston News-Letter, 06-03-1756; 06-10-1756; 06-17-1756.

Boston Evening Post, 05-24-1756.

Ran away from Capt. Samuel Cottman, last Sunday Night, the Ninth Instant, a Negro Man Slave called Nicola; when he went away he had on a blue lappelled Coat, a scarlet Waistcoat and grey Breeches, all with yellow Metal

Buttons, a white Shirt ruffled at the Bosom, black Ribbon about his Neck, talks a little smattering of French. If any Person takes up said Negro, and brings him to his Master in Winter Street, near the Common in Boston, he shall have THREE DOLLARS Reward, and all necessary Charges paid: And publick Notice is hereby given to forewarn all Masters of Vessels, and others, not to take on board or harbour said Negro, otherwise they may depend on being prosecuted as the Law directs.

Boston, May 11, 1756.

Boston Evening Post, 05-31-1756 (Supplement).

Ran away the 22d Day of this Instant May, two Negro Men Servants from Newbury, the one belonging to Mr. Joseph Swasey of Newbury, of a light pale Complection, and of midling Stature: Had on whet he went away, a homespun Coat, Swanskin Jacket, and a white Jacket and Trowsers, named Cebrew.---The other from Timothy Greenleaf of Newbury, of midling Stature, and black as most Negroes are, a fat plump lusty Fellow; he has a sly Look with his Eyes, wears the Button of his Hat before, a white Jacket with black Spots in it, and one striped jacket and a pair of Cloth Breeches, named Newport.

Whoever shall take up the said Negroes, or either of them, and convey them to either of said Masters, shall have TWO DOLLARS Reward for each, and and all necessary Charges paid. Joseph Swasey,

Timothy Greenleaf.

All Masters of Vessels and others are forbid carrying off said Negroes, or concealing them, on Penalty of the Law provided.

Reprints: Boston Evening Post, 06-07-1756; 06-14-1756.

Boston Evening Post, 08-16-1756.

Lately taken up in Rehoboth, a likely Negro Man, about 20 Years of Age, 5 Feet and 2 Inches high, very black, and has a sly Look: He plays on a Fiddle, and has on an old brown Jacket, old Trowsers and a pair of old Pumps. He was born in this Country, and speaks good English. Whoever has lost such a Fellow, may enquire of the Printer of this Paper, who will inform where he may be had.

Reprint: Boson Evening Post, 08-23-1756.

Boston Evening Post, 08-29-1757 (Supplement).

Ran away on the 23d of this Instant, from his Master Charles Ward Apthorp of Boston, a Negro Man named Cato, sturdy well set Fellow, about 5 Feet and an half high, bandy legg'd and splay fotted, talkative, but speaks bad

English. He took with him a blue cloth Jacket and whitish cloth Breeches, both trm'd with red, and metal Buttons, a blue and white check'd linen Coat, a Cloth coloured Camblet Coat, and Drab Surtout Coat with Horse Hair Buttons, and affects to dress smart. Whoever takes up the said Negro, and secures him in any Goal or Bridgewell or delivers him to Ambrose Vincent, shall have THREE DOLLARS Reward, and all reasonable Charges paid by said Vincent. All Masters of Vessels and others are hereby warned against carrying off or concealing said Negro.

N.B. He formerly belonged to Mr. Thomas Hawding, Ropemaker, deceased, and is pretty well known. Boston, Aug. 29 1757.

Reprint: Boston Evening Post, 09-05-1757.

Boston Evening Post, 10-10-1757.

Ran away from his Master James Dalton of Boston, on the first Instant, a Negro Man named Ulysses, speaks good English, about 5 Feet 8 Inches high, turns his Toes a little in, somewhat bow-legg'd. Whoever apprehends him and brings him to his said Master, shall have Three Dollars Reward and all necessary Charges paid.

Oct. 10, 1757.

Reprints: Boston Evening Post, 10-17-1757; 10-24-1757.

Boston Evening Post, 04-03-1758.

Ran away from his Master, John Gray of Boston, Ropemaker, on the 30th of March, and was seen going over the Neck, a Negro Man Servant named Cato, suppos'd to be about 20 Years of Age, he very much resembles an Indian, not only in his Complexion, but is very quick at Rapartee. He had on when he went away, a Felt Hat, a check'd homespun Shirt, a cloth colour'd Kersey Jacket, lined with red Baize, and white flat Metal Buttons, a strip'd homespun Jacket, a pair of Leather Breeches, very much tarr'd, a pair of yarn Stockings, he is splaw footed, and treads upon one side of his Shoes. Whoever shall apprehend the said Servant and will bring him to his Master, shall be handsomely rewarded for their Trouble, and all necessary Charges paid. All Masters of Vessels are hereby cautioned against carrying off said Servant as they would avoid the Penalty of the Law. April 1, 1758.

Reprints: Boston Evening Post, 04-10-1758; 04-17-1758.

Boston Evening Post, 06-04-1759.

Ran away from John Lloyd of Stamford, a Negro Man named Cyrus; he is a tall well made Fellow, slender waisted, large Legs and Feet, some of his Fore Teeth missing, aged about 28 Years: He has a remarkable stammering in his

Speech, took with him a brown Irish Camblet Coat. Whoever takes up and secures said Servant so that his Master may have him again, shall be well rewarded for their Trouble and all reasonable Charges paid by

JOHN LLOYD.

Reprints: Boston Evening Post, 06-18-1759; 06-25-1759.

Boston Evening Post, 07-30-1759.

Ran AWAY FROM Mr. Thomas Cave of Middleton, on the 24th Instant, two Negro Men Servants, one named Caesar, about 25 Years of Age, and 5 Feet 6 Inches high; he had on a striped cotton Wool Jacket, Dearskin Breeches, light blue Stockings, and no Hat, and talks good English. The other Negro named Titus, about 23 Years old, and near the same heighth with the other, he is a very spry active Fellow, stammers very much in his speech, had on a Woollen Jacket and Breeches, dark blue Stockings, and a Felt hat, and Pewter Buttons on all their Cloathing.

Whoever shall take up said Negroes and convey them to their said Master at Middleton, shall have TWO DOLLARS Reward for each, and all necessary Charges paid.

All Masters of Vessels and others, are hereby cautioned not to conceal, entertain, or carry off said Servant as they would avoid the Penalty of the Law.

Middleton, July 28, 1759.

Reprints: Boston Evening Post, 08-06-1759; 08-13-1759; 08-20-1759.

Boston Evening Post, 08-13-1759.

Ran away from Robert Wilson of Lincoln, as he was travelling through Woodstook, a likely Negro Man named Jack, who once belonged to Mr. Nathaniel Curtis of Wallingsford, but now belongs to Mr. David Cook: He had on when he Ran away, a brown Great Coat, white Shirt, black Tow Trowers, a pair of old Stockings and Pumps, a check'd Linen Cap, no Hat, and is of a middling Stature, very well set, has some Pits of the Small Pox, and speaks good English.—Whoever will take up said Negro and confine him, and send Word to the Subscriber, so that he may have him again, shall have a handsome Reward, and all necessary Charges paid. Robert Willson.

N.B. The Subscriber lives 20 Miles from Boston near Sudbury. July 31, 1759.

Reprints: Boston Evening Post, 08-20-1759; 08-29-1759. This notice was also printed in the Boston News-Letter, 08-16-1759; 08-23-1759; 08-30-1759; Boston Post Boy, 06-02-1759; 07-09-1759; 07-16-1759; 07-30-1759; 08-06-1759.

Boston Evening Post, 08-13-1759.

Ran away from his Master Joseph Swasey of Newbury, a Negro Man named Scarbrough; he is light colour'd for a Negro, has one crooked Finger, is about 5 Feet 7 Inches, and speaks good English.

Whosoever shall take up said Negro and bring him to his said Master, shall have FIVE DOLLARS Reward, and all necessary Charges paid by me, JOSEPH SWASEY.

All Masters of Vessels and others are hereby cautioned against harbouring or carrying off said Negro as they would avoid the Penalty of the Law.

Newbury, July 27, 1759.

Reprints: Boston Evening Post, 08-20-1759; 08-27-1759.

Boston Gazette, 10-02-1750.

Ran-away from his Master William Brown of Framingham, on the 30th of Sept. last, a Molatto Fellow, about 27 Years of Age named Crispas, 6 Feet two Inches high, short curl'd Hair, his Knees nearer together than common; had on a light colour'd Bearskin Coat, plain brown Fustian Jacket, or brown all-Wool one, new Buckskin Breeches, blue Yarn Stockings, and a check'd woollen Shirt.

Whoever shall take up said Run-away, and convey him to his abovesaid Master, shall have ten Pounds, old Tenor Reward, and all necessary Charges paid. And all Masters of Vessels and others, are hereby caution'd against concealing or carrying off said Servant on Penalty of the Law. Boston, October 2, 1750.

Reprints: Boston Gazette, 11-13-1750; 11-20-1750.

Boston Gazette, 11-20-1750.

Ran-away from his Master Josiah Stowell of Watertown, on the 13th Instant, a Molatto colour'd Servant, named Edward Stanley, between 16 and 17 Years of Age, about 5 Foot 4 Inches high: Had on when he went away, a light colour'd Duroy Coat with red Lining, a dark Cloth colour'd Jacket and Breeches, a white Linnen Shirt, light blue yarn Stockings, a Felt Hat, almost new, and a pair of thick Shoes with brass Buckles. He has thick bushy black Hair. Whoever shall take up said Servant, and convey him to his abovesaid Master in Watertown, shall have ten Pounds old Tenor Reward, and all necessary Charges paid. And all Masters of Vessels & others are hereby caution'd against concealing or carrying off said Servant, on Penalty of the Law. Boston, Nov. 19, 1750.

Reprint: Boston Gazette, 01-07-172.

Boston Gazette, 08-20-1751.

Ran-away from his Master Capt. Job Prince of Boston, a Negro Man named Sipio, about 27 Years, speaks good English; he was bred from 10 Years in Nantucket, has lived since at Hingham, and at Weymouth with Mr. Jonathan White: He had on when he went away, a white Flannel Jacket, a pair of wide Trowsers, check Shirt. Whoever shall apprehend said Negro and convey him to his Master, or John Kneeland, jun. in Boston, shall have Ten Dollars Reward, and all necessary Charges paid by John Kneeland, jun.

All Masters of Vessels & others, are hereby caution'd against concealing or carrying off said Servant on Penalty of the Law.

N.B. Said Negro has been gone about a Month.

Boston Gazette, 08-04-1752.

Ran away from Benj. Bird, Esq; of Dorchester on the 28th of May last, a Servant Man named George Michael Hobbatt, he is a short black Man with black Hair; had on when he went away, a white Woollen or check'd Shirt, a blew & white strip'd jacket, & white Trousers.

Whoever shall take up said Servant and return him to his said Master again, shall have 20f. Lawful Money Reward, and all necessary Charges paid, by

Benj. Bird.

And all Masters of Vessels and others, are hereby caution'd against con-cealing or carrying off said Servant on Penalty of the Law.

Reprint: Boston Gazette, 08-18-1752.

Boston Gazette, 09-18-1753.

Ran-away from his Master Capt. Benjamin Reed, of Lexington, on the 14th of this Instant September, a Negro Man Servant, named Sambo, but calls himself Samuel Hank's, and pretends to be a Doctor, about 30 Years of Age, of a middling Stature, speaks good English: Had on when he went away, a brown homespun Coat with brass Buttons, a brown Holland Jacket, new Leather Breeches, a pair a blue clouded seam'd Stockings, a new course Linnen Shirt, and a Holland one, Trowsers, and an old Castor Hat: has lost some of his fore Teeth. He carry'd with him a Bible, with (Samuel Reed) wrote in it, with some other Books.

Whoever shall take up said Runaway Servant, and convey him to his abovesaid Master in Lexington, shall have Four Dollars Reward, and all necessary Charges paid.

And all Masters of Vessels and others are hereby caution'd against concealing or carrying off said Servant on Penalty of the Law. Lexington, September 17, 1753.

Boston Gazette, 10-23-1753.

Ran-away from his Master, on the 7th of October Instant, a Negro Man called Hazzard, who formerly belong'd to Deacon Benjamin Wadworth, a well set Fellow, speaks good English, and can read: Had on when he went away, a Lead colour'd Pea Jacket, and linen Trowsers, and is known to have been Lurking about Millton, the first Week of his Absence, he was at several Huskings, he has a scar on one of his Arms, where he was Inoculated for the Small-Pox, he keeps in the Woods in the Day Time.

Whoever shall secure said Run-away, and inform the Printer hereof, so that his Master may have him again, shall have five Pounds old Tenor Reward, and all necessary Charges paid.

And all Masters of Vessels and others are hereby caution'd against concealing or carrying off said Servant on Penalty of the Law. October 23, 1753.

Reprint: Boston Gazette, 10-30-1753.

Boston Gazette, 11-13-1753.

Ran-away on the 16th of October, from his Master, Stephen Turner of Hartford, a Negro Man called Primas, about 37 Years of Age, a stout, tall, well set Fellow, had on when he went away, a Brown double brested Jacket, with mettle Buttons, and a strip'd Holland Jacket under it, a check'd Holland shirt, ruffled with the same, a pair of strip'd Trowsers, a pair of Blewish worsted Stockings, Calf skin Shoes with Buckles, a Caster Hatt, a white Holland Cap, has lost the first Joint of one of his great Toes.

Whoever shall take up said Runaway, and secure him so that his Master may have him again, shall have twenty Pounds old Tenor Reward, and all necessary Charges paid by me,

Hartford, November 5, 1753.

Stephen Turner.

N.B. Said Negro is a good Fidler, & had his Fidle with him.

Reprint: Boston Gazette, 11-20-1753.

Boston Gazette, 11-20-1753.

A Negro Man named Pompey, about 23 Years of Age, belonging to John Wire of Charlestown, went away on Friday Night last, from Mr. Ridgaway, Bricklayer in Boston, with whom he has labour'd the Summer past: He is a stout well set Fellow, and had on a blue under Serge Jacket, and an old patch'd one over it. Whoever shall give Intelligence of said Negro to his Master, or to Mr. Ridgaway, they shall be well rewarded.

Reprint: Boston Gazette, 11-27-1753.

Boston Gazette, 05-14-1754.

Ran-away from Dr. Thomas Dean of Exeter, May 1753, a Negro Man named Quom, suppos'd to be forty Years or upwards, a well set Fellow, something slow in Motion, a wrinkled Face and a Mouth full of Teeth, and a large Eye which he turns up when he is earnest in Speaking. He speaks brokenly, the Tops of two his Fingers are froze off. He had on when he went away a light colour'd Bearskin Coat, a striped Jacket, (the Stripes going round,) a white woollen Shirt and light Stockings.

Whosoever shall bring said Negro, to me the Subscriber in Haverhill, shall have 3 Dollars Reward, and all necessary Chages paid by,

John White, Junr.

Haverhill, May 8th, 1754.

Boston Gazette, 05-21-1754.

Ran-away from his Master Mr. Lemuel Sturtevant, of Hallifax, in the County of Plymouth, on April 25th 1754, a Mallatto Man Servant named Shubal Lawrence, aged 18 Years, a stout lusty Fellow, had on when he went away a Felt Hatt, and a curled Head of Hair, a strait Bodied or mixed colour'd Great Coat with Pewter Buttons, a striped Jacket without Sleeves, white woollen Shirt, his Breeches the same with his Coat, light colour'd blue Stockings, and a Mark on his upper Lip, in form of Figure 3 something resembling an M:

Whoever shall take up said Servant, and bring him to his Master in Hallifax, shall have ten Pounds old Tenor Reward, and all necessary Charges paid.

Halifax in the County of Plymouth, May 15, 1754.

Reprint: Boston Gazette, 10-01-1754.

Boston Gazette, 12-03-1754.

Ran away from Mr. Philip Curtis of Stoughton, on the 18th of November Instant, a Negro Man Servant about 24 Years old, named Scipio Congo, his Left Arm shorter than his Right, can read and write, of a Copper Colour, middle Stature, and with Teeth irregular: When he went away, he had on, an old Hat, a grey Woollen Coat, with Brass Buttons, a strip'd black and white Jacket, and white West coat laced round him, Linnen Breeches and Trousers, blue Stockings and old Shoes.

Whoever shall take up said Negro, and him safely convey to his Master aforesaid, shall have Four Dollars Reward, and handsomely paid for all necessary Charges.

P.S. And as he threatned to go to Sea, 'tis desir'd no Masters of Vessels would receive him, as they would shun the Penalty of the Law.

Stoughton, November 30th 1754.

Boston Gazette, 01-28-1755.

Ran-away from his Master Mr. James Bayley of Watertown, a Negro Man Servant named Constant, between 30 & 40 Years of Age: Had on when he went away a blue Pea Jacket: a pair of Buck-Skin Breeches, a pair of large flower'd Brass Buekles, check hSirt, carry'd away with him a light blue Duroy coat, & a pair of cheek plush Breeches, speaks English; a very spry Felow.

Whoever shall take up said Run-away, and him safely convey his abovesaid Master, or commit him to either his Majesty's Goal, shall have six Dollars Reward, and all necessary Charges.

James Bayley.

And all Masters of Vessels and others, are hereby caution'd against concealing or carrying off said Negro, on Penalty of the Law.

N.B. He has a large Scar in his Neck.

Watertown, January 21, 1755.

Reprint: Boston Gazette, 03-25-1755.

Boston Gazette, 02-18-1755.

Ran-away from his Master Cord Wing of Boston, a Negro Fellow named Portland, about 35 Years of Age, of a middle Stature, speaks bad English, much pock-broken, had on an old Leather Cap, dark Cloth Coat, red lining, flat mettle Buttons, woollen speckled Shirt. Whoever shall take up said Fellow, and return him to his Master, shall have two Dollars Reward, paid by

Boston, Feb. 17, 1755.

Cord Wing.

And all Masters of Vessels are herehy cautioned against carrying off said Servant on Penalty of the Law.

Boston Gazette, 06-28-1756.

RUN-away from the Subscriber at Boston, the 24th Inst. a Negro Fellow named Abboo, about 40 Years of Age, of a small Size: He had when he went away, a white Flannel Jacket, check'd Shirt, a Pair of light colour'd Cloth Breeches; he formerly belonged to Dr. William Douglass, late of Boston.

Whoever will secure said Run-away, so that his Mistress may him again, shall have ONE DOLLAR Reward, and all necessary Charges paid. All Masters of Vessels and others, are caution'd against concealing, harbouring, imploying or carrying off said Negro, as they would avoid the Penalty of the Law.

Kathrin Kerr, living in the Green-Dragon House.

Reprint: Boston Gazette, 07-05-1756.

Boston Gazette, 02-28-1757.

RUN-away from Joseph Syas of Durham, in the Province of New-Hampshire on the Evening of the 24th of February 1757, a Negro Man named George, of a midling Stature, Mulatto Complection, about 35 Years of Age: Had on when he Ran-away, a Soldier's red Coat, worsted Cap, Felt Hat, a brownish Cloth Great Coat, and speaks good English. Who shall apprehend said Runaway, and confine him in any of His Majesty's Goals, so that his Master may have him again, shall have TWO DOLLARS Reward, and all necessary Charges paid, by

JOSEPH SYAS.

Reprints: Boston Gazette, 03-07-1757; 03-14-1757.

Boston Gazette, 06-13-1757.

Ran-away from his Master, Ebenezer Webster of Bradford in the County of Essex, a black Slave, Native of the East-Indies, named James; speaks good English, about 21 Years of Age, wears long bushy Hair, of middling Stature, has a Scar on the left side of his Forehead which enters under his Hair: Had on a light Oznabrigs Coat, a brown homespun Jacket, with brass Buttons, black plush Breeches, a pair of new Pumps, a new Felt Hat, and a white Linnen Shirt.—He formerly belong'd to Mr. Elijah Collins of Boston.

Whoever has taken up the said Servant, or may take him up, and convey him to his said Master, or to Mr. Benjamin Harrod of Boston, shall have Three Dollars Reward, and all necessary Charges paid.—

All Masters of Vessels and others are hereby caution'd not to conceal or carry off the said Slave, as they would avoid the Penalty of the Law. June 7th 1757.

Reprints: Boston Weekly Newsletter, 06-09-1757; 06-16-1757; and 06-23-1757.

Boston Gazette, 07-04-1757.

Ran-away from his Master Mr. Joseph Lynde jun. of Malden, on the 22d of June Instant, a Negro Man Servant named John, about 35 Years of Age, a Pock-broken Fellow, with small Pitts on his Nose; and has a great Scar on one of his Shins: He is a well sett short Fellow: Had on when he went away a Silk Grogram Coat, a white Pair of ribb'd Stockings, and a Pair of Channel Pumps, has lost one of his Fore Teeth, and pretends to be a Doctor. Whoever shall take up said Negro, and convey him to his abovesaid Master, shall have FOUR DOLLARS Reward, and all necessary Charges paid.

All Masters of Vessels and others are hereby caution'd against conceal-ing, entertaining or carrying off said Servant on Penalty of the Law. Malden, June 28, 1757.

Reprints: Boston Gazette, 07-11-1757; 08-01-1757; 02-28-1758; 03-13-1758.

Boston Gazette, 08-08-1757.

Portsmouth, August 2, 1757.

RUN from James Dwyer of Portsmouth, in the Province of New-Hamp-shire, Truckman, this Day, a Negro Man Servant, named Scipio, about 35 Years old, about 5 Feet 8 Inches high, well sett, and of a yellowish Complec-tion. He was born and bro't up among the English; he understands Husband-ry, mows well, and affects to be tho't a Man of Sense: He had on and carried with him, a Saxon blue frize jacket lin'd with Baize, flash Sleeves and small Metal Buttons, a brown Fustian Jacket without Sleeves, a Pair of scarlet everlasting Breeches, and a Pair of Deerskin Breeches, yarn Stockings, a Pair of new Shoes, and new turn'd Pumps, one white Cotton and Linnen, and one Woolen checkt Shirt, an old Hat and Cap. Whoever shall apprehend said Runaway, and bring him to his said Master in said Portsmouth, or secure him so that his Master may have him again, shall have TWENTY SHILLINGS Sterling Reward, and all necessary Charges paid, by

JAMES DWYER.

N.B. If the said Scipio will of his own Accord (without putting me to the Charge of the above Reward) return home, he shall be kindly received, and have his absconding himself forgiven.

Reprints: Boston Gazette, 08-15-1757; 08-22-1757. This notice was also printed in the New-Hampshire Gazette, 08-05-1757.

Boston Gazette, 08-29-1757.

Ran-away from his Master Mr. Ichabod Chesley of Durham, a Negro Man named Toney, about 30 years of Age, speaks good English, a lusty stout Fellow: Had on when he went away, a black and blue full'd Cloth round tail Jacket, a stripped Cotton Jacket, grey Yarn Stockings, a Pair of new Pumps, and Brass Buckles; has lost one Joint of his Fore-Finger of his Right Hand. Whoever shall take up said Runaway, and convey him to his said Master, or Mr. Abner Clough of Salisbury, in the County of Essex, shall have Three DOLLARS Reward and all necessary Charges paid by

New-Hampshire, August 11, 1757.

ICHABOD CHESLEY.

Reprints: Boston Gazette, 09-12-1757; 09-19-1757. This notice was also printed in the New-Hampshire Gazette, 08-19-1757; 09-02-1757; and 09-16-1757.

Boston Gazette, 09-12-1757.

Ran-away, on the 14th of August last, at Night, from his Master Captain Peter Bourn, of the Sloop Bilboa, (then lying in the Harbour of Halifax) a Negro Man named Cuff, about 5 Feet 8 Inches high: Had on a stript Flannel Jacket, a Pair of thick Canvas Trowsers, a checkt Shirt, a stript Cap, and a Pair of Boots; he goes stooping forward, and has a Bunch on the Knuckle of his left Wrist, and is about 20 Years old.

Whoever takes up said Negro, and brings him to his Master, or to Capt. William Wimble of Boston, (but now bound for New-York) shall have TEN DOLLARS Reward, and all necessary Charges paid.

And all Masters of Vessels and others, are hereby cautioned against harbouring, concealing or carrying off said Servant, as they would avoid the Penalty of the Law in that Case made and provided.

N.B. 'Tis tho't he is gone to New-York.

Reprint: Boston Gazette, 10-19-1757.

Boston Gazette, 10-10-1757.

JOHN GRELEA, jun. Clk.

RUN-away from the Subscriber last Thursday Night, a Negro Man named JOSEPH, a well sett Fellow, and of a pleasant Countenance for a Negro; he can speak but little English, but can speak good French; he has Holes in both Ears, with several Turns of brass Wire through them, and has lost some of his fore-Teeth: Had on when he went away, a felt Hat, and a Handkerchief about his Head, a blue double-breasted Jacket, and a strip'd homespun ditto, a cotton and linen Shirt, brown Serge Breeches, a Pair of polish'd Steel Knee Buckles, and red Garters to be seen below his Breeches, speckled Yarn Stockings, and a Pair of work'd Shoe Buckles which look like Silver.—He carried with him sundry other Cloaths, viz. Blue Cloth Breeches, broad check'd linen Trousers, Oznabrigs ditto, a Frock, a cotton and linnen check'd Shirt, and white ditto French made, with which he can shift his Apparel. Whoever can give the Printers, or Owners, any Intelligence of him, so that he may be had again, shall have TWO DOLLARS Reward, and all necessary Charges paid. 'Tis tho't he is conceal'd by some Person, most likely a French Neutral, as he can't speak English sufficient to travel by himself. All Masters of Vessels and others, are hereby caution'd against harbouring, concealing, entertaining or carrying off said Servant, on Penalty of the Law. Boston, October 10, 1757.

FORTESQUE VERNON.

Reprints: Boston Gazette, 10-17-1757; 10-31-1757.

Boston Gazette, 04-03-1758.

Ran-away from the Subscriber, on Saturday the 25th of March ult. a Mulatto Servant Man 23 Years of Age: He is a spry, likely-looking Fellow, but has been guilty of running away; and as he is not very Black, he passes for a free Man. He formerly went by the Name of Worrison, but has since changed it to Jonathan Spane: He had on when he went away, a small Felt Hat, new Worsted Cap, an old out-side Dubblet, and striped Waistcoat, new Trowsers, blue Stockings, and double sol'd Shoes. Whoever shall take up said Runaway, and bring him to his Master in Cape-Ann, or secure him 'till' his Master can send for him, shall have TEN DOLLARS Reward, and all necessary Charges paid, by me JOSEPH FOSTER

All Masters of Vessels and others are hereby caution'd against concealing or carrying off said Servant on Penalty of the Law. Boston, April 1st, 1757.

Reprint Boston Gazette, 04-10-1758.

Boston Gazette, 06-26-1758.

RUN-away from his Master Samuel McClellan, of Woodstock in Connecticut, on the 6th Instant, a Negro Man Servant named Cesar, about 22 Years of Age: Had on when he went away, a blue grey stait bodied Coat, and Breeches of the same, a red Shag double-breasted Jacket, stript woollen Cap, and an old Beaver Hat; and carried a Violin with him. Whoever shall take up the above Runaway, and convey him to his said Master, shall have FOUR DOLLARS Reward, and all necessary Charges paid, by SAMUEL McCLELLAN.

Reprints: Boston Gazette, 07-03-1758; 07-10-1758.

Boston Gazette, 07-10-1758.

RUN-away from Thomas and Benjamin Forsey, Merchants in Albany, a Negro Man that did formerly belong to Dr. Donald Cummings of Caseo-Bay, known by the Name of Phenix, five Feet nine Inches high, about 26 years of Age, speaks good English; Had on when he went away, a stript Flannel Waistcoat, Oznabrigs Shirt, ditto Trowsers, a little lame, one Ancle a little larger than the other, with a Speck in one Eye. Whoever shall take up said Negro, and bring him to his Masters, or send them Intelligence so that he may be had again, shall receive Five Dollars Reward, and all reasonable Charges paid by,
    Albany, June 2, 1758.

                                 Thomas & Benjamin Forsey.
    Reprints: Boston Gazette, 07-17-1758; 07-24-1758.

Boston Gazette, 04-09-1759.

RUN-away from his Master Mr. Timothy Goodwin of Charlestown, on the 2d Instant, a Negro Man named Gosport, about 25 Years of Age, a stout Fellow, and has had the Small-Pox. Had on when he went away, a green Cab, blue Coat, and red Bayse Waistcoat, Leather Breeches with hard-metal Buttons, light gray Stockings, hard-metal Buckles, and an old rusty Hat. Whoever shall take up said Runaway and carry him to Mr. Leasenby's in Boston Common, shall have TWO DOLLARS Reward, and all necessary Charges paid. He was seen in Boston last Friday.

Boston Gazette, 05-21-1759.

Ran-away from the Subscribers, two Negroes, one a Boy about 16 Year old, nam'd Coff, with an old Kersey jacket, plays well on the Violin; the other Negro is also nam'd Coff, about 26 Years old, yellow Complection, both have red Great Coats, and talk good English: Whoever takes up said Negroes, and bring or send them to Boston to their Masters, shall have Three Dollars for each, and all necessary Charges paid, by STEPHEN DEBLOIS,
                                       LEWIS DEBLOIS.

Boston Gazette, 07-23-1759.

TAKEN up by Benjamin Corham, a Run away Negro, who is confin'd in his Majesty's Goal in Providence, George Taylor, Esq; his Dialect hardly intelligible, calls himself Tom, and says he belongs to Master Waddam, but don't tell of what Place: He is a slim, tall strait limb'd Fellow, seems about 30 Years old, a Scar in the Middle of his Forehead, his Cheeks mark;d with his Country Scars. Has on a Crimson short Jacket, a ragged blue Coat, an Homespun old grey Great Coat. Has with him in an Oznabrigs Wallet, a dark brown Broad Cloth Coat about half worne, a new Dowlas Shirt, and a Flannel one, and old course red Pair of Breeches, which is all the Description we can give his Master. Providence, July 18, 1759.

Reprints: Boston Gazette, 08-06-1759; 08-13-1759.

Boston Gazette, 08-20-1759.

RUN away from his Master Peter Hay of Stoneham, on the 11th Instant, a stout Negro Man named Tom, about 25 Years old, born in this Country, and has red Eyes: Had on when he went away, a Tow Shirt, a strip'd Jacket, and a grey Jacket, all Wool, and a Pair of Trowsers; He took with him besides, a brown Coat and Jacket, and a red Jacket, two Pairs of Stockings, a red Cap, and a Felt Hatt. He went away with an Indian Woman, named Hannah Simyar. Whoever shall take up said Run-away, and convey him to his Master aforesaid, shall have TEN DOLLARS Reward, and all necessary Charges paid. All Masters of Vessels and others, are hereby caution'd against concealing or carrying off said Negro on Penalty of the Law.

Reprints: Boston Gazette, 08-27-1759; 09-03-1759.

Boston Gazette, 09-17-1759.

RUN away the 12th Instant from his Master Joseph Gould of Lynn, a Negro Man named George, formerly belonging to Isaac Royall, Esq: of Medford, who had on when he went away, a stript worsted Cap, a coarse Linnen fly Coat, red Waistcoat, a Fustian Pair of Breeches, Yarn Stockings, and a Pair of a Shoes. His Stature is short and small, speaks broken English, his Age between thirty and forty Years. Whoever will apprehend and take up said Negro, or bring him to me his said master, shall have TWO DOLLARS, and all necessary charges paid.

JOSEPH GOULD.

Lynn, Sept. 15, 1759.

Reprints: Boston Gazette, 09-24-1759; 10-01-1759. This notice was also printed in the Boston News-Letter, 08-10-1758; 08-17-1758.

Boston Gazette, 09-17-1759.

RUN away Yesterday from his Master Thomas Church, of Little-Compton, in this Colony, a Negro Man named Boston, about 28 Years of Age, tall, slim, and well liim'd. Had on and carried with him when he went away, a Cloth-colour'd Worsted Coat with a Red Flannel Linnen, a striped Tow and linen Jacket and Breeches, a Pair of Homespun Broad Cloath Breeches, with worsted Buttons, a Pair of white Trowsers, Stockings and Shoes, a Soldiers Knapsack, a fine Linen Shirt, a Tow Shirt, and a Felt Hat.

Whoever apprehends said Negro, and confines him in any of his Majesty's Goals, and gives Notice thereof or conveys him to his Master, shall receive Four Dollars as a Reward, paid by the said Church.

N.B. All masters of Vessels and others, are forwarned carrying off said Slave, as they will answer it at their Peril. Newport, September 12, 1759.

Reprints: Boston Gazette, 09-24-1759; 10-01-1759.

Boston Gazette, 10-08-1759.

RUN away from Major Edmond Matthis of Albany, in the Province of New-York, the following People, viz. a servant Man named William Fairfield, of a dark Complection, down look, black Hair, and of a middling Stature. Also a Negro Man and Woman, and a white Girl with them, about 14 Years of Age, who talks good English, high and low Dutch; the Negro Man is much pitted with Small Pox, and speaks good English; tis suppos'd they are all together: They took with them a great many Cloaths, and its probable they will often alter their Dress. Whoever takes up said Runaways, and safely conveys them to their abovesaid Master, shall have Ten Pounds (25 Dollars) New York Currency Reward, and all necessary Charges paid. Albany, Octob. 1, 1759.

Edmond Matthis.

Reprints: Boston Gazette, 10-22-1759; 11-05-1759.

Boston Weekly News-Letter, 09-06-1750.

Ran-away Yesterday from Capt. Francis Bramham, a Negro Man, named York, of a low Stature, of about 26 or 27 Years of Age, round Face, and some rotten Teeth: Had on when he went away, a green Ratteen Jacket, a Cap, a pair of large white Trowsers, and a large pair of brass Buckles in his Shoes, use to sweep Chimneys in the Winter. Any one that bring said Negro to his Master, or to the Printer hereof shall have FIVE POUNDS old Tenor, Reward, and all necessary Charges paid by Francis Braham.

All Masters of Vessels and others are hereby caution'd against entertaining, harbouring, concealing, or carrying off said Negro, as they would avoid the Penalty of the Law. Boston, September 6, 1750.

Boston Weekly News-Letter, 04-04-1751.

Ran-away from his Master Johnson Jackson of Boston, Distiller, on the 24th Instant, a Negro Man named Titus, of middle Stature, born at Nantucket, speaks softly: He had with when he went away, two Jackets, one of a light colour which he wore outside, with mettal Buttons and a Patch on the shoulder, the other Jacket of a dark colour, and a pair of Breeches of the same, a pair of Leather Breeches with mettal Buttons, a pair of Trowsers, two pair of Stockings, one pair blue very fine, the other grey patched on the Feet, two Shirts, one check'd woollen, the other cotton and linen, and a narrow Beaver Hat; it is suppos'd that a free Negro Woman named Hannah is along with him, who goes lame; and 'tis tho't they lye by in the Day-time and travel at Night, and design for Rhode-Island or Nantucket. The Fellow plays well upon a Violin.

Whosoever will take up said Negro, so that his Master may have him again, shall receive TEN POUND old Tenor, Reward, and all necessary Charges paid,

Johnson Jackson.

All Persons are hereby caution'd against harbouring, entertaining or concealing said Servant, as they would avoid the Penalty of the Law.

Reprints: Boston Weekly News-Letter, 04-11-1751; 04-18-1751.

Boston Weekly News-Letter, 05-23-1754.

Fifty Pistoles Reward.

Annapolis, in Maryland, March 25, 1754.

Ran away on the 18th Instant with the Sloop Hopewell, belonging to the Subscriber, William Curtis, Master, the two following Convict Servants, and a Negro Man, viz.

John Wright, a White man, of a swarthy Complexion, very lusty, talk hoarse, and is much pitted with the Small Pox.

John Smith, also a lusty White Man, with short black Hair.

Toney, a yellowish Negro, and not quite so lusty, pretends to be a Portuguize, speaks good English and pertly, is a good Hand by Water, also can do Cooper's Work, Butchering, &c. Had on or with him, a Dove colour'd Surtoot Coat.

They may have sundry Cloaths, Wigs, Linnen, Cash, &c belonging to the Captain, as it is believed they have murdered him; and the above Wright was seen with the Captain's Cloaths on, which were red; tho' he had Cloaths of sundry Colours with him; He also had a neat Silver hilted Sword, and Pistols mounted with Silver.

The Captain had the Register of the Sloop with him, but he was not indorsed thereon, as he was to return here to make up his Load, and clear at the proper Office.

They were seen off Patuxent on the 22d Instant, at which Time the said Wright assumed Master, and took two Men with them, belonging to a Schooner of Mr. James Dick's and Company; one a White Man, belonging to the said Dick, and the other a Negro belonging to Captain William Strachem of London-Town, who went on board with some Bread for them, at which Time they hoisted Sail, and cut their Boat adrift and carried them off.

They had some Lumber on board, such as Staves, Heading, & Plank; also Rum, Molasses, Sugar, Linnen, &c. &c.

The Sloop is about 45 Tons Square Stern'd, with a Round House, with a Partition under, dividing the Cabin and Steerage, the Waste black, yellow Gunwales and Drift-Rails, and the Drift and Stern blue.

Whoever secures the said Sloop and Goods, so that the Owner may have her again, and the three White Servants, and two Slaves, so as they may be brought to Justice, shall have FIFTY PISTOLES Reward, paid by,

Patrick Creagh.

Boston Weekly News-Letter, 04-24-1755.

RUN away this Morning from his Master, a Negro Man Slave named Hazard, 25 Years of Age, speaks good English, and can read; he hath the Scar of Inoculation on the inside of his left Arm; is a short well set Fellow, had on a woolen chec'd Shirt, Deer skin Breeches and old Trousers over them, two striped woolen Wastcoats, a Pair of white Yarn Stockings, newly footed, and old Shoes. He also carried with him a cotton and linnen, and a Garlick Shirt, a Pair of new white Yarn Stockings, and old strip'd ditto, a Sailor's Waist-coat, and new Shoes: He formerly belong'd to Dr. Stevens; and hath for some Time had a mind to inlist. Whoever shall secure the abovesaid Negro, and inform the Printer hereof, so as his Master may have him again, shall have FIVE DOLLARS Reward, and all necessary Charges paid. All Masters of Vessels and others are caution'd against being deceiv'd by him; it's tho't he will try to hide in some Vessel.

Boston Weekly News-Letter, 09-18-1755.

Ran-away from his Master Hugh McLallen of Gorham-Town, alias Narra-gansett Township No. 7, in the County of York, a Negro Man named Jube, on the 24th Day of August last past; of low Stature, somewhat slender Body, and thin-favour'd; speaks English but poorly, aged about 25 Years: Besides other Cloathing carried away with him a blue Broad-cloth Jacket, and a Pair of strip'd Linnen Trowser. Whoever shall tak up said Negro, and convey him to Col. Ezekiel Cushing in Falmouth in Casco Bay, or to me said Hugh McLallen, shall have SIX DOLLARS Reward, and all necessary Charges paid.

Gorham-Town, Sept. 8th 1755. Hugh McLallan.

Boston Weekly News-Letter, 11-20-1755.

Ran-away the beginning of October last, from his master Johnson Jackson, of Boston, Distiller, a Negro Man named Boney or Bonny [faded]: He is about five Feet 9 or 10 Inches high, has had the Small Pox, speaks good English, lame in his right Leg, by a kick from a Horse: Had on when he went away a Cloth-coloured Fly Coat, a Callico jacket with small brass Buttons, a pair of blue Breeches, a pair of white and a pair of blue Stockings, old Shoes with brass Buckles: He has been seen at Natick several Times with some ladies [faded,] and suppos'd to be [faded] by them, or else gone towards Rhode-Island: Whoever shall secure the said Servant or bring him to his said Master shall have FOUR DOLLARS for their Trouble, and all necessary Charges paid.

                                                    Johnson Jackson.
    All Masters of Vessels and others are hereby cauion'd against harbouring, concealing or carrying of said Servant as they would avoid the Penalty of the Law.

Boston Weekly News-Letter, Thursday November 10, to Friday November 18, 1757.

Ran-away from his master Capt. John Nicholson of Cumberland, in the Colony of Rhode-Island, on the 8 th of October last, a Negro Man Servant named Joxet, about 40 Years of Age, of a middling Stature, speaks good English, has a peculiar Mark just above one of his Ears, about the Bigness of a Walnut, and in Form of a Man's Ear: Had on when he went away, a blue Coat and Jacket, and otherways well-cloath'd. He was seen Yesterday fe'ennight at Natick, & the Friday following at Sudbury, and 'tis tho't he may be gone towards Albany. Whoever shall take up said Negro so that his Master may have him again, shall have FIVE DOLLARS Reward, and all necessary Charges paid by John Nicholson.

    ALL Masters of Vessels and other are forbid harbouring or carrying off said Servant, to void the Penalty of the law. November 9, 1757.

    Reprints: Boston Weekly News-Letter, 11-18-1757; 12-01-1757. This notice was also printed in the Boston Post Boy, 11-14-1757; 11-21-1757; 11-28-1757; 12-05-1757.

Boston Weekly News-Letter, 09-28-1758.

Ran away from the Ship Sharp, Richard Maitland Master, on Sunday Night, between the 24th and 25th Instant, a Negro Servant Man named Thomas Morro, about 27 or 28 Years of Age, and about 5 Feet 5 Inches high. He had on Sailor's Cloathing when he left the Ship: He was born at Barbadoes, and liv'd long at Venice in Italy.

Whoever apprehends the said Negro Servant, so he may be deliver'd to Mr. Nathaniel Taylor, shall receive of him FIVE DOLLARS Reward, and all necessary Charges. Richard Maitland.

N.B. All Persons are forbid harbouring, concealing or carrying off said Servant, as they may depend upon being Prosecuted as the Law directs.

He robb'd said Ship of her Boat.

Boston Weekly News-Letter, 10-26-1758.

BROKE out of the Workhouse last Night, TWO NEGRO BOYS. Whoever take them up, and return them there again, shall be well Rewarded for their Trouble.

Boston Weekly News-Letter, 11-02-1758.

Ran away from Powers Mariott in Cornhill, a Negro Boy named Quam; a tall Lad with a yellow Face; he had on a blue German Serge Jacket and Breeches, a speckled Shirt, a good Beaver Hat, light worsted Stockings, and wrought brass Buttons, a dark Bearskin Coat with white Mettal Buttons. Whoever takes up said Negro, and returns him to his Master, shall be well rewarded for their Trouble. N.B. All Masters of vessels and others are caution'd against carrying off, or harbouring or concealing said Negro Lad, as they would avoid the Penalty of the Law. Boston, November 1, 1758.

Boston Weekly News-Letter, 06-07-1759.

Ran-away from Henry Charlton, of Milton, on the 20th Instant, a Negro Man, named Portsmouth; about five Feet and a half high, near Forty Years of Age, speaks good English, goes something stooping, with his right Foot very much out; had on when he went away, a blue Jacket, leather Breeches, white Shirt, a green Cap, a Soldier's old Hat, and an old great Coat.

Whosoever shall take up said Run-away, and bring him to his said Master, shall have FOUR DOLLARS Reward, and all necessary Charges paid by me,

Milton, May 22, 1759.

Henry Charlton.

Reprints: Boston Weekly News-Letter, 06-14-1759 and 07-12-1759.

Boston Weekly News-Letter, 09-13-1759.

Ran-away from Capt. John Diamond at Marblehead, on Tuesday the 11th of September Instant, a Spanish Negro Fellow, named Cuffe, about 25 Years old, speaks broken English, and can talk the Spanish language: He is a tall slim Fellow; had on a new Felt Hat, striped homespun Jacket and Breeches, new Shoes, with square Buckles. Whosoever will bring or send the said Negro to Mr. Norwood, Innholder, at Lynn, shall have TWO DOLLARS Reward, and all necessary Charges paid.—All Masters of Vessels and others, are caution'd not to conceal or carry off the said Negro, as they would avoid the Penalty of the Law.

Reprint: Boston Weekly News-Letter, 09-20-1759.

Boston Post Boy, 07-23-1750.

Ran-away the 19th of July, from Ichabod Goodwin of Berwick, in the County of York, a Negro Man named Pompey, about 40 Years of Age, a short well-set Fellow, speaks good English, he had on a pair of Pot-hooks when he went away, a pair of Trowsers, a homespun Jacket, and a check'd woolen Shirt, and has one of Ears cut. Likewise a tall slim young Fellow named William Nason, of light Complection and light Hair: Whoever takes up said Servants and delivers them to their Master, or secures them so that they may be had again, shall have Ten Pounds Old Tenor Reward, with all reasonable Charges paid by

Ichabod Goodwin.

N.B. All Masters of Vessels are hereby forewarned carrying them off, as they may expect to answer it at their Peril.

Reprints: Boston Post Boy, 07-30-1750; 08-06-1750.

Boston Post Boy, 08-20-1750.

Ran-away from Capt. Thomas Bloss, last Night, Two Negro Men, one named Phillip, the other Ned, both Sailmakers. Phillip is a tall spare Fellow, and walks a little lame. Ned is a spry young Fellow of about 19 Years of Age: They both talk broken English: They carried away with them sundry Wearing Apparel that belong'd to some of the Hands of the Vessel from which they run, such as Jackets made of coarse Blanketing and strip'd Homespun, speckled Shirts, Trowsers and Breeches, Hats, &c. but have neither Stockings or Shoes unless they have Mogizeens. Whoever shall take up said Negroes and bring them to their Master on board the Schooner Success lying at Col. Wendell's Wharf, or Mr. Benjamin Hallowell in Boston, shave have FIVE POUNDS old Tenor Reward for each, and all necessary Charges paid.

All Masters of Vessels and others are hereby caution'd against harbouring, concealing or carrying off said Servant as they would avoid the Penalty of the Law. Boston, August 20, 1750.

Boston Post Boy, 08-27-1750.

Ran-away on the 9th of August from Robert Thompson of the Town of Durham in the Province of New Hampshire, a Negro Man, named John Batter, of a midling Stature, talks pretty good English, and can speak French: He carried away with him a Gun and Ammunition; and had on a grey home-spun Jacket a pair of Leather Breeches, a white woollen Shirt and a felt Hat. Whosoever will take up said Negro and secure him so that he may have him again, shall have TEN POUNDS old Tenor and all necessary Charges paid by me Robert Thompson.

Reprints: Boston Post Boy, 09-03-1750; 09-10-1750.

Boston Post Boy, 08-27-1750.

Ran-away on the 9th Instant from Aaron Davis of Durham, in the Province of New Hampshire, a Negro Man named Quam, of a middling Stature, talk good English, he carried away with him, a Gun and Ammunition; he had on a grey homespun Jacket a white woolen Shirt, a Felt Hat. Whoever will take up said Negro and secure him so that he may have him again, shall have TEN POUNDS old Tenor, and all necessary Charges paid by me Aaron Davis.

Durham, August 23, 1750.

Reprints: Boston Post Boy, 09-03-1750; 09-10-1750.

Boston Post Boy, 09-17-1750.

Ran-away on the 3d of September, from Doctor John Ross of Portsmouth, in the Province of New-Hampshire, a Negro Man, named Pomp, about six Feet high, about 28 Years of Age, speaks good English; He had on when he went away, striped homespun under-Jacket, and old upper blue Jacket, a pair of Leather Breeches, has a Sore upon his left Shin, and a Scar if not a Sore on his right Shin, another Scar on his left Check, near his Ear, with oftentimes issues Water: He designs for the Sea. Whoever will take up said Negro, and secure him so that his Master may have him again shall have TEN POUNDS old Tenor Reward, and all necessary Charges paid by John Ross.

N.B. All Masters of Vessels and others are caution'd from concealing or carrying off said Negro, as they would avoid the Penalty of the Law.

Reprints: Boston Post Boy, 09-24-1750; 10-01-1750.

Boston Post Boy, 01-28-1751.

RUN from Abigail Walker of Portsmouth in the Province of New-Hamp-shire, on Sunday the 20th Instant, a Negro Man Servant named Cato, about 40 Years old, the End of his Thumb on his right Hand has been cut off near the Root of the Nail, one of his fore Teeth is out, and he is something bow knee'd: He had on when he run a black broad-cloth Coat with round cuffs, a grey homespun Jacket with large bell-mettle flat Buttons, a blue Under-jacket of Baize, pewter Buttons, the Button-holes work'd, with white black cloth Breeches, black yarn Buskins, a felt Hat, and a blue and white woollen Shirt. Whoever shall apprehend said Negro so that the said Abigail shall have him again, shall have FIVE POUNDS old Tenor Reward, and necessary Charges paid by

Abigail Walker.

N.B. All Persons are caution'd against harbouring, concealing or carrying off said Servant, as they will answer the same at their Peril.

Reprints: Boston Post Boy, 02-04-1751; 02-11-1751.

Boston Post Boy, 06-03-1751.

Ran-away from his Master Richard Dodge of Wenham, in County of Essex, on Wednesday last, a likely Negro Man-Servant, named Hazard, of a yellow-ish Complection, middling Stature, about 30 Years of Age, speaks pretty good English, well set: Had on when he went away, a white cotton and linnen Shirt, a homespun Coat mix'd with a cast of Blue, tow Trowser, blue worsted Stockings, a dark Wig, a Beaver Hat, and a Pair of Pumps, with large silver Buckles mark'd D.H. He has a Scar across the middle of each of his Legs of two Inches long, cut by an Ax. He carried off with him a fine large Bay Horse, Fourteen Hands high, valued at 200l old Tenor, a natural Pacer, us'd to Drawing, and has a Sore in the middle of his Back; the said Horse being the Property of his Master. Whosoever shall take up the said Servant and Horse and return them to the said Dodge in Wenham, shall have Five Pounds old Tenor Reward for each, and all necessary Charges paid.

Wenham, May 30th 1751. per me, Richard Dodge.

N.B. All Persons whatsoever are hereby caution'd against concealing or carrying off said Negro and Horse, as they would avoid the Penalty of the Law.

Reprint: Boston Post Boy, 06-10-1751.

Boston Post Boy. Date: 09-02-1751.

Ran-away from his Master Capt. Job Prince, of Boston, the latter End of July last, a Negro Man named Scipio, aged 27 Years, speaks good English: he was bred from ten Years old in Nantucket, has lived since at Hingham, and at Weymouth with Mr. Jonathan White: He had on when he went away a white Flannel Jacket, a Pair of wide Trowsers, a check Shirt.

Whoever shall apprehend said Negro, and convey him to his Master, or John Kneeland, jun. in Boston, shall have TEN DOLLARS Reward, and all necessary Charges paid by John Kneeland, jun.

All Master or Vessels and others, are hereby cautioned against concealing or carrying off said Servant on Penalty of the Law.

Reprints: Boston Post Boy, 09-09-1751; 09-23-1751.

Boston Post Boy, 09-09-1751.

RUN away on the 12th of last Month, from William Oakford, at the Head of Alloway's Creek, Salem County, a Servant-Man, named Joseph Steel, an English Man, about 28 Years of Age, of middle Stature, and black curled Hair: Had on when he went away, and took with him, three Coats, one grey, the other two blue, and three Jackets, two blue, and the other of a light colour, a pair of Leather Breeches, a Leather Jacket, and two pair of Trowsers, thread and worsted Stockings, and Calf-skin Shoes, three coarse Shirts, two Hats, one Castor, the other Felt. "Tis probable he will pass for a Ship-Carpenter, or Caulker, having with him some Caulker's Tools. He took with him a Negro Lad, named Caesar, about 18 Years of Age: Had on when he went away, a Coat and Jacket, thick Cloth, of a Lead colour, Leather Breeches, and short Trowsers, thread Stockings, and half-worn Shoes, two Shirts, the one white, the other brown, and two Felt Hats. They took with them a Rifle-Barrel Gun, and a large new bag: Whoever takes up and secures said Servants, so that their Master may have them again, giving Notice thereof to Caspar Wistar, in Philadelphia, shall have TEN POUNDS Reward, or Five Pounds for the white Man, and Five Pounds for the Negro, and reasonable Charges, paid by WILLIAM OAKFORD.

N.B. The Negro can speak good Dutch: All Masters of Vessels are forbid to carry them off at their Peril.

Reprint: Boston Post Boy, 09-23-1751.

Boston Post Boy, 07-06-1752.

RUN-away the 11th Instant from his Master Jeremiah Brown of South-Kingstown, in this Colony, a Mustee Fellow, named Simon, aged about 20 Years, something short of Stature, and round favoured. Had on when he went away, an old blue Coat, striped Flannel Jacket, pretty good Hat, black Wig, Linen Trowsers, white Yarn Stockings, and an old Pair of mended Shoes.

Whoever shall take up said Run-away, and deliver him to his said master, or secure him, so that he may be had again, shall have Twenty Pounds, old Tenor Reward, and all necessary Charges paid by Jeremiah Brown.

Reprints: Boston Post Boy, 07-13-1752; 07-20-1752.

Boston Post Boy, 06-18-1753.

Ran away the 19th Instant from Isaac Fowler, of North Kingstown, a dark Mustee Fellow, named Caesar about 21 Years of Age, well-set, has a thick short neck, and a down Look. Had on when he went away, an old Felt Hat, striped Flannel Jacket, and a Full-cloath dark grey Jacket, Check Shirt, Leather Breeches, white Thread Stockings, and old Shoes; took with him a Frock and Trowsers. Whoever takes up and secures said Fellow, so that his Master may have again, shall have TWENTY POUNDS Reward, and all necessary Charges, paid by,

Isaac Fowler.

Reprint: Boston Post Boy, 06-25-1753.

Boston Post Boy, 01-14-1754.

Ran-away from his Master Robert Stone, Innholder, living at the Royal Exchange Tavern in Boston, on the 11th Instant, a Negro Fellow named Dan, about 20 Years of Age, 5 Feet high, a well-set Fellow, much pitted with the Small-Pox, having lately had it, has a very stern Countenance, and speaks good English, was born in Plymouth in New-England: Had on when he went away a red and white worsted Cap, an old Beaver Hat, a dark Bearskin Pea-Jacket, with brass Buttons, and piec'd on the right Elbow, a red and white Swanskin Jacket, a white cotton and linnen Shirt, a blue and white strip'd Handkerchief, a pair of light Buckskin Breeches, a pair of mix'd Yarn Stockings, a pair of good Shoes and brass Buckles.

Whoever shall take up the said Runaway, and him safely convey to his said Master, shall have three DOLLARS Reward, and all necessary Charges paid: And all Masters of Vessels and others are hereby caution'd against harbouring, concealing, or carrying off said Negro, as they would avoid the Penalty of the Law.

Boston, January 14, 1754.

Reprints: Boston Post Boy, 01-21-1754; 01-28-1754.

Boston Post Boy, 10-14-1754.

RUN-away the 3d Instant from his Master Joseph Dennis of Portsmouth, on Rhode-Island, a Mustee or Molatto Man Servant, named Pero, about 27 Years of Age, very large of Stature; hath a Scar on each Thumb, which causes them to stand crooked, and a round large Scar on the outside of the Calf of his left Leg, resembling the Scar of a Burn. Had on when he went away a Homespun full-cloth grey-coloured double breasted Jacket, with large flat Brass Buttons, notch'd or scollop'd round the Edges, a Pair of Tow

Trowsers, and a Tow Shirt. Whoever takes up said Molatto, or secures him, so that his Master may have him again, shall have TEN POUNDS old Tenor Reward, and all necessary Charges, paid by me, Joseph Dennis.

Reprints: Boston Post Boy, 10-21-1754; 10-20-1754.

Boston Post Boy, 10-16-1758.

Ran away from me the Subscriber, on the 11th of this Instant, a Negro Boy named Cuff, about 14 Years of Age, plays well on the Violin: He had on when he went away, a Duroy Coat, stript Jacket and Leather Breeches. Whoever shall take up said Negro, so that his said Master may have him again, shall be well Rewarded, and all Charges paid by

STEPHEN DEBLOIS.

N.B. All Masters of Vessels and others are forbid harbouring, concealing or carrying off said Negro, as they would avoid the Penalty of the Law.

Reprint: Boston Post Boy, 10-23-1758.

Boston Post Boy, 05-21-1759.

Ran away from the Subscribers two Negroes, one a Boy about 16 Years old, named Cuff; had on when he went away, an old Kersey Jacket, plays well on the Violin: The other named Cuff, about 26 Years of Age, yellow Complection, both have red Great-Coats, and talk good English; suppos'd to be about Ispwich, or to the Eastward. Whoever takes up said Negroes, and will bring or send them to Boston to their Masters shall have THREE DOLLARS for each, and all necessary Charges paid by

STEPHEN DEBLOIS.

Boston, May 21, 1759

GILEERT DEBLOIS.

Boston Post Boy, 07-30-1759.

Ran away from Edmund Leavenworth on the 23d of June last, a Negro Man named Pomp, a short well-set Fellow, about 28 Years of Age, speaks good English, can both read and write, and it's likely may have wrote himself a Pass; he carry'd off with him one striped linnen and one brown vest, without Sleeves, a light colour'd Flannel Great-Coat, and a fly Coat of the same without Lining, and a pair of Tow Trowsers, a pair of blue woolen Stockings, and one black ditto with a blue Streek round the top, one new pair single sole Shoes with square Brass Buckles in them. Whoever takes up and secures the said Negro, so that his Master may have him, shall have Forty Shilling Lawful Money Reward, and all reasonable Charges paid by EDMUND LEAVENWORTH.

Reprints: Boston Post Boy, 08-06-1759; 08-13-1759; 08-20-1759.

Boston Post Boy, 08-20-1759.

Ran away last Saturday Evening from George Russell, Master of the Ship St. Kitts Merchants, Thomas Rawlinson, born in Scotland; a likely Lad, about 18 Years of Age; thick and well set, of a ruddy Complection. Had on when he went away a red Waistcoat and Trowsers, check Shirt, and his Hat bound with yellow Quality-binding.—Also Ran-away from the same Ship some Time ago, Nicholas Cunningham, a West-India Molatto, about 40 Years of Age, about 5 Feet 4 Inches high, thin favour'd, and had on a Sailor's Habit, has short curl'd black Hair, and his Hat bound with yellow Quality. Whoever shall apprehend the said Run-aways, and bring them to the Master on board said Ship, shall have Four Dollars Reward for each or either of them, and all necessary Charges paid by GEORGE RUSSELL.

N.B. All Masters of Vessels and others are hereby caution'd against harbouring, concealing or carrying off said Servant, as they would avoid the Penalty of the Law.

Reprints: Boston Post Boy, 08-27-1759; 09-03-1759.

Boston Post Boy, 10-29-1759.

Ran away from Joseph Hall of Wallingford, in Connecticut, a Molatto Slave, 26 Years of Age, middling Stature, speaks clear and quick, and can read well: Had on when he went away, and carried with him, a check't flannel Shirt, one Holland ditto, and one white ditto, a light brown Duroy Coat lin'd with red, a dark brown ditto, light blue Stockings, and a white bed Blanket. Whoever will take up said Runaway, and bring him home, or secure him so that I may have him again, shall have Twenty Shillings Lawful Money, and all necessary Charges paid by Joseph Hall.

Reprints: Boston Post Boy, 11-05-1759; 11-12-1759.

Boston Gazette, 03-31-1760.

Ran-away from William Rhodes, of Craston, in the Colony of Rhode-Island, on the 13th Inst. a Mulatto Fellow of 16 Years Old, named Pete Cuchip, very stout and large for that Age. Had on when he absconded, a pair o white Stockings, a Duffles Waistcoat double breasted, with Leather Buttons upon it, an old Kersey Jacket over the other, a Flannel Shirt, a pair blue Breeches, and a Felt Hat. Whoever shall take up, secure and forward Home said Mulatto Fellow, shall have two Dollars Reward, besides all necessary Charges paid, by me William Rhodes.

Boston Gazette, 04-14-1760.

Came to the House of the Subscriber, on the 4th Inst. a Negro Man, aged about 50, a thick-sett Fellow, of about 5 Feet Stature: Had on, an old Felt Hat, a white mill'd Cap, a red Shag Great Coat, a green Jacket, an old checkt Shirt, and a Pair of black Cloth Breeches. Said Fellow says he belongs to Mr. John Green of Concord, who has given him a Pass to obtain Business. His Master may have him again paying the Charges. Ipswich, April 10, 1760.

THOMAS BORDMAN.

Boston Gazette, 08-18-1760.

RUN-away from his Master Jacob White of Springfield, the 6th Day of August Current, a Negro Man Servant, 18 or 19 Years old, of a middling Stature, his Knees incline much inwards : Had on when he left his said Master, a blue Broad Cloth Coat, lined with red, and Brass Buttons, and a blue Waistcoat, lined with red. Whoever will take up and secure the said Negro, so that his Master may have him, shall have FOUR DOLLARS Reward, and necessary Charges paid,

Springfield, Aug. 8, 1760.

By Jacob White.

Reprints: Boston Gazette, 08-25-1760; 09-01-1760.

Boston Gazette, 11-10-1760.

TWO DOLLARS Reward.

RUN-away last Friday Evening, a Negro Boy called Boston, a very well set, strong, well-made Boy, about 18 years old : He had on when he went away, a cloth coloured Pea-jacket lined with red, and white metal Buttons, with a strip'd Waistcoat under ; cotton and linnen Shirt, brown breeches under Trowsers, blue Stockings, large Brass Buckles ; his Hat and Shoes generally in the Mode. Whoever will bring the above Boy to W. D. Cheever, or give Intelligence where he may be had, are intitled to the above Two Dollars, and all necessary Charges. Nov. 10, 1760.

N. B. As he has been sometime at Sea, this serves to caution all Masters of Vessels and others, from harbouring or concealing him.

Reprints: Boston Gazette, 11-17-1760; 06-25-1770; 07-02-1770; 07-09-1770; 10-01-1770; 10-08-1770.

Boston Gazette, 03-09-1761.

Ran-away on the 19th Day of February last from Captain Ezibilon Ross of Dover, in Dutches County in New York Government, two Negro Fellows, on about 27 Years old, 5 Feet 6 Inches high ; had on an all Wool Coat, lined with Flannel, and a red double Breasted Jacket, his left Leg is less than his right, and his Foot turns out ; --The other about 17 Years old, and has lost one of his Fingers on his right Hand. Whoever shall take up said Fellows, and convey them to the Subscriber, in Dover aforesaid, or to Jeremiah Ross in Windham in Connecticut, shall have Forty Shillings York Money Reward, and all necessary Charges paid. EZIBILON ROSS.
    Reprints: Boston Gazette, 03-16-1761; 03-23-1761.

Boston Gazette, 06-08-1761.

Ran away from his Master, Capt. Ephraim Holmes of Halifax in the County of Plymouth, about 10 Days ago ; a Negro Man named Abel, about 21 Years of Age, a strait limb'd Fellow, of a common Stature, pretty light Complexion for a Negro, and had very short Hair or Wool : Had on when he went away, a red Broad Cloth Jacket very fine, a white Holland Shirt ruffled in the Slits, a Pair of Buckskin Breeches, grayish Stockings, and an old Beaver Hat. Whoever shall take up said Fellow, and convey him to Mr. Morton at the Sign of the White Horse in Boston, or to his said Master in Halifax, shall have Four Dollars Reward, and all necessary Charges paid, by
                                                    EPHRAIM HOLMES.
    All Masters of Vessels and others are hereby caution'd against concealing or carrying off said Servant on Penalty of the Law.
    Note, he lately belonged to Major James House of Hanover, in the above County.
    Reprint: Boston Gazette, 06-15-1761.

Boston Gazette, 07-06-1761.

Ran-away on the 28th Day of June 1761, from his Master Ephraim Swift of Falmouth in the County of Barnstable, a Negro Man Servant named Peter, about 27 or 28 Years old, speaks good English: had on when he went away a Beaveret Hat, a green worsted Cap, a close bodied Coat mill coloured, with a green narrow Frize Cape, a Great-coat, a black and white homespun Jacket, a flannel check'd Shirt, grey yarn Stockings ; also a flannel Jacket, and a Bundle of other Cloaths, and a Violin. He is a very tall Fellow.
    Whosoever shall apprehend the said Negro Fellow, and commit him to any of his Majesty's Goals, or secure him so as that his Master may have him again, shall have FIVE Dollars Reward, and all necessary Charges paid.

Ephraim Swift.

All Masters of Vessels and others are cautioned not to carry off or conceal the said Negro, as they would avoid the Penalty of the Law.

Reprints: Boston Gazette, 07-13-1761; 07-20-1761. This notice was also printed in the Boston News-Letter, 07-02-1761; 07-09-1761; 07-16-1761.

Boston Gazette, 09-07-1761.

Ran away from his Master Obadiah Sprague, of Providence, on the 30th Day of August last past, a Negroe Man, named Cumber, about 35 Years of Age, of a middling Stature, has a pretty old Look ; had on when he run away a bluish colour'd full'd Cap, a woolen Jacket of a grayish Colour, short linnen Breeches, and a pair of old Shoes, has a small Bunch on the left Side of his Face, near his Ear, and speaks very bad English.—Whoever shall apprehend the said Negroe, and convey him to his said Master in Providence, or give Intelligence where he may be had, shall have FOUR DOLLARS Reward, and all necessary Charges paid by OBADIAH SPRAGUE.

Reprints: Boston Gazette, 09-14-1761; 09-21-1761.

Boston Gazette, 09-21-1761.

RUN-away from the Subscriber (about a Month since) a well set likely Negro Fellow, of a middling Stature, named Cesar, aged about 25 Years. Said Runaway had on when he went away, a blue Kersey Coat with blue Lining, flat Brass Buttons, a stript homespun Waistcoat without Sleeves, a Pair of Moose Skin Breeches, ript on the back Part of the Thigh, a Cotton and Linnen Shirt, grey Yarn Stockings, and is suppos'd to be in some of the neighbouring Towns, as he has been frequently seen, and prevented Persons taking of him up as a Runaway, by telling them he was there Working for his Master.—Whoever shall take up said Runaway, and convey him to his Master, shall have TWO DOLLARS Reward for their Trouble, and necessary Charges paid, by

THOMAS DAWES.

Boston, September 14, 1761.

N. B. All Persons whatsoever are hereby forewarned from harbouring, concealing or carrying off said Servant on Penalty of the Law.

Boston Gazette, 11-16-1761.

Ran-away from Joseph Cottle of Newbury, a negro man named Daniel, a sturdy thick set fellow, about 28 years of age : Had on when he went away, a check shirt, a brown coat and jacket, and 'tis supposed he has changed his clothes ; he has been gone six weeks. Whoever will apprehend said negro, shall have TWO DOLLARS reward, and all necessary charges paid. And all persons are cautioned against entertaining, harbouring, concealing or carrying off said negro, as they would avoid the penalty of the law.

Newbury, October 30, 1764.

JOSEPH COTTLE.

Reprints: Boston Gazette, 01-25-1762; 02-01-1762.

Boston Gazette, 03-29-1762 (Supplement).

SIXTY DOLLARS REWARD

Run-away from Messieurs Bodkin and Ferral of the Island of Santa Croix, on the 1st Day of July 1760, a Negro Man named Norton Minors, is by Trade a Caulker and Ship Carpenter, was born and bred up at Capt. Marquand's at Nebury, who sold him to Mr. Craddock of Nevis, from whom the above Gentlemen bought him, is about 5 Feet 10 Inches high, about 30 Years of Age, speaks good English, can Read and Write, and is a very sensible, smart, spry Fellow, has a remarkable bright Eye, he has been seen in and about Newbury sundry Times since his Elopement. Whoever takes up and secures the said Negro Man, so that he may be delivered to the Subscriber, shall receive SIXTY DOLLARS Reward, and all reasonable Charges paid, by

HENRY LLOYD.

N. B. All Persons whatever are cautioned against harbouring or concealing said Negro, or carrying him off, as they may depend on being prosecuted to the utmost Rigour of the Law.

Boston, March 29, 1762.

Reprints: Boston Gazette, 04-05-1762; 04-12-1762. This notice was also printed in the Boston Post Boy, 12-01-1760; 03-29-1762; 04-05-1762; 04-12-1762; and in the New-Hampshire Gazette, 05-21-1762; 05-28-1762; 06-04-1762.

Boston Gazette, 04-26-1762.

Ran away from Zacheus Gates of Rutland, on Thursday the 15th of April Current, a Negro Man named Cesar, about 5 Feet 9 Inches high, goes something stooping, has large Bones, has a small Scar on his Cheek Bone, talks pretty good English, and is about 25 Years of Age : His Cloathing when he went off was an all Wool brown Coat, a blue and white striped double breasted Jacket, a light coloured Camblet Jacket, a Pair of grey home-made Cloth Breeches, a Pair of blue Stockings, a striped woolen Shirt, a checkt Linnen ditto, a black Wig, and a woolen Cap. Whosoever shall take up said Negro, and convey him to his said Master at Rutland aforesaid, or otherways secure him, and send Word to his said Master so that he may receive him again, shall receive FOUR DOLLARS Reward, and all necessary Charges paid, by

Rutland, April 16, 1762.

ZACHEUS GATES.

And all Masters of Vessels and others, are hereby cautioned against concealing or carrying off said Servant as they would avoid the Penalty of the Law.

Reprint: Boston Gazette, 05-03-1762.

Boston Gazette, 08-30-1762.

Fifteen DOLLARS Reward.

Ran-away from his Master Lieut. Joseph Sias of Durham, a Negro Man, named Surrinam, about Twenty-five Years of age, speaks good English, a thick set Fellow, one Leg less than the other, with a small Scar on the small Leg, and a joint of one of his Thumbs is off ; had on when he went away, a check'd cotton and woolen Shirt, two Jackets, one striped and the other Fustian, and a pair of Moose Skin Maugersons ; Whoever will take up said Negro, and convey him to his said Master, shall have Fifteen Dollars Reward,and all necessary Charges paid by me,

Durham, July 3, 1762. JOSEPH SIAS.

N. B. All Masters of Vessels and others are forbid to entertain, conceal or carry off said Negro.

Reprints: Boston Gazette, 05-03-1762. This notice was also printed in the New-Hampshire Gazette, 07-09-1762; 07-15-1762; 07-23-1762; 07-30-1762.

Boston Gazette, 10-18-1762.

Ran-away from his Master, Mr. Brackley Read of Boston, Block-Maker, a Negro Lad named CATO, about 5 Feet 6 Inches high, speaks pretty good English, though something stammering : Had on when he went away, a red Jacket with a green [?] under it, a Felt Hat, Leather Breeches, yarn Stockings, and old Shoes. Whoever shall take up said Negro, and return him, or secure him in any of his Majesty's Goals, shall be handsomely rewarded for their Trouble. And all Masters of Vessels and others are caution'd against harbouring, concealing or carrying off said Negro, as they would avoid the Penalty of the Law.

BRACKLEY READ.

Boston Gazette, 12-13-1762.

Ran away on Sunday Night the 5th of December Instant, from Widow Martha Jerauld, of Medfield, a Mulatto Servant, named CESAR about 4 Feet 9 Inches high, born in Medfield, aged 30 Years, speaks fast and thick : Had on when he went away, a thick all wool Coat, a blue Broad Cloth Jacket, and an old Felt Hat, wears a Cap. Whoever shall take up said Fellow, and convey him to the Subscriber, shall have TWO DOLLARS Reward and all necessary Charges paid,
Per MARTHA JERAULD.
Medfield, December 11, 1762.
Reprint: Boston Gazette, 12-20-1762.

Boston Gazette, 05-09-1763.

Ran-away from the Subscriber, at North-Kingstown, in the Colony of Rhode Island, a young Negro Man named Dimas, born in this Country, well-set, has a down Look, thin jaw'd, and a visible Scar from the Bridge of his Nose, over his Cheek, reaching beyond the Corner of his Mouth: He had on when he absconded, a new Jacket and Breeches of Snuff colour'd Broad Cloth, trim'd with Horn Buttons, his Jacket is double breasted ; has a low brim'd Hat, and affects the Sailer. He is a subtle artful Fellow, and has got a forged Pass. Whoever takes up and secures said Fellow so that he may be recovered, shall receive a Reward of SIX DOLLARS, with necessary Charges paid by
LODOWICK UPDIKE.
North Kingstown, April 26th, 1763.
Reprints: Boston Gazette, 05-16-1763. This notice was also printed in the Providence Gazette, 04-30-1763; 05-07-1763; 05-14-1763; 05-21-1763.

Boston Gazette, 07-11-1763.

Ran-away last Night from his Master Othniel Gorton, Esq ; of Warwick, in the County of Kent, in the Colony of Rhode Island, a Negro Man Servant named Peter, about 28 Years of Age, of a small slim Stature, not tall, speaks good English born in this County ; he has a small Bunch on his Forehead, and also another small Bunch on one of his Wrists : Had on when he went away, one old striped linsey Woolsey Jacket, without Sleeves, one new full Cloth Jacket, of a redish Colour, and an old Beaver Hat ; he carried away a new full Cloth Great Coat, of the same Colour as the Jacket ; likewise, two new Tow Cloth Shirts, and two Pair of Tow Cloth Trowsers, which last were made pretty wide and short ; he also took with him one fine white Shirt.— Whoever shall take up said Negro Man Servant and return him to his Master shall have FIVE DOLLARS Reward, and all necessary Charges paid by me

OTHNIEL GORTON.
Reprints: Boston Gazette, 07-18-1763. This notice was also printed in the Newport Mercury, 06-20-1763; 07-04-1763; 07-11-1763.

Boston Gazette, 08-01-1763.

RUN away from Col. John Read, of Fairfield, in Connecticut, two mulatto fellows, one named Titus, aged 22, is of a middling stature, longish and pale visage, his hair cut off, plays well on a fiddle, had one with him.—Had on a blue flannel coat with flat pewter buttons, a brown camblet vest with horn buttons.—The other named Daniel, aged 16, large of his age, broad face, high cheek bones, long black hair but cut off on the top of his head ; had on a brown camblet coat with red lining, a white linnen and a mixt colour'd flannel vest—both had blue great coats with yellow metal buttons, and leather breeches—Any person that will take up and return them to their said master or secure them so that he may have them, shall have Five Pounds New York Money Reward and Fifty Shillings for either of them, singly, and all needful charges paid. They had a Gun with them and forged pass, were seen to cross Hudson's river & travel westward. Whoever takes them are desired to secure them well or they will give 'em the slip, and also to search well for and secure said pass, for which Two Dollars shall be added to said reward. Any person that hath a mind to purchase them, that can take and secure them, and send me word, shall have them at a reasonable price : they are healthy, able bodied, and well understand husbandry business. All Masters of Vessels are forbid to carry them off.
Fairfield, July 13, 1763.

JOHN READ.

Reprint: Boston Gazette, 08-08-1763.

Boston Gazette, 09-19-1763.

Ran-away from his Master Capt. Richard Baxter, this Day, a Negro Man, named Sancho, about 21 Years of Age, about 5 Feet 10 Inches high: He speaks good English. Had on when he went away, a brown Jacket, and a streaked Under Jacket and Breeches, an old Pair of Shoes and Stockings, an old Beaver Hat and a check Woolen Shirt and carried a small Bundle with him. Whoever will take up said Servant, and bring him to his said Master in Yarmouth, or confine him in any of his Majesty's Goals, so that his Master may have him again, shall have FOUR DOLLARS Reward, and all necessary Charges paid. (Signed) RICHARD BAXTER.

Boston Gazette, 03-05-1764.

Ran-away on Saturday Morning the 11th of February, a Negro Man nam'd Jacob, belonging to George Wray at Albany. He had on when he went off, a Blanket Coat with red Stripes, Buckskin Breeches, green Leggins, a pair of Moccasins and red Worsted Cap; and tis suppos'd he had a black & white spotted Dog with him, answering to the Name of Venture. Said Negro is about 24 Years old, 5 Feet 6 3.4 Inches high without Shoes, has a Scar on the right Side of his Forehead, another on the left Temple, both just in the Edge of his Hair, and another on the Crown of his Head, two large Pock-marks under his left Eye, high Cheek-bones, crooked Legs, the Calves of his Legs remarkably high, a Lump on each Shoulder by being flogg'd some Time past, hangs down his Head, and stoops forward in walking speaks good English, some French, a little Spanish, but little or no Dutch ; has a stammering in his Speech when in Liquor, to which he is much addicted ; is very artful and apt to feign plausible Stories, and may perhaps call himself a free Negro. Whoever apprehends the said Negro, and secures him in any Goal, or brings him to his Master in Albany, shall receive FIVE DOLLARS Reward, and all reasonable Charges paid by me, GEORGE WRAY.

The above Negro was bought of Isaac Kibbe the 3d of Enfield in the County of Hartford, and has been going that Road.

Reprints: Boston Gazette, 07-23-1764.

Boston Gazette, 07-09-1764.

Ran-away from Amos Gardner, a Negro Man named Cambridge, he is a short thick set Fellow, about 24 Years of Age; he had on when he went away, a flannel Shirt and Jacket, blue & white striped, without Sleeves; and a thick black Jacket Homspun made, and a pair of wide Trowsers, a pair of old Stocking Leggins, a pair of new Shoes, and a Worsted Cap, and no Hatt. Whoever takes up said Fellow, and secures him in any of his Majesty's Goals, shall have Four Dollars Reward, and all necessary Charges paid, by me

AMOS GARDNER.

Reprints: Boston Gazette, 07-23-1764. This notice was also printed in the Providence Gazette, 07-21-1764; 07-28-1764; 08-04-1764.

Boston Gazette, 04-08-1765.

RUN away from Jacob Fowle, Esq; the Twenty-ninth ult. a Negro Boy, about Eighteen Years old, was born in Hopkington, and brought up by the Rev. Mr. Barret; his name is Ishmael, he has been a Soldier at the Lake, is thick sett, has thick Lips, and goes limping by Reason of the great Toe of his right Foot being froze and not quite well. He had on when he went away, a striped Jacket, leather Breeches, checquered woolen Shirt, blue under Jacket, light coloured Stockings, brass Buckles in his Shoes, and an old mill'd Cap. He is an artful Fellow, and is supposed will endeavour to pass for a Soldier, as he carried off with him a Firelock and Blanket.—Whoever shall take up said Negro and bring him to his Master, or confine him in any of his Majesty's Goals so that his Master may have him again, shall have FOUR DOLLARS Reward, and all Charges paid.

Marblehead, April 2, 1765.

JACOB FOWLE.

Reprints: Boston Gazette, 04-15-1765; 04-29-1765. This notice was also printed in the Boston News-Letter, 04-04-1765; 04-11-1765; 04-19-1765.

Boston Gazette, 07-08-1765.

Run-away from his Master Peter Bourn, the 2d Instant, a Negro Man named Sambo, 30 Years of Age, about 5 Feet 10 Inches high. He had on when he went away, a check Woollen Shirt under a Frock, a pair of light reddish Breeches under a pair of Trowsers, and a blue mill'd Cap. Any Person that takes up said Negro, and brings him to his Master at the North End of Boston, or gives Intelligence where he may be found, shall have Two Dollars Reward, and all necessary Charges paid by me,

Boston, July 5. 1765.

PETER BOURN.

Reprints: Boston Gazette, 07-15-1765; 07-22-1765.

Boston Gazette, 08-19-1765.

Ran-away from his Master Nathan Parker of Reading, on the 7th Instant at Night, a Negro Man named COLE, about 27 Years of Age, and about 5 Feet 6 Inches high, well-sett, speaks good English, and has a demure Countenance. Had on and took with him, a light blue Coat, and also a light Coat, a check Holland Jacket without Sleeves, a Pair of check and a Pair of white Trowsers, a new check and an old white Shirt, and a new Felt Hatt.—He took with him a very good Gun, with the Name of his Master engrav'd at large on the Thumb Piece which was Silver and an old Sword. Whoever takes up said Negro, and will convey him to his said Master, shall have TWO DOLLARS Reward and all necessary Charges paid. NATHAN PARKER.

All Masters of Vessels and others are hereby cautioned against harbouring, concealing or carrying off said Servant, on Penalty of the Law.

Reprints: Boston Gazette, 08-26-1765; 09-02-1765; 09-09-1765.

Boston Gazette, 04-07-1766.

FIVE DOLLARS REWARD.

New Haven, March 27, 1766.

RUN-away, from Doris Van Wyck of Oyster Bay, on Long Island, a Negro Man, named Dick, but now calls himself John Dickerson ; He is of a middle Stature, has a wildish whitish Look with his Eyes especially when frightened, a likely Fellow, about forty Years of Age. HE talks as if he has a Cold, and had on when he went away grey yarn Stockings, Pumps, large Silver Buckles, blue Broad Cloth Breeches, a blackish thickset Jacket, a whitish Broad Cloth Coat, and a grey Homspun great Coat, a Cap and a large Beaver Hat, cock'd. About a Fortnight ago he went over Milford Ferry, with a false dirty pass all written by one Hand, with the Names of 6 or 7 Long Island Justices of the Peace, at the Bottom. He enquired the Road to Boston and 'tis supposed he is gone that Way, to see an Acqaintance. Whoever secures the said Negro so that his Master may have him again, shall have Five Dollars Reward, and all reasonable Charges. And 'tis desired he may be delivered to Michael Peck, of Milford, living at the Ferry, who will pay the Reward and Charges, for the said

DORIS VAN WYCK.

Reprints: Boston Gazette, 04-14-1766; 04-28-1766.

Boston Gazette, 10-06-1766.

Run-away from the Subscriber, a well-set likely Mulatto indented Servant Lad, about 17 Years of Age. He wore a blue Pea Jacket, red under Jacket, short Trowsers, and a Seaman's Bonnet; He also took with him a Pair of red Breeches, a good Hat and other Cloathing. He has a white Spot high on his Forehead over the left Eye which he endeavours to conceal. He speaks English and can speak Dutch—Whoever apprehends said Servant, and conveys him to me, living in Battery March Street Boston, shall have EIGHT DOLLARS Reward, and all necessary Charges paid.—All Masters of Vessels and others, are hereby cautioned against harbouring concealing or carrying off said Servant, as they would avoid the Penalty of the Law in that Case made and provided.

Boston, Sept. 26, 1766. JOHN PECK.

Reprint: Boston Gazette, 09-29-1766.

Boston Gazette, 03-02-1767.

Ran away from me the Subscriber, a Negro Man named Tom about 5 Feet 7 or 8 Inches high : Had on when he went away, a red Great Coat, a light colour'd Pea Jacket, lined with striped Homspun, a Hair Plush Jacket, green

Colour, short Trowsers blue Yarn Stockings, a Pair of square silver Buckles ; speaks good English; and was seen going over Roxbury Neck last Wednesday Morning with a Bridle in his Hand.

Whoever takes up said Servant, and secures him in any of his Majesty's Goals, so that his Master may have him again or brings him to the Subscriver shall have FOUR DOLLARS Reward and all necessary Charges paid, by SIMEON POLLY.

All Masters of Vessels and others, are hereby cautioned against harbouring, concealing or carrying off said Servant on Penalty of the Law.

Boston, February 24, 1767.

Reprints: Boston Gazette, 03-09-1767; 03-16-1767; 03-30-1767; 04-06-1767; 12-20-1773; 12-27-1773; 01-03-1774.

Boston Gazette, 05-11-1767.

Ran-away from his Master Daniel Goodhue of Ipswich, on Thursday the 7th Instant, a Negro Man Servant named Jack, sometimes calls himself John Baptize : He is a Fellow of a middle Stature, speaks good English, and has been branded in the Forehead with the Letter B, the Scar whereof still remains ; and to hide the same, he wears his Cap very low on his Forehead. He had on when he went away, a grey all-wool outside Jacket, and a red under Jacket, grey yarn Stockings, a Pair of old Shoes, a Pair of white Trowsers and blue Cloth Breeches under them. He carried away with him a light coloured Coat, with sundry other Cloaths in a Bundle. Whoever shall take up said Negro, and him convey to his said Master, or secure him in any of his Majesty's Goals, shall have FOUR DOLLARS Reward, and all Charges paid.

N. B. All Master's of Vessels are hereby forbid carrying off said Negro, or secreting him, on the Penalty of the Law, in that Case provided.

Ipswich, May 8, 1767.

Reprints: Boston Gazette, 05-18-1767; 05-25-1767; 07-06-1767; 07-20-1767. This notice was also printed in the New-Hampshire Gazette, 07-24-1767; 07-31-1767.

Boston Gazette, 06-15-1767.

Ran away from me the Subscriber, on Thursday the 4th of this Instant, a Negro Man named Caesar, about 5 Feet 9 Inches high ; had on when he went away, a Serge Cloth-coloured Coat, a striped Jacket, and striped Holland Trowsers, and almost a new Beaverrit Hatt, and also a Pair of Silver Shoe Buckles ; said Fellow is very black, hath a Scar on one of his Cheeks, and is well proportion'd every Way, about 33 Years of Age, and is by Trade a Blacksmith, but principally follows Anchor-making. Whoever apprehends said Fellow, and secures him in any of his Majesty's Goals, or brings him to me, shall have Eight Dollars Reward, and all reasonable Charges paid, by me,

EBER SWEET.

Reprint: Boston Gazette, 06-22-1767. This notice was also printed in the Providence Gazette, 06-27-1767; 07-11-1767; 07-18-1767; 07-25-1767; 08-01-1767; 08-15-1767; 08-22-1767; 08-29-1767; 09-05-1767; 09-12-1767; 09-19-1767; 09-26-1767; 10-03-1767; and in the Newport Mercury 06-22-1767 to 06-29-1767. In these variant notices, it is noted that Caesar "can read and write."

Boston Gazette, 09-14-1767.

Ran-away from his master Nathaniel Smith of Eppen, in the Province of New Hamsphire, a Negro Man Servant named William Mingo, about 29 Years old, speaks good English, born in New-England, about 5 Feet 8 Inches high, something slim—Had on when he went away, a blue Homespun Coat, a blue Jacket without sleeves, Leather Breeches, light Worsted Stocking. Whoever takes up said Negro Servant, and will convey him to the Subscriber, shall have FIVE DOLLARS Reward, and all necessary Charges paid.

All Masters of Vessels and others are hereby cautioned against harbouring, concealing or carrying off said Servant on Penalty of the Law.

Eppen, 23d August 1767. NATHL SMITH

Reprints: Boston Gazette, 09-07-1767; 09-14-1767.

Boston Evening Post, 02-10-1766.

Newport, December 30, 1765.

Ran-away from the Subscriber, on Monday the 21st Instant, a short thick well made Negro Man named LONDON, about 20 Years of Age; had on when he went away, a light frize double-breasted Jacket, blue baize under ditto, a pair blue Plush Breeches, brown yarn Stockings, tow cloth Shirt, and a pair new Shoes with brass Buckles.—Whoever apprehends said Negro, and brings him to his Master, shall have EIGHT DOLLARS Reward, and all necessary Charges paid

by BENJAMIN BRENTON

All Masters of Vessels and others are forbid to conceal or carry off said Servant, as they will answer it at their Peril.

Reprints: Boston Evening Post, 09-21-1767; 09-28-1767. This notice was also printed in the Boston News-Letter, 01-09-1766; the Boston Weekly News-Letter, 01-16-1766; 01-23-1766; and in the Newport Mercury, 12-30-1765.

Boston Gazette, 11-23-1767.

Ran-away last week from his Master in Hopkington, in Rhode Island Government, A NEGRO MAN 'bout 5 Feet 7 Inches high, 36 Years old, of a yellowish Black, well set, remarkably large Feet, speaks good English, carry'd off a light colour'd Cloth Coat, cut Velvet Waistcoat, a white Holland and a striped Shirt, besides sundry old Cloathing, addicted to be funny in his Talking; he is particular in shaving true his Forehead. Whoever will take up said Runaway, and bring him to his master, or commit him to any of his Majesty's Goal in New England, so that his Master may have him again, shall have FIVE DOLLARS Reward, and all necessary Charges paid by me,

Hopkinton, 20 Nov. 1767 (6w) JZDIAH DAVIS
Reprint: Boston Gazette, 11-30-1767.

Boston Evening Post, 08-08-1768.

Five Dollars Reward

Ran-away from the Subscriber in Northkingston, in the Colony of Rhode-Island, on the 11th Day of this Instant July 1768, a Negro Man named CUFF, about 18 Years of Age, a short thickset Fellow, between 4 and 5 Feet high, a long built Head; had on a Tow Cloth Shirt, red and white striped Flannel; long Trowsers, an old Beaver Hat, a large red and white spotted silk Handerchief, a check Linen ditto, a Pair mixt blue Worsted Stockings, a Pair new Leather Pumps.—It is suspected that some evil minded Person has given him a Pass, and also some Clothing, as he carried away no other than abovesaid. Whoever will secure him in any of his Majesty's Goals, and give Notice thereof, or deliver him to his Master, shall have FIVE DOLLARS Reward, and all necessary Charges paid, by

IMANUEL CASE
Reprints: Boston Gazette, 08-01-1768; 08-08-1768.

Boston Gazette, 08-22-1768.

Newbury-Port, August 13, 1768.

Last Night Ran away from his master the Subscriber a Negro Boy named LONDON, about 18 Years of age, about 5 Feet 4 Inches in Height, of a thin lean Make, he was born in the Country, is very artful and likely to tell a good Story. He had on a blue outside Jacket, and a striped Woolen under-Jacket, a dirty white Shirt, and a Pair of long Trowsers.—Whoever will take up the said Boy, and convey him to his Master, or secure him so that he may be come at, and give Information of it to his Master, shall have EIGHT DOLLARS Reward, and all necessary Charges paid.

All People are warned from harbouring the said Boy, who has been guilty of Theft, as they will in all Respects expose themselves to the Penalties of the Law. JOHN WOOD.

Reprint: Boston Gazette, 08-29-1768.

Boston Gazette, 09-19-1768.

Ran-away from me the Subscriber, a Negro Man names PRIMAS, about 21 Years of Age, a likely spry Fellow; had on when he went away, a Pair of Pot-Hooks round his Neck, a blue Serge coat, a green Plush Jacket, and a Pair Leather Breeches: whoever will take up the said Servant, and commit him to any of his Majesty's Goals, shall have TWO DOLLARS Reward, and all necessary Charges paid by me

DANIEL MESERVE, junr.

P.S. All Masters of Vessels and others, are hereby Cautioned against harbouring, concealing or carrying off said Servant, as they may depend on being Prosecuted to the utmost rigour of the Law.

Portsmouth, September 13, 1762.

Reprints: Boston Gazette, 09-26-1768; 10-03-1768.

Boston Gazette, 10-24-1768.

Ran-away a Negro Man named Sam, about 5 Foot 6 Inches high, full faced had on a blue Jacket with a red one under it, long Trowsers, and a slopt Hat with a blue Garter round the Crown.

Whoever will secure and deliver him to Mr. Nathaniel Cary, in Boston, shall have Three Dollars Reward, and all reasonable Charges paid.

All Masters of Vessels and others are hereby caution'd against harbouring, concealing, or carrying off said Negro, as they would avoid the Penalty of the Law.

Boston, October 17, 1768.

Reprints: Boston Gazette, 10-31-1768; 11-07-1768.

Boston Gazette, 11-14-1768.

A Runaway NEGRO.

The 11th instant left his Master John Gallison, Esq; of Marblehead, and on the Road towards Boston told some of his Acquaintance he was going there.—NERO, a large Negro Man, the Property of said Gallison, about 25 Years of Age, speaks good English, clothed in an Olive-coloured German Serge Coat lined and cuffed with red, black Waistcoat, Leather Breeches, and white worsted Stockings, Cotton and Linnen Shirt, a Hat (or Cap) doubleSole Shoes.

-A Reward of EIGHT DOLLARS,with all necessary Charges, is offered to any one who will take up said Negro and commit him to any of his Majesty's Goals, or to Bridewell, and will give Information of the same either to said Gallison at Marblehead, or to Melatiah Bourn, esq; of Boston, of his being secured, shall receive the Reward.—

All Persons are cautioned not to conceal, harbour, or transport said Negro over Sea, as they will be called to answer such Conduct.—If taken up at or near Boston, it is desired Information may be immediately given to Melatiah Bourn, who will take proper Care of him.

Marblehead, 12th November, 1768.

Reprint: Boston Gazette, 11-28-1768.

Boston Gazette, 12-12-1768.

FIVE DOLLARS Reward.

Ran-away from his Master the 25th Day of November last, at North-Kingston, in the Colony of Rhode Island, a well-set Negro Man Slave, named Isaac, about 5 Feet 6 or 7 Inches high, with a Scar on his Forehead, between 30 and 40 Years old, thick Beard, can play on a Fiddle, and loves strong Drink; had on and carried with him a lightish-colour'd Thickset Coat, a blue Ratteen Jacket without Sleeves, Flannel Shirt, stript Flannel Trowsers, grey yarn Stockings, and single Channel Pumps. Whoever will secure said Slave in any of his Majesty's Goals, or deliver him to the Subscriber, his Master, shall have FIVE DOLLARS Reward, and necessary Charges paid.

Per, SAMUEL ROSE.

Masters of Vessels, and others, are hereby forbid carrying off or securing said Slave, as they would avoid the Penalty of the Law. December 5, 1768.

Reprints: Boston Gazette, 12-19-1768; 12-26-1768.

Boston Gazette, 04-17-1769 (Supplement).

BOSTON, April 10, 1769.

This Morning Ran-away from the Subscriber, a Negro Boy named ROB-IN, about 5 Feet 6 Inches high, between 16 & 17 Years of Age, a yellow Complection, and likely Fellow, has Hair. Had on when he went away, a dark blue German Serge Coat with Mohair Buttons of the same Colour, a red Plush Jacket, check Shirt, dark Breeches, light-coloured blue Worsted Stockings, and small round Silver Buckles in his Shoes: and has carried with him a green flower'd Russel Banyan, blue Serge Breeches, a pair light blue Stocking, and an Ozenbrigs Frock. He speaks good English, and has lately serv'd 4 Years with James Purrington, Shoemaker, of Lynn. Whoever may take up said Negro, and return him to the Subscriber, or secure him in any of his Majesty's Goals, shall have FOUR DOLLARS Reward, and all reasonable Charges paid by WILLIAM VERNON

N.B. All Masters of Vessels and others, are hereby cautioned against carrying off, harbouring or concealing said Negro, as they would avoid the Penalty of the Law.—It is supposed he has been enticed away by some evil minded Person, and gone to Chelsea to one who the said Negro said strove to entice him away last Fall.

Reprint: Boston Gazette, 05-01-1769.

Boston Gazette, 07-24-1769.

Ran-away from his Master, Capt. Henry Herrick, of Beverley, on Wednesday the 19th of July Instant, a Negro Servant, named James, about 21 Years of Age, a stout, lusty, well-made Fellow, about 5 Feet 9 Inches high: Had on when he went away, a short green Ratteen Jacket double-breasted without Sleeves, a Pair of dark Woolen Breeches patched on each Knee with a black Stocking, blue Yarn Stockings, large Brass Buckles in his Shoes, a white Shirt, and a Bilboa mill'd Cap. Whoever takes up said Fellow, and will return him to his Master in Beverly, or confine him in any of his Majesty's Goals, shall have EIGHT DOLLARS Reward, and all necessary Charges paid by me HENRY HERRICK.

Beverly, July 21, 1769.

All Masters of Vessels and others, are hereby caution'd against harbouring, concealing or carrying off said Fellow, as they would avoid the Penalty of the Law.

Reprints: Boston Gazette, 07-31-1769; 08-07-1769; 08-21-1769; 08-28-1769.

Boston Gazette, 10-09-1769.

Ran-away from William Barber of Charlestown on the 25th of September last, a Negro Man named Abram, about 33 Year old, of a light Complection, about 5 Feet 9 or 10 Inches high, a thick well-set Fellow, had on when he Ran-away, a tarr'd Hat, a Worsted Cap, a Baize double-breasted Waistcoat without Sleeves, and a dark snuff-colour'd Waistcoat lin'd with the same, a check Shirt, and strip'd Homespun Breeches; he has a large Scar on his Breast. Whoever shall take up said Negro, and safe convey him to his Master, shall have THREE DOLLARS Reward, and all necessary Charges paid by me WILLIAM BARBER.

All masters of Vessels and others, are hereby caution's against harbouring, concealing, or carrying off said Negro on Penalty of the Law. October 9, 1769.

Reprints: Boston Gazette, 10-16-1769; 10-23-1769; 11-06-1769; 11-13-1769; 11-20-1769.

Boston Weekly News-Letter, 03-27-1760.

Ran-away on the 26th of March, from Henry Charlton, of Milton, a Negro Man, named Peter, between 40 and 50 Years of Age, about 5 Feet high, thick-set, goes something stooping: Had on a red Shag Great Coat, a blue Jacket, old Camblet Breeches, or a Pair of Trowers, grey yarn Stockings, Shoes with Straps; he had both a red and a green Cap. Whoever shall bring the said Negro to his Master, shall have EIGHT Dollars Reward, and all necessary Charges paid by me

Henry Charlton

All Masters of Vessels and others are cautioned against harbouring, concealing or carrying off said Negro, as they would avoid the Penalty of the Law.

Reprints: Boston Weekly News-Letter, 04-04-1760; 04-10-1760.

Boston Weekly News-Letter, 06-12-1760.

Ran-away on Tuesday May 27th 1760, from her Master the Rev. Aaron Whittemore of Pembrook (alias Suncook) in the Province of New-Hampshire, a Negro Girl named Rhode; about 20 Years of Age, of a middling Stature, and pretty thick set, of a brownish Complexion, speaks good English.—She had on when she went away and took with her, a striped woollen Gown, a blue Shalloon guiled Petticoat, lined with Woollen, with several Caps, Shifts and sundry other Things.

Whoever shall take up said Girl, and convey her to her said Master, shall be well rewarded, and have all necessary Charges paid.

N.B. It is suspected that somebody has forged her a Pass. Aaron Whittemore

Reprints: Boston Weekly News-Letter, 06-19-1760; 07-03-1760.

Boston Weekly News-Letter, 05-07-1761.

On Friday the 1st Inst. A Negro Servant, named Rumford, lately belonging to Capt. Nathaniel Patten of this Town, broke into the Cabin of the Snow Hibernia, John Troy, Master, and took from said Troy's Pocket Book sundry Papers among which were the third Drafts of five Sets of Bills of Exchange for £ .100 sterling each, drawn by William Edington Esq; in favour of Capt. John Troy, on Colebrook and Nesbit in London: Dated Louisbourg, December 1, 1760—Also an Indenture for the said Servant, for Seven Years.—And as the Fellow has been strictly examined and no satisfactory Account can be yet obtained from, if any Person shall come to the Knowledge of any of the above Bill, or Indenture, or any other Papers belonging to said Troy, they are desir'd to give Information thereof to him, or to the Printer, and they shall be well rewarded for their Trouble.

The lost Papers can be of no use to any Person but said Troy.

Reprints: Boston Weekly News-Letter, 05-14-1761; 05-21-1761.

Boston Weekly News-Letter, 04-08-1762.

TEN DOLLARS Reward.

Ran-away from his Master Christopher Prince of Boston, a Negro Fellow named Caesar, about 25 Years of Age, who lately lived with Mr. Joseph Hapgood, of Marlborough: When he went away had on a grey Great Coat, Leather Breeches, a Hat, striped Cap. Leather Apron, and a speckled Woolen Shirt. Of a midling Stature, talks very good English, of a smooth Skin, and very Likely, can Read and Write---Whoever brings him to his Master shall have TEN DOLLARS Reward, and all necessary Charges paid by me

Boston, April 7, 1762. CHRISTOPHER PRINCE.

N.B. ALL Masters of Vessels and others are hereby Cautioned against harbouring, concealing or carrying off said Negro, as they would avoid the severest Penalty of the Law.

Boston Weekly News-Letter, 06-10-1762.

Ran-away from the Subscriber, on the 16th of May last, a Negro Man named Juba; about Five Feet and half high, thickset; had on a homespun Kersey Fly coat, light-colour'd, with Pewter-Buttons; old Leather Breeches; and took with him a Pair of blue Plush Breeches, a doubled-breasted Waistcoat without Sleeves, one half green the other scarlet Broad-Cloth, much faded;--was cut on one leg with a Scythe, and healed with a high Scar, the Flesh soft and spungy under the same. Whoever secures the said Negro Slave in any of His Majesty's Goals, shall have FIVE DOLLARS Reward, and Charges paid by the Subscriber.—All masters of Vessels are hereby cautioned not to carry off said Negro.

Dated in Killingworth, Benja. Gale.

June 2d 1762.

Reprints: Boston Weekly News-Letter, 06-17-1762; 06-24-1762.

Boston News-Letter, 07-29-1762.

Run-away from the Subscriber of Waterbury, on the Night after the 19th Instant, (Monday) a Mulatto Servant Man, named George Tankard; a spry, well-built Fellow, about 26 or 27 Years old, near five Feet 10 Inches high, has had the Small Pox, has a Small Scar on his Forehead, and another on his Nose, is lame in his left Ancle; had with him when he went away, a blueish homespun Coat, a new brown Shear Cloth Waistcoat, an old grey Kersey ditto, a Pair of flower'd ditto without Sleeves, a Striped CottonShirt, a Pair of Tow Trowsers, a Pair of Leather-Breeches, a Pair of Worsted Stockings, a Pair of Blue Yarn ditto, and a Pair of white Thread ditto, a Butternut Colour'd Kersey Great Coat, the Buttons set five Inches from the Breast, a large Barcelona Handkerchief, a Silk ditto, and a flower'd Cotton ditto, a Pair of Pumps, with a large Pair of Brass Buckles. He took with him a sorrel Mare about 14 Hands high, something Wind broke, branded I on the left Shoulder, and I P on the left Thigh, a Hunting Saddle with a quilted Buck Skin Seat, a Seal-Skin Housing, and a new Briddle; he also took a new Beaver Hat, an old felt ditto, and a good Gun with a Quantity of Ammunition.

   *** Whoever will take up said Runaway, and confine him in any of his Majesty's Goals, or secure him so that his Master may have him again, shall have a Handsome Acknowledgement, for their Trouble, besides all necessary Charges paid by me. CALEB HUMASTUN.

   Reprints: Boston Weekly News-Letter, 08-05-1762; 08-19-1762.

Boston Weekly News-Letter, 09-16-1762.

Ran-away from his Master, Jabez Hatch, Wharsinger, of Boston, a Negro Man named Newport; He is not very black, but is a very likely short well-set Fellow; He had on a Gold Lace hat, black Wigg, a greyish Bearskin Coat, a green Jacket with Gold Vellum Button-Holes, red Breeches, he carried with him other Cloathing, several white Shirts, Pairs of Stockings and Shoes.

   Whoever apprehends and secures said Negro, so that his Master may have him again, shall have FIVE DOLLARS Reward, and all necessary Charges paid. Boston, Sept. 16, 1762. Jabez Hatch. All persons are cautioned against harbouring or carrying off said Negro.

   Reprints: Boston Weekly News-Letter, 09-23-1762; 09-30-1762.

Boston Weekly News-Letter, 09-16-1762.

RUN-away from his Master Capt. Samuel Chapman of Tolland, a Negro Man Servant named Newport, about 35 Years of Age, of middling Stature, pretty well set, of a swarthy Complexion, has a Scar on one of his Ankles and on one of his Wrists, has had the Top of one of his Fingers shot to pieces, had a bad cut on his little Finger of his left Hand ; he speaks good English, can play on a Violin ; he had on a brown Camblet Coat with a Velvet Cape, jet Glass Buttons, yellow Lining, a Pair of green Plush Breeches, one Linnen and and one Woollen check'd Shirt, a Pair of blue yarn Stockings, a pair of black worsted ditto ; an old pair of Pumps, a Castor Hat, and a silk Cap.

Whoever shall take up said Negro, and return him or secure him so that I may him again, shall have FIVE Dollars Reward, and necessary Charges paid by me. Samuel Chapman. All Masters of Vessels and others are forbid harbouring or carrying off said Negro.

Boston Weekly News-Letter, 10-14-1762.

TAKEN up at Milton, a Negro Fellow, about 40 Years of Age, talks very little English ; had on a striped Jacket laced together instead of Buttons, a blue Cap, he calls himself Bungo, and belongs to Providence : The Owner of said Negro by applying to William Sumner of Milton, may have him again paying Charges.
    Reprints: Boston Weekly News-Letter, 10-21-1762.

Boston Weekly News-Letter, 11-04-1762.

Ran-away from the Subscriber on the Evening of the 1st Instant, a Negro Man named Essex, about 15 Years of Age: Short in Stature, but very sprightly and active ; was born in this Country, and speaks good English. He had on when he went away a blue coarse cloth Jacket, with Breeches of the same, speckled Shirt, grey worsted Stockings, and wore a Seal Skin Jockey Cap with the Hair on. Whoever will take up said Servant and confine him in any of his Majesty's Goals, or bring him to me the Subscriber in Boston, shall have THREE DOLLARS Reward, and all necessary charges paid by JAMES BARRICK.
    All Masters of Vessels and others are cautioned against harbouring, concealing, or carrying off said Servant on Penalty of the Law. Boston, November 3, 1762.
    Reprints: Boston Weekly News-Letter, 11-11-1762; 11-18-1762.

The Boston News-Letter, 06-02-1763.

Ran away from his Master Daniel Sharley, of Boston, on Monday last, a Negro Fellow about 35 Years of Age, named Sam, has a large Bump over his right Eye: — He had on when he went away a blue Surtout Coat, a strip & home-spun Jacket, light coloured Velvet Breeches, with a Pair of Trowsers, black Stockings ; but it is probable he may change his Dress : He has been used to grind Chocolate, and carry it about for Sale. Whoever takes up said Negro, and will bring him to his Master, shall have TWO DOLLARS Reward, and all necessary Charges paid by DANIEL SHARLEY.

The Boston News-Letter, 09-15-1763.

RUN-away from the Subscriber, of Cloverack in the County of Albany, a Negro Man about 19 Years old, speaks good English and low Dutch, he is about 6 Feet high ; had on when he went away a red Great coat, a woolen Shirt, blue mill'd Stockings, old leather Breeches, and had with him another pair of blue mill'd Stockings, and a woolen check'd Shirt. Whoever takes him up and will bring him to his Master, shall have FIVE DOLLARS Reward, and all charges paid by me. Killiaen Muller of Cloverack.

Reprint: Boston Weekly News-Letter, 09-15-1763.

The Boston News-Letter, 05-31-1764 (Supplement).

Ran-away from me the Subscriber, a Negro Man named Tom, had on when he went away a cloth colour'd Jacket, a striped homespun Ditto Also, a pair of Leather Breeches and a woolen check Shirt and blue grey Stockings, about Five ten Inches high and has lost one of his upper fore Teeth: *** WHOEVER will take up the said Negro shall have THREE DOLLARS Reward and all necessary charges paid, by EBENEZER TIDD. ALL Masters of Vessels and others are heareby cautioned against concealing or carrying offered Negro as they would avoid the Penalty of Law. Myslick, May 26 1764.

Reprints: Boston Weekly News-Letter, 06-07-1764; 06-14-1764.

The Boston News-Letter, 07-12-1764.

Ten Dollars Reward,
For taking up a Molatto Slave belonging to Jerathmeel Rowers Esq; of Boston: The said Slave Ran away on the 26 th of June last, his Name is Oney, about 24 Years of Age, a tall slender Fellow, with black curling Hair, has a slow hoarse Voice: he had on a red baize short under Waistcoat, and a dark outside Jacket, with white Pewter Buttons, a check'd linnen Shirt, grey yarn Stockings, large round rim brass Buckles in his Shoes: He had a Violin with him. Whoever apprehends said Servant, and brings him to the Printers hereof, shall have TWO Dollars Reward, and all necessary Charges paid.

All Masters of Vessels and others are cautioned a-gainst harbouring, concealing, or carrying off said Servant, as they would avoid the Penalty of the Law.

Boston News-Letter, 12-06-1764.

Scituate, December 4th, 1764, Ran away from his Master Benjamin Jacob, a Negro Fellow named Prince, not very black, about 26 Years old, has an Impediment in his Speech: Had on when he went away, a brown homespun Coat with brass Buttons, a Pair of new Shoes, a black Jacket lin'd with

Figure 1.1.   Oney, Boston News Letter, July 12, 1764.

yellow, brown Breeches, an old light blue Great Coat. Whoever shall take up said Negro, and bring him to his Master in Scituate, or to Mr. Benjamin Cudworth in Boston, shall be well rewarded, and have all necessary Charges paid.

All Masters and Vessels and others are forbid concealing, harbouring or carrying off said Servant, as they will be prosecuted for so doing.

Reprint: Boston Weekly News-Letter, 12-13-1764.

The Boston News-Letter, 12-20-1764.

Ran-away from his Master, Benjamin Faneuil jun'r of Boston, on Tuesday the 18th Instant, a Negro Man, named Harry ; a likely well sett Fellow, about 24 Years of Age, speaks broken English, and a little French, being purchased at Martinico : He had on when he went away, a blue freize Jacket lined with a blue Baize pretty much worn, and underneath a white flannel Waistcoat, a pair of yellow leather Breeches, blue yarn Stockings, a yellow Shoe and knee Buckles, a striped worsted Cap – he was Seen Yesterday-noon in Roxbury street. ANY Person who will secure the said Negro and deliver him to his Master in Boston, shall receive FIVE DOLLARS Reward, and all Necessary Charges paid, by Benja. Faneuil, jun'r.

Boston, Dec. 19, 1764.

Reprints: Boston Weekly News-Letter, 01-03-1765; 01-10-1765.

Boston News-Letter, 06-13-1765 (Supplement).

Ran away from his Mistress Isabel Caldwell, of Rutland District, in the County of Worchester, the 25th of May last, a Negro Man about 30 Years of Age, named Mingo, speaks middling good English, a sprightly little Fellow, about five Feet and five or six Inches high : Had on when he went away, an all wool brown colour'd great Coat with large white metal Buttons, and an all wool Jacket of the same Colour ; a blue and white striped woolen Shirt, and a worsted Cap, an old Hat, A Pair of leather Breeches, and light blue Stockings ; a Pair of Shoes about half worn, tied with leather Strings.

Whoever shall apprehend said Run away, so that I may have him again, shall have FOUR DOLLARS Reward, and all necessary Charges paid by me, Isabel Caldwell.

Reprints: Boston Weekly News-Letter, 06-13-1765; 06-20-1765.

Boston News-Letter, 11-07-1765 (Supplement).

RUN-away from his Master Capt. Thomas Gilbert of Brookfield, on Thursday Evening the 24th of October last, a Molatto Slave named Moses Attacks, about 38 Years of Age; a Stout well-built Fellow, with Streight black Hair, with a small Scar on one of his Eye-brows ; had on when he went away, a mixed coulor'd blue and white Coat, with white Buttons, a blue Jacket, leather Breeches, a felt hat, a check woollen Shirt ; carried away one strip'd linnen Shirt, one pair of blue rib'd Stockings, and an Indian Blanket ; WHOEVER shall take up said Servant, and convey him to his said Master, or confine him and give his Master intelligence, shall have FOUR DOLLARS Reward, and all necessary Charges paid by me.

Brookfield,

November 4th, 1765 Tho. Gilbert.

Reprints: Boston Weekly News-Letter, 11-21-1765; 02-27-1766; 03-06-1766; 03-13-1766.

Boston News-Letter, 09-11-1766.

Ran away from Subscriber, a Negro Man named George, about 19 years of Age, of a Molatto Colour, something short and thick, he had a Scar on the End of his Nose. He had on a check woolen Shirt, with a Frock and short wide Trowsers.

    Whoever takes up said Negro and will bring him to his Master shall have SIX Dollars Reward, and all necessary Charges paid. Ebenezer Pope.

    N.B. If he is taken up near Boston, by applying to Mr. Seccombe of Medford, the Reward will be paid. – All Masters of Vessels and others are hereby cautioned against harbouring or carrying off said Servant, as they would avoid the Penalty of the Law.

    Reprints: Boston Weekly News-Letter, 09-18-1766; 10-02-1766.

Boston News-Letter, 02-05-1767.

RUN-away from Henry Holland's Place on the North Side of Staten-Island, in the Colony of New York, on the First of October last, a Negro named Cyrus, between 25 and 30 Years of Age, about 5 Feet 8 inches high, he has a mean Look with a Monkey Face, he can read and write, has learn'd some Latin, and knows the Greek Characters: It is supposed he is gone towards Boston where he was born, in the Rev. Samuel Auchmuty's Father's Family : Whoever apprehends him, so that his said Master may have him again, shall have Fifteen Spanish Dollars Reward. If the Negro should be taken up near Boston, it is desired that he may be secur'd and Notice given to R. & S Raper, Printers.

    Reprints: Boston Weekly News-Letter, 02-12-1767; 02-19-1767.

Boston News-Letter, 07-14-1768.

Ran-away from the Subscriber in Dartmouth, on the 20th of this Instant, a Molatto Fellow named Gideon Halley or Gideon Cheat, about 5 Feet and six Inches high, about 30 Years old, a thick built Fellow, wears long Hair tied up; had on when he went away, a brown Kersey Flannel Jacket, strip'd Flannel Shirt, strip'd Flannel Trowsers, and a Beaver Hat much worn, looks much like an Indian, brags much of his being in the Army Westward the last War. Whosoever will secure him in any of his Majesty's Goals or deliver him to his Master shall have FOUR DOLLARS Reward and all necessary Charges paid by JOSEPH RUSSEL. Dartmouth, June 24, 1768.

    Reprints: Boston Weekly News-Letter, 07-21-1768; 07-29-1768.

Boston News-Letter, 08-04-1768.

Ran-away from his Master, Jabez Hatch, of Boston, on the 25th Inst. a Negro Man named Caesar, a stout well set Fellow, speaks good English: had on when he went away, a Froost and Trowsers, check Shirt, no Stockings, an old pair Shoes. Whoever will bring said Negro to his Master, or secure him so that he may have him shall have TWO DOLLARS Reward, and all necessary Charges iaid. Jabez Hatch.

Boston News-Letter, 08-04-1768.

Eight Dollars Reward. Ran-away the 24th of July Instant from Zaccheus Clough of Durham, in New Hampshire, a Negro Man partly Molatto named Primus, about Thirty Years of age, a well set Fellow, born in this Country, speaks good English; (said Negro was lately own'd by the Rev. Mr. Coffin of Kingslen,) had on when he went away a blue Serge Coat, a grey lappell'd Jacket lin'd with red Baise, a pair of Deerskin Breeches, of a light colour, a Beaver-Hat, a pair of blue yarn Stockings : He can play well on a Violin. Whoever apprehends sad Negro and brings him to his said Master, shall have EIGHT DOLLARS Reward and all necessary Charges paid by: ZACCHEUS CLOUGH. N.B. All Masters and Vessels and others, are cautioned against secreting or carrying off said Negro, as they would avoid the penalty of the Law. Durham, July 30th, 1768.
    Reprints: Boston Weekly News-Letter, 08-11-1768; 08-18-1768.

Boston News-Letter, 10-06-1768.

Ran-away from Capt. Silvier, about four Weeks ago, a Negro Girl, about 17 years of age, she had on when she went away, a dark short homespun Gown, and a light coloured Petticoat, and the Wool on her Head clipt very short : her name was formerly Redisher. Whoever will take up said Run-away and return her to her Master's in Cold Lane, shall be handsomely rewarded.

Boston News-Letter, 03-30-1769.

Eight Dollars Reward. Ran away from the Subscriber, the 17th instant, a likely Negro Fellow, (named CATO) about five feet seven inches high, about twenty years old, had on when he went away, a grey bear-skin double-breasted Jacket, with large white metal buttons, and striped under ditto, long striped trowsers with leather breeches under them, a sailor's Dutch cap; he has pimples in his face, speaks good English, very nice about the hair, tells a very plausible story upon any extraordinary occasion, and pretends he has a pass signed by John Watson.

Whoever may take up said Servant, and return him, to his Master, shall have EIGHT DOLLARS reward, and all necessary charges paid by GEORGE WATSON. Plymouth, March 25, 1969.

N.B. It is supposed he went away with a Molattoe Wench ; about the same age, (named Kate Daniel).

All Masters of Vessels and other are hereby cautioned against carrying off or concealing said Servant, as they would avoid the Penalty of the Law.

Reprints: Boston Weekly News-Letter, 08-11-1768; 08-18-1768.

Boston News-Letter, 12-07-1769.

Ran away from Dr. Whitworth, a Negro Fellow named Tom, about 20 Years of Age, a short, well-set Fellow, with large Lips: Had on when he went away green Plush Breeches, cloth-coloured Kersey Pea-Jacket, Hat, Stockings, Shoes, &c.

Whoever takes up said Negro and will bring him to his Master, shall have TWO DOLLARS Reward, and all necessary Charges paid. Boston, Dec. 6. 1769.

Boston News-Letter, 12-28-1769.

Ran-away from his Master Edward Bardin, a Negro Man named Cuffe, about 22 years of Age, a tall Fellow his Legs crooked the small of them bending out, talks good English : Had on when he went away a white cloth Jacket, short skirts, a red Waistcoat under it, white Shirt, his Hat with a Gold wash'd Loop and Button, he formerly lived with Issac Winslow, Esq; of Roxbury, Whoever apprehends said Negro, and will bring him to his said Master living at the King's Arms on Boston Neck, shall have a Dollar Reward, and all necessary Charges paid.

All Masters of Vessels and other are heredy cautioned against harbouring, concealing or carrying off said Servant as they would avoid the Penalty of the Law. Edward Bardin.

Boston Post-Boy, 02-11-1760.

Ran away from his Master Thomas Poynton of Salem, a Negro fellow about 25 Years of Age, a short thick set Fellow, not very black, something pitted with the small Pox, speaks bad English; had on when he went away a dark colour'd Cloth Coat, lined with red Shalloon, with mettal Buttons, a blue Sailors Jacket, and a flower'd German Serge Jacket, black knit Breeches, a pair of grey Stockings, newly stock'd, an old Beaver Hatt : carried with him an old drab great Coat. Any Person that shall take up said Negro and convey him to Salem, or secure him in any Goal shall be well Rewarded, and all necessary Charges paid. N. B. All Masters of Vessels and others are hereby caution'd against harbouring, concealing and carrying off said Negro, as they would avoid the Penalty of the Law. Thomas Poynton Salem, Feb. 6. 1760.

Reprints: Boston Post Boy, 02-18-1760; 03-03-1760; 03-10-1760. This notice was also printed in the Boston Gazette, 02-11-1760.

Boston Post-Boy, 03-17-1760.

Ran away from his Master David Parsons of Amherst Hadley, a Negro Man Servant named Pomp, about 26 Years of Age; a Fel[low] of the tallest Stature, judged six Feet and half High, has been long in the Country, can Read and Write, speaks good English : Had on when he went away two Jackets, one of Leather, and under all a Flannel Jacket. Whoever takes up the said Runaway and will bring him to his said Master shall have THREE DOLLARS Reward, and all necessary Charges paid by me David Parsons.

N. B. All Masters of Vessels and others are hereby caution'd against harbouring, concealing,or carrying off said Servant as they would avoid the Penalty of the Law. Amherst Hadley, Feb. 25. 1760.

Reprints: Boston Post Boy, 03-10-1760; 03-17-1760.

Boston Post-Boy, 04-28-1760.

Ran-away from the Widow Rogers of Rumford, in New-Hampshire, about a Month ago, a Negro servant Man, belonging to Major Robert Rogers, named Prince, of a middling Stature, about 30 Years of Age, has had the Small-Pox, looks very serious and grave, and pretends to a great deal of Religion.— Since his Departure, he has sold the most of his Cloaths, and now is but meanly dressed ; he was in the Service the last Year, and has offer'd to inlist sundry Times, pretending himself to be a Free-man : He was lately taken up, but by his insinuating Discourse made his Escape again.

Whoever will take up and secure said Servant, and convey him to the Widow Rogers at said Rumford, or to Capt. James Rogers, or to Col. Doty at the Sign of the Lamb in Boston, shall have FIVE DOLLARS Reward, and all necessary Charges paid.

Boston, April, 23d 1760.

James Rogers.

N. B. All Masters of Vessels and others are caution'd against concealing or carrying off the said Servant, as they would avoid the Penalty of the Law.

Reprints: Boston Post Boy, 05-05-1760; 11-22-1762; 11-29-1762; 12.6.62. This notice is also printed in the Boston Newsletter, 04-24-1760; 05-01-1760; 05-08-1760.

Boston Post-Boy, 05-05-1760.

Ran away from his Master Capt. Edward Arnold of Cranston, the 28th of April, A Negro Man named Portsmouth, about 27 Years of Age, about 5 Feet 6 Inches high, strait limb'd, speaks pretty good English : Had on when he went away a homespun brownish colour'd Waistcoat and Breeches, and inside strip'd Flannel Waistcoat, a strip'd Flannel Shirt, Shoes and Stockings ; he also carried with him a light colour'd Camblet Coat, and strip'd Holland Waistcoat, and one white Shirt. Whoever shall apprehend said Negro, and convey him to his said Master at Cranston, or either of his Majesty's Goals in the Colony of Rhode-Island, shall have EIGHT DOLLARS Reward, and all necessary Charges paid by me EDWARD ARNOLD.

N. B. All Masters of Vessels and others are hereby caution'd against harbouring, concealing or carrying off said Negro, as they would avoid the Penalty of the Law.

Reprints: Boston Post Boy, 05-19-1760; 06-02-1760. This notice was also printed in the Boston Gazette, 05-05-1760; 05-19-1760.

Boston Post-Boy, 06-02-1760.

RUN away from his Master, John Moor, of Londonderry, in the Province of New-Hampshire, on the Evening of the 30th of May, a Negro Man, named Simond, 20 Years of Age, of a Molatto Colour, about 5 Feet 7 Inches high. Had on when he went away, a blue Sarge Jacket, a striped Cotten and linnen ditto, a Check linnen Shirt, dark colour'd Cloth Breeches, dark Stockings, & c. Whoever will take up said Negro, and bring him to Samuel Allison of Boston, or convey him to his Master, shall have FOUR DOLLARS Reward, and all necessary Charges paid by John Moor.

N. B. All Masters of Vessels and others, are caution'd against harbouring, concealing or carrying off said Slave, as they would avoid the Penalty of the Law.

Londonderry, May 31, 1760.

Reprints: Boston Post Boy, 03-10-1760; 03-17-1760.

Boston Post-Boy, 06-23-1760.

Ran away from his Master, Edmand Leavenworth, a Negro Man named Pompy, aged 28 Years, about five Feet and a half high, or there abouts; high, well set, of a middling Black Colour, talks good English, he can read and write, and it is likely that he hath got a Pass, and will pass for a free Man. Whoever shall take up said Negro, and secure, or send him to his Master in Stratford, shall have FIVE POUNDS Lawful Money Reward, and all reasonable Charges paid by me the Subscriber. Edmand Leavenworth.

Reprints: Boston Post Boy, 06-30-1760; 07-07-1760.

Boston Post-Boy, 09-29-1760.

Ran away from me the Subscriber, on the 25th of September instant, a young Negro Fellow named Chester, about 18 Years of Age. Had on when he went away, a Felt Hatt, a cloth colour'd Kersey Jacket, seam'd with Canvis, a pair of Ozenbrig Trowsers, a pair of old Shoes and no Stockings, has very large and full Eyes, thick Lips, great Mouth, and speaks good English. Whoever will take up said Negro, and convey, or cause him to be convey'd to the Subscriber, the said Fellows Master, shall have a Reward of FIVE DOL-LARS, and all Charges paid.

JOHN LEE.

N. B. All Masters of Vessels and others are hereby caution'd against harbouring, concealing, or carrying off said Servant, as they would avoid the Penalty of the Law.

Manchester, September 27, 1760.

Reprints: Boston Post Boy, 10-06-1760; 10-13-1760; 10-10-1760. This notice was also printed in the Boston Gazette, 09-29-1760; 10-13-1760; 10-05-1772; and, 10-19-1772; the Essex Gazette, 09-22 to 09-29-1772; 09-29 to 10-06-1772.

Boston Post-Boy, 05-25-1761.

Ran away from the House of Col. Bradstreet, on Tuesday last, a Negro Boy, named Spruce, of a yellow Complexion, about 8 Years of Age, and speaks good English. Had on when he went away, a dark colour'd Livery, cuff'd with red Plush, and white mettal Buttons, black Stockings, and black Buckels in his Shoes. Whoever will take up said Negro Boy, and bring him to his Master's House again, near Concert-Hall, or give Information where he may be had again, shall be well Rewarded.

N. B. All Masters of Vessels and all others are forbid to harbour or conceal him.

May 25, 1761.

Boston Post-Boy, 06-08-1761.

Ran away on the 26th Instant from his Master Benjamin Faneuil, Esq; of Cambridge, a Negro Man servant, named Peter, about 25 Years of Age, a small limb'd likely Fellow, very sprightly and active, born and bred in the Country, used to all kind of Husbandry, speaks very good English, a wide Mouth, shows his Teeth much when he speaks, very light Complection for a Negro, has something of a Roman Nose.—He carry'd off with him, a mix'd colour'd Coat, blue Jacket, a pair Leather Breeches with Brass flower'd

Buttons, a pair of Shoes newly Soled, two or three pair Stockings, two or three Shirts, one of which made of striped Holland, with Gussets and Collar of broad figur'd Checks. He robbed his Master of considerable Sums of Money and other Articles.—Whoever will apprehend said Run-away and bring him to his Master at Cambridge, or to Mr. Benjamin Faneuil, jun. Merchant, at Boston, shall receive FIFTEEN DOLLARS Reward, and all necessary Charges paid. Cambridge, May 28, 1761.

Reprint: Boston Post-Boy, 06-15-1761.

Boston Evening-Post, 10-19-1761.

RUN-away on the 5th Instant from John Lloyd of Stamford, in the Colony of Connecticut, a Negro Man Servant named Cyrus, about 5 Feet 9 Inches high, well built, but rather slim waisted, Leggs and Feet somewhat large, has lost one or more of his Fore Teeth, about 30 or 32 Years of Age, long Visage, very black, active and ingenious in all sorts of Country Business, and is a good Butcher, bred in the Country, and speaks good English and a little French, but stammers when frighted or confused; had on when he went off, and Iron Collar, riveted round his Neck, with a Chain fastened to it; carried away with him a red Cloth Jacket, and another of brown Frize, both considerably worn, black Everlasting Breeches almost new, Tow Trowsers, white Cotton or Linnen Stockings, coarse Tow Shirt. 'Tis not unlikely he may consort with any Deserter, or other straggling Fellow he may meet with, as about 2 years ago he Ran off with two Deserters, and was taken up at Philadelphia, whoever takes up said Negro is desir'd not trust him a Moment till he is put in Irons and secured in some of his Majesty's Goals, otherwise (his Crime being great) he will certainly give them the Slip; and upon sending me word, so that I may have him again, such Person shall have FIVE POUNDS New-York Money Reward and all reasonable Charges paid

October 6, 1761. By JOHN LLOYD.

N. B. As inserting advertisements in the several News Papers is judged the most expeditious Method of spreading them far & near, if any Gentlemen will be so good, when they have read their Papers, to cut out this Advertisement and set it up in the most public Place, it will be esteem'd as a Favour: All Masters of Vessles and others are caution'd against Harbouring or Carrying him off, as they will answer it at their Peril.

Reprints: Boston Post-Boy, 10-26-1761. This notice was also printed in the Boston Gazette, 10-26-1761; the Boston Newsletter, 10-22-1761; 10-19-1761; and in the Connecticut Gazette, 10-17-1761; 10-31-1761; and 11-07-1761.

Boston Post-Boy, 10-26-1761.

Ran-away the 15th of this Inst. from Andrew Hunter, of Newport, Rhode-Island, a Negro Man named Robert, about 5 Feet 9 Inches high, well built and very square Shouldered, has a scar or Mark something like a Burn, between his Cheek and the Corner of his Mouth, wants the middle Tooth of the upper Row; speaks good English being born in Jamaica, is very artful and insinuating, had sundry sorts of Apparel, therefore cannot describe him by any particular. Whosoever shall apprehend and bring him to his abovesaid Master, or to Mr. Peter Mumford, or secure him in any of His Majesty's Goals, so as his Master may have him again, shall have TEN DOLLARS Reward, and all necessary Charges paid by, Andrew Hunter,
Newport, Rhode Island, Octo. 19, 1761.
Reprint: Boston Post-Boy, 11-02-1761; and in the Connecticut Gazette, 11-07-1761; 12-12-1761; and 12-05-1761.

Boston Post-Boy, 10-01-1764.

10 DOLLARS REWARD
Ran away from his Master Jonathan Norwood, of Gloucester, (Cape-Ann) on the 22d of September Inst. a very likely Negro Man named Newport, about 5 Feet and half high, a strait limb Fellow, about 35 Years of Age, very likely in the Face ; had on when he Ran away a good Castor Hat, clean white Frock, a woolen Shirt, white short Trousers, white ribb'd worsted Stockings, pretty good Pumps, very large Silver Buckels in his Shoes, plays well on a Violin, and is a very active Fellow, and as he has Money with him, 'tis likely he will change his Dress, as he took other Cloaths with him.

Whoever apprehends the said Negro, and will bring him to his said Master, or secure him, shall have Ten Dollars Reward, and all necessary Charges paid by
Jonathan Norwood.

All Masters of Vessels and others, are hereby cautioned against harbouring, concealing or carrying off said Negro, as they would avoid the Penalty of the Law.

Gloucester, Sept. 24, 1764.
Reprints: Boston Post-Boy, 06-21-1762; 06-28-1762; 07-05-1762; 10-01-1764; 10-08-1764. This notice was also printed in the Boston Gazette, 06-21-1762.

Boston Post-Boy, 06-28-1762.

Twenty Dollars Reward.

Ran away from his Master William Miller, of Wallpool in Damarscotty, at the Eastern Part of this Government, on the 20th Day of June past, a Negro Man named Boston, he is of a large Stature, no Mark on him except one of his great Toes was Froze and cut off ; the Cloaths he carried away with him were a Coat of a light Colour, with white mettel Buttons, a brown Jacket, a pair of Trousers, a Wolleen Shirt, Hatt, and Cap. Whoever shall apprehend the said Negro and bring him to his said Master, or confine him in any of His Majesty's Goals, and send Word as aforesaid, shall have Six Pounds, Lawful Money Reward, and all necessary Charges paid by William Miller.

All Masters of Vessels and others, are hereby caution'd against harbouring, concealing, or carrying off the said Negro, as they would avoid the Penalty of the Law,

Wallpool, June 21. 1762.

Reprints: Boston Post-Boy, 07-05-1762; 07-12-1762.

Boston Post-Boy, 05-02-1763.

Ran away from his Master, John Amiel of Boston, last Thursday Night, a Negro Fellow named Peer, he had on when he went away a cloth colour'd Coat, lin'd and trim'd with red, a black broad cloth Waistcoat without sleeves, a yellow pair of leather Breeches, a large pair of silver Buckels, and a good Beaver Hat ; he is a thick set Fellow, has very large Feet and Legs, and spe ks good French and English Whoever will apprehend the said Negro and bring him to his Master in Boston, shall have TWO DOLLARS Reward, and all necessary Charges paid by

John Amiel.

All Masters of Vessels and others, are hereby forbid to harbour, conceal or carry off said Negro servant, as they would avoid the penalty of the Law. Boston, May 2.

Reprints: Boston Post-Boy, 05-09-1763; 05-16-1763.

Boston Post-Boy, 10-17-1763.

FIVE DOLLARS Reward,

RUN away from Moses Cooper of Gloucester, in the County of Providence, on the 2d of October in the Evening, a Megro Man named Jack, about 26 Years of Age, of a small Stature, is of the Pawpaw Tribe, his Teeth filed sharp, has a Scar on the right side of his Forehead, and is marked up and down on each side of his Cheeks, and holes in both Ears, and is blacker than common ; had on when he went away, a dark kersey Coat, a blue and white striped Cotton Jacket, a pair of Leather Breeches, and carried away another pair of Breeches of the same of the Jacket. Whoever takes up said Fellow and conveys him to his said Master in Gloucester, or secures him in any of his Majesty's Goals so that he may be had again, shall have FIVE DOLLARS Reward, and all necessary Charges paid by Moses Cooper.

N. B. All Masters of Vessels and others, are hereby forewarned Secreting or Carrying off said Fellow, as they will answer it at their Peril. Providence, October 7, 1763.

Reprints: Boston Post-Boy, 10-24-1763; 10-31-1763; 11-07-1763. This notice was also printed in the Providence Gazette, 10-15-1763; 10-22-1763.

Boston Post-Boy, 02-20-1764.

Run away from his Master, Dr. Miles Whitworth, of Boston, a Negro Man about 25 Years of Age, named York, formerly a Servant of Thomas Sawl, Esq; of Halifax, a thin made Fellow, with Hair extending low down his Cheeks;--had on when he went away, a white Shirt, a Bearskin Coat, a Cloth Waistcoat, with a worsted Lace on it much worn, Leather Breeches, light blue Stockings, and Silver Buckles.—Whoever will take up said Negro, and convey him to his said Master, shall be handsomely rewarded, and all necessary Charges paid.—

N. B. All Masters of Vessels and others are forbid to entertain, conceal, or carry off said Negro.

Reprints: Boston Post-Boy, 03-05-1764. This notice was also printed in the Boston Gazzette, 02-20-1764; 02-27-1764; 03-05-1764.

Boston Post-Boy, 06-25-1764.

10 DOLLARS REWARD

Ran away from his Master John Miller, of New-London in Connecticut, on the 2d Inst. a Negro Man named PRIMUS, about 23 Years of Age, of a middling Stature, has a defect in his left Wrist ; had on when he went away, a Kersey Jacket with Leather Buttons, a check't Shirt, a pair of short Trousers, a new Felt Hatt, and an old pair of blue Stockings. Whoever shall take up said Negro and secure him so that his Master may have him again, shall have TEN DOLLARS Reward, & all necessary Charges paid, by JOHN MILLER.

N. B. All Masters of Vessels and others, are hereby caution'd against harbouring, concealing or carrying off said Negro, as they will answer it as their Peril.

New-London, June 4th 1764.

Reprints: Boston Post-Boy, 07-02-1764; 07-09-1764. This notice was also printed in the Providence Gazette, 06-03-1764; 07-07-1764; 07-14-1764; 07-21-1764; 07-28-1764.

Boston Post-Boy, 08-27-1764.

Eight DOLLARS Reward.

Ran away the 16th Inst. from James Dwyer of Portsmouth, a Negro Man named Scipio, about 40 Years of Age, a Subtle well set Fellow, five Feet ten Inches high, speaks good English, he carried with him 4 woollen check Shirts, one white ditto, 2 new under Jackets, one white lapelled Jacket bound with black, one new blue Kersey lapelled Jacket lined with red Baise and trimed with Metal Buttons, a brown Coat with Metal Buttons, one pair of black Plush Breeches, Worsted Cap and 2 pair of Shoes, &c. &c.

Whoever apprehends said Negro, and brings him to his Master, shall receive Eight Dollars Reward and all necessary Charges paid by

JAMES DWYER.

N. B. All Masters of Vessels and others, are cautioned against secreting or carrying off saidNegro, as they would avoid the penalty of the Law.

It is supposed he is in Company with Seneca, a Negro Man of Mr. Hall's.

Portsmouth, August 20th, 1764.

Reprint: Boston Post-Boy, 09-03-1764.

Boston Post-Boy, 08-27-1764.

Six Dollars Reward.

Ran away from his Master Samuel Hall of Portsmouth, on Tuesday last, a Negro Man named Seneca, a thick set Fellow, about Thirty-six Years of Age, and five Feet eight Inches high, with a Scar over his left Eye ; he took with him one Coat, five Jackets,three pair of Breeches, one pair of Trowsers, five pair of Stockings, two pair of Shoes, two Hatts and Caps and three Shirts : Whoever will take up said NEGRO, and bring him to his said Master shall have SIX DOLLARS Reward and all necessary Charges paid.

N. B. All Masters of Vessels and others are forbid carrying off said Negro, as they will answer the Penalty of the law.

If he will return of his own Accord his Fault shall be forgiven. July 16th.

Reprints: Boston Post-Boy, 09-03-1764. This notice was also printed in the Boston Gazette, 08-27-1764; 09-03-1764; 09-10-1764.

Boston Post-Boy, 10-22-1764.

Ran away from the Subscriber Yesterday, being Friday the 19th Instant at Noon, a Negro Boy named POMPEY, a thickset well-made Fellow, about 22 Years of Age, about 5 Feet 8 Inches high, speaks pretty good English, his Face cut with one large streak in each Cheek.—Had on when he went away, a cloth-colour'd Kersey out-side Jacket, striped homespun under Jacket, Tow

Shirt, Leather Breeches and a pair of Oznabrigs ditto over them, grey yarn Stockings, double soled Shoes, Brass Buckles, his Hat (if any) almost a new Castor one ; no Cap.

Whoever will take up said Negro Boy, so that the Subscriber may have him again shall receive THREE DOLLARS Reward and all necessary Charges paid.

All Masters of Vessels and others are hereby cautioned against concealing or carrying off said Negro Boy, as they would avoid being prosecuted with the utmost Rigour of the Law by

FITCH POOL.

Boston, October 20, 1764.
Reprints: Boston Gazette, 10-22-1764; 10-29-1764; 11-05-1764.

Boston Post-Boy, 01-07-1765.

Ten Dollars Reward.

Ran away from John Peirce, jun'r of Dighton, a Negro Man, named Prince, about 35 Years of Age, five feet nine Inches High, a well set Fellow, with a remarkable Roman Nose, speaks good English : Had on when he went away, a grey double breasted Jacket, a Flannel under Jacket strip'd with black Wool, an old white Flannel Shirt, a pair of old light colour'd thick Breeches, a pair of Tow Trowsers, a pair of black Stockings, a pair of double soal'd Shoes tap'd, has some gray hairs in his Head : 'Tis supposed he has a Counterfeit pass. Whoever will apprehend said Negro, and secure him so that his Master may have him again, shall have TEN DOLLARS Reward, and all necessary Charges paid. John Peirce, jun'r.

All Masters of Vessels and others are hereby forbid against carrying off said
Negro. Dighton, December 1, 1764.

Reprints: Boston Post-Boy, 01-14-1765; 01-21-1765. This notice was also printed in the Newport Mercury, 12-31-1764; 01-07-1765; 01-21-1765; and in the Providence Gazette, 12-29-1764; 01-05-1765; 01-12-1765; and 01-19-1765.

Boston Post-Boy, 01-14-1765.

Eight Dollars Reward.

Ran away from his Master, Capt. Daniel Rogers of Durham, a Negro Man, named CATO, born in the Country, a middling Size, and a spry Fellow ; had on when he went away, a greyish homespun Coat, lin'd with strip'd homespun, a light colour'd Jacket, Leather Breeches, white yarn Stockings ; he is about 35 Years old, and had a Scar a cross his Throat, (lately done by a fall from a Horse) –WHOEVER will take up said Negro, and bring him to his said Master, or confine him so that he may be had, shall have EIGHT DOL-LARS Reward and all necessary Charges, paid by

DANIEL ROGERS.

N. B. All Masters of Vessels and others, are cautioned against secreting or carrying off said Negro, on Penalty of the Law.

Durham in New-Hampshire, Jan. 1, 1765.

Reprint: Boston Post-Boy, 01-21-1765. This notice was also printed in the Newport Mercury, 01-21-1765; 01-28-1765; 02-04-1765; 02-11-1765; 02-18-1765; 02-25-1765; and in the New-Hampshire Gazette and Historical Chronicle, 01-04-1765; 01-11-1765; 01-18-1765; 06-05-1767.

Boston Post-Boy, 08-12-1765.

Run away the 5th inst. from Samuel Paine, a Negro Man named Will, lately a Servant to Mr. John Gray, Ropemaker. He is a stout Fellow near 6 Feet high, about 23 Years of Age, speaks good English, has large Nostrils : Had on when he went away an old double-breasted grey Jacket with Pewter Buttons, small Trowsers, and an old Shirt. Whoever will take up said Negro and return him to his said Master near Bull's Wharff or to Robert Pierpoint at the South-End, shall have FOUR DOLLARS Reward and all necessary Charges paid by

Boston, Aug. 10, 1765. SAMUEL PAINE.

All Masters of Vessels and others are cautioned against concealing or carrying off said Negro on Penalty of the Law.

Reprints: Boston Post-Boy, 08-19-1765; 08-26-1765.

Boston Post-Boy, 03-30-1767.

10 Dollars Reward.

Ran away from his Master, Benjamin Cobb, of Boston, on the Evening of the 29th of March Inst. a likely Negro Fellow, named Jackson Ebet, about 18 or 19 Years of age, 5 Feet 6 Inches high, speaks good English, and was born in New England---Had on when he went away, a blue Shag great Coat, and a grey Jacket with Pewter Buttons, a dark brown double-breasted Jacket with-out sleeves, a check'd Linnen Shirt, red cloth Breeches, and mixt yarn Stock-ings, had one Pewter Buckle and one yellow metall flower'd ditto in his Shoes which were above half worn.

Whoever will apprehend the said Negro and bring him to his said Master in Boston, shall have TEN DOLLARS Reward and all necessary Charges paid.

BENJA. COBB.

All Masters of Vessels and others are hereby cautioned against harbouring, concealing or carrying off said Negro, as they would avoid the Penalty of the Law. Boston, March 31, 1767.

Boston Post-Boy, 12-21-1767.

Ran away from his Master Lieut. Matthew Caldwell on the 25th of November last, a stout Molatto Negro Slave, named Step, aged 27 Years, 5 Feet 10 Inches high, his Head wooly, a large Nose, speaks very thick, but good English : He had on and carried with him when he went away, a Felt Hat and yellow Wig, a homespun light-color'd KerseyCoat with metal Buttons, a strip'd cotton and linen Jacket with the stripes downwards, a strip'd worsted and wool Jacket with the Stripes cross-ways, a pair of Sheepskin Breeches, one white tow Shirt, one linen check Shirt, and two worsted & wool Shirts, two pair blue yarn Stockings, two pair Pumps with brass Buckles.

Whoever takes up said Runaway, and will bring him to his Master, or secure him so as he may have him again, shall have SIX DOLLARS Reward, and all necessary Charges paid by Matthew Caldwell.

All Masters of Vessels and other Persons are hereby caution'd against harbouring, concealing or carrying off said Servant, as they would avoid the Penalty of the Law.

Reprints: Boston Post-Boy, 01-04-1768. This notice was also printed in the Boston, 12-21-1767; 12-28-1767; 01-04-1768; in the Boston News-Letter, 12-24-1767; 01-07-1768.

Boston Post-Boy, 06-27-1768.

Worcester, June 14, 1768.

Ran away from his Master, Robert Barber of Worcester, this Morning, a Negro Man named Mark, of a middling Stature, about 35 Years of Age, very much Pock-broken, and can read and write; he carried away with him two blue Coats, one lined and bound with red, the other not lined, a pair of green plush Breeches, a pair of Trowsers, and an old Beaver Hatt.—Whoever shall take up said Runaway, and convey him to his said Master, shall receive SIX DOLLARS Reward, and all necessary Charges paid. ROBERT BARBER.

N. B. ALL Masters of Vessels and others, are hereby cautioned against harbouring, concealing, or carrying off said Runaway, as they would avoid the Penalty of the Law.

Reprints: Boston Post-Boy, 06-27-1768; 07-18-1768.

Boston Post-Boy, 08-08-1768.

Ran away from Samuel Lee of Manchester, on the 4th Inst. a likely Negro Fellow, about 20 Years of Age, short, pretty thick set, and spry, understands the Farming Business, and is something bow-legg'd, born in New-England. Had on when he went away, a Check Woolen Shirt, striped Cotton and Wool Jacket, blue Yarn Stockings, with a red Camblet Jacket trimm'd in Silver.— Whoever shall take up said Negro and confine him in any of his Majesty's Goals, or send him to the Subscriber, shall have FIVE DOLLARS Reward, and all Charges paid by SAMUEL LEE.

Manchester, Aug. 6, 1768.

Reprints: Boston Post-Boy, 08-15-1768; 09-19-1768. This notice was also printed in the Boston Gazette, 08-08-1768; 08-15-1768; 08-22-1768.

Boston Post-Boy, 10-03-1768.

Ran away from her Master John Desilvier, on Friday the 9th instant, a Negro Girl named Violet, about 17 Years of Age; she is a sprightly Girl speaks good English and had on when she went away a dark stript Cotton short Gown, light colour'd Quilted Petticoat, blue Yarn Stockings, and Mens Shoes : Whoever will apprehend said Negro Girl, and bring her to her said Master's House in Cole Lane shall be handsomely Rewarded.

Boston, Sept. 26, 1768.

Reprints: Boston Post-Boy, 10-10-1768; 10-17-1768.

Boston Post-Boy, 03-13-1769.

Ran away from the Subscriber, of Roxbury, on Monday Morning the 30th of January last, a Negro Man Servant named Prince, about 18 Years of Age, and Five Feet high, well built, except small Legs ; with one of his upper Fore Teeth broke off nigh half way to his Gum, and a large Scar on his Belly occasioned by a Scald ; talks good English :— He carried off with him a blue Broadcloth Coat and Waistcoat, with plain yellow Metal Buttons, a double breasted striped Flannel Jacket, and a plain brown ditto, one Pair of white Yarn Stockings, one pair of blue ditto, two Pair of Shoes, one of said Pair with Shoe-Strings, two striped Woollen Shirts, and a Felt Hat.——

Whosoever shall take up said Servant and bring him to me the Subscriber, at Roxbury, or confine him, and notify the same, so that his Master can have him, shall have FOUR DOLLARS Reward, and all necessary Charges paid, by me,

ELEAZER WELD.

Roxbury, Feb. 1st. 1769.

N. B. All Masters of Vessels, and Others, are hereby cautioned against harbouring, concealing, or carrying off said Servant.

Reprint: Boston Post-Boy, 03-20-1769.

Boston Post-Boy, 06-05-1769.

Ran away from me the Subscriber of Glocester, the first of this Instant June, a Negro Man named Titus, about 21 Years of Age, of a midling stature, Stutters considerable when he Speaks, and hath lost Part of his great Toe on one Foot ; had on when he went away, a grey Coat, a striped blue and white Cotton and Linnen Jacket with Pewter Buttons, a light colour'd new Pair of Serge Breeches with flat Pewter Buttons, a fine Shirt, a light blue Pair of Yarn Stockings, a new Pair of Shoes, also wore away a Felt Hatt.—Whoever will take up said Negro, and him safely keep or convey to his said Master, shall have TWO DOLLARS Reward, all necessary Charges paid by me the Subscriber. Thomas Jaques.

  N. B. All Masters of Vessels and others, are hereby cautioned against harbouring, concealing or carrying of said Negro, as they would avoid the Penelty of the Law.

  Reprints: Boston Post-Boy, 06-12-1769; 06-19-1769; 07-03-1769.

Boston Post-Boy, 08-21-1769.

CAESAR a Negro Fellow noted in Town by having no Legs, is supposed to be strolling about the Country: If he can be brought to the Printer for One Dollar, besides necessary Expences, it shall be paid.

  Reprints: Boston Post-Boy, 09-11-1769; 09-18-1769. This notice was also printed in the Boston Gazette 08-21-1769; 08-28-1769; in the Boston News-Letter, 08-24-1769; 08-31-1769.

Boston Evening Post, 07-16-1770.

To all worthy Brothers and other Generous Commanders of Ships or other Vessels Sailling between the Poles, — as also to all the valourous Sons of Zebulon and others, whoever dispers'd upon the wide surface of old Ocean, or upon any island or Main-land upon this habitable Globe, into whose Hands these may chance to fall. Note well — THAT on the 23d of May 1770, SCIPIO, a Negro Man near 23 Years old, Ran from the Subscriber — He is five feet and 3 or 4 inches high, little more or less, and well set, his Hair or Wool (unless shav'd) comes low upon his Cheeks, his Fore Teeth rather Splaying, has an Incision mark on one of his Arms, where he was Inoculated, and 2 or 3 Scars in one of his Legs where he was lanced, is pretty black, with a flattish nose, tho' not that flat so peculiar to Negroes, is very artful — Speaks plain but something inward and hollow, inclines much to the Sea, will make an able Seaman, and is a Cooper. —If he returns voluntarily he shall not be whipt as he deserves, but I will either sell him to a good Ship Master, or let him as he shall chuse, till he has earnt his prime Colt &c. when I will give him his Freedom — but if any shall bring or convey him to his Master, shall be paid EIGHT DOLLARS, by SAMUEL SWIFT.

Reprints: Boston Evening Post, 06-04-1770. This notice was also reprinted in the Boston Gazette, 07-16-1770; 07-20-1770; 07-23-1770; in the Massachusetts Gazette, 06-28-1770; 07-05-1770; 07-12-1770; 07-19-1770.

Boston Evening Post, 06-11-1770.

Ran away from his Master, Captain Joseph Hale of Newbury, the first day of June 1770, a Negro Man, named Peter, about 23 Years of Age, about 5 Feet 3 Inches high, thick set, speaks English well, had on when he went away a snuff coloured Coat with Brass Buttons, a green Ratteen Waistcoat, a pair of brown Fustian Breeches, he carried away with him a pair of light blue Stockings, and white ditto, a large Linen Shirt, brown Wig, and a Castor Hat, and he had a Scar on the Backside of his Neck. Whoever will take up the said Negro, and convey him to his Master at Newbury, or secure him in any of his Majesty's Goals, shall have FIVE DOLLARS Reward, and all necessary Charges paid by me the Subscriber. JOSEPH HALE.

All masters of Vessels and others, are caution'd against harbouring, concealing, or carrying off said Servant, as they would avoid the Penalty of the law.

Reprints: Boston Evening Post, 06-18-1770; 06-25-1770. This notice was also printed in the Boston Gazette 06-11-1770; 06-25-1770; 07-02-1770; in the Massachusetts, 06-07-1770; 06-14-1770.

Boston Evening Post, 06-11-1770.

Ran away from his Master, Joseph Moody of Newbury, a Negro Man, named Prince, about 30 Years of Age, 5 Feet 9 Inches high, a well set Fellow, has had his Jaw Bone broke, it is an Obstruction to him in Eating, has had his right Leg broke & is a little crooked, has lost two or three Toes of his left Foot, had on when he went away, a light color'd Homespun Coat, a Scarlet Ratteen Waistcoat, a pair of yellow Buckskin Breeches, a black Wig, and Felt Hat, and Linen Shirt. Whoever will take up the Said Negro, and convey him to his Master at Dummer School in Newbury, or confine him in any of his Majesty's Goals, so that his Master may have him again, shall have FIVE DOLLARS Reward, and all necessary Charges paid by me the Subscriber. JOSEPH MOODY.

All Masters of Vessels and others, are hereby cautioned against harbouring, concealing, or carrying off said Servant, as they would avoid the Penalty of the law.

Reprints: Boston Evening Post, 06-18-1770; 06-25-1770. This notice was also printed in the Boston Gazette 06-11-1770; 06-25-1770; 07-02-1770; in the Massachusetts, 06-07-1770; 06-14-1770.

Boston Evening Post, 06-11-1770.

Ran away from Daniel Moors of Bedford, in New Hampshire, a likely Negro Man, about 32 Years of Age, about 5 Feet 10 Inches high. Had on a green Ratteen Coat with red Trimming, a Thickset Jacket, and blue Breeches. Whoever shall take up the said Negro and bring him to said Moors, shall have EIGHT DOLLARS Reward and all necessary Charges paid. Bedford, May 15, 1770.
   Reprint: Boston Evening Post, 06-25-1770.

Boston Evening Post, 03-25-1771.

Ran away from Hugh M'Lean of Milton, a Negro Man, named Peleg Abby, about 26 Years of Age; had on when he went away a light Brown Great Coat without any Cape, very much torn about the Sleeves, a Corded Fustain Olive color'd close-bodied Coat, a Homespun Stript Jacket, two Stript Cotton Shirts, a Pair ribb'd Yarn Stockings, 1 Pair mill Stockings, a Pair of old blue & white Yarn ones, and 2 Pair of pretty good Shoes, and a Pair of Pumps. Whoever will apprehend said Runaway and bring him to the Subscriber in Milton near the Slitting Mill, shall have SIX DOLLARS Reward and all Charges paid. He is about Five Feet Six Inches high, speaks good English, was born in Rhode-Island Colony, but lately has lived at St. George's at the Eastward, Burning of Lime. Milton, March 25, 1771. HUGH M'LEAN.
   Reprints: Boston Evening Post, 04-01-1771; 04-08-1771.

Boston Evening Post, 08-19-1771.

Ran away from John Hunt of Watertown, on Tuesday last, a Negro Man named Prince, a tall straight Fellow, walks with a small Hitch. He is about 33 Years old, has been used to farming Business, is a handy Fellow on most Accounts, talks pretty good English — Had on when he went away a striped Jacket, a Frock & Trowsers almost new. — His Design was to get off in some Vessel so as to go to England, under the Notion if he could get there he should be Free. Whoever takes up and secures said Fellow so that his Master receives him again shall be well rewarded for their Trouble. He carried with him a good Pair of Deerskin Breeches.
   All Masters of Vessels are cautioned against carrying off said Servant, as they would avoid the Penalty of the Law. August 19, 1771. JOHN HUNT.

Reprints: Boston Evening Post, 08-26-1771; 09-02-1771; 09-09-1771. This notice was also printed in the Boston Gazette, 08-19-1771; 08-26-1771; 11-18-1771.

Boston Evening Post, 11-25-1771.

Ran away from the Subscriber on the 9th of November Instant, a Negro Man Servant named CROMARTIE, commonly called CRUM, who formerly belonged to Mr. Brackett, Inholder in School-Street Boston. He is a likely well-made Fellow, rather short of a middling Stature and about 27 Years of Age; carried with him an old Hat, a good grey Frock of Beaver Coating, a red Cloth short Waistcoat, double breasted, an old brown-coloured short Coat, much worn, an old striped Woollen Waistcoat, a Cloth-colour'd Great Coat, three white Linen Shirts ruffled at the Bosom, a new Cotton & Linen and an old striped Cotton & Linen Shirt, a Pair of Buckskin Buff coloured Breeches, almost new, a Pair of mixt-coloured Yarn Stockings, and two Pair of brown Thread Stockings. Whoever shall take up said Runaway, and return him to me his Master in Boston, or secure him in some public Goal, & give Notice thereof to me, so that I shall have him again, shall have TEN DOLLARS Reward and all necessary Charges paid. And all Masters of Vessels and others, are hereby cautioned not to carry off or harbor said Fellow, who is a Slave for Life. Boston, Nov. 16, 1771. SAMUEL FITCH.
Reprints: Boston Evening Post, 11-25-1771; 12-02-1771. This notice was also printed in the Boston Gazette, 11-18-1771; 11-25-1771; 12-02-1771.

Boston Evening Post, 08-03-1772.

Ran away from his Master William Maynard of Framingham, on the 16th of July last, a Negro Boy about 15 Years of Age, small of Stature, speaks good English, and has a Scar on one of his Temples: Had on when we went away only a Shirt and a Pair of Trowsers. Whoever will take up said Boy and convey him to his Master shall have TWO DOLLARS Reward and all necessary Charges paid. All masters of vessels and others are hereby cautioned against harbouring, concealing or carrying off said Runaway, as they would avoid the Penalty of the Law. Framingham, Aug 1, 1772.
Reprint: Boston Evening Post, 08-10-1772.

Boston Evening Post, 08-24-1772.

GEORGE PENN (a Mulatto) aged 30, five Feet nine Inches, and remarkably stout for his Height. Whoever shall apprehend all or either of the above Persons, and him or them commit to any of His Majesty's Goals in the Province of Massachusetts Bay, shall receive for each TEN DOLLARS Reward. RICHARD SALTONSTALL, Sheriff.

Reprints: Boston Evening Post, 08-31-1772; 09-07-1772. This notice was also printed in the Boston Gazette 08-31-1772; 09-07-1772; in the Massachusetts Gazette, 08-27-1772; 09-03-1772.

Boston Evening Post, 05-03-1773.

Ran away from Admiral Montagu on Saturday Evening last, a Negro Man named John Polite, about 23 or 24 Years of Age, well made, about 5 Feet 8 Inches high ; had on a green Livery Coat, a red Waistcoat, both with Brass Buttons, a new Pair of leather Breeches, and a new Hat, with a Brass Button. Whoever will apprehend the above Negro, and bring him to Admiral Montagu, shall have EIGHT DOLLARS Reward.

Reprints: Boston Evening Post, 05-10-1773; 05-17-1773.

Boston Evening Post, 07-12-1773.

Last Thursday Night deserted from on Board the Sloop Little Bob, William Ham, Master, from St. Croix and Tucks Island, a Negro Man Servant, named DICK, about 28 Years of Age, a strait limb'd Fellow, pitted a little with the SmallPox, speaks good English; and had on when he went away a blue Jacket and long Canvas Trowsers. Whoever apprehends the said Negro so that he may be returned to his Vessel, now lying at Tilestone's Wharf, shall receive THREE DOLLARS Reward and all necessary Charges paid, by the said Master.

N.B. All Masters of Vessels and Others are hereby cautioned against concealing or carrying off said Servant as they would avoid the Penalty of the Law.

Boston, July 12th, 1773

Reprints: Boston Evening Post, 07-19-1773; 07-26-1773.

Boston Evening Post, 07-19-1773.

Ran away from Subscriber, on Friday the 9th Day of July Instant, a Molatto Woman Slave nam'd Violetus, aged about 32 Years, of short Stature, and Hair of a yellowish colour: She had with her when she went away a Chints Gown and Cooler, and a Couple of Quilts, one of a blue, the other of a brown Colour, two Pair of Shoes, and divers other Things. — If any Person shall inform where she is, that her Master may have her again, they shall be rewarded ; and all Masters of Vessels and others are hereby warned not to harbor or conceal said Slave. — N.B. It is suspected she is in Company with one Henry Traveller, a free Negro. Bridgewater, July 12, 1773.

ABIA KEITH.

Reprints: Boston Evening Post, 07-26-1773; 08-02-1773.

Boston Evening Post, 08-30-1773.

Ran-away from me the Subscriber, on Tuesday the 13th of May last, a NEGRO Woman SLAVE named Nancy: She is a tall Woman, aged about 22 Years, and had on when she went away, a blue and white loose Gown; and did about two Years ago belong to Mr. Samuel Willis of Bridgewater. – Whoever shall bring said Runaway to me the Subscriber shall be well rewarded for their Trouble by Francis Perkins.

    Bridgewater, Aug 28, 1773.

    N.B. All Persons are forbid Harbouring, concealing or carrying off said Slave, as they may depend upon being prosecuted as the Law directs. F.P.

    Reprints: Boston Evening Post, 09-06-1773; 09-13-1773; 09-20-1773.

Boston Evening Post, 05-30-1774.

Ran away from his Master on Tuesday Evening last, a Negro Boy, named Goree, about 16 Years of age, 5 Feet, 3 Inches high, had on when he went away, a brown Cloth Coat, dark Velvet Waistcoat, white Shirt, white Linen Breeches, grey Yarn Stockings, a pair of Shoes tore at the Heels, with Pinchbeck Buckles, an old Felt Hat. Whoever will take up said Run away, and secure him, and give Information to the subscriber, so that he may have him again, shall have a handsome Reward and all necessary Charges paid by DANIEL VOSE.

    All Masters of Vessels and others are hereby cautioned against harbouring, concealing, or carrying off the above Negro, as they would avoid the Penalty of the Law. May 30, 1774.

    Reprints: Boston Evening Post, 06-06-1774. This notice was also printed in the Boston Gazette 05-30-1774; 06-13-1774; 06-20-1774; in the Essex Gazette, 05-24 to 05-31-1774; 05-31 to 06-7-1774.

Boston Evening Post, 06-06-1774.

Lately broke out of Bridewell, a sturdy well set Negro Fellow, about 27 Years of Age, well known in Town by the Name of Pomp Fleet: — He has had the SmallPox, the Marks of which appear very distinct in his Face, being much darker than the other Parts of his Skin ; is about 5 Feet 6 Inches high ; had with him a good dark brown Coat, white Breeches and Stockings, also black ditto, and often has his Wool dressed in the Maccaroni Taste : — He is supposed to be lurking about with an Indian Wench, whom he calls his Wife. — Whoever will take him up and commit him to Bridgewell, or to any of his Majesty's Goals, shall be rewarded for their Trouble by the Printers hereof.

All Masters of Vessels and others, who shall harbour, conceal, or carry off said Fellow, (Who is a servant) may depend on being prosecuted to the extent of the Law. June 4, 1774.

Boston Evening Post, 06-20-1774.

Ran away from his Master, Capt. Jonathan Brewer of Waltham, a Negro man named Boston, about 25 Years of Age, about 5 Feet and a half high, walks stooping, speaks quick; had on when he went away, a dark colour'd Serge Coat and Drawboy Jacket, a Pair of Buff colour'd Sheepskin Breeches, one Pair of Yarn Stockings and a Pair of Pumps. — Whoever will take up said Negro and return him to his Master, shall have TWO DOLLARS Reward and all necessary charges paid.

All Masters of Vessels and others are hereby forbidden to carry off, conceal, entertain or trust said Servant at the Peril of the Law.

Reprints: Boston Evening Post, 06-27-1774. This notice was also printed in the Massachusetts Gazette, 06-09-1774; 06-16-1774; 06-23-1774.

Boston Evening Post, 07-18-1774.

Ran-away last Evening a Negro Girl of middling Stature, a Cast in her Eye; had on when she went away a short strip'd Homespun Gown, an old Camblet Coat, and an Ozenbrigs Apron. — Whoever shall take up and return said Negro shall be handsomely rewarded. Inquire at the Printers.

Reprint: Boston Evening Post, 07-25-1774.

Boston Evening Post, 08-01-1774.

FOUR DOLLARS Reward,

Ran away from her Master, Francis Shaw, a likely tall Negro Woman, known by the Name of Violet Shaw, about 25 Years old; has a Blemish in one Eye, carried away with her a white Calico Riding Dress, a strip'd Calico Gown, a Claret colour'd Poplin Gown, a strip'd blue and white Holland Gown, a Bengal Gown, and many other valuable Articles of Apparel. — Whoever apprehends her, and will return her to her Master in Boston, shall have Four Dollars Reward, and all necessary Charges paid. All Persons are cautioned against harbouring or carrying off said Negro Servant, as they would avoid the Rigor of the Law. Boston, July 29, 1774.

Reprint: Boston Gazette 08-01-1774.

Boston Gazette, 05-28-1770.

Run-away from his Master the 23d Instant, a Negro Fellow about 22 Years old, has since chang'd his Cloaths. His Hair of Wool grows pretty much on his Cheecks, smooth-fac'd, his Fore-teeth jet out a little, is artful and good natured, went towards Providence. Whoever conveys him to his Master, shall be rewarded by SAMUEL SWIFT.

N.B. It is taken for granted all Captains of Vessels will Discountenance him. Boston, May 26, 1770.

Reprints: Boston Gazette, 06-04-1770; 06-11-1770; 06-18-1770.

Boston Gazette, 06-25-1770.

RUN away from the Subscriber last Night, a Negro Wench named Philis, a likely smooth handsome Face, but not vey black one. Had on and carried away with her, one old striped Homespun Coat, one Quilted Coat dark on one Side, and the other Side red Baize; two short Gowns or Jackets striped, two Shirts, one white Apron, white Stockings clock'd with blue, heel'd Leather Shoes. Any Person taking and securing the said Negro, and giving Notice, shall receive Four Dollars Reward, and all necessary Charges paid by JAMES MUGFORD. Marblehead, June 22.

Reprints: Boston Gazette, 07-02-1770; 07-09-1770.

Boston Gazette, 07-23-1770.

Ran-away from MILES WHITWORTH, a Negro Man named YORKE. Had on when he went away a brown Fustian Frock, cloth-colour'd Waistcoat, and Leather Breeches. His Wool extends far on his Face, and of a sallow Complexion. Whoever takes up said Negro, and brings him to his Master, shall have TWO DOLLARS Reward, and all necessary Charges Paid. All Masters of Vessels and others, are cautioned against harbouring, concealing, or carrying off said Negro, as they would avoid the Penalty of the Law. July 23.

Reprint: Boston Gazette, 07-30-1770.

Boston Gazette, 10-01-1770.

Ran away from his Master last Saturday Night, a Negro named Duke, is a well set Fellow, about 19 Years of age, has a pleasant Countenance, speaks good English, had on and carried with him 2 Homespun Jackets, 2 pair of Ravens Ducks Trowsers, 2 pair of grey Yarn Stockings, old Shoes, 2 pair of cloth Breeches, a round Dutch Sap. He is about 5 Feet 6 Inches high. Whoever shall take up said Servant and will bring him to the Printer's hereof, shall have TWO DOLLARS Reward.

N.B. All Masters of Vessels are hereby cautioned against concealing or carrying off said Negro on penalty of the law. Boston, Oct 1st, 1770.

Boston Gazette, 10-01-1770.

TWO DOLLARS REWARD.

Ran-away last Night, a Negro Man called BOSTON. He is a short, well-set, strong made Fellow of about 27 Years of Age. He had on when he went away, a new cloth-coloured Pea Jacket, with a striped blue and white under Waist Coat, a Cotton and Linnen Shirt, a pair of white Dimothy Breeches, white thread Stockings, a pair of pumps, with large Brass Buckles. Whoever will take up the above Fellow and bring him to the Printers hereof, shall be Intitled to the above Reward.

N.B. All Masters of Vessels and others are hereby caution'd against carrying off said Servant as they would avoid the penalty of the law. October 1st, 1770.

Reprints: Boston Gazette, 10-08-1770; 10-15-1770.

Boston Gazette, 10-15-1770.

Ran-away from the Subscriber on the 11th Instant at Night, a Negro Man Servant, named POMP, about 5 Feet 7 Inches high, speaks good English, has a large Scar on one part of his Forehead, and about 23 Years of Age: Had on when he went away, a dark colour'd Broad Cloth Coat, which has been turn'd, a home-made Cotton and Linnen Jacket of a mixt colour, a pair of Black Knit Breeches something worn, it is supposed he stole a Horse near the place he went from with a Saddle and Bridle. Said Horse is about 14 ½ Hands high, of a Sorrel Colour, with a light Mane and Tail, lately Shod, and trim'd with a Hog'd Mane. Whoever shall take up said Negro and Horse, or either of them, shall have TWO DOLLARS Reward for each, and all necessary Charges paid them. AARON WAIT.

All Masters of Vessels and others, are hereby caution'd against harbouring, concealing, or carrying off said Negro as they would avoid the Penalty of the Law. Salem, 11th October, 1770.

Reprints: Boston Evening Post, 10-22-1770; 10-29-1770. This notice also printed in the Providence Gazette, 11-03-1770 to 11-10-1770, and 11-10-1770 to 11-17-1770.

Boston Gazette, 04-01-1771.

Twenty Dollars Reward

Ran away from the Subscriber, (living in Second-Street, between Market and Arch Streets) about the latter end of last June, a negro fellow named Toby, about 24 Years of age, 5 feet 6 or 8 inches high, a likely well-set fellow, very talkative and complaisant, especially when in liquor, has been brought up to house work. He was taken up at New York, the 19th of Aug. last, and made his escape from goal the same day. It is supposed he is there got on board some Vessel bound to the West Indies, or went towards Albany or New England. Any Person who shall take up said Negro, so that his master may get him again, shall be entitled to the above reward and all reasonable charges. JOHN BAYARD

N.B. His clothing are not described, as he took nothing but his common apparel, which is supposed by this time he has worn out or changed. He can write, and perhaps he may change his name & pretend to be free negro.

Reprints: Boston Gazette, 04-08-1771; 04-15-1771. This notice was also printed in the Connecticut Courant, 03-19-1771 to 03-26-1771.

Boston Gazette, 05-27-1771.

Ran-away from the Subscriber living at Woodbridge, East New Jersey, on the 2d Day of June last past, a Negro Man named Dick or Richard, about 5 Feet 7 Inches high, about 26 Years of Age, a well-looking and well-shaped Fellow, right Negro, but little on the yellow, speaks very good English, and that very handsomely; he was seen in the Stratford in Connecticut a few Days after, and shewed a Pass in Stratford, and their being in said Pass a grand Contradiction, he made off for Boston. – The Pass, Singer and Evidences being all of one Hand Writing, and sign'd by his Master after his Death; he being a crafty Fellow may get some evil-minded Person to give him another, as he did before. Had on when he went away, blue Coat, black Velvet Jacket and Breeches, with Sundry other very good Cloaths. – Whosoever shall take up said Negro, and send him to New York, so that his Master may have him again, shall have Ten Pounds. New-York Money Reward, and all reasonable Charges, paid by me, DAVID EDGAR.

Or by James Wilmot, in Hanover-Square, New-York. Dated the 5th Day of May, A.D. 1771.

Reprint: Boston Gazette, 06-17-1771.

Boston Gazette, 07-01-1771.

Twenty Dollars Reward.

Ran-away from Capt. Daniel Campble, on the Island Grenada, a Negro Man named Boston: He is a strong-made, well-set, straight-lim'd, likely Fellow, of about 28 Years of Age, 5 Feet 4 Inches high, smooth-fac'd, small Eyes, well-set in his Head, and a low Forehead; when he speaks he seldom opens his Teeth; he has a remarkable small but very hard hand, and was brought up to the Sugar-Baking Business in this Town, but for his Bad Behavior was sent to the West-Indies, from thence its thought he has got on board some Vessel bound to some Part of this Continent. – In Cafe any Person, through the whole Coast of America, will secure the above Fellow, so that he can be brought to me, or to the Printers hereof, they are intitled to the above Reward, with all reasonable Charges. JAMES SMITHWICK.

N.B. The above Fellow speaks good English; he can read in a Psalter, and at Times very fond of Singing Psalm Tunes —He has a very serious Look and can lie without Stuttering.

Reprints: Boston Gazette, 07-08-1771; 07-15-1771.

Boston Gazette, 07-29-1771.

Ran-away from his Master JONATHAN GREEN of Chelsea on the 17th Instant, a thick well-set Negro Man named Cesar, about 24 Years of Age, speaks very good English:--Had on when he went away, a blue Coat, brown Jacket, and dark Claret colour'd Breeches, blue Yarn Stockings seem'd, and old Shoes, a white Linnen Shirt, and old Caster Hat.—He was seen at Cambridge on Commencement Day, and the two following Days.—Whoever shall take up said Run away, and bring him to his Master in Chelsea aforesaid, shall have Three Dollars Reward, and all necessary Charges paid by JONATHAN GREEN.

All Masters of Vessels and others, are hereby cautioned against harbouring, concealing or carrying off said Servant, on Penalty of the Law.

Chelsea, July 26, 1771.

Reprints: Boston Gazette, 08-05-1771; 08-21-1771.

Boston Gazette, 09-09-1771.

Ran-away from the Subscriber, on the Second of September Instant, a Negro Man named PRIMUS, about 5 Feet 10 Inches high, speaks good English, pretty black, long Limbs, and very long Finger Nails. Had on when he went away, a striped cotton and wool under Waistcoat, a gray black and blue Coat, or a lapell'd brown all-wool outside Jacket, Trowsers &c.- Whoever will take up said Negro, and bring him to his Master in Beverly, shall have FOUR DOLLARS Reward, and all necessary Charges paid by Doctor ISRAEL WOODBURY.

N.B. All Masters of Vessels are forewarn'd not to carry off said Negro. He is 42 Years Old.

Beverly, September 4, 1771.

Reprint: Boston Gazette, 09-23-1771.

Boston Gazette, 02-10-1772.

Ran-away from the Subscriber living in Marblehead, a Negro Man about 34 Years old, about 5 Feet and half high: Had on when he went away last Monday Se'nnight, a mill'd Cap, an old Ratteen Jacket, and an Homespun under Jacket, both lin'd with red Baize, Homespun Breeches and Cotton Shirt, and grey Yarn Stockings. Whoever will take up and secure said Negro, and send me Word, so that I can have him again, shall have FIVE DOLLARS and all Charges paid, by CHRISTOPHER BUBIER.

All Persons are forbid entertaining, and Masters of Vessels carrying off said Negro at their Peril.

Marblehead, Feb 8. 1772.

Reprints: Boston Gazette, 02-17-1772; 02-24-1772.

The Boston Gazette, 05-10-1773.

Ran-AWAY from his Master John Foster, on Long-Island, about three Months since a Negro-Man Named Cush, about five Feet nine Inches high, his Complexion got very black, one or two of his fore Teeth out, a Scar upon one of his Ears, Speaks good English, has Forg'd a Pass; had on when he went away a blue Mill'd Cap, a blue outside Jacket, and a red Bays Shirt. – It is likely he may have chang'd his Dress, as he has broke open his Master's Store, and Stole to the value of 100 Dollars in Cash and Goods.

Whoever shall apprehend said Negro and commit him to any of his Majesty's Goals, shall have 10 Dollars Reward, and all necessary Charges paid; and for securing the Pass 20 Dollars, if it can be prov'd who was the Forger of it, Paid by me JOHN FOSTER.

All Masters of Vessels and others are hereby Cautioned against harbouring, concealing or carrying off said Servant as they would avoid the Penalty of the Law. South-Hampton, April 28, 1773.

Reprint: Boston Gazette, 05-10-1773.

Boston Gazette, 11-15-1773.

Twenty Dollars Reward.

Ran-Away from the Subscriber on the Evening of the 16th Oct. a Negro-Man named BRISTOL, is about 30 Years of Age, five Feet six Inches high, well fet, of a light Complexion, and speaks good English; carried off with him one short Coat, of a mix'd colour, and a Number of other Cloathing, is by Trade a Barber, Shaves well and can Dress Hair :— Whoever will take up said Negro and return him to me shall have the above mentioned Reward. SAMUEL SWAN.

N.B. All Masters of Vessels and others, are Warned against harbouring or carrying off said Negro-Man, as they would avoid the Penalty of the Law.

Reprints: Boston Gazette, 11-08-1773; 11-15-1773. This notice was also printed in the Massachusetts Gazette, 10-21-1771; 10-28-1773; 11-04-1773.

Boston Gazette, 11-15-1773.

Ran away last Night from on Board the Schooner 'Two Williams, lying at the Hon. John Hancock, a Elq'rs Wharff, a Negro Man, named Nath. of a yellow Complexion, about five Feet seven Inches high, 28 Years of Age; a likely well made Fellow, and a good Sailor. – Had on when he went away, a blue Wasitcoat, lin'd with Red.

Whoever will apprehend and secure him, so that his Owner may have him again, shall have SIX DOLLARS Reward. And all Masters of Vessels and others are hereby cautioned against entertaining or concealing said Negro, as they may depend on being prosecuted according to Law. SAMUEL LIGHT-BOURN. Boston, Nov 13, 1773.

Reprint: Boston Gazette, 11-29-1773.

Boston Gazette, 05-09-1774 (Supplement).

Ran-away from William Thompson of Billerica, on the 24th ult., a Negro Man named Caesar, about 5 Feet 7 Inches high, carried with him two Suits of Cloaths, homespun all Wool, light coloured, with white Lining and plain Brass Buttons, the other homespun Cotton and Linnen Twisted. Whoever takes up said Negro and secures him, or returns him to his Master, shall be handsomely rewarded, and all necessary Charges paid by JONATHAN STICKNEY.

N.B. All Masters of Vessels and others, are cautioned from carrying off or concealing said Negro, as they would avoid the Penalty of the Law.

Reprints: Boston Gazette, 05-09-1774; 05-16-1774. This notice was also printed in the Massachusetts Gazette, 04-28-1774; 05-05-1774; 05-19-1774.

Boston Gazette, 06-06-1774.

Ran-away from the Subscriber, living in Gorham, which joins Falmouth, Cumberland County, in the Massachusetts Province, a short Negro Man named Prince, about 26 Years of Age, 5 Feet some Inches high, talks broken English, has remarkable small Ears and a Jewel Hole in one of them. Had on almost a new Felt Hat, a reddish grey home made Cloth Coat Jacket and Breeches with silk knee Garters, a dark Callicoe under Jacket, a white Linnen Shirt, red Collar and Cuffs to his Coat with Metal Buttons, white Cutton Stockings, Calf-Skin Pumps. It may be he has a Pass. Said Negro plays tolerable well on a Violin. Whoever will take up said Negro, or bring him to his Master shall have Sixteen Dollars Reward, and all Charges paid by WILLIAM M'LENNEN

N.B. Said Negro Leaving done some Damage at the House where the Negroes met to hold their Frolick on Election Day, did not return to his Master again. All Masters of Vessels are forewarned not to carry him off at their Peril. May 26, 1774.

Reprints: Boston Gazette, 06-13-1774; 06-20-1774.

Boston Gazette, 06-20-1774.

Ran away from the Subscriber on the Eighth of June Instant, at Night, a Negro Boy, about Seventeen Years of Age: Had on when he went off, a dark coloured cloth Jacket and Trowsers, and is branded on the Breast Dehamote, very remarkable: said Fellow speaks tolerable good English, and some French. Whoever takes up said Fellow and Secures him in any of his Majesty's Goals, or Returns him to the Subscriber, shall have FIVE DOLLARS Reward, and all necessary charges paid by ALLIN BROWN. Providence, June 10, 1774.

Reprints: Boston Gazette, 06-20-1774 (Supplement); 06-27-1774; 07-04-1774; 07-11-1774. This notice was also printed in the Providence Gazette, 06-11-1774; 06-18-1774; and 06-25-1774.

Boston Gazette, 06-20-1774 (Supplement).

Ten Dollars Reward.

Ran AWAY from the Subscriber, Joseph Moors, of Groton, in the County of Middlesex, and Province of Massachusetts-Bay, a Mulatto Man Servant, named TITUS, about 20 Years of Age, of a middling Stature, wears short curl'd Hair, has one of his Fore Teeth broke out, took with him a blue Surdan, a Snuff-coloured Coat, and a Pair of white wash'd Leather Breeches, a Pair of new Cow-Hide Pumps and a Furr'd Hat with large Brims, and Sundry other Articles of Wearing Apparel. – Whoever will take up said Servant and confine him in any of his Majesty's Goals, so that the Owner may have him again, shall have TEN DOLLARS Reward and all necessary Charges paid, by JOSEPH MOORS.

All Masters of Vessels and others, are hereby Caution'd against Harbouring, Concealing, or carrying off said Servant, as they would hereby avoid the Penalty of the Law.

Reprints: Boston Gazette, 06-20-1774; 06-27-1774.

Boston Gazette, 07-25-1774.

Four Dollars Reward.

RANAWAY from his Master MARK HUNKING of Barrington, in New Hampshire, a Negro Servant named CAESAR : — Had on when he went away, a striped homespun lappel'd Waistcoat, a Tow Shirt, black Serge Breeches, grey Jacket, a pair of Breeches and Jacket of a black and Hemlock dye, striped Tow Trowsers, black and white Yarn Stockings. He is a straight Limb'd Fellow about 5 Feet nine Inches high, very white Teeth, smiling Countenance ; was bro't up to Farming Work. — Whoever shall take up said Runaway, and secure him so that his Master may have him again, shall have Four Dollars Reward, and all necessary Charges paid by MARK HUNKING.

N.B. All Masters of Vessels and others are forbid carrying him off, as they would avoid the penalty of the Law. Barrington, July 12, 1774.

Reprints: Boston Gazette, 08-01-1774; 09-08-1774. This notice was also printed in the Essex Gazette, 07-19 to 07-26-1774; 07-26 to 08-02-1774; 08-02 to 08-09-1774.

Boston Gazette, 08-29-1774 (Supplement).

Ran-away from his Master, on the 25th Instant, a Negro Fellow named CATO, about 20 Years of Age, about 5 Feet 8 Inches high, a thick well set Fellow. Had on when he went away, a thin Homespun Coat, a Woollen Shirt, and Tow Trowsers. – Whoever shall take up said Runaway and convey him to his Master in Salem, shall have TWO DOLLARS Reward and all necessary Charges paid by Me. DANIEL MALLOON.

All Masters of Vessels and others, are hereby cautioned against concealing, harbouring, or entertaining said Runaway, on Penalty of the Law. SALEM, August 29, 1774.

Reprints: Boston Gazette, 09-05-1774; 09-12-1774.

Boston Gazette, 09-12-1774.

Ran away from the Subscriber, at Manchester, Yesterday; two Negroes, viz. CHESTER, alias TITUS, about 30 Years of Age 5 Feet 9 Inches high, well Limb'd, a stammering Speech, and one or more of his toes partly lost by Frost. Had on when he went away, and carried with him, a brown colour'd all Wool Coat, light colour'd Broad Cloth ditto, trim'd with Green, two striped Jackets, blue Breeches and a Pair of Trowsers. — CAESAR, a slim Boy about 17 Years of Age. Carried with him a light colour'd Broad Cloth Coat, trimm'd with Green, Leather Breeches, two under Jackets, one Calico, the other whitish Broad Cloth with Metal Buttons, a Pair of Trowsers &c.

Whoever shall take ups said Run-aways or either of them, and return them to their Master at Manchester or Secure them in any of his Majesty's Goals, and give notice thereof shall have Four Dollars Reward for each Negro, and all necessary Charges paid by JOHN LEE. Manchester, Septem. 8, 1774.

N.B. All Masters of Vessels and others are cautioned against Harbouring or Carrying off said Servants on Penalty of the Law.
Reprint: Boston Gazette, 09-26-1774.

Boston Gazette, 10-03-1774.

FOUR DOLLARS REWARD.

Ran-AWAY from the Subscriber on the 22d of September, at Night, a Negro Man Servant, by the Name of CATO, about Five Feet and Eight Inches high, very thick Lips, speaks broken, and Walks as if he was lame in his Heels. Had on when he went away, a Cloth colour'd Coat, with Pewter Buttons, old Leather Breeches, a Tow Shirt, old Shoes with Silver plate Buckles, wore a Cap, and shoves around his Neck, and very high on his Forehead : Carried with him a Callico Banyan, fine Linen Shirt, Check Linen Trowsers, grey Wigg, also carries or Wears a Felt Hatt with a Silver Lace on it, had a Violin and carries it in a green Bays Bag. Whoever will return the Runaway to his Master in Winchenden, shall have the above Reward and all necessary Charges paid by LEVI NICHOL. Winchenden, Sept 23, 1774.
Reprints: Boston Gazette, 10-10-1774; 10-17-1774.

Boston Gazette, 10-24-1774.

FIFTEEN DOLLARS REWARD.

Ran-AWAY from me the Subscriber on Thursday the Twentieth of October Instant, a Negro Man named CAESAR, about 26 Years Old, five Feet four Inches high: had on when he went away, a Green Ratteen Coat, Red Everlasting Jacket, White Linnen Breeches, Blue Yarn Stockings, he has a Mark or Scar over one of his Eyes, the little Finger of his left Hand is a little crooked by the Cut of a Sickle; it is suspected that some one assisted him by changing Cloaths or gave him a pass: Whoever will take up said Negro and return him to me, or confine him to any of his Majesty's Goals, so that he may be return'd to me, shall have the above Reward and all necessary Charges paid by SIMEON HAZELTINE. Hardwick, October 21, 1774.
Reprints: Boston Gazette, 10-31-1774; 11-07-1774; 01-16-1775. This notice was also printed in the Essex Gazette, 10-18 to 10-25-1774; 10-25 to 11-01-1774; 11-1 to 11-08-1774.

Boston Gazette, 2-06-1775 (Supplement).

RANAWAY on Thursday last, from her Master Capt. Nathaniel Patten, a Negro Woman, named Dillar, about 30 Years of Age: She carried off with her a Child, about 5 Years of Age, she had on homespun Clothes, and took with her two Callico and one Cambleteen Gown:—Whoever will return said Negroes to their Master at New Boston, shall have TWO DOLLARS Reward.—

All Persons are cautioned against harbouring, concealing, or carrying off said Negroes, as they would avoid the Penalty of the Law.

Boston Gazette, 04-03-1775.

Ran-away from the Subscriber, on the Evening of the 12th Instant, a Negro Man, named PRIMUS, about 52 Years old, he carried away with him a light brown Coat, a green Ratteen Outside Jacket, and a red Broad Cloth Waistcoat, and a pair of Short Trowsers, and is supposed to have a bundle of Cloaths with him, he is about five Feet eight Inches high. Whoever shall take up said Negro, and secure him in any one of his Majesty's Goals, shall have ONE DOLLAR Reward paid by JOSEPH HOYH.

All Masters of Vessels and all others are hereby cautioned against harbouring, concealing or carrying off or employing said Negro as they would avoid the Penalty of the Law. Newbury-Port, March 23, 1775.

Reprints: Boston Gazette, 04-10-1775; 04-17-1775.

Boston Gazette, 07-24-1775.

Ran away from the Subscriber on Thursday last, a Negro Man named Quamono (but calls himself Jack) about 23 Years old, and near 6 feet high, short limb'd. — He had on when he went away, and took with him, a thick blue jacket, a red ditto, two strip'd ditto, a pair of long trowsers, a red baize shirt, and a small old Beaver hat. He has a small scar between his eyes, just over his nose. Whoever will take up said Negro and convey him to his master in Lynn End above said shall have FOUR Dollars Reward and all necessary Charges paid by NEHEMIAH SKILLINGS.

Reprints: Boston Gazette, 07-31-1775; 08-07-1775.

Boston Gazette, 12-04-1775.

BROKE Goal last Night the following Prisoners, Thomas Smith, and William Benson, a Negro Man. Said Smith is a very noted Thief, hast been in almost all the Goals on the Continent; had on when he broke Goal, a blue Jacket, a Pair of Striped Trowsers, sandy coloured Hair, about 5 Feet 4 Inches high. Said Benson the Negro had on when he went away, a dark coloured old Coat a Pair of old black knit Breeches, about 5 Feet 6 Inches high. Whoever shall take up said Prisoners and return them to said Goal shall have TWO DOLLARS Reward paid by. ISAAC BRADDISH, Under Keeper.

Reprints: Boston Gazette, 10-30-1775; 11-06-1775; 12-04-1775; 12-11-1175.

Boston Gazette, 03-25-1776.

Ran away from the Subscriber on the 16th of this Instant, a likely young Negro Man named Mile, strait limb'd about 5 Feet 10 Inches tall, and has remarkable large Feet. Had on when he went away a check'd woollen Shirt, a blue double-breasted Jacket without Sleeves, and blue Breeches, yarn Stockings, and a red Duff Great Coat. — Whoever will take up said Negro, and bring him to his Master, shall receive a handsome Reward, and all Expenses paid him. Warning is further hereby given for no Person or Persons to harbour, conceal, or hide said Negro, do they must take the consequences arising from said Practices. And all Officers are also directed not to inlist said Negro nor to hire him as a Waiter, but seeing him forth coming shall be intitled to the Reward and Expenses accruing and will highly oblige. SAM ZEAGERS.

N.B. Whoever shall take up said Negro and confine him in any Goal, and acquaint his Master therewith shall be entitled to the Reward. Little Cambridge, March 22, 1776.

Reprints: Boston Gazette, 04-01-1776; 04-08-1776.

Boston Gazette, 06-10-1776.

Ran away from Joshua Somers in this town, a Negro Boy, belonging to James Mugford of Marblehead, named Jack ; about fifteen years of age, walks a little knock kneed : Had on when he went away, a crow colour'd cloth coat, with red cuffs, striped shirt, white Jacket, red breeches with stockings & shoes. — Whoever will take up said negro, or give information so that the subscriber may have him again, shall have TWO DOLLARS reward and all necessary charges paid by JAMES MUGFORD.

N.B. All Persons are forbid entertaining or carrying off said negro, he says he is free, that his father and mother is dead.

Reprints: Boston Gazette, 06-17-1776; 06-24-1776; 11-04-1776; 11-11-1776; 11-18-1776.

Boston Gazette, 07-01-1776.

RUN away from me the Subscriber upon the eighteenth instant June, a Negro Man named CAESAR, about fifty Years of Age, five foot seven inches high, took away with him a short blue Coat with yellow Buttons, a cotton and linen Waistcoat yellow & white stript one blue do, a pair of black serge Breeches, and red snug Surtout, two wolloen Shirts, a Beaver hat, and Wig: - One that speaks English Tongue well, also Reads and Writes ; Whoever shall take up said Runaway and return him to the Subscriber shall have SIX DOLLARS Reward and all necessary charges paid. WILLIAM WALKER. Worchester, June 18, 1776.

Boston Gazette, 08-05-1776.

TEN DOLLARS REWARD.

Ran away the first instant, a Negro man named SAMSON, and stole betwixt fifty and sixty pounds in Continental and other bills. He had on when we went away, a blue coat & scarlet jacket, and white linnen breeches, and stockings, and a new fashion cock'd hat ; he is about five feet eight inches high, speaks good English, and is sprightly and active ; when he speaks he has a learing under look with his eyes. Whoever will apprehend said Negro, and return him to Simon Elliot of Boston, or secure him in any of the State Goals, and send word to his Master, shall have TEN DOLLARS reward, and all necessary charges paid by said Elliot. Boston, August 5, 1776.

Reprints: Boston Gazette, 08-12-1776; 08-19-1776.

Boston Gazette, 08-19-1776.

Ran away from the Subscriber the 13th Instant, a Negro Man, named Constant, about 5 Feet 10 Inches high, about 25 Years of Age : He had on when he went away, a Tow cloth Shirt and long Trowsers, a Pair of old Shoes, and plated Buckles : He carried with him a blue broad Cloth Coat with red cuffs and cape, and Brass Buttons, and the Button holes work'd with red, and dark brown Cloath Jacket and Breeches, a red Cloth Jacket, a light colour'd Sturton, a white Shirt, a pair of Silver Shoe Buckles mark'd C.I. and a Violin. Whoever will take up said Negro, and convey him to his Master in Boston, shall have FIVE DOLLARS and all necessary Charges paid by me the Subscriber: JAMES IVERS.

All Masters of Vessels and others are cautioned against harbouring, concealing, or carrying off said Negro, as they would avoid the Penalty of the Law. N.B. He was seen in Walham last Wednesday. Boston, August 15, 1776.

Reprints: Boston Gazette, 08-26-1776; 09-02-1776.

Boston Gazette, 09-02-1776.

Ran away on the 8th of July last, from his Master in Boston, a Negro Man named POMPEY. He had on when he went away, a fashionable new cock'd Beaver Hat, a blue Whitney half lapell'd on blue Jacket, with white Metal Buttons, and a tasty slash Pocket, a blue & white striped under Waistcoat, white Leather Breeches, with blue yarn Stockings, and Brass Buckles in his

Shoes. He is about 24 Years old, stout and strong made, his natural Colour quite Black but when challeng'd and he going to Lie, his Eyes will twinkle, and his Face change Colour. 'Tis apprehended he is at Work, or lurking about in the same of the Country Towns. Whoever will bring said Negro to the Printer, that his Master may have him again, shall receive Three Dollars and all reasonable Charges paid.

Reprints: Boston Gazette, 09-09-1776; 09-16-1776.

Boston Gazette, 09-16-1776.

About the first of August Ran away from me the subscriber, a negro man named Newport, about 5 feet 5 inches high, speaks good English, had on a brown homespun round tail jacket, tow shirt, tow long trowsers and a pair of Mooseskin Breeches. Said Negro is scar'd in his temple, which was done in Guinea ; he had a felt hat on. All officers of privateers are forbid inlisting said Negro and all other officers of the United States are forbid inlisting said Negro ; he is about 34 years of age. Whoever will take up said Negro, and convey him to me, or confine him in any of the State goals, so that I may have him again, shall have FIVE DOLLARS reward and all necessary charges paid by me. TILLEY HIGGINS.

Reprint: Boston Gazette, 09-16-1776.

Boston Gazette, 04-21-1777.

This day Ran away from John Tyng, Esq; a negro man servant named Boston, about 26 years old, about 5 feet 6 inches high; had on when he Ran away, a brown homespun jacket, leather breeches, and yarn stockings. Whoever shall take up said Negro, and return him to his master at Dunstable, shall have eight DOLLARS reward, paid by JOHN TYNG

Dunstable, April 14, 1777.

The Massachusetts Spy, 04-24-1777.

Ran away from me the Subscriber on the 9th day of April, a Negro Man, who calls himself Harry, but his right name is London, is about four feet, 5 inches high, has on when he went away a cloth coloured jacket. C[?ret coloured] waistcoat and mooseskin Breeches: He st[ole] before he went off, a fine castor hat, a fine linen, and a Wollen shirt a st[blurred text] ring set in Gold, and a pair of Silver sleeve buttons. Whoever takes up said Negro and will Convey him to the Subscriber in Oakham shall have all Charge paid. JAMES AMES.

Boston News-Letter, 02-22-1770.

Ran-away from the Subscriber, about ten Months ago, a large Negro Man, named Joseph Coffee, aged 37 Years, — he has lost both of his great Toes : He had with him a small Indian Squaw. Whoever will take up said Negro and commit him to any of his Majesty's Goals, so as the Owner can have him again, they shall have TEN DOLLARS, as a Reward, and all other necessary Charges paid. Harwich, Febr. 7, 1770. THEOPHILUS HOPKINS.
Reprint: Boston News-Letter, 03-01-1770.

Boston News-Letter, 06-14-1770.

Ran-away from her Master the 3d Instant, a Negro Girl, named Violet, Eighteen Years of Age, about five Feet three Inches in Height; had on at the time of her going away, a dark strip'd Homespun Jacket and a Quilted Petticoat: — Whoever will convey her to the Subscriber, shall be well Rewarded. RICHARD JENNYS.
All Masters of Vessels and others, are hereby caution'd against concealing, or carrying off said Negro, as they would avoid being Prosecuted. Boston, June 6th, 1770.

Boston News-Letter, 06-28-1770.

TWO DOLLARS Reward.
Ran-away from the Subscriber on the Sixteenth Instant, a Negro Man named Caesar, about 25 Years of age ; had on when he went away, a blue cloth Coat with Brass Buttons, leather Breeches, and a strip'd cotton and linnen Shirt, he also took with him a light cloth Coat, and a pair of long oznabrigs Trowsers ; — He is small and very Talkative, and has a Number of Scars on his Cheeks : — Any Person taking and securing the said Negro, and giving Notice shall Receive the above Reward. WILLIAM HOMES.
All Masters of Vessels and others are hereby cautioned against harbouring, concealing, or carrying off said Negro, as they would avoid the Penalty of the Law.
Reprints: Boston News-Letter, 07-05-1770; 07-12-1770.

Boston News-Letter, 07-26-1770.

Ran-away from his Master, Capt Daniel Hoar, of Westminster; a Negro Fellow named Jack, about 22 Years of Age, walks very upright, is about six Feet high, very black, had with him three suits of Cloaths, a fiddle and some other Articles: - Whosoever shall take up said Negro and convey him to his Master, shall have THREE DOLLARS Reward and all necessary Charges paid by DANIEL HOAR. Westminster, July 23d, 1770.

N.B. All Persons whomever, are hereby forbid harbouring, concealing, or carrying off said Servant as they will be prosecuted as far as Law will allow.

Reprints: Boston News-Letter, 08-02-1770; 08-16-1770.

Boston News-Letter, 08-16-1770.

Ran away from the Subscribers in Plainfield, in Connecticut, the Evening after the 8th Inst, two Negro Men, one named Boston, about 30 Years old, a thin well set Fellow, of a middling Stature, very black, carried with him one check'd linen Shirt, one streaked ditto, one old fine Holland ditto, one Pair Leather Breeches, one Pair streaked long Breeches, 4 Pair stockings of divers Colours, one old beaver Hat, velvet Waistcoat, snuff colour'd horn Buttons, one other ditto, something worn, strait body'd Coat, brownish, a new Great Coat, brownish Colour, trim'd with flour'd Metal Buttons.

The other named Newport, a well-set Fellow, not quite so tall as the Former, and about 24 Years old, red Broadcloth Waistcoat, crimson trim'd, Lincey woolcey strip'd ditto, 2 strip'd tow Shirts, Frock and Trowsers, 1 Pair Cotton Stockings seem'd, Pair mix'd seem'd ditto, 2 Pair Shoes, a good Felt Hat, two Silk Handkerchiefs. Whoever will take up said Fellows, and secure them in any of his Majesty's Goals, so that we can receive said Negroes, shall have a Reward of SIX DOLLARS, and all necessary Charges paid by us, ISSAC COLT, ROBERT KINSMAN.

N.B. It is suspected said Negroes have got a forg'd Pass. Plainfield, August 10, 1770.

Reprint: Boston News-Letter, 08-23-1770; 08-30-1770. This notice was also printed in the Connecticut Courant, 08-27-1770.

Boston News-Letter, 09-06-1770.

Taken up by Henry Stone of Stoughton on Thursday last, a NEGRO MAN, calls himself Jeffry, and says he belongs to Mr. John Reed, jun. of Freetown; an Account has been sent thither, but no Answer returned; it is therefore suspected he belongs to some other Person : He is a well-set Fellow about 22 Years of Age, had on a mill'd Cap without a Rim, a pair of long striped Trowsers, thick Moggasins, no Stockings, a cloth cloured home made Jacket.

Whoever owns said Negro are desired to send for him to said Stone, where they may have him, paying the Charges. Sept 4. Henry Stone.

Reprint: Boston News-Letter, 09-13-1770; 09-20-1770.

Boston News-Letter, 09-27-1770.

Ran away from the Subscriber, on the 17th Inst, at Night, a Negro Man named Jack, about 6 Feet high, near 50 Years of Age, speaks bad English, and born in Martinico; had on when he went away, a blue Coat with Mohair

Buttons, a black Jacket with black Glass Buttons, blue Breeches with white metal Buttons, and a red Worsted Cap, but may have changed his Cloaths, as he had more at Beverly. — Whoever shall take up said Negro, and deliver him to Mr. Brown, Deputy-Sheriff, in Salem, shall have Two Dollars Reward, and all necessary Charges paid them.

All Masters of Vessels, and others are cautioned against carrying said Negro off, as they would avoid the Penalty of the Law. JOSEPH HOMAN.

Reprint: Boston News-Letter, 10-04-1770; 10-18-1770.

Boston News-Letter, 2-28-1771.

Ran-away from Thomas Dick of Pelham, in the County of Hampshire on the 21st Day of February 1771, a Molatto Servant, named Samuel Simons, about 19 Years of Age, strait limb'd bushy black Hair ; Had on a mix'd coloured, called Pepper and Salt, Coat bound with green Binding, a Felt Hatt with white Loops, a Flannel Jacket, Leather Breeches, Yarn Stockings, and a Pair of Pumps: He took with him a Gun, Pistol, Flute, and a considerable of Money. Whoever shall take up said Run-away and secure him or bring him to the Subscriber, shall have THREE DOLLARS Reward and all necessary Charges paid. THOMAS DICK. Pelham, February 25, 1771.

All Masters of Vessels and others, are hereby cautioned against harbouring, concealing, or carrying off said Servant, as they would avoid the Penalty of the Law.

Reprints: Boston News-Letter, 03-07-1771; 03-14-1771.

Boston News-Letter, 03-28-1771.

Two Runaways.

Ran-away from Job Clap of Scituate, the 21st of March, a Molatto Fellow named Abraham, about 5 Feet and ten Inches high, aged 26 Years, thick and well-set, with a small Scar in the Corner of his Forehead, good set of Teeth, wears his own Hair: Had on when we went away, a brown homespun Coat lined with the same colour, white metal Buttons, a blue short Jacket, lined with striped Woolen, old Leather Breeches, a Pair of new long striped Linen Trowsers, and took with him a new homespun brown lappel Coat and Breeches lined with the same colour, and brass Buttons, the Collar lined with red Quality, black Calamanco Jacket, and a homespun Great Coat with metal Buttons, and divers Pair of Stockings, striped Woolen Shirt and a white linnen ditto.

Reprints: Boston News-Letter, 04-04-1771; 04-11-1771.

Boston News-Letter, 03-28-1771.

Ran-away the same Day from Benjamin Jacob of Scituate, a Negro Man, named Prince, about 26 Years of Age, not very black, tall and slim, wears his Hair, had a Beaver Hat, buff Cap, a new brown lappel Coat, an old brown Great-Coat, three Shirts, two white Woolen, one Linnen ditto, three Pair of Breeches, blue and brown.

Whoever shall take up said Servants and bring them to their above Masters, or to Mr. Olis Goalkeeper in Boston, shall have THREE DOLLARS Reward for each, and all necessary Charges Paid.

N.B. All Masters of Vessels and others are hereby cautioned against harbouring, concealing, or carrying off either of said Servants, as they would avoid the Penalty of the Law.

Reprints: Boston News-Letter, 04-04-1771; 04-11-1771.

Boston News-Letter, 4-11-1771.

Ran-away from his Master John Sober, Esq; on Monday the 8th of April Inst. A Negro Man Servant, named Cato, formerly owned by Mr. William Cooper of Boston, and well known by the Name of Mrs. Betty Cooper ; — Whoever takes up said Negro, and will bring him to the Subscriber shall have TWELVE DOLLARS Reward, and all necessary Charges paid. Boston April 12, 1771. JOHN SOBER.

Boston News-Letter, 05-30-1771.

Ran-away in the Night of the 19th of May, from the Subscriber living in Dunstable, a Negro Man, named Leath, about 22 Years of Age, 5 Feet 7 Inches high: he is of a very modest Look. – Had on when he went away, a blue Coat with yellow Brass Buttons, black Jacket and Breeches. Whoever apprehends said Negro, and returns him to the Subscriber (or to Mrs. Martin on Jamaica Plains to whom he belongs) shall have SIX DOLLARS Reward, and all necessary Charges paid by Archibald Robertson.

Reprint: Boston News-Letter, 05-30-1771; 06-05-1771.

Boston News-Letter, 07-16-1772.

Ran away from the Sloop Lois, John Alden, Master, on Monday last, a Negro Fellow named Cudjoe, about 25 Years old, branded upon each Cheek, lately from the West Indies, and speaks pretty good English, middle Size having very small Legs: Had on when he went away, a green frize double-breasted Jacket, a Pair of striped Woolen Trowsers, Oznabrig's Shirt, a blue and white

Kilmarnock Cap. Whoever takes up said Servant and will convey him to Mr. George Minot, on the T. shall have THREE DOLLARS Reward, and all necessary Charges paid. JOHN ALDEN. Boston, May 15, 1772.

All Masters of Vessels and others are cautioned against harbouring or carrying off said Servant as they would avoid the Penalty of the Law.

Reprints: Boston News-Letter, 07-23-1772; 07-30-1772.

Boston News-Letter, 08-13-1772.

Ran-away from Capt. Richard Walker, on the 27th of last Month, a Negro Man, about 40 Years of Age, named Imanuel: He had on a green Jacket, and carried with him a striped Jacket, three Shirts, a Saw and an Ax. Whoever shall take up said Negro and convey him to his said Master at the North End of Boston, shall have TWO DOLLARS Reward, and all necessary Charges paid by, RICHARD WALKER. Boston, Aug. 12, 1772.

Reprints: Boston News-Letter, 08-20-1772; 08-27-1772.

Boston News-Letter, 11-19-1772.

Ran-away from the Subscriber on the 15th Instant, a Negro Fellow named Sarvis, about 5 Feet 10 Inches high, a stout Fellow, much marked with the Small-Pox; had on when he went away, a light colour'd double-breasted Jacket, a brown Waistcoat, and a pair of Velvet Breeches, and carried away with him, one pair of white Breeches, one blue Coat, and two white Shirts : Whoever takes up the said Run-away, and conveys him to his Master shall have TWENTY DOLLARS Reward, and all necessary Charges paid by WM. McNeill.

All Masters of Vessels and others are hereby cautioned against carrying off or harbouring said Negro, as they would avoid the Penalty of the Law.

Reprint: Boston News-Letter, 12-04-1772; 12-10-1772.

The Boston News-Letter, 12-17-1772.

Broke out of his Majesty's Goal in Boston, the last Night, the following Prisoners,

Robert Anderson, an Irishman, with short black Hair, about five Feet five Inches high, walks lame with his right Leg, poorly cloathed, was charg'd with Robbery.

Thomas Williams, an Irishman, five Feet four Inches high, wore a Cap, his outside jacket made of an old striped Blanket, had no Shoes or Stockings, charged with Theft.

John Hopkins, an Irishman, had long black Hair, was about five Feet four Inches high, had on a blue Coat, was charged with Theft.

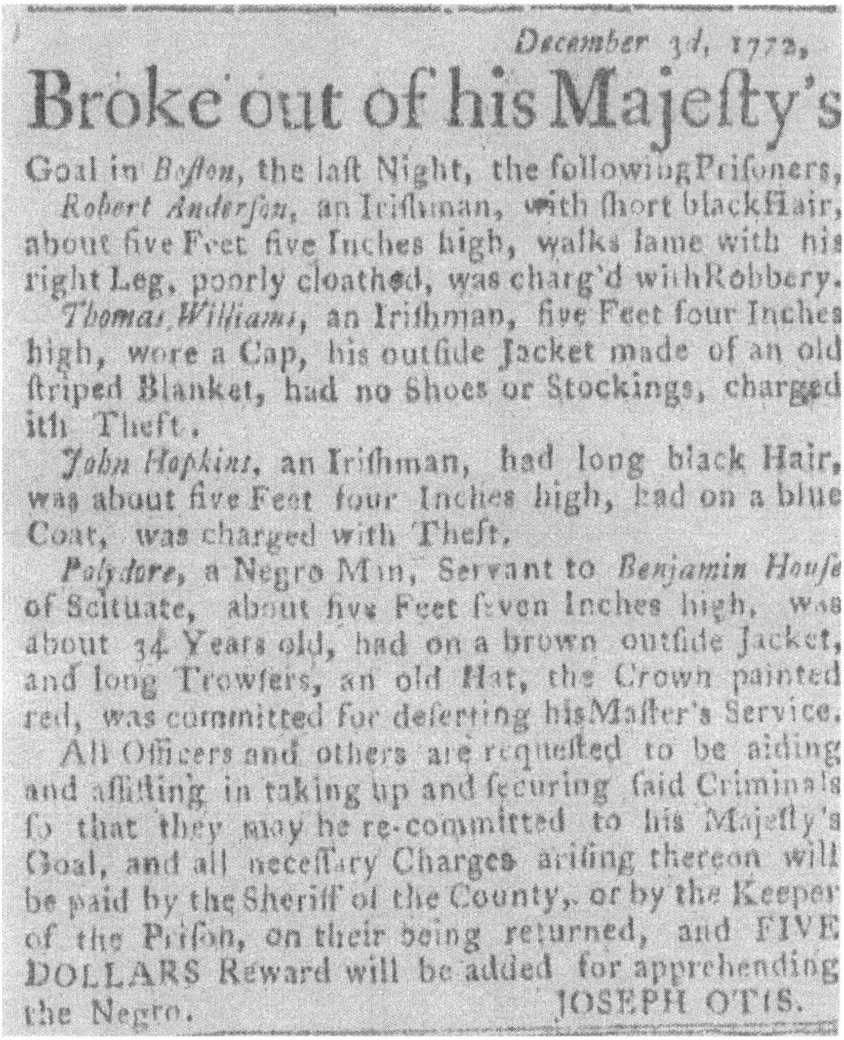

Figure 1.2.   Polydore, Boston News Letter, December 17, 1772.

Polydore, a Negro Man, Servant to Benjamin House of Scituate, about five Feet seven Inches high, was about 34 Years old, had on a brown outside Jacket, and long Trowsers, an old Hat, the Crown painted red, was committed for deserting his Master's Service.

All Officers and others are requested to be aiding and assisting in taking up and securing said Criminals so that they may be re-committed to his Majesty's Goal, and all necessary Charges arising thereon will be paid by the Sheriff of the County, or by the Keeper of the Prison, on their being returned, and FIVE DOLLARS Reward will be added for apprehending the Negro.

JOSEPH OTIS.

Boston News-Letter, 04-22-1773.

Ran-away from his Master, John Caldwell, of Rutlant District, in the County of Worchester, Esq; a Mulatto Fellow, named Harry, Part Indian and Part Negro, aged about 23 Years, speaks good English, a straight limbed well-set Fellow, about five Feet ten Inches high, his Hair pretty long and curl'd but cut short on the fore Part of his Head: Had on when we went away, one large Jacket and one small Jacket, all Wool, a lightish Colour, and yellow Buttons, a Pair of old Shoes, a Castor Hat almost new, a Pair of old cloth Breeches near the same Colour of his Jackets, a Pair of Stockings a little darker than his Jackets, a striped all wool Shirt. – Whoever take up said Servant and conveys him to his said Masters or confines him in any of his Majesty's Goals, so that his said Master may have him again shall be handsomely Rewarded for their Trouble, and all necessary Charges paid by his said Master.

N.B. All Masters of Vessels and others are hereby cautioned against harbouring, concealing, or carrying off said Servant, as they would avoid the Penalty of the Law. April 6th, 1773.

Reprints: Essex Gazette, 04-13 to 04-20-1773; 04-20 to 04-27-1773; 04-27 to 05-04-1773.

Boston News-Letter, 07-08-1773.

Ran-away Yesterday Afternoon, a Negro Boy about 15 Years old, a stout well set Fellow, had on an old dark brown Jacket without Sleeves, a white Shirt torn in both Shoulders, a good Pair of brown Broad-Cloth Breeches, was bare-footed, his Wool cut close to his Head. — He may be gone towards Concord, from whence he was lately brought into Boston, if not gone off in some Vessel. — Whoever will bring Intelligence to the Printer, concerting said Boy, called Dick, shall be rewarded therefore.

Boston News-Letter, 08-12-1773.

Four Dollars Reward.

Ran-AWAY from the Subscriber, at Skenesborough, on Sunday the 11th Instant, a Spanish Negro Man named NED; he is about Six Feet high, of a Robust make and dark Olive Complexion; his Breast and Body scarified after the Manager of his Country: He travels with a false Pass signed James McCoy, Captain in one of his Majesty's Regiments: Has a large Pack, with a red Jacket and long Trowsers and a blanket Coat, talks broken English. It is conjectured that he will attempt to get to the Sea Coast, therefore, all Masters of Vessels are forbid to carry him off, or any other Person to harbor him at their Peril.

Whoever will apprehend and secure the said Negro so that the Owner may have him again, shall receive FOUR DOLLARS Reward, and all reasonable Expences paid by ANDREW P. SKENE.

Skenesborough, July 14, 1773.

N.B. If the said Servant is taken up near Boston, they may apply to GERSHAM BEECH, at Mr. Moore's at the Sign of the Lamb. Boston.

Boston News-Letter, 05-05-1774.

Ran-away from the Subscriber, on the 18th Instant, a Negro Man named David, about 6 Feet high, goes a little Lame, had on when he went away, a grey Cloth Coat and Jacket, Deer-Skin Breeches, and grey Hose, a Pair of Silver Buckles in his Shoes.

Whoever takes up said Servant, and secures him so that his Master may have him again, shall have ONE GUINEA Reward, per JOSIAH STARR. Weston, April 20th, 1774.

Boston News-Letter, 10-06-1774.

Ran-away from Joshua Barker of Hingham, a Negro Man, named Champain, about 35 Years old, a slim, handsome made Fellow, about 5 Feet, eight Inches high, one of his Ears bored for a Jewell, and the Hole broke out, he speaks good French. He carried with him, a scarlet Cloth Coat, turned up with Yellow, a blue Cloth Coat, Silver laced Hat, Buff Leather Breeches, with Sundry other kind of Cloathing. Whoever will take up said Negro, and bring him to his Master, at Hingham – or secure him so that his Master may have him again, shall be handsomely rewarded for their Trouble, and Charges by JOSHUA BARKER.

Reprints: Boston News-Letter, 10-13-1774; 11-03-1774.

Boston News-Letter, 11-03-1774.

SIX DOLLARS REWARD.

Ran-away from the Subscriber last Night, a Negro Man, an indented Servant for six Years, named Pomp, a well made Fellow, (about 25 Years of Age) of middling stature, lively and active, speaks quick and something broken English, can talk a little Dutch, has lost the upper part of his left

SIX DOLLARS REWARD.

RAN away from the fubfcriber, laft night, a Negro man, an indented fervant for 6 years, named POMP, a well made fellow, of middling ftature, lively and active, about twenty-five years old, fpeaks quick, and fomething broken Englifh, can talk fome Dutch, has loft the upper joint of his left thumb, the nail turns down partly over the end of the fame ; carried away with him a home made mix-colöured blue and red coat, lined with blue fhalloon, trimmed with yellow metal buttons, cloth-coloured duroy jacket and breeches, two pair of leather-breeches, a new felt-hat laced with yellow tinfel, old ditto not laced, a white fhirt, and ftriped ditto, checked linen trowfers, cloth coloured great coat, much worn, a pair of turn'd pumps, and double foled fhoes, filver-plated fhoe buckles, and fundry pair of ftockings :——Whoever will take up faid Negro, and bring him to his mafter, or fecure him, and give notice thereof to his mafter, fhall have the above reward, and all neceffary charges, paid by the fubfciber. All mafters of veffels, and others, are forbid carrying off, or harbouring, faid Negro, at their peril.

SAMUEL BROWN, jun.

Stockbridge, Oct 9, 1774.

Figure 1.3.   Pomp, Boston News Letter, November 3, 1774.

Thumb, the Nail turns down partly of the End of the same; carried away with him, a Home made coloured red and blue Coat, lined with blue Shalloon, and trim'd with yellow Metal Buttons, cloth colour'd Duroy Jacket and Breeches, two pair Leather Breeches, one old and dirty, the other new Buff colour'd, were made at Philadelphia; a new felt Hat laced with yellow Tinsel, old ditto not laced, white Shirt and strip'd ditto, Check linnen Trowsers, cloth colour'd Great Coat much wore, turn'd Pumps and double soled Shoes, silver plated Shoe Buckles and Sundry Pair of Stockings. — Whoever will take up said Negro and bring him to his Master, or secure him and give Notice, to his Master, so that he can have him, shall have the above Reward, and all necessary Charges paid by the Subscriber.

All Masters of Vessels and others are forbid carrying off, or harbouring said Negro at their Peril.

Stockbridge, Oct. 9, 1774. SAMUEL BROWN, jun.

Reprints: Boston News-Letter, 11-17-1774; 12-08-1774. This notice was also printed in the Connecticut Courant, 09-15-1772 to 09-22-1772; 09-22-1772 to 09-29-1772; and in the Newport Mercury, 10-31-1774.

Continental Journal, 06-26-1777.

TEN DOLLARS REWARD.

RANWAY from me the subscriber on Saturday, the 31st of May last, a NEGRO MAN named ROBIN, about 23 years of age, and about 5 feet 10 inches high, pretty stout, and well made, had a wh[itish] spot on his forehead between his eye-brow, speaks good English; had on when he went away a claret coloured coat and jacket, coat with red lappels and cuffs, and flowered pewter buttons, leather breeches, white linnen shirt, and white tow stockings, a new felt hat, and new calf skin shoes.—Whoever shall take up said NE-GRO and convey him to me at Brookfield, or confine him in any of the goals in these States, and give me notice, so that I may have him again, shall receive TEN DOLLARS REWARD, and all necessary charges paid. And all masters of vessels and others are hereby forbid to harbour, conceal or carry off said NEGRO, as they would avoid the penalty of the law.

Brookfield, June 3, 1777. Phineas Upham.

Continental Journal, 08-20-1778.

TWENTY DOLLARS REWARD.

Ran away from his Master a Negro Man about thirty Years of Age, a likely strait limb'd Fellow, about 5 Feet 6 or 8 inches high. Had on when he went away a strip'd home-spun Jacket, and a Pair of strip'd Overalls, and carried with him a variety of other Clothing.—Twenty Dollars and all necessary Charges shall be paid to any Person who shall take up said Negro and bring him to his Master.

Boston, Aug. 6. SAMUEL WHITWELL.

N.B. All masters of Vessels and others, are forbid concealing or carrying off said Negro as they would avoid the Penalties of the Law.

Continental Journal, 11-27-1778.

Ran-away from the subscriber last Sabbath-day morning, a Negro Fellow named CATO, about 25 years of age, about 6 feet high—had on when he went away a hair cap, a short blue coat, with blue horn buttons, and lin'd with red baize, a pair of long cloth coloured duffled trowsers—he carried off a black hair knapsack, part of the hair wore off. Whoever shall take up said Negro and bring him to subscriber, shall have THIRTY DOLLARS reward, and all necessary charges paid by EDWARD CARNES.

Boston, November 25, 1778.

Essex Gazette, Tuesday, August 7, to Tuesday, August 14, 1770.

Ran away from the Subscriber, on the 5th Inst, a Negro Man named Phero, of a very light Complection, something scar'd in the Face, and 5½ Feet in Height, and 18 Years of Age, remarkable for the Fingers of his Right Hand (more especially his Thumb) being crooked; carried off with him a red broadcloth Jacket and Breeches, and a Pair of Pepper and Salt homespun ditto, with sundry other Things.—Whoever will return or secure said Runaway, shall have Four Dollars Reward, and all Charges paid.

SAMUEL DEVEREUX.

N.B. All Masters of Vessels and others are hereby cautioned against concealing or carrying off said Runaway, as they would avoid the Penalty of the Law.

Marblehead, August 6, 1770.

Reprints: Essay Gazette, 08-14 to 08-21, 1770; 10-20 to 10-27-1772; 10-27 to 11-09-1772.

Essex Gazette, Tuesday, September 18, to Tuesday, September 25, 1770.

Runaway from the Subscriber, on the 17th Inst. at Night, a Negro Man, named Jack, about 6 Feet high, near 50 Years of Age, speaks bad English, and born in Martinico; had on when he went away, a blue Coat with Mohair Buttons, a black Jacket with black Glass Buttons, blue Breeches with white metal Buttons, and a red worsted Cap, but may have changed his Cloaths, as he had more at Beverly. – Whoever shall take up said Negro, and deliver him to Mr. Brown, Deputy-Sheriff, in Salem, shall have Two Dollars Reward, and all necessary Charges paid them.

All Masters of Vessels, and others, are cautioned against carrying off said Negro, as they would avoid the Penalty of the Law. JOSEPH HOMAN. Marblehead, Sept. 22, 1770.

Reprints: Essay Gazette, 09-25 to 10-02-1770; 10-02 to 10-09-1770.

Essex Gazette, Tuesday, October 9, to Tuesday, October 16, 1770.

It is thought that a Negro named POMPEY, but commonly called Pomp, has taken Mr. Turner's Horse, advertised above, with a double Bridle, a Saddle and a green Cloth Housing with a green Fringe, all about half worn, and Brass Stirrups. Said Negro belongs to me the Subscriber, and was formerly

Capt. Kent's and Mr. David Waitt's, both of Charlestown, where he was born. Said Negro is about 23 Years old, hath a Scar on his Forehead, and had on a dark cloth Coat that had been turn'd, a cotton and linen mix'd coloured Jacket, and a Pair of black worsted Breeches, much wore and tore. Whoever shall take up said Negro, and bring him to said Waitt in Salem, shall have TWO DOLLARS Reward, and all Charges paid them by AARON WAITT.

Reprints: Essay Gazette, 10-16 to 10-23-1770; 10-23 to 10-30-1770; 10-30 to 11-06-1770.

Essex Gazette, Tuesday, May 14, to Tuesday, May 21, 1771.

Ran away from Subscriber, on the 4th of May, Negro Man named Cato, of a middling Stature, has loft the Sight of his left Eye, had on a kersey Jacket and leather Breeches. Whoever shall take up said Negro, and bring him to his Master in Salem, shall have Two Dollars Reward, and all Charges paid by William Hunt.

Reprints: Essay Gazette, 05-14 to 05-21-1771; 05-21 to 05-28-1771.

Essex Gazette, Tuesday, November 5, to Tuesday, November 12, 1771.

RUN-away from the Subscriber, about 15 Days ago, a Negro Boy, of the yellow Sort, about 16 Years old; had on a blue half-thick Jacket, homespun Waistcoat & Breeches, and a lopp'd Hatt; speaks bad English. — Whoever takes up said Runaway, so that his Master may have him again, shall have THREE DOLLARS Reward. WILLIAM BODEN. Marblehead, November 11, 1771.

Essex Gazette, Tuesday, February 4, to Tuesday, February 11, 1772.

RUN away from Christopher Bubier, last Monday, a Negro Man named Prince; had on a white cotton Shirt; gray Stockings; striped homespun Jacket lined with Baize, and Breeches of the same; light-coloured great Jacket, lined with Baize, much wore, and mill Cap. Whoever may take up said Negro and deliver him to Mr. Brown, D. Sheriff, in Salem, shall have Two Dollars Reward, and all necessary Charges paid by CHRISTOPHER BUBIER. Marblehead, Feb 3, 1772.

Reprints: Essay Gazette, 02-04 to 02-11-1772; 02-11 to 02-18-1772.

Essex Gazette, Tuesday, June 9, to Tuesday, June 16, 1772.

A Negro Man, named Prince, Ran away the 29th of last Month, from his Master, JOHN HIGGINS of Berwick: He is a well set Fellow, about 25 Years of Age, has a Scar in his Forehead over his left Eye: Had on a Kersey round tail'd Jacket of a dark Colour, a Woolen Under Jacket, and Moose

Skin Breeches. — Whoever takes up said Fellow and conveys him to his Master, or commits him to Goal, shall have Four Dollars Reward, and necessary Charges paid by me JOHN HIGGINS.

Reprint: Essay Gazette, 06-09 to 06-16-1772.

Essex Gazette, Tuesday, June 23, to Tuesday, June 30, 1772.

RUN away from Mark Haskall, of Ipswich, last Saturday se'nnight, a Negro Man named Cato, 22 Years old, middling Stature, thick sett, plays upon a Violin, has some White Spots on his Shins. Whoever apprehends said Negro, and will confine him, or convey him to the said Mark Haskall, in Ipswich, shall have Three Dollars Reward, and all necessary Charges paid.

N.B. All Masters of Vessels and others are hereby cautioned against concealing or carrying off said Negro, as they would avoid the Penalty of the Law.

Reprints: Essex Gazette, 06-30 to 07-07-1772; 07-07 to 07-14-1772.

Essex Gazette, Tuesday, May 25, to Tuesday, June 1, 1773.

RUN-away from John Hodges, last Wednesday, a Negro Boy named Scip, about 20 Years old; had on when he went away, a ragged Jacket, a Speckled Shirt, velvit Breeches, white Stockings, and a small Hat, the Brim about 2 Inches wide. Whoever takes up said Negro, so that the Owner may have him again, shall have all necessary Charges paid. Salem, May 31, 1773.

Reprints: Essay Gazette, 06-01 to 06-08-1773.

Essex Gazette, Tuesday, January 18, to Tuesday, January 25, 1774.

RUN away from William Stinson of Dunbarton, in New-Hampshire, a Negro Man, named Jack, about 40 Years of Age, 5 Feet 6 Inches high; had on a dark mixed, homespun Coat, with Striped Lining; a striped homespun Jacket, washed Leather Breeches, and a Beaver Hat. Whoever will take up said Negro, and confine him in any of his Majesty's Goals, or convey him to Mr. Darius Abbot of Andover, in the Massachusetts Government, so that his Master may have him again, shall have TEN DOLLARS Reward, and all necessary Charges paid, by WILLIAM STINSON.

Reprints: Essay Gazette, 01-25 to 02-01-1774; 02-01 to 02-08-1774.

Essex Gazette, Tuesday, March 1, to Tuesday, March 8, 1774.

RUN away from the Subscriber, last Saturday, a Negro Man named Obed, about 25 Years old, somewhat tall, his Skin very black, his Nose more in the shape of a white Person's than a Negro's; he was born at Cohasset in this Province: It's uncertain what Cloathes he had on, as he carried a considerable

Quantity with him, among which were a red Coat with brass Buttons, green Jacket and Breeches, with white Buttons. Whoever will take him up and secure him, or return him to his Master, shall have Three Dollars Reward, and all necessary Charges paid. RICHARD DERBY. Salem, Feb 25. 1774.
Reprint: Essay Gazette, 03-08 to 03-15-1774.

Essex Gazette, Tuesday, September 13, to Tuesday, September 20, 1774.

Four Dollars Reward.

RUN away from his Master, Issac Pool, of Gloucester, in the County of Essex, a Negro Servant named Anthony; had on when he went away a green, lapell'd, outside Waistcoat; a Calico under Waistcoat, Leather Breeches and Worsted Stockings; he is about five Feet high, a lively Eye, one of his upper fore Teeth gone; a well-set, smart Fellow, about 22 Years of Age; plays on a Fife, which he carried with him. Whoever shall take up said Runaway, and secure him, so that his Master may have him again, shall have FOUR DOL-LARS Reward, and all necessary Charges paid, by ISSAC POOL.
N.B. All Masters of Vessels and others are forbid carrying him off, as they would avoid the Penalty of the Law. Gloucester, September 12th, 1774.
Reprints: Essay Gazette, 09-13 to 09-20-1774; 12-13 to 12-20-1774.

Essex Gazette, Tuesday, November 29, to Tuesday, December 6, 1774.

RUN away from the Subscriber on the 28th ult., a Negro Man named Lon-don, about 22 Years of Age, five Feet nine Inches high; had on when he went away, a brown colour'd all-wool Coat & Jacket, new Moose-skin Breeches, and blue yarn Stockings; his Ears were both froze last Winter; he has a large Scar on his right Shin; it is supposed he has a forged Pass with him. Whoever will take up and secure said Negro, so that I may have him again, shall have Eight Dollars Reward, and all necessary Charges paid. JOHN PATCH 3d.
All Masters of Vessels, and others are hereby cautioned against conceal-ing or carrying off said Negro, as they would avoid the Penalty of the Law. Ipswich, December 5, 1774.
Reprints: Essay Gazette, 12-06 to 12-13-1774; 12-13 to 12-20-1774.

Essex Gazette, Tuesday, March 14, to Tuesday, March 21, 1775.

RUN away from the Subscriber, a Negro Man about 28 Years of Age, has several Pits in his Face, about 5 Feet, 10 Inches in Height, a stout, well made Person, had on when he went away, a short blue double-breasted Waistcoat, and cotton velvit Breeches. Whoever will secure the said Runaway, and bring him home to his Mistress, shall be handsomely rewarded. ELIZABETH CA-BOT. Beverly, February 20, 1775.

Reprints: Essay Gazette, 03-14 to 03-21-1774; 03-21 to 03-28-1775.

Independent Ledger, 06-21-1779.

FIFTY DOLLARS REWARD.

Ran-away from the Subscriber, in the night of the 10th June, a Negro Man named POMP, about 20 years of age, talks good English, a scar under his eye: Had on a snuff colored short Coat, a pea green Jacket, white Breeches, or Trousers, with a Blanket, and other Cloaths. Whoever shall take up said Negro, and convey him to me in Boston, shall receive the above Reward.— All Masters of Vessels and others, are forbid to harbor or carry off said Negro, without giving me Notice, if they would avoid the Penalty of the Law. SAMUEL SELLON
Boston, June 14, 1779.

The Massachusetts Spy, 11-05-1772.

Ran away from his master, on Saturday last, a young NEGRO MAN, named NEWPORT, had on when he went away, a striped homespun jacket, shoes, but no stockings, a small sailor's hat bound with red. He is a likely, well-shaped Fellow, about five and a half feet high, one or both the calves of his legs full of scars, he is a new negro and can speak but little English. Whoever will apprehend said negro, and deliver him to the subscriber shall be well rewarded, and all necessary charges by B.M. HOMES.

N.B. All masters of vessels and others, are hereby cautioned against concealing or carrying of said negro, as they would avoid the penalty of the law. Boston, November 5, 1772.

The Massachusetts Spy, 02-24-1774.

Ran away last night from the Subscriber, a NEGRO LAD, about twenty years of age, about five feet and a half high, had on when we went away, an old blue great coat, a mixed coloured jacket, blue cloth breeches, a checked linen shirt, blue yarn stockings. Whoever will take up said NEGRO, and deliver him to the subscriber shall have TWO DOLLARS reward and all charges paid. JOHN ROBINSON.

Massachusetts Spy, 07-07-1774.

Run away from the subscriber on Monday last a NEGRO MAN, who goes by the name of Charles perril. He is small of stature, remarkable white skin for a negro, pitted with the small pox, about 27 years of age, and very talkative: Had on when he went away, an old hat, check shirt, a blue jacket, and long striped trowsers. Whoever takes up the said Negro, and will bring or send him to me, shall have Two Dollars reward, and all necessary charges paid. ISAIAH THOMAS.

Reprint: Massachusetts Spy, 06-15-1774.

The Massachusetts Spy, 10-27-1774.

Ran away from Newbury-Port, a Negro Man, named CHARLESTOWN, about five Feet six Inches high; had on a blue Jacket, and Dussel Breeches, Bilbog Cap, a very black Fellow, one of his Fingers made crooked and stiff by Means of a Fellon. Whoever secures him, so that I may have him again, shall have SIX DOLLARS Reward, and all necessary Charges paid. JOSEPH LEATHERS.

Reprints: Massachusetts Spy, 11-03-1774; 11-10-1774; 11-17-1774; 11-24-1774. This notice was also printed in the Essex Gazette, 10-18 to 10-25-1774; 10-25 to 11-01-1774; 11-01 to 11-08-1774.

Massachusetts Spy, 06-14-1775

Ran away the 7th of June from the Subscriber, a NEGRO MAN, named TOWER. He is about five feet seven inches high. Had on when he went away a patched blue coat and jacket, a pair of leather Breeches. Said Negro talks pretty slow, he has a little scar on one side of his cheek. Whoever will take up said Runaway shall be handsomely rewarded, and all reasonable charges paid by Capt. NATHANIEL READ, of Worcester.

Reprint: Massachusetts Spy, 06-21-1775.

Massachusetts Spy, 01-05-1776.

Ran away from the Subscriber, on the 11th of November last, a likely negro man, named Harry, about five feet ten inches high, speaks good English, wore away a lightish coloured broad cloth coat and veil, a good beaver hat, large pack, with an Indian wampam belt for a tumploin ; a wagon maker by trade, and can work very well at the carpenter's business; heard since he went away, that he has a red great coat, likewise he, as I hear, has a counterfeit pass. Whoever takes up said negro and returns him to me, living on the Mohawk River, Tryon-County, shall have ten dollars reward and all necessary charges paid by me, ABRAHAM HODGES.

N.B. Said Negro is about 30 years of age.

Reprints: Massachusetts Spy, 01-12-1776; 01-19-1776.

Massachusetts Spy, 11-26-1778.

Ran away from the subscriber the tenth of October, a negro man, named Prince, aged about twenty-four years. He is a short well-set fellow, has a large scar on the head in which no hair grows. Had on a brown home made coat and waistcoat, long trowsers and frock home-spun linen, stockings and shoes. Whoever will take up said fellow and return him to me, or secure him in any goal in the United States, and send me word, or the Printer hereof, shall have TWENTY DOLLARS reward, and all charges paid by LEVI ALLEN.

Duchess County, State of New-York. Oct. 31

New-England Chronicle, Thursday, June 22, to Thursday, June 29, 1775.

Run away from the subscriber, on the 18th of June, two Negro Men, one named Exeter, the other Ireland, and a Wench called Flora, with a small Child; one of the Negro Men is about six Feet high, the other five Feet and nine Inches, with each of them a Gun, and poorly cloathed. Whoever will take up said Negroes and secure them so that I may have them, or bring them to me, shall receive Twenty Dollars Reward, and all necessary Charges paid by me.

Willisbourge, on the west Side WILLIAM GILLILAND.

of the Lake Champlain 20 Miles to the Northward of Crown Point.

Reprint: New-England Chronicle, 06-29 to 07-06-1775.

New-England Chronicle, Thursday, June 29, to Thursday, July 6, 1775.

Ran away from me the Subscriber, on Sunday Night the 25th of June, a Negro Man named Scip, about 30 Years of Age, about six Feet high, well set, speaks good English; he hath two Scars on his Temple, between his Eye and his Ear: He carried away with him a large Pack, two Suits of Cloaths, one blue Chat lined with Red, one Coat of a brown colour, one calico lined Jacket, a black Jacket, one Pair of Mooseskin breeches, a Pair of black and white Breeches, besides a great Coat and other Jacket, Shirts and Trowsers, and a set hat. It is suspected he has a Pass.—whoever will take the said Negro and convey him to his Master, or commit him to Goal, so he may be returned to me, shall have Four Dollars Reward, and all necessary Charges paid by me, JOHN LUMMUS June 25, 1775.

Reprints: New-England Chronicle, 07-06 to 07-13-1775; 07-13 to 07-21-1775.

New-England Chronicle, Thursday, July 6, to Thursday, July 13, 1775.

Run away from me the subscriber, a Negro Man named Dolphin, about five Feet high; had on when he went away a black Jacket, a pair of dirty leather Breeches, blue Stockings, and Shoes without Buckles. Whoever will secure said Negro so that I may have him again, shall have five Dollars Reward. ISAAC BRADISH

Cambridge, July 11, 1770.

Reprints: New-England Chronicle, 07-13 to 07-21-1775; 07-21 to 07-27-1775.

New-England Chronicle, Thursday, July 13, to Friday, July 21, 1775.

Brookfield, July 13, 1775

Ran away from their Masters, this Day, three Men Servant: The one named Peter, who is thick-set Fellow, very black, and much bow-legged, 22 Years of Age, a good Fiddler, talke plain English.—Another named Abner, who stiles himself Abner Hybra, a Malatto, of a middle Size, about 5 Feet and half high, well built, walks clumsy, and turns his Toes out, talks good English (with Deliberation) has a small Blemish in one of his Eyes; had with him a good blue Coat of fine Drab Cloth, trimmed with plain hard-metal Buttons, a nankeen Jacket, and another summer Jacket striped with Red, one Pair of new cotton Stockings, and two Pair of woolen ditto, two Pair of Shoes, two fine Shirts; he is about thirty-six Years of Age.—The other named Cuff, a Negro Servant (a Fiddler) about 25 Years old, talks good English.—Whoever shall apprehend said Servant, and return them to the Subscribers at Brookfield, shall receive as a Reward for their Trouble and Expence the Sum of FIFTEEN DOLLARS, or Five Dollars for either or each of them so returned

PHINEAS UPHAM
FRANCIS FOXCROFT,
JABEZ UPHAM

Reprints: New-England Chronicle, 07-21 to 07-27-1775; 08-03 to 08-10-1775.

New-England Chronicle, Thursday, October 19, to Thursday, October 26, 1775.

TEN DOLLARS REWARD.

Ran away from the Subscriber, a Negro Man, named PETER LONG, about 25 Years of Age, talks good English, about six Feet high; had on when he went away a light-coloured homespun Coat, knit Jacket, and dark brown

Breeches. Whoever will take up said Negro, and confine him in any of his Majesty's Goals, so that his Master may have him again, shall have the above Reward, and all necessary Charges paid, by

Rye, Oct. 16 1775. MERIFIELD BERRY.

Reprint: New-England Chronicle, 11-02 to 11-09-1775.

New-England Chronicle, Thursday, November 16, to Thursday, November 23, 1775.

Ran away from me the Subscriber, 23d September last, a Negro man about 40 years of age, of a short stature, a yellowish black, very artful in his turn, took away with him a blue jacket and breeches, check shirt, and one white Holland ditto, a felt hat with large brime, and a great coat of a butternut colour, and a pair mixt colour'd yarn stockings. Whoever will secure him so that I may have said Negro again shall be handsomely rewarded, and all necessary charges paid by me,

New-Haven, 16th Nov. 1775. ESTHER MORRIS.

Reprints: New-England Chronicle, 11-16 to 11-24-1775; 12-14 to 12-21-1775; 12-21 to 12-28-1775.

New-England Chronicle, Thursday, November 30, to Thursday, December 7, 1775.

Ran from the Subscriber, the 23d of this Instant, a negro man named Cesar, about 22 years of age, 6 feet high, has two scars upon the back of his head, also several scars on his cheeks, talks English well, a very artful fellow, carried off a coat almost new, of a butternut colour, a Jacket of the same, sundry Jackets and breeches of various colours, sundry pair of stockings, among the rest a pair of cotton, almost new. All persons are cautioned against harbouring or concealing him. Any person that will return him, or secure him so that I may have him again, shall be handsomely rewarded by me the subscriber and all necessary charges paid by

SAMUEL GERRISH

Newbury, Nov. 24, 1774.

Reprints: New-England Chronicle, 12-07 to 12-14-1775; 12-14 to 12-21-1775; 12-21 to 12-28-1775.

New-England Chronicle, Thursday, December 7, to Thursday, December 14, 1775.

Ran away from his master, a negro man, named Briton, about twenty-seven years of age, a stocky, well built fellow, 5 feet 6 inches high, is cut in both his cheeks, from his temples as low as his chin, formerly lived with Rev. Dr.

Appleton in Cambridge; had on when he went away, a brown coat, with white buttons, buff leather breeches & green brize waistcoat. Whoever will secure said fellow so as he may be delivered to the subscriber, shall be handsomely rewarded & necessary charges paid.

Salem, 13th December JOSEPH VINCENT.

Reprints: New-England Chronicle, 12-14 to 12-21-1775; 12-21 to 12-28-1775.

New-England Chronicle, Thursday, December 14, to Thursday, December 21, 1775.

RUN away from the Bell tavern, the 3d instant, a negro man named Pomp, 28 years old, of a middling Stature, was born in Boston, speaks good English, can read tolerably well, carried away a green coat with metal buttons, a handsome hat, cut small, a durey coat, 2 kersey jackets lined with red baize, a black serge jacket, a lapel'd striped holland jacket, a sailor's white knotted jacket, a white holland shirt, a striped cotton and linen shirt, 2 check linen shirts, 2 woolen ditto, a pair of black knit breeches, 2 pair of shoes, a pair of silver shoe and knee buckles. Whoever will bring said negro to the Bell tavern in Danvers, or secure him so that he may be recovered, shall have four dollars reward and all necessary charges paid by me,

Danvers, Dec. 12

ELIZABETH SYMONDS.

'Tis tho't he carried away a piece of sprig'd stuff.

Reprints: New-England Chronicle, 12-14 to 12-21-1775; 12-21 to 12-28-1775.

New-England Chronicle, Thursday, January 11, to Thursday, January 18, 1776.

FIFTEEN DOLLAR Reward.

RUN AWAY from Col. Jonathan Moulton of Hampton in the colony of New Hampshire, in October last, a negro boy named Cato, about 18 years old, and about 5 feet and an half high, or something more; a more likely, strait limb'd, well built and active a boy is seldom to be seen, and plays well on a fife; he is very apt to scowl, or knit his brows, and has had the small-pox by inoculation, which he shows but little in his face, but the place on his arm where he was inoculated is plain to be discovered. Since he Ran away he was taken up at Durham, and in conveying him to his master he made his escape; since that he was at head quarters, and offered to inlist, but not meeting with success, he went from thence to Lexington, where he offered his service to Mr. John Buckman, innholder in that town, and called himself Elijah Bartlet, and said that he was free born; Mr. Buckman suspecting him to be a runaway, which the boy perceiving, he stopped but a few days, and went off privately, which was some time in November last, and his master has had no intelligence of him since. He had on when he went away, a blue duffel round jacket, with cuffs, and without lining, a blue serge jacket, both almost new, and a pair of leather breeches, and carried with him 3 check shirts, 2 of which were cotton & woolen, and the other linen, with large checks &c. but it appears he has exchanged some of his outside clothes for other of another colour.

Whoever will take him said runaway and convey him to his master, or secure him in any of the colony goals, so that his master can have him again, shall have fifteen dollars, and all necessary charges paid by

JONA. MOULTON

Hampton, January 1, 1776

N.B. As the boy was born at New-York, and from some other reason it's likely he is thence making his way; but it's more likely he will offer himself to work by the month or Year in some part of the colony of Massachusetts-Bay or Connecticut, and whoever may have the opportunity of taking up said runaway is cautioned to take particular care lest he make his escape again, as he is so artful and cunning a boy.

Reprints: New-England Chronicle, 01-11 to 01-18-1776; 01-18 to 01-25-1776. This notice was also printed in the New-Hampshire Gazette, 11-02-1775 and 11-08-1775.

New-England Chronicle, Thursday, February 29, to Wednesday, March 6, 1776.

Ran away from the subscriber, on the 24th of February, a Negro fellow, named Jack, of a small stature, has lost his upper teeth; had on when he went away, a blue coat, with large white buttons. Whoever will take up said Negro and convey him to the subscriber in Stoneham, shall have three dollars reward.

JOSEPH BRIANT, jun.

Reprints: New-England Chronicle, 03-06 to 03-14-1776; 03-14 to 03-21-1776.

New-England Chronicle, Thursday, March 21, to Thursday, March 28, 1776.

Ran away, last Saturday evening, a Negro woman, named Nell, about 24 years of age, of a large size; carried off with her four gowns, viz. one brown homespun, one homespun linen, one black and yellow stuff, and a red and white calico; also a light blue quilted coat, red coak, blue ridinghood, four yards of yellow tammy, and a black bonnet. Whoever shall take up said runaway, and bring her to her master, shall have all necessary charges paid by me the subscriber.

Woborn, Mar. 4, 1776

TIMOTHY WINN.

Reprint: New-England Chronicle, 03-21 to 03-28-1776.

New-England Chronicle, 06-11-1778.

Ran away from me the Subscriber, on the 4th Day of May Instant, a Negro Girl named VENUS, in the 19th Year of her Age. All Persons are hereby cautioned and forbid against harbouring, concealing or employing said Negro, as they would avoid the Penalty of the Law.

EPHRAIM FULLER.

Middleton, May 28, 1778.

New-England Chronicle, 04-22-1779.

Ran away from the Subscriber, in Woodbury, State of Connecticut, on the 28th of March, a Negro Man named Pomp, about 23 Years old, a trim built Fellow and grey black, a small round Nose, a little pitted with the small Pox on his Nose had a Butternut coloured great Coat, and Overalls of the same Colour; yellow Button on his Har, and had with him a Number of Clothes; talks good English: is about 5 Feet 9 or 10 Inches high. Whoever will take up said Negro, and return him to me, shall have one Hundred Dollars Reward, paid by me OBADIAH WHEELER.

Woodbury, April 8, 1779.

The Boston Evening-Post, 12-07-1782.

RUN away from his Master, at Colonel John Marston's, last Evening, a NEGRO MAN, named PRINCE, about 22 Years of age, well set; had on a white Coat, faced with white---Whoever will apprehend and return him to Comte de SPAUT, Captaine au Regt. Royal a Ponts, at the Bunch of Grapes, shall be generously rewarded. Dec. 7.

Reprint: The Boston Evening-Post, 12-21-1782.

The Boston Gazette, 09-30-1782.

Ran away from the Subscriber, a Negro Man, an indented Servant; he is a tall slim fellow, pleasant looking, and of a good Black, speaks bad English, is a native of Senegal, and answers to the Name of Pier Sanno: had on, old blue Breeches and Stockings, strip'd Shirt, and a short Oznaburgh Coat. Whoever may apprehend said Negro and confine him or return him to the Subscriber, or Joseph Henderson Esq; of Boston, shall receive a handsome Reward. THO' THOMPSON.

Portsmouth, New Hamsphire, Sept. 2, 1782.

The Boston Gazette, 10-14-1782.

Ran-away, about the 23d of the last Month, a Molatto Boy, named JOE, about 10 Years old, thick set; had on when he went away a dark Waistcoat and Trowsers. Whoever will take up said Boy, and bring him to the Printers hereof, shall be handsomely rewarded for their Trouble.

N.B. All Masters of Vessels are hereby forbid carrying off said Lad, if they will avoid the Penalty of the Law.

The Boston Gazette, 05-26-1783.

Ran away from the Subscriber last Saturday Evening, a Negro Boy, named FIVE, about 17 Years old, about 5 Feet high, strait Limb'd and well set;-- Had on when he went off, a brown mix'd Homemade Cloth Jacket and Trowsers of the same. Whoever will take up said Runaway, and secure him, or will convey him to his Master, shall have One Guinea Reward, and all necessary Charges paid, by

SHUBAEL DOWNS.

Boston, May 26, 1783.

N.B. He may be well known by being at his Master's, when he kept a House of public Entertainment, at Walpole.

Reprint: The Boston Gazette, 06-02-1783.

The Boston Gazette, 12-21-1789.

Absconded from his Master's Service,

A NEGRO servant lad, named William, about nineteen years of age, belonging to CORNELIUS DURANT, of St. Croix.—He carried off with him a superfluity of Wearing Apparel.—All and every person or persons are hereby forbid and cautioned against harbouring said Servant, or hiring, or in any way employing him, unless by the previous consent of [Mr.] CHARLES MILLER for his hire, to be paid him as Agent to the Subscriber.—Therefore if any person should after the Date hereof, employ or hire said Servant, without such previous agreement with said MILLER, [they] may depend upon being prosecuted to the utmost severity of the Law. CORNELIUS DURANT.

Boston, Dec. 14, 1789.

Reprint: The Boston Gazette, 12-28-1789.

Continental Journal, 06-29-1780.

BROKE out of the Goal in Boston, on the evening of the 27th instant, DAVID PHELPS of Sherburne, about 40 years of age, black hair, about 5 feet 9 inches high, had on a brown homespun great coat, and striped trowsers, was committed for betering counterfeit bills—JACOB YOUNG of Broad-Bay, confin'd for being inimical to the United States, about 5 feet 5 inches high, round face, had on a short blue jacket, and long trowsers—ROBERT ALLEN, confin'd for theft, about 5 feet 7 inches, a thin face, black strait hair, wears it loose in his neck, broke out very much with the itch, had on a chocolate colour'd coat, white flannel waistcoat and breeches.—JOHN PAINE, confin'd for theft, about 5 feet 6 inches high, black hair, about 21 years of age, had on a hat with a gold button and loop, light coloured cloathes—STEPHEN PAINE, confin'd for theft, about 5 feet six inches high, brown hair, about 19 years of age, had on a brown coat faced with blue, light colour'd waistcoat and breeches.—JAMES DENNIS, a molatto, about 5 feet 8 inches high, wore a wig, brown short coat and long trowsers.—Whoever will take up and secure said villains, that they may be brought to justice, shall receive FIVE HUNDRED DOLLARS for PHELPS—THREE HUNDRED DOLLARS for YOUNG—and TWO HUNDRED DOLLARS for each of the four last, and all charges paid by
    JOSEPH OTIS, Dep Goaler.

Boston, June 28, 1780.

Continental Journal, 01-31-1782.

Ten Dollars Reward

Ran away from the subscriber, an indented NEGRO BOY, about 12 years old, a likely smart boy, had on a green waistcoat and Overalls, a jockey-cap and white surtout.—Whoever will apprehend said Boy, and return him to his Master shall receive the above reward and all necessary charges paid.

All Masters of Vessels and others are caution'd against harbouring or concealing said indented servant, as they would avoid the penalty.

D.D. ROGERS.

Boston, January 29, 1782.

Reprints: Continental Journal; 02-07-1782; The Independent Chronicle and the Universal Advertiser, 06-20-1782 (Supplement); 06-27-1782; 07-04-1782 (Supplement).

The Independent Chronicle and the Universal Advertiser, 04-27-1780.

Ran away from Willam Cotton, of Portsmouth, a Negro Man named GARRACK, about five Feet ten Inches high, something of a yellow Colour, his little Finger on the left Hand squat off half way the Nail, speaks broken and very grum, about 25 Years old, has two Streets round his Middle, with Notches cut between, from his Navel to Navel; had on when he went off, a light coloured cloth Jacket, lined with check'd homespun Cloth, his under Jacket blue Cloth, Leather Breeches, striped Trowsers, woolen Shirt, grand about his Hair. Whoever will take up said Negro, and convey him to his Master, or secure him in some Goal, shall have Forty-Five Pounds, L.M. for their Trouble, and necessary Charges paid, by

WILLIAM COTTON.

Portsmouth, Aprill 27, 1780.

The Independent Chronicle and the Universal Advertiser, 12-07-1780.

One Joe Reward.

Ran away from the Subscriber, a Negro Man, about 5 and a half Feet high, Coal black, Bermuda born, goes by the Name of WILL STILES of WILL PORT. Whoever will take up said Negro, and confine him in any Goal, and give Notice to the Printer hereof, shall receive one Joe Reward, and all Charges.

JOHN LITHBOURN.

Nov. 30.

The Independent Chronicle and the Universal Advertiser, 12-28-1780.

TWENTY ROUND DOLLARS REWARD,
and all reasonable Charges.

Ran away from the James Mitchell, of Weathersfield, in the State of Connecticut, two Servants one a Molatto Boy, about 15 Years old, named PRINCE very large of his Age, had on when he went from home, white Yarn Stockings with small Seams, Leather Breeches, a light Waist and Country Coat, and light Great Coat, grey Wool Hair, striped Woolen Shirt, and Copper Buckles.—The other a middling Size well set, named ROBIN, rather black, with a light brown Great Coat, and very old Breeches, when new a Legwood-colour, a Blemish in one Eye, so that he keeps it always shut.— Any Person that takes up said Negroes, and secures them so that I may them again, shall be entitled to the above Reward, or Ten Dollars for either.—All Masters of Vessels are cautioned against harbouring or carrying off said Negroes. Boston, Dec. 20, 1780.

Reprint: The Providence Gazette, 01-10-1781.

The Independent Chronicle and the Universal Advertiser; 03-29-1781.

Ran away from his Master in Suffield, on the Evening of the 3d Instant, a Negro Man named BOSTON, about 27 Years old, had on when he went away, a light brown broad cloth Coat which had been turned, a dark brown broad cloth Vest, a pair of light-brown camblet breeches, white yarn Stockings, and a white Holland ruffled Shirt. Said Negro is about 5 Feet 6 Inches, thick set, well built, speaks good English, plays poorly on a Violin, of a Copper Colour, whoever will take up said Negro and return him to me, shall have 500 Dollars Reward, and all necessary Charges paid, otherwise secure him in any Goal and give me Notice thereof, shall have 150 Dollars and Charges paid by me, SHEM BURBANK.

Suffield, Feb. 6, 1781.

The Independent Chronicle and the Universal Advertiser, 11-07-1782.

Ran from the Subscriber, of Freetown, on the 10th of July last, a female negro Servant, named Selah, of about 50 Years of Age, a little cross-eyed. Whoever will take up said Servant, and return her or secure her, so that her Master may have her again, shall have two Dollars Reward, and all necessary Charges paid, by

PHILIP HATHWAY.

Reprint: The Independent Chronicle and the Universal Advertiser, 11-14-1782.

The Independent Chronicle and the Universal Advertiser, 06-19-1783.

TEN DOLLARS REWARD.

Ran away from the subscriber, a negro man named ZEB, about 30 years old, five feet seven or eight inches high, carried off with him a horse, saddle and bridle, very black, full ey'd, had on a brown duroy coat, black short breeches, patch'd, checkd linen draws over them, blew ribb'd stockings. Whoever will take up said runaway, and confine him in any of the goals in the United States, so that his master may have him again, shall be intitled to the above reward, and all necessary charges paid by me.

JOSEPH GORDON.

N.B. Said Negro Ran away some time ago, went to Marblehead, and returned again.

South-Kingston, May 30, 1783.

Reprints: The Independent Chronicle and the Universal Advertiser, 06-26-1783; 07-03-1783.

The Independent Chronicle and the Universal Advertiser, 05-13-1784.

Ran away from me the Subscriber, on the 19th Day of April, 1784, molatto Fellow, named PRINCE, in the 21 st Year of his Age, is of a middling Stature, had on when he went off, a woolen striped Shirt, a blue Plush Jacket, a blue Coat, and a Pair of thick Leather Breeches—had with him another Suit of blue, all Wool, home made.—All Persons are likely forbid harbouring, trading with, or trusting said Boy, on my Account. JAMES PENNIMAN.

The Independent Chronicle and the Universal Advertiser, 09-09-1784.

One Hundred Dollars reward.

Ran away from the Subscriber, on the 31st of May last, a very dark Mulatto fellow, named JAMES (generally called JIMMY) about 5 feet 6 or 7 inches high, 29 years old, square and strong made, sensible and well spoken, is an exceeding good joiner, at coach, phaeton and chair work, is a good house-joiner, carver, wheel-wright and painter, and is a tolerable Negro fiddler; he has the scar of a burn on his buttock, about the size of a heater, which burnt him when a child; also the scars of axe-cuts on the lower part of one of his legs, and one raised up in a ridge on his great toe; he wore away a long bushy head of hair, inclining to wool. He was taken up in June, and committed to Baltimore goal, at which time he confessed himself to be my property, and called himself JAMES LUCAS; he was soon after released by a Mr. Simpson, of Virginia, from whom he made his escape at Elk-Ridge Landing, and as he has not been since heard of, it is more than probably he has made towards Philadelphia, or engaged with some workman in the above branches. Whoever delivers the said Fellow to me, near Boyd's Hole, King George County, Virginia, if taken out if this state, shall receive the above reward; but if taken in this state, shall be entitled to FORTY DOLLARS.

WILLIAM FITZHUGH.

Marmion, (Virginia) Aug. 12, 1784.

The Independent Chronicle and the Universal Advertiser, 07-28-1785.

Five Dollars Reward.

Ran away from the subscriber, a Mulatto Fellow, in the 20th year of his age, named Joseph Pito, is about 6 feet high; carried with him, 1 blanket, 1 brown great coat, 1 brown strait-bodied coat, 1 white and 1 striped linnen Waistcoat, a pair trowsers, and 3 shirts. Whoever will take up said runaway, and return him to me the subscriber, shall receive the above reward, and all necessary charges paid.

WILLIAM ALLIS.

Hatfield, July 19, 1785.

The Independent Chronicle and the Universal Advertiser, 09-14-1786.

Ran away, on the night of the 29th ult. From Martha's-Vineyard, a Negro Man, named NED, about 30 years old, speaks good French and English, about 5 feet 8 inches high, very slim.---Said Negro secreted himself on board the brig Active, Capt. Fuller, from Aux-Cayes, and was not discovered until 24 hours after she sailed; says he formerly belonged to Rhode-Island.— Whoever will take up and return him to said Fuller, at Kingston (county of Plymouth) shall receive THIRTY DOLLARS reward, and all necessary charges.
    Sept. 13, 1786.

The Independent Ledger, 09-04-1780.

Two Hundred Dollars Reward.
    Ran-away from the Subscriber, living in Berkly in the County of Bristol, a Negro Boy named Titus, about 15 Years old, had on when he went away, a white Shirt, a pair of striped Trowsers pretty much worn, and a round painted Hatt—Whoever will take up said Negro, and secure him in any Goal in this State, or bring him to me, shall receive the above Reward, and all necessary Charges. JAMES NICHOLLS.

Massachusetts Spy, 01-29-1784.

Ran away from the subscriber, on the night of the 16th of December, a NEGRO GIRL named DIDO, about 22 years of age, having with her a large bundle of clothing; I therefore forbid all persons harbouring or trusting her the said Negro on my account, and thereby avoid all trouble, as I will not pay any thing of her contracting, MARGARET TUFTS.
    New-Braintree, Jan. 10, 1783.

Massachusetts Spy, 04-28-1785.

ONE DOLLAR REWARD.
    Ran away from his master, JOHN CALDWELL, of Barre, in the county of Worcester, on the 11th of April last, a negro man named TITUS; twenty one years of age; a tall stout looking fellow, of a redish complexion, has lately had a large wart cut off his left jole or cheek, a scar in his forehead, stammers some in his speech; carried away with him two woollen shirts, one white do. pair of woollen breeches, a pair of leather do. and a pair of white ditto; a good coat of a lightish colour, five pair of stockings, and a number of other clothing and things allowed to be for his use, and supposed to carry off feloniously a large white silk handkerchief belonging to his said master: Whoever will return said handkerchief to the said Caldwell, shall receive the

above reward; and I forbid all persons harbouring or trusting him on my account, for I will not pay one farthing that he shall contract. JOHN CALD-WELL.

Barre, April 19th, 1785.

Reprint: Massachusetts Spy, 05-12-1785.

Massachusetts Spy, 08-11-1785.

TWENTY DOLLARS reward.

Ran away from the Subscriber, on Wednesday the 13th ult. a negro servant woman, about twenty years old, with her a female child, about eighteen months old, almost white.—The wench is a smart likely girl, about five feet five inches high, slim built, speaks but little, has a sore on her right arm which appears to be a scald; was bred on the island of Barbadoes, and in all probability will try to make that place again.—All persons are forbid harbouring her;--masters of vessels are requested to pay a particular attention, as they will answer it at their peril. JOHN CAPE.

N.B. Have heard that she had made an acquaintance with a negro man from the eastward.—All charges will be paid.

New-York, July 15, 1785.

Reprints: Massachusetts Spy, 08-18-1785; 08-25-1785. This notice was also printed in the Connecticut Journal, 08-10-1785; 08-17-1785.

Massachusetts Spy, 11-30-1786.

Ran away from his Master, on the 10th of October, a Mulatto fellow, about 17 years of age, five feet two inches high, named LEMUEL WOOD, had on when he went away a dark brown coat, with light green lining and bright buttons, a light brown jacket, a pair of round silver-washed buckles, a pair of mixed yarn stockings, long trowsers, and a poor felt hat. Whoever will take up said runaway, and return him to the subscriber, shall FIVE DOLLARS reward, and all necessary charges paid, by DAVID LOTHROP.

Bridgewater, [Oct.] 12th, 1786.

Reprint: Massachusetts Spy, 11-09-1786. This notice was also printed in the Providence Gazette, 10-28-1786.

Massachusetts Spy, 04-24-1788.

Ten dollars reward.

ON the night of the 10th inst. the store of the subscriber was broken open, and a number of articles taken out, to the value of Fifty Dollars, supposed to be done by two Negroes, one named CAESAR, about 30 years old, small of stature; the other named CUF, about 22 years old, nearly same height with the other, but thicker set. Said Negroes are supposed to be gone towards Boston. Whoever will take up and secure them, so that they may be brought to justice, shall have TEN DOLLARS reward, and all necessary charges paid, by

DAVID HOLMES.

N.B. Said Negroes had each of them a violin.

Woodstock, April 14th, 1788.

Reprints: Massachusetts Spy, 05-01-1788; 05-08-1788

Connecticut Notices 1755–1789

Monday, December 3, 1764

The CONNECTICUT COURANT.

Containing the freshest Advices, Foreign and Domestick.

HAMBURGH, Sept. 4.

THEY write from Silesia, that cannon and warlike stores are daily arriving there; that the King of Prussia has reviewed the regiments which were encamped under Briege; and that a body of Austrians, commanded by Gen. Loudoun, is forming in Upper Silesia, while another body of the same troops is assembling in Moldavia, near Olmutz.

Letters from Thorn of the 31st of August, and those from Berlin of the 5th of September mention not a word of the election of the King of Poland.

LONDON, September 6.

At the three places of rendezvous lately opened at Wapping, for entertaining sailors, none are admitted but those who are good and able seamen, well cloathed, and have likewise chests and bedding.

Sept. 11. Letters from Upper Silesia bring advice, that on the 12th ult. there happened the most violent storm that ever was known, attended with thunder and lightning, the latter of which penetrated into 50 places in the circuit of 27 English miles. Several buildings were set on fire, and in the castle of Jagerndorff it occasioned a very great one. A great number of people were killed and wounded, and other very considerable damages done.

We hear from Constantinople, that a Moore, who had been 20 years a slave at Marseilles, and afterwards remained near as long in Egypt, has presented a plan to the Grand Vizier, the design of which is to shew, that the ancient passage from the Mediterranean into the red sea, which was completed by the Caliph Omar, A. D. 635, and which was shut up on the side of the sea by the Caliph Abugiafar Almanzor, A. D. 755, may be very easily restored, rendered navigable, and become thereby, not only a means of keeping Egypt in subjection, but of adding largely to the revenue of the Turkish empire. It is however apprehended, that this specious proposition will be liable to many political objections.

We are assured that 10,000 seamen will forthwith be raised, in order to man the fleet that is now getting ready with all expedition.

It is computed that there are not less than 40,000 persons in the several goals in this kingdom for debt.

Sept. 23. It is said a regiment of Highlanders will soon be raised, in order to embark for the East Indies.

It is said the Rt. Hon. the Earl of Halifax will be appointed Lord Lieutenant and Custos Rotulorum of the county of Hertford, in the room of Earl Cowper, deceas'd.

We are informed that Capt. John Forbes, the nephew of John Wilkes, Esq; has been promoted by his Portuguese Majesty to the command of a regiment of foot in that service. The same information says, that he narrowly escaped that assassination from five Portuguese, since he received that command.

Wednesday the Right Hon. the Earl of Bute made a present to her Royal Highness the Princess Dowager of Wales of two pair of Portugal pigeons and a parrot; one pair of the pigeons was a fine red.

Sept. 29. Yesterday Thomas Harris, and Brass Crosby, Esqrs. the two new sheriffs of this city, were sworn into their office at Guildhall.

Extract of a Letter from New-England, July 27.

"All our money is gone and going to England to pay our debts. No money is like to be in the country. Our trade to the French and Spanish islands, from whence we used to get money is stopped; men of war being placed along our coasts for that purpose. Husbandry is discouraged, for there is no vent for provisions, Merchants and Farmers are breaking, and all things going into confusion."

Oct. 2. A letter from Paris says, " The codfishery on the Newfoundland bank has been this year equally plentiful and advantageous to the persons concerned in it. The people of St. Malo in particular have made cent. per cent. of it ; which no doubt will encourage our merchants to fit out next year a greater number of vessels for this trade.

By the last French mail there is advice, that the number of their vessels employed in the Newfoundland fishery, amounts to upwards of 500 sail, from 150 to 300 tons, as appears from the following list : 50 from St. Maloes, 10 from Granville, 64 from St. Martin's 49. from the isle of Rhee, 110 from Bayonne, 70 from St. Jean de Luz, 38 from Sibour 90 from Rochefort, and, a large number of small craft from the different ports of inferior note along the coast ; and their cargoes have sold from 30 to 36 livres the quintal.

The whale fishery at Bermudas has this summer turned out extremely advantageous.

Letters from Cadiz, by Friday's mail, mention the sailing of the Glorious and Subtile men of war, with 1000 troops on board, for Carthagena, in New-Spain.

The merchants are afraid of a rupture with the Algerines; our court, not being satisfied, by any means with the Divan's condemnation of the Genoese polacre taken under an English pass, and the Dey seeming absolutely determined not to give up the point in still being us the liberty of granting passes to the vessels of other nations.

Three additional companies of foot, and a large quantity of artillery, embarked at Jamaica the fourth of August last, to reinforce the English settlements on the Mosquito shore, and to erect some strong batteries on the Spanish side. By this account it appears we are not idle, but always ready to defend our rights ; and the Gazette confirms it.

According to an authentic account, Spain and France have already sent 20 ships of the line, to the West Indies since signing the treaty of Versailles.

If some Indian priests were to take orders here, & go to America, it would not be amiss ; as the Indians, perhaps, would be readier to receive instructions from their own people than ours ; as they would be better able to inculcate the principles of our worship in them.

On Sunday last died on a visit at the Rev. Mr. Spicer's, at Durham, Mr. Robert Dossley, author of Cleone, the tragedy, the King and the Miller of Mansfield, and several other pieces of a moral tendency, and late an eminent book seller, in Pall Mall.

Wednesday died at her house at Greenwich, Mrs. Wolfe, relict of Colonel Edward Wolfe, and mother to the late heroic General of the same name.

It is reported that two light horse, Commoners will soon retire from business, with pensions and titles.

The conductors of the French fishery at Newfoundland, have, we are told, made grievous complaints of the unmannerly intrusion of our cruizers at the isle of St. Pierre and Miquelon, who, it seems, are determined not to suffer them, to take on board any quantities of fish for Europe which are not actually of their own catching ; such English boats as are detected on this illegal traffic, are publickly burned at St. John's.

Oct. 2. An alteration in the Austrian ministry, and a marriage between the King of the Romans and a Princess of Portugal, are both now said to take place.

Sunday his Royal Highness the Duke of Cumberland, the Rt Hon. the Earl and Countess of Northumberland, and several other persons of distinction, set out for New-market to be present at the races.

Saturday se'night died in Dublin, Lieut. Gen. Dejean, Col. of the 3d regiment of Light Horse, in the 85th year of his age.

Thursday morning died at Bath, of the gout in his stomach, John Lord Trevor, Baron of Bromham, and F.R.S. His Lordship, leaving no issue male, his title and estate descends to his Brother the Hon. Robert Hampden, Esq; Post-Master-General, how Lord Trevor, married, (May 31. 1731) Elizabeth, daughter to the late celebrated Sir Richard Steel, ; by whom he had an only daughter named Diana.

We are informed, that all the noble family of the York's have joined the Majority.

It is expected that the 44th regiment of foot, which has been for many years past, and now is on duty in North-America, will very soon receive orders to embark for Europe.

We are assured that 10,000 seamen will forthwith be raised, in order to man the fleet that is now getting ready with all expedition.

Figure 1.4.   Cover page: Connecticut Courant, 12-03-1764.

Chapter Two

Connecticut Notices

Connecticut Courant, 10-07-1765.

RANAWAY from Stephen Hopkins of the Nine-Partners, a Negro Man named Simon, about 24 Years of Age, near 6 Feet high, well proportioned, had on when he went away, a blue Coat, brass Buttons with round Tops, a light-colour'd, double-breasted Waistcoat, a white Tow Shirt, short Tow Trowsers, black and white Stocking, two Threads twisted together, an old felt Hat with a small Brim. Whoever shall take up said Negro, and secure him in any of his Majesty's Goals, so that his Master may have him again, shall have Five Dollars Reward, and all necessary Charges paid, by
STEPHEN HOPKINS.

Connecticut Courant, 06-30-1766.

Last Thursday Evening, made his Escape at Middletown, (from Capt. Edward Clack of Rutland, in the County of Worcester, and Province of Massachusetts Bay) a Molatto Slave, about 18 Years old, bushy Hair, of a middling Stature, well made and sturdy; has lost the first Joint of one of his Fore-Fingers, speaks good English, had on a red Baize Jacket without Sleeves, Leather Breeches, blue Stockings, and a Pair of Pumps. Whoever shall take up said Runaway, and secure him in any of his Majesty's Goals and send me Word, or convey him to me at Rutland, shall receive three Dollars Reward, and all necessary Charges paid by
June 30, 1766.

EDWARD CLARK.

Connecticut Courant, 09-08-1766.

RUN away from the Widow Elizabeth Porter of Hadley, a Negro Man named Zebulon Prut, about 30 years old, about five feet high, a whitish Complexion, suppos'd to have a Squaw in Company: Carried away with him, a light brown Camblet Coat, lin'd and trimm'd with the same Colour—a blue plain Cloth Coat, with Metal Buttons, without Lining—a new redish brown plain Cloth Coat, with Plate Buttons, no Lining—a light brown Waistcoat, and a dark brown ditto, both without Sleves—a Pair of blue Yarn Stockings, and a Pair of Thread ditto—two Pair of Shoes—two Hats—an old red Duffel Great Coat.—Whoever will take up said Negro, and bring him to Mrs. Porter, or to Oliver Warner, of said Hadley, shall have Ten Dollars Reward, and all necessary Charges paid, by OLIVER WARNER.
    Reprint: Connecticut Courant, 09-15-1766 (Supplement); 09-22-1766.

Connecticut Courant, 10-27-1766.

RUN-away from Josiah Griswold, of Weathersfield, the Night after the 24th Instant, an Apprentice Boy about 17 Years of Age, about 5 Feet three Inches high, dark Complexion, wears his own long black Hair, had on, and carried with him, light colour'd old Great Coat, an new Castor Hat, with a very wide Brim a short, pale blue Coat, a cut velvet Waistcoat, a Pair of Deerskin Breeches, and a Pair of black Stockings.—Also a Negro Man about 19 Years old, had on a long brown Coat, and carried with him a Pair of thin Sheepskin Breeches, and a Pair of black ditto, a Pair of black Stockings, and an old blue Great Coat. Whoever shall take up and secure said Run-away in any of his Majesty's Goal, or return them to the Subscriber in Weathersfield, shall have Five Dollars Reward, and all necessary Charges paid, by JOSIAH GRIS-WOLD.

Connecticut Courant, 02-27-1769.

RUN-away from the subscriber of Hartford, on the 15th instant, a negro man, named NERO, about 35 years of age, about 5 feet 4 inches high, speaks bad English. Had on when he went away, a light colour'd great coat, a pair of buckskin breeches, a mill'd cap, and woolen shirt his other cloaths forget as to the colour of them. Whoever shall take up said Negro, and return him to his master, or secure him, so that he may have him again, shall have two dollars reward, paid by SAMUEL FARNSWORTH.

Connecticut Courant, 10-02-1769.

Farmington, Sept. 12, 1769.

RUN-Away from the subscriber of Farmington, on the 1st of Sept. inst. a Molatto, Indian and Negro blood, named John Way, about 30 years of age, about 6 feet high, slim built, speaks good English, small voice, wears his own black hair, quiew'd behind the fore part of his head shav'd—Had on when he went away an old felt hatt, a light flannel waistcoat, without sleeves, a check'd linnen shirt, shirt, short white tow trowsers, blue yarn stockings, a pair single soal'd shoes.—Whoever will take up said servant, and secure him in any of his Majesty's goals, or return him to his master, shall be reasonably rewarded, and all necessary charges paid, by ELIAKIM DEMING.

Connecticut Courant, 10-02-1769.

Weathersfield, Sept. 23, 1769.

RUNAWAY from me the subscriber of Weathersfield, on Monday the 25th inst. a Servant Lad, about 11 or 12 years of age, had on when he went away an old Hat, a light blue Jacket, a pair of white tow Trowsers, no shoes when he went away. Whoever takes up said Negro Lad and brings him to his master, shall have TEN DOLLARS Reward, and all necessary charges paid, by me

JOSIAH BUCK.

N.B. All persons are Strictly forbid harbouring, concealing or carrying off said Negro, as they must answer the consequences at their Peril.

Connecticut Courant, 07-30-1770.

RUN-AWAY

FROM their Master, Benjamin Hale of Glastenbury, the Night after the 29th Inst. a Negro Man and Woman named Robin and Jin: the Negro Man about Forty Years of Age, of a middling Stature strait Limb'd carried away with him one dark brown Coat one Great Coat light blue two blue Jackets, one white Cotton ditto one Beaver Hat, 5 Shirts, 2 Pair of Breeches, and sundry other Cloaths.—The Negro Woman about 34 Years of Age of a middling Size, carried away with her, 4 Gowns, one white one Chince one Wollen strip'd, a Shalloon Quilt of a light Blue, a Pair of Stays, and many other Things, they both speak good English. Whoever shall up said Runaways, and return them to their Master, shall have Twenty Shillings Reward, paid by

BENJAMIN HALE.

Glastenbury, 30th July 1770.

Connecticut Courant, Tuesday, April 9, to Tuesday, April 16, 1771.

RAN-away from the subscriber of Claverack, on the 1st day of instant April, a negro man named Harry, about 5 feet high, had on when he went away, a greyish coloured coat, a pair of buckskin breeches, green Indian stockings, large brim'd beaver hatt, something worn.—Whoever shall take up said Negro, and convey him to Col. John Ashley of Sheffield, or confine him in any of his Majesty's goals, and send word to the subscriber, shall have Three Dollars reward, and all necessary charges paid, by

JOHN UPHAM.

Claverack, April 10, 1771.

Connecticut Courant, Tuesday, June 25, to Tuesday, July 2, 1771.

RUN away from the subscriber hereto, the evening following the 12th of May last past from Milford, in the colony of Connecticut, in New England, a negro man named Newport, aged 29 years, a stout well set, broad shoulder'd fellow, for height about middling, rather stoops when walking, if carefully observed was born in Newport, Rhode Island, talks plain. He carried with him, one brown homespun flannel coat and breeches almost new and one scarlet broad cloth vest, with flowered pewter buttons also one coarse cinamon colour'd lappel'd broad cloth coat with metal buttons, one blue and white striped lappel'd linen vest, one such shirt, one fine white ditto. Three coarse check'd woolen ditto, one course flannel outside jacket, and great coat mix'd, black and white wool, two pair ribb'd stockings, one pale blue worsted, the other brown thread, one old beaver hat, with a white metal button, and silver'd loop. The same night went from the same house, a large white feemale, aged about 27 years, red hair, stoops as she walks about her housework.—Carried off with her sundry aprons some blue and white small check linen, and some white, one scarlet broad cloth short cloak, much worn with a silver lace about the same, and a woman's black fitten bonnet almost new. She had of her own with her, sundry new tow cloth smocks, several petticoats, striped new linen blue and white gown, some blue and white woolen aprons, two check linen handkerchiefs is some near sighted, wore men's shoes. They were seen about 14 miles to the northward. Whoever will take up said negro, and convey him to the subscriber, or secure him so that he gets him again, if taken in this colony shall receive Five Dollars, if out of this colony Eight Dollars reward and all necessary charges—and if any of the articles supposed stolen by the feemale be taken and return'd the person that returns them shall receive half the value of what may be so returned. The foregoing reward shall be paid by EDWARD ALLEN.

N.B. If said negro hears of this advertisement and shall return to his duty within one month from the date, he shall be received into his master's service, without corporal punishment.

Milford, June 18, 1771.

Connecticut Courant, Tuesday, June 25, to Tuesday, July 2, 1771.

Runaway from Daniel & Israel Lewis of Charlotte Precinct, in Dutches county, province of New York, a Negro man named ISAAC, between 30 and 40 years of age, had on when he went away, a brown vest, and check shirt, a pair leather breeches, and a small pack of other cloaths, any person that shall take up said negro and confine him so that the owners may have him again or return him to said owners, shall receive twenty shillings reward and all necessary charges paid by us.

Daniel Lewis,
Israel Lewis.

Charlotte Precinct, June 17th, 1771.

Connecticut Courant, Tuesday, October 8, to Tuesday, October 15, 1771.

Runaway from me the subscriber, a negro man, named TOM, a little on the molatto colour, aged 19 years, speaks good English, and low Dutch, has a blemish in one eye. Had on when he went away, a light bluecoat white Philadelphia buttons, and vest of the same colour. Whoever takes up said negro, and brings him to me, shall have five dollars reward, and all reasonable charges paid by me.

JOHN DELAMETTER.

Dutchess County, Amenia, Oblong, Oct. 25, 1771.

Connecticut Courant, Tuesday, November 19, to Tuesday, November 26, 1771.

New Haven, November 22d, 1771.

Runaway last evening from the subscriber two Negro Fellows, one named Peter, the other Primas. Peter is a stout fellow, of a yellow complexion, about thirty-nine years of age, bushy head of hair, took with him a suit of light cloth clothes, and some other articles of apparel not possible to be described. Primas is about 27 year old, trim built fellow, something yellowish; has pretty long hair for a negro, and I think has lost one of his toes: he lately run away from the Jersies and was taken up in this town, where he was purchased. He took with him a souff colour'd coat and breeches lined with red coating, a black velvet waistcoat, &c. he is a handy fellow, and pretty good carpenter; 'tis likely he may have a pass, and change his name from Primas to Charles. Whoever shall take up said negroes, and confine them, and give their master intelligence where they are, or convey them home, shall be rewarded in a very generous manner, and received the thanks of their humble Servants

                                                              RALPH ISAACS.
     Reprint: Connecticut Journal, 11-22-1771.

Connecticut Courant, Tuesday, June 16, to Tuesday, June 23, 1772.

Ran-away from the Subscriber the Evening of the 4th Instant a Negro Man named Tony, about 25 Years of Age, about 5 Feet 10 Inches high, well set and very Black; took with him when he went away, a new Coat, and Vest of a claret Colour, mixed with red and white, yellow metal Buttons, and one gray ditto some wore, and a Vest striped red and white; one pair Deer Skin Breeches, and check'd long Trowsers, two Holland Shirts, and one strip ditto and one check'd ditto, speaks good English, and as he walks lops very one side and the other. Whoever will take up said Negro and secure him in any of his Majesty's Goal or return him to his Master, shall have Three Dollars Reward, and all reasonable Charges paid by Samuel Gilbert, jun.
     NB. All Masters of Vessels and other Persons are forbid harbouring or carrying off said Negro, as they will answer the consequences at their peril. Hebron, June 5, 1772.
     Reprints: Connecticut Courant, Tuesday, June 16, to Tuesday, June 23, 1772.

Connecticut Courant, Tuesday, July 14, to Tuesday, July 21, 1772.

                                   Six Pounds Reward.
     Runaway from their Master John Northrop, of Newtown, and John San-ford, of Reading, in Fairfield County, on the 31st May last, two Negro Men: the one belonging to John Northrop, was about 5 Feet 9 Inches high, about 25 years old, has a Scar over his right Eye, had on when he went away, a yellow and black Coat and Waistcoat, a blue Coat, white linnen Shirt, one striped Woolen ditto, one white seam'd pair Stockings, two pair blue and white ditto, a pair brown Fustian Breeches, and a pair Buckskin ditto, two pair shoes, and a pair Cooper Buckles. The other about 5 Feet 8 Inches high, about 30 Years old, well set, has a hair Mole on one of his Cheeks near his Ear, one of his great Toes cut off, his cloaths were nearly alike with the above, except a pale blue Waistcoat, a pair black everlasting Breeches, & a pair silver shoes buckles. They have each a good castor hat, and speak good English.— Whoever shall take up said negroes and return them to their Masters, shall have ten dollars reward for each, and all necessary charges paid, by

John Northrup.
John Sanford.

June 11, 1772
'Tis supposed they have each of them a forged pass.

Connecticut Courant, Tuesday, September 15, to Tuesday, September 22, 1772.

RUN away from the subscriber the 13th instant a negro man named POMP, about 25 years old, a thick, well set fellow, about 5 feet 6 inches high, speaks quick and broken English, he has lost the first joint of his right thumb, so that the nail turns down; had on when he went away, a mix'd colour'd blue & red homemade coat, lined with blue shalloon, with yellow mettle buttons, an old brown camblet, lapell'd jacket, a pair buckskin breeches, a pair steel plated buckles flower'd and somewhat wore, and a felt hat.

Whoever will take up said negro, and return him to his master, shall have five dollars reward, and all necessary charges paid, By SAMUEL BROWN, jun.

Stockbridge, Sept. 14, 1772.

N.B. All masters of vessels are hereby warn'd against concealing or carrying of said negro, on their peril.

Reprint: Connecticut Courant, Tuesday, September 22, to Tuesday, September 29, 1772.

Connecticut Journal, 10-09-1772.

September 30, 1772.

RAN-AWAY from the Subscriber (of Bedford, in the County of West-Chester, and Province of New-York,) on the Night after the 24th of September, Instant, a Negro Man named STEPTH, about 6 Feet high, about 30 Years old, this Country born, has two Scars on his Head, his Cloathing can't be particularly described as he took with him various Kinds; he speaks good English, loves strong Drink, and is very noisy, and is supposed to have a forg'd Pass. Whoever shall take up said Servant, and return him to his Master, or secure him in Gaol, so that I have him again, shall have Three Dollars Reward, and all necessary Charges paid, by ELIJAH HUNTER.

Reprints: Connecticut Journal, 10-16-1772; 10-23-1772.

Connecticut Courant, Tuesday, August 17, to Tuesday, August 24, 1773.

Runaway last night from his master John Williams of Somers, a negro servant named Peter, a stout well set fellow, betwixt 30 and 40 years of age, very black, he took a considerable quantity of cloathing with him. He can read and write well, it is not unlikely he may have a forg'd pass; he can play well upon a fiddle and took a good one with him. If any person will take him up and bring him to his said master, they shall have 8 dollars reward.

per me, John Williams.

Somers, August 12, 1773.

Reprint: Connecticut Courant, Tuesday, September 14, to Tuesday, September 21, 1773.

Connecticut Courant, Tuesday, August 31, to Tuesday, September 7, 1773.

16 Dollars Reward.

RAN away from the subscriber of Pittsfield in the county of Berkshire, on the Instant June last, two Molatto Servants one named Edward Peters, about 35 years old, of a middling stature, round shouldered, bushy hair, and has lost his fore teeth; had on when he went away a brown jacket with small cuffs, wollen shirt, black leather breeches, and an old bever hat. The other named Rufus Cooper, about 21 years old, a strait trim built fellow, 5 feet 9 or 10 inches high, has remarkable light eyes and curl'd hair for a molatto; had on when he went away, a blue coat with basket buttons, striped waistcoat, striped cotton shirt, wash'd leather breeches, and a castor hat.

Whoever shall take up said servants, and return them to the subscriber in Pittsfield, or secure them in any of his Majesty's goals, and send word to the subscriber, so that he may have them again, shall have the above Reward, or eight dollars for either, paid by EZEKIEL ROOT

All masters of vessels and others are hereby forbid harbouring, concealing or carrying said servants, as they would avoid the peril of the law.

September 2, 1773.

Reprint: Connecticut Courant, Tuesday, September 21, to Tuesday, September 28, 1773.

Connecticut Courant, Tuesday, September 21, to Tuesday, September 28, 1773.

Run-away from the subscriber in Wethersfield, a Negro Man named CATO, about the age of 27 years, is about 6 feet high, is a handsome well made fellow—Had on when he went away, a light brown jacket and a green under ditto—blue German serge breeches, and speckled worsted stockings, and old shoes—a striped shirt, and an old strip'd felt hat. He had with him a dark brown homespun great coat, he talks very good English, he was seen last at West Windsor, the evening after the 19th instant. Whoever shall take up said fellow, and bring him to me, or secure him so that I may find where he is shall have four Dollars reward, and all necessary charges paid, by me

WAIT ROBBINS.

Wethersfield, Sept. 15, 1773.

Reprints: The Newport Mercury, 10-11-1773 and in the Providence Gazette, 10-02-1773; 10-09-1773.

Connecticut Courant, Tuesday, September 21, to Tuesday, September 28, 1773.

Ten Dollars Reward.

RUnaway from the subscriber, the night after the 22d instant, a Molatto fellow named PERO, about 23 years old, well set has short curl'd hair, lately cut, about 5 feet 4 inches high, had on when he went off a light brown coat, a stript linen waistcoat, shoes and stockings, a white tow shirt, strip'd woolen ditto, a Pair of tow trowsers, a newish felt hat, and some other cloathing. Whoever will take up said Fellow, and deliver him to me, or confine him in any of his Majesty's goals, and send me word, shall have the above reward, and all necessary charges paid, by me.

SAMUEL TURNER.

Hartford, August 23d, 1773

All Masters of Vessels and other are forbid harbouring, concealing, or carrying off said Fellow at their Peril.

Reprint: Connecticut Journal, 09-10-1773.

Connecticut Courant, Tuesday, April 19, to Tuesday, April 26, 1774.

RUN away from Elihu Hyde of Spencer Town on the 17th day of instant April, a Negro Man about 26 years of age, had on when he went away a mix'd colour'd short coat, black and blue, an under double breasted waistcoat, one side of it plaid, dirty leather breeches, blue stockings and double soal'd shoes, his hair com'd out and tied up, an old brown wool hat, about 5 feet 8 inches high, round shouldered, carries his head stooping forward. Whoever shall take up said negro and deliver him to said Hyde, shall have Seven Dollars reward and all necessary charges paid, by

April 18, 1774

ELIHU HYDE.

Reprint: Connecticut Courant, Tuesday, April 26, to Tuesday, May 3, 1774.

Connecticut Courant, Tuesday, May 17, to Tuesday, May 24, 1774.

TEN DOLLARS REWARD.

RUN away from the subscriber living in Simsbury, in Hartford county, on the day before the election at Hartford, a negro man about 27 years of age, about 5 feet and 8 inches high, and lisps some in his speech; had on when he went away a brown coat and red waistcoat, a white holland shirt, new castor hat, a new pair of leather breeches, a pair of blue stockings, carried away with him a blue vest, two pair of stockings the one pale blue the other deep blue, two pair of shoes. Whoever shall take up said negro and return him to me shall have ten dollars reward and necessary charges paid, or secure him in any of his majesty's goals and send me word so that I may have him again shall have five dollars reward and necessary charges paid, by

TIMOTHY MOSES.

N.B. His fore teeth are gone—he carried a fiddle with him. All persons are hereby forbid to harbor said negro on penalty of the law.

Connecticut Courant, 06-07-1774.

RUN away from the Subscriber in Cornwall, in Litchfield County, a Negro Man named Prince, about 27 Years old, about five Feet high, this Country born, he is thin faced, with a large Pimple or Wart on one Side of his Nose, speaks good English, is a good Fidler. Had on and took with him a coarse brown kersey Coat, with smooth yellow Buttons, one Pair Leather Breeches, one Pair brown ribb'd worsted Stockings, one ditto white Linen, ribb'd, has a small Foot, and wears yellow Metal Buckles in his Shoes: He is supposed to have a forged Pass with him. Whoever will take up said Negro, and return him to his Master, or secure him so that he may have him again, shall have five Dollars Reward, and all reasonable Charges paid by me,

STEPEHEN ROYCE.

Cornwall, May 24, 1774.

Reprint: Connecticut Courant, 06-14-1774; 06-21-1774 (Supplement)

Connecticut Courant, 08-08-1774.

RUN-away from Stephen Goodwin of Goshen, in the county of Litchfield, in the evening of the 2d of June instant, a negro servant about 25 years of age, named JEFFERY, speak tolerable good English.—He took with him one check linnen shirt; one pair strip'd linnen trowsers; one pair brown plain cloth breeches; one mix'd colour'd plain cloth coat; one brown plain cloth waistcoat; one blue broadcoat waistcoat; one pair turn'd pumps; one pair double soled shoes. Said Negro also at the same time stole and rode away from his master, a small iron grey horse, three years old, no brand. Said Negro was born in Colchester, and is a short thick well set fellow. Any person that will take up said fellow, and confine him in any of his Majesty's goal in this colony, so as that his master can have him again or return him to his said master, shall be entitled Six Dollars reward for the said Negro, and Four Dollars for the said Horse, and all necessary charges paid, by

STEPHEN GOOWIN.

Goshen, June 3, 1774.
Reprints: Connecticut Courant, 06-14-1774; 06-21-1774 (Supplement); 06-21-1774 (Supplement); 08-09-1774.

Connecticut Courant, 07-05-1774.

TEN DOLLARS REWARD.

RUN away from the Subscriber in Canterbury, on the Night following the 26th Instant a Mulatto Slave named Sampson, about 5 Feet 8 Inches high, and thirty Years of Age. He is a Slender built Fellow, has thick Lips, a curled, Mulatto Head of Hair, uncut, and goes stooping forward. He had on and carried with him, when he eloped from his Master, a half wore Felt Hat, a black and white Two Shirt, a dark brown Jacket, with Sleeves cuffed, and Pewter Buttons down before, a Butter Nut coloured Great Coat, with Pewter Buttons, a Pair of striped long Trowsers, and a Pair of short white Ditto, a Pair of white Tow Stockings, and a Pair of single channel Pumps. Whoever will take up said Slave, and deliver him to the Subscriber, in Canterbury, shall have the above Reward, and all necessary Charges, paid by me

DANIEL TYLER.

CANTERBURY, June 27, 1774.
Reprint: Connecticut Courant, 07-12-1774.
*An earlier, variant notice for Sampson appeared in the Connecticut Courant, 09-03-1770; 09-17-1770.

Connecticut Courant, 08-09-1774.

Run-away from the subscriber of Hartford West-Division, on the night following 6th instant, a Molatto servant man named JUDE, about 21 years old, about 5 feet 8 inches high, had on a claret colour'd coat and waistcoat, and a light colour'd waistcoat, one pair of check'd linen trowsers, two pair tow ditto, a pair good leather breeches, one white shirt, two check'd ditto, and is supposed to have a forged pass. TWENTY DOLLARS Reward and all necessary charges will be paid to any person who shall take up and return said Fellow to

STEPHEN SEDGWICK.

N.B. All Masters of vessels are forbid carrying off said fellow.

Connecticut Courant, 08-23-1774.

Run-away from the subscriber of Canaan, in Litchfield County, a Negro man named BOND, about 27 Years old, 6 Feet high, well sett, one of his upper Fore Teeth broke out, this Country born, had on a homespun Butternut Colour'd Jacket, speaks good English, but has a small impediment in his speech.

Took a considerable sum of Money with him. Whoever will take up said Negro, and return him to his Master, or secure him so that he may have him again, shall have Five Dollars reward, and all necessary Charges paid, by TIMOTHY HURLBURT.

All Masters of Vessels are forbid to transport said Negro, as they will answer it at their Peril.

N.B. Said Negro pretends to be free, and has a forg'd pass. Canaan, August 14, 1774.

Reprint: Connecticut Courant, 09-06-1774. This notice was also printed in the Connecticut Journal, 08-25-1774; 09-09-1774.

*Earlier variants of this notice appeared in the Connecticut Journal, 05-06-1774; 05-13-1774.

Connecticut Courant, 09-12-1774.

Ran-away from the subscriber Samuel Chapman of Tolland, in Hartford county, the night after the 28th of August last, a Molatto servant named ISRAEL, a strong well built fellow, about 18 years of age, something strait-ish hair for a Molatto, carried with him a false tail to tie on his hair, one or more small scars on his forehead, wore and carried with him a red black and white mix'd grey colour'd coat, a lappel'd waistcoat with horn buttons brown colour'd, one grey ditto with pewter buttons, 2 pair of streaked linnen trowsers, 1 pair wool ditto, 2 pair stockings, 1 pair twitted black and white, the other red and white, and a pair of thin shoes tap'd, 4 shirts, 2 striped woolen 1 striped linen ditto, 1 check'd ditto, 1 old bever hat, and a buff cap. He went away with a servant boy belonging to William Hatch of said Tolland, named Joseph Robins, a short thick set fellow, about 17 years old, carried a large pack of cloathing. Whoever will take up said runaway, and return them to their masters shall have 4 Dollars reward for the Molatto, and a handsome reward for the boy; and all necessary charges paid, by me
SAMUEL CHAPMAN.

N.B. All masters of vessels and others are fore warned harbouring said servants.

Dated, Tolland, September 2, 1774.

Reprints: Connecticut Courant, 10-03-1774.

Connecticut Courant, 10-10-1774.

RUN-away from the Subscriber the 21st of September Instant, a New Negro Man, about 25 Years old, 5 Feet 9 Inches high, well sett, talk but a little English, calls himself a Portuguese, and talks a little of the Tonque—Had on a white flannel Jacket without Sleves, a Check Shirt, and a blue buff Mill Cap. Whoever will take up said Negro and return him to his Master, shall have FIVE DOLLARS Reward, and necessary Charges paid, by

Samuel Boardman.

Wethersfield, September 26, 1774.

A Negro answering the above Description has let himself to Mr. Jeffe Leavenworth of New-Haven.

Connecticut Courant, 10-17-1774.

Middletown, September 27, 1774.

RAN away from the subscriber a Negroy Boy named PITCHFORD, about 14 or 15 years of age, has one of his little toes cut off, and a dent in his forehead, (he can frame a ready lie for an excuse)—he had on a frock and trowsers only when he left home. Whoever shall take up said runaway and deliver him to me or order here, shall have Two DOLLARS reward and all necessary charges paid, by SAMUEL WILLIS.

Reprints: Connecticut Courant, 10-24-1774 and 10-31-1774.

Connecticut Journal, 11-04-1774.

RUNAWAY from the Subscriber, on the 23d Instant, a Negro Boy named Dunstable, about fifteen Years of Age, pretty large and somewhat pitted with the Small Pox on the Nose, which is to be seen if carefully observed; had on when went off a blue Coating Jacket, lined with blue Bays, with small Pewter Buttons, a Pair of Raven Duck Trowsers, pretty much worn, and an Ozna-brigs Shirt. Whoever will take up said Boy and bring him to me the Subscrib-er, shall have three Dollars Reward, and all reasonable Charges paid by ASHBEL BURNHAM.

N.B. It is supposed that the Boy went off with another Boy, belonging to Capt. Willis of this Place, as they were seen together the Evening he went off.

Middletown, October 26th, 1774.

Connecticut Courant, 11-21-1774.

Ten Dollars Reward.

RUN-away last night from the subscriber, a Negro servant, named BRIS-TOL, about 34 years of age; carried with him two suits of Cloaths, two pair of Leather Breeches, one pair mill dress'd; a red Great Coat, a Castor Hat, and a Violin.—The above reward and necessary charges shall be paid to any person that shall return him, to ROBERT BRECK.

N.B. All masters of vessels are forbid harbouring or carrying off said Negro.

North-Hampton, November 14, 1774.

Reprint: Connecticut Courant, 11-28-1774.

Connecticut Courant, 01-02-1775.

RUN away from Subscriber at Goshen, on the 24th day of November past, a Negro Man named York, upwards of fifty years of age, about five feet eight inches high, had on when he went away a black jacket, brown coat, leather breeches, and duffil great coat, whoever will take up said fellow and deliver him to me, shall have Two Dollars Reward, and all necessary Charges paid by

JOSIAH WILLINGBY.

Goshen December 26, 1774.

Connecticut Courant, 05-22-1775.

RUN away from the subscriber, on the 27th inst. a negro man named Prince, about 25 years old, near 5 feet 10 inches, well set, had with him a red great coat and a violin, on which he plays well, has a small scar in his forehead, and speaks good English. Whoever will take up said negro and return him to his master, shall have a handsome reward and all necessary charges paid, by

Elisha Jones.

Pittsfield, April 28, 1775.

Reprints: Connecticut Courant, 05-15-1775. An earlier variant of this notice appeared Connecticut Courant, 05-08-1775.

Connecticut Courant, 08-07-1775.

Runaway [from the subscriber, Daniel Olcott, the night] after the 26th of July instant, a Negro Man Servant, named JACK, about 22 Years of Age, is about 5 Feet 8 Inches high, a lively, smart Fellow, a cooper by Trade, his Hair dressed in the Macoaroni Taste, carried with him a brown homespun Coat, with a red Collar, a red Jacket, brown Jacket and Breeches, two Pair two cloth Trowsers, one blue broad Cloth Coat, 1 Felt & 1 Beaverett Hat, with a Silver Band round it, and many other Articles of Apparel. Whoever will secure said Servant, so that his Master may have him again, shall have TEN DOLLARS Reward, and all reasonable charges paid by

DANIEL OLCOTT.

Hartford, 31st July, 1775.

Connecticut Courant, 11-06-1775.

Run away from the subscriber on the 20th day of October last a Negro named Cato, about 22 years old, about 6 feet, handsome but great eyes, is a Popow Negro, has been in the country 5 years, talks poor English, had on when he ran away a brown waistcoat, a striped woolen ditto, check'd woolen shirt, check'd linnen trowsers, snuff colour'd breeches, and an old blue great coat.—Whoever will take up said Negro and return him to me at Say-[?]ook ferry shall have FOUR DOLLARS reward and all necessary charges payed by SAMUEL SANFORD.

Connecticut Courant, 06-17-1776.

Runaway from the subscriber, on the 29th of May last, a negro man named Sye, about 5 feet 11 inches high, blind with his right eye; had on when he went away, striped linen shirt, linsey woolsey trowsers, an old felt hat; he carried with him two swanskin jackets, has a violin with him, on which he plays very well. Whoever will take up said negro and return him to his master, or secure him shall have five dollars reward, and all necessary charges paid by PETER BUCKLEY, jun.
　Colchester, June 1, 1776.

Connecticut Courant, 06-17-1776.

(Twenty Dollars Reward)
　RUNAWAY from the subscriber, a Mustee Fellow named SY, about 5 Feet 5 Inches high, about 25 Years of Age, has short cul'd Hair nearly resembling a Negroes, well built, had on when he went off, a thick Jacket of a mix'd Colour, black and white, striped trowsers, Buckles in his shoes, a striped flannel under jacket, a check linen shirt blue and white, a white Holland shirt, a felt hat, has a fiddle with him, his upper lip very short, and has altered his name to Joseph Symonds. Whoever takes up said Negro, secures him, or returns him to his Master, shall have TWENTY DOLLARS Reward, and all necessary Charges paid by JAMES ROGERS, late of New London, Great-neck.
　New-London; March 8, 1776.

Connecticut Courant, 07-01-1776.

RUN away from the subscriber at Dover, in Dutchess County, and Province of New-York, on the 16th inst. a Negro man named Prince, had on a round beaver hat, a short white broad cloth coat, a red inside jacket, green superfine breeches, white shirt, black and white worsted stockings, new shoes, about 25 years of age, 5 feet 5 or 6 inches high, well set, speaks good English. Whoever shall take up said Negro, and secure him so that his master may have him again shall have five dollars reward and all reasonable charges paid by me,

W. Conroy, jun.

Dover, June 20, 1776.
Reprint: Connecticut Courant, 07-29-1776.

Connecticut Courant, 09-16-1776.

A Negro MAN, named LONDON, aged about 21 years, a well set fellow, about 5 feet 9 inches high, serveral negro scars in his face, speaks good English, had on when he went away a light colour'd coat and vest, with him one pair leather breeches, two pair trowsers, two pair shoes, and a busscap, run away from the subscriber the 6th instant. Whoever shall take up and return said negro to me, shall have 5 dollars reward. SAMUEL HOOKER.
Kensington, Sept. 14, 1776

Connecticut Courant, 01-27-1777.

TWENTY DOLLARS REWARD.

RUNAWAY from the subscriber the 5th of September last, a Negro man named DICK, about 22 years old, about 5 feet 9 or 10 inches high, a large scar on one of his feet.—Had on when he went away, a home-made coat of a redish colour, and a pair buck skin breeches. Whoever will take up said Negro and return him to his master shall have Twenty Dollars reward, and charges paid, by

FRANCIS CLARK.

Middletown, January 14, 1777.

Connecticut Courant, 01-27-1777

RUN away from the subscriber the 4th of [unreadable], a negro man named BOSTON, 5 feet 4 inches high, had on an old brown camplet [unreadable] blue and white woolen jacket, check'd woolen [??] blue and white mixt stockings, calf skin pumps [and a] beaver hat, speaks very quick and polite, and [plays] well on the fiddle. Whoever takes up the said negro [and] returns him to me, shall have ten dollars reward, [and] all charges paid by Josiah Smith.

Great-Barrington, Jan. 6, 1777.

Connecticut Courant, 05-05-1777.

RUN-AWAY from the subscriber in the night of the 16th of April, a Negro boy named LIVERPOOL; had on a brown jacket, a blue cap, blue stockings and red vest: is a short thick fellow, about 18 years of age. Whoever will take up and secure said Negro so as his master may have him, shall have FIVE DOLLARS reward, and all reasonable charges paid by me his master, living near Salisbury, Furnace on the Oblong in Dutchess County. JOSHUA DA-KINS.

APRIL 26, 1777.

Reprint: Connecticut Courant, 05-12-1777.

Connecticut Courant, 05-26-1777.

RUN away from the subscriber the 22d instant, a negro man named WILL, 22 years of age, talks something broken English; had on a red scarlet broad cloth coat, one old scarlet soldier coat, the buttons marked with the number 40, two brown vests, two pair leather breeches, one pair white ditto, one pair blue ditto, one pair new trowsers, five pair stockings, 2 pair deep blue other pale blue, one pair shoes, one pair half boots, a fiddle, one new black Barcelona handkerchief, one spotted ditto, one grey surtout coat, and sundry other articles. Whoever will take up said negro, and return him to me, or secure him so that I may have him again, shall receive TEN DOLLARS reward, and all necessary charges paid, by ALEXANDER MCNIEL.

N.B. Said Negro is supposed to be made off towards the enemy. Litchfield, May 23, 1777.

Reprint: Connecticut Courant, 06-02-1777.

Connecticut Courant, 05-12-1778.

RUNAWAY from the subscriber, a Negro woman, named Hannah, about 19 years old country born, had on when she went away a striped tow and linnen gown an old red shag short cloak, a linnen and woolen peticoat, and a striped tow apron. Whoever will take up said Negro and deliver her to the subscriber in the middle parish of Killingly or secure her and send me word shall have 4 dollars reward and all necessary charges paid, by NATH'L PACKARD.

N.B. All persons are forewarned not to harbour or conceal said servant.

Connecticut Courant, 07-21-1778.

Deserted from William Retter, conductor of a party of men engaged in the nine month service belonging to the Continental army in the march from the county of Worcester to the Fish kill at landlord Scotts in Palmer, on the evening of the 5th instant, a negro man belonging to said party from the town of Licester, known by the name of Sambo, about five feet five inches high, well set, between 20 and 30 years of age, talks very broken English; had on an old Straw Hat, a dark coloured old Surtout, and Leather Breeches, has lost the joint of one Thumb. Whoever will take up said negro, and send him to Gen. Warner, at Fish kill, or confine him in any public goal, and give information of the same, shall have a handsome reward, and necessary charges, paid by me

WILLIAM RITTER.

Palmer, July 14, 1778.

Connecticut Courant, 08-25-1778.

AUGUST 18, 1778.

TEN DOLLARS REWARD

RUN away from the subscriber, living in New Hartford, Litchfield county, the night following the 16th inst. a negro man, named Neptune, 24 years of age about 5 feet 7 inches high, well set, something pock broken, has scars on his knees, the toes on each foot almost gone, part of two toes grow together on one foot, and speaks good English. Had on when he went away a strip'd woollen shirt, linen frock and trowsers and a light horseman's hat, with No. 62 on it. Whoever will take up said negro, and secure him so that his master may have him again shall receive the above reward, an all necessary charges, paid by ABRAHAM PETTIBONE.

Connecticut Courant, 01-05-1779.

TWENTY DOLLARS REWARD.

RAN-AWAY from the Subscriber, in October last a Negro Man named PRINCE, twenty-three years old, Guinea born, a remarkable scar on his head: Had on a light brown coat and vest of homespun, round felt hat, trowsers and shirt, or rather a frock of homespun linen; a short well set fellow. Whoever will take up and secure said slave, in any goal, or return him to me, or give information to the Printers, shall have the above reward, and charges paid, by

LEVI ALLEN.

Dutchess County, State of New-York
November 3, 1778.

Connecticut Courant, 03-30-1779.

RUN-away from the subscriber in Woodbury, a Negro Man, about 23 years of age, very black and trim built, a small head and flat nose and pitted on the nose with the small pox; he is about 5 feet 9 or 10 inches high; took away with him a butternut coloured great coat, a strait bodied coat and overhalls of the same colour, the coat has yellow buttons and a yellow button on his hat; a large quantity of other cloaths of all sorts. Whoever will take up said Negro and confine him or deliver him to me, shall have One Hundred Dollars Reward. OBADIAH WHEELER.

April 7, 1779.

Reprint: Connecticut Courant, 05-04-1779.

Connecticut Courant, Date: 06-08-1779.

Three Hundred DOLLARS Reward.

LAST night ran away from the subscriber, a Negro man and Negro girl, the man about 25 year old, thick, well built, speaks low, and shews his teeth when he speaks, has a down look, this country born, his name is BUD, the girl, the girls name is NABEY a short thick sett full faced girl, about 20 years old, low spoken, subtle crafty creature: it is most likely their design is to get on board some privateer, and its probable the girl may be dress'd in mens cloaths; the man is about 5 feet 8 inches high, both well cloathed. Whoever shall take them up and return them to me, or give such notice of their being secured, as I can obtain them, shall have the above reward of three hundred dollars, two hundred for the man only, or one hundred for the girl only, and reasonable charges paid, by EDWARD HINMAN.

Woodbury, May 31, 1779.

Fifty dollars reward will be given to any one who will return to the subscriber in Woodbury, a Negro girl named LETTICE, about 24 years of age, trim built and speaks good English, who it is supposed went away with the above Negroes. EDWARD HINMAN.

Connecticut Courant, 08-10-1779.

RUN away from the subscriber on the night after the 22d day of July, a young negro man, called his name ROGERS, about 5 feet 10 inches high, light colour'd hair, slow of speech; had a blue coat and vest check shirt, stripe trowsers, a larger pair of diamond silver shoe buckles, and an old fashioned large watch, and a large pock, with a pillow coat knapsack, with a rope tump line, and a great coat. Stole from the subscriber one white shirt, one check do. one pair blue broadcloth breeches, one pair of thread stockings, one pair striped long trowsers. Whoever will take up said fellow and commit him to any goal so that the subscriber may have him, shall have 50 dollars reward and all necessary charges paid, by SETH GARY. Enfield, July 23, 1779.

Reprint: Connecticut Courant, 08-17-1779.

Connecticut Courant, 10-05-1779.

RUN away from the subscriber a Negro Man about 40 years of age, about 5 feet 4 inches high, the grizle of his nose eat out, and the top sunk in. Whoever will take up said run away and confine him so that his master can have him again, shall have one hundred dollars reward, and all necessary charges paid, by ABRAHAM CASE. West Simsbury, Sept 29, 1779.

Connecticut Courant, 12-07-1779.

RAN-AWAY from the Subscriber, a Negro Fellow, named WOODER about 22 years old, this country born, about 5 feet 8 inches high, thick lips, something long favoured, has a scar on the back of one of his hands, (that was burnt when he was a child) when stoops down the small of his back sticks up as though it had been broke; wore away a full cloth butternut coloured jacket, striped blue and white under jacket without sleves, striped blue and white woolen shirt, and checkt trowsers much the same: carried off a checkt linen shirt, two striped black and white woolen jackets much worn. Whoever will take up said fellow, and confine him in goal and notify me thereof, or convey him to me, shall have ONE HUNDRED and FIFTY DOLLARS Reward, and all necessary charges, paid by

JOSHUA POWERS.

Lime, October 16, 1779.

Reprint: Connecticut Courant, 12-14-1779.

Connecticut Courant, 03-14-1780.

RUN away from me the subscriber about the 28th of February last, a Negro Man named LONDON, about 50 years of age, had on when he went away, a strait bodied blue coat and leather breeches, as to his other cloathing I am not certain: he is a middling sized fellow, speaks faint and slow, but tolerable good English, is a crafty subtle sly fellow, and has and can pretend sickness when well. Whoever will apprehend said Negro and bring him to me in Hartford, or secure him in any goal in this or the neighbouring States and send me word so that I may have him again, shall have 50 dollars reward and all necessary charges paid. I also forewarn all persons from either harboring, secreting or employing said Negro, as they will answer the same at the peril of the law. H. LEDLIE

Hartford, March 13, 1780.

Connecticut Courant, 02-12-1782.

RAN AWAY on the 15th of September last, my Negro man LANKTON, about thirty-two years of age, talk but indifferently, handsomely pitted with the smallpox, has his two for teeth remarkable sharp, being filed in his youth to a point, his wool, the fore part, gray by sickness, walk very upright.— Whoever will take up said Negro, and return him to the subscriber, shall have TEN DOLLARS reward, and all necessary charges paid, by
    JOHN BELDEN.
                                        Weathersfield, January 16, 1782.

Connecticut Courant, 07-30-1782.

Five Dollars Reward,
    RANAWAY from the subscriber, living in Sharon, about the 20th of June last, a NEGRO MAN, named DARBY, about five feet six inches high, 25 years of age, speaks broken; had on when he went away, a tow cloth shirt and trowsers only; he formerly belonged to Canterbury, and is supposed to have gone that way; and as he had an inclination to enter into the service, it is likely he will attempt to inlist.—Whoever will take up said Negro and secure him in any goal in the United States, so that the owner may have him again, shall be entitled to the above reward, and necessary charges paid, by
    LEMUEL BRUSH.
    Sharon (State of Connecticut) July 16th 1782.

Connecticut Courant, 08-06-1782.

RAN AWAY from the Subscriber, on Sunday night, the 21st ult. A NEGRO MAN, named DICK, stout built, a scar on the right side of his neck, another on his ancle bone; carried off with him a Grey Coat, a red Under Jacket, a Linen Do. and old Woollen Shirt, a pair of Woollen Trowsers, a pair of Cotton Do. two pair of Thicken Breeches, a pair of Shoes and brass Shoe Buckles, three pair of Stockings, and an old Caster Hat.—Whoever will take up said Negro and return him to the subscriber, shall be handsomely re-warded, and all necessary charges paid, by
                                        GIDEON LEET, ad.
    N.B. All masters of vessels or others, are forbid harbouring or carrying off said Negro, on penalty of the Law.
    Saybrook, July 27, 1782.

Connecticut Courant, 11-19-1782.

RAN away on Monday Night the 28th Instant, a negro Man named DERRY, about 27 years of age, six feet and about 2 inches high, pretty slim, looks a little cross eyed, his feet very extraordinary large and long, carried with him one caster Hat, two checked woolen Shirts, one old checked Holland Do, one white homespun Do. one streaked linen Do. two pair of old brown linen Trowsers, one pair of striped linen Do. one darkish brown woolen Vest and one dark do. one short outside dark woolen Jacket with white lining, one darkish woolen Coat with white lining without pockets lids, one mixed Surt-out, one pair of brown wolen Breeches, and striped cotton Vest, one pair of pale blue Stockings, one pair of white cotton Do. one pair of mixed blue and white Do. one bark silk stampt Handerchief, one checked linen Do. marked D, and one fiddle, and plays some but not well. And another negro man named DAN, about 5 feet 8 inches high, pale complexion, about 22 years old, took with him two checked woolen Shirts, a calf-skin under Jacket, a knapsack, brown under Jacket, and one pair blue seemed wolen Stockings.— Whoever will take up said negroes, and return them to subscribers in Chat-ham, shall have a generous reward and necessary expences

JOSEPH BLAGUE.
JONATHAN BUSH.

N.B. They have had a mind to go to sea, and it is supposed that they ran away for the same purpose. This is therefore to forbid all masters of vessels and others harbouring them on their peril.

October 19th.

Reprint: Connecticut Courant, 11-26-1782. This notice was also printed in the Boston Evening Post, 11-16-1782; 11-23-1782; 11-30-1782 and in the Providence Gazette and Country Journal, 11-16-1782; 11-23-1782.

Connecticut Courant, 12-17-1782.

RANAWAY, the 2d instant, from the subscriber, a NEGRO MAN, named JACK, about 19 years old, upwards of 5 feet 4 inches high, has a blemish in one of his eyes, speaks quick; had on and carried away a whitish coloured Coat, one striped red and white Jacket, one white do. one pair white Stock-ings, and one pair mixed do.—Whoever will take up said Negro, and return him to the subscriber, or secure him in any goal in this State, shall receive FIFTEEN DOLLARS reward, and necessary charges paid, by JABEZ SWAN.

East-Haddam, December 12, 1782.

Connecticut Courant, 12-31-1782.

RUN away from the Subscriber, on the night after the 15 instant, a Servant Boy, named ROBERT SMITH, about 18 years of age, about 5 feet 4 inches high, dark hair and eyes, had on and carried with a light coloured great Coat, two brown homespun body Coats, two Vests do. two pair Breeches do. one pair speckled calico Breeches, one Vest do. two check'd Shirts, one white do, two pair blue yarn Stockings, one pair white do. one furr Cap, and one caster Hat.—Also, a Negro Man named DICK, about 5 feet high, thick set, talks broken, one of his toes on each foot grows above the rest, had on and took with him, two brown homespun Coats, two Vests do. two pair Breeches do. one velvet Vest, one old great Coat, two check'd woolen shirts, one pair blue yarn stockings, one pair white do. one old hat. Whoever will take up and return to me in Hartford, or secure in any goal in this state, said Boy and Negro, and give me notice, shall be entitled to a reward of Ten Dollars and all reasonable charges paid, or Five Dollars each.

    ISAAC SHELDON.

                                          Hartford, Dec. 21

Connecticut Courant, 01-07-1783.

Twenty Dollars Reward.

RANAWAY from the subscriber, on the 1st instant, a NEGRO MAN, named PRINCE, about 6 feet high, well built, speaks good English, about 23 years old; took with him a short light brown Coat, the buttons marked U.S.A. a grey Great-Coat, an old dark brown Vest and Breeches, one pair of Leather Breeches, one pair of black and blue Stockings, one pair white linen do. a striped linen Coat and Vest, an old beaver Hat, six yards and an half of cloth, mensware, of a fresh colour, marked T.I. Whoever will take up said Negro, and return him to the subscriber, shall be entitled to the above reward.

                                      TIMOTHY IVES.

    January 4, 1783.

    Reprint: Connecticut Courant, 01-21-1783.

Connecticut Courant, 01-28-1783.

RANAWAY from the Subscriber on the night after the 30th Day of Sept. last, a MOLATTO PRENTICE MAN, above five feet high, well sett, had about two Years and a half to serve when he ran away, and was bound to me by the Authority of the Town. His name was called JACK: he has lately been in the Continental Service near a Year; there he called his Name JOHN

JOHNSON; he is well cloathed, had a large brown great Coat; he is now in Boston, as I have lately heard. Whoever takes up said Fellow and returns him back to the Subscriber, shall have Two Dollars Reward, paid by

ELIZUR TALLCOTT.

Glastenbury, Jan. 24.

Connecticut Courant, 02-11-1783.

RUN away from the Subscriber, on the night of the 20th inst. a Negro Boy Named JUBA, 18 years of age, 5 feet 8 inches high, had on when he ran away, a white Jacket with sleeves, a brown corduroy Vest, a pair of buckskin Breeches, a pair of [shoes,] a white holland Shirt, and an old beaver Hat. Also took with him a small horseman Portmanteau containing the following articles viz. a superfine scarlet broadcloath Coat, faced with blue and trimed with prussion binding and white buttons, a pair of blue cloath Breeches, a white cloath Vest, a striped silk and linnen do. one holland Shirt ruffled, 3 white Stocks, a black leather do. with a false collar, a short blue Jacket with sleeves, a pair of Shoes, Shoe-Brush and Black-Ball. Whoever will take up said Negro and deliver him to me, or to John Whiting, Esq; of Windham, shall receive a generous reward and all necessary charges paid by their humble servant, FRED J. WHITING, A. 2d. R.L.D.

Newtown, January 7, 1873.

Connecticut Courant, 02-18-1783.

TEN DOLLARS REWARD.

RUN away from the subscriber, on the 9th instant, a Negro Man named BILL, about 6 feet 9 inches high, well built, about 26 years of age, talks good English, had on when he went away, a white Shirt, white Jacket and Breeches, and blanket Coat, white yarn Stockings, Silver Shoe and Knee Buckles, but may change his dress, as he took all his cloaths with him, it is supposed he will endeavour to get into New-York, as he was taken at the capture of Cornwallis. Whoever will secure said Negro, or give information so that his Master may get him again, shall receive the above reward and all reasonable charges.

REUE CROSUIER.

Albany, February 10, 1783.

Connecticut Courant, 06-03-1783.

Thirty Dollars Reward!

RUN away from the Subscriber on the 26th of April last; a Negro MAN servant, named SCIP, about 23 years of age, middling stature, well sett, born in the country, speaks good English, and can read tolerable well; had on when he went away and carried with him, one pair of blue broadcloth Breeches, a red Waistcoat, a light mixt coating doublebreasted Jacket, with buttons covered with blue cloth, two striped Shirts, one white do. one pair of blue seemed Stockings, one pair of white do. a white Jacket, a green broadcloth Coat, a pair of brown linen breeches, a small beaver Hat, and one felt do. Whoever will take up and return said servant to me in New-London, north parish, shall have the above reward and all reasonable charges paid—

All masters of vessels and others, are forbid to carry off or harbor said servant.

WILLIAM PRINCE.

New-London, May 15, 1783.

Connecticut Courant, 06-10-1783.

RUN away from the subscriber, a Negro Man named SAY, about 21 years of age; had on when he went away a blue Broadcoat Coat edged with white, white flannel Jacket and Breeches, silver buttons on his Jacket, and a number of every day cloaths. Whoever will take up said Negro and return him, or give information where he may be found, shall have Ten Dollars reward, and all charges paid, by ALEXANDER CATLIN.

Litchfield, June 3, 1783.

Connecticut Courant, 07-08-1783.

RUN away from Levi Booth and Samuel Tudor, of East-Windsor, the evening after the 23d of this instant June, two Negro men, the one belonging to the said Booth, was named HECTOR, about 20 years of age, a pretty well built fellow, pitted a little with the small pox, of a yellow complexion, this country born, talks pretty good English, had on when he went away, a brown linen short Coat, Jacket and Breeches, white Shirt, black Handkerchief, a new felt Hat with large brims; the other, belonging to the said Tudor, about 20 years of age, 5 feet 10 inches high, named LONDON, this country born, talks pretty good English, yellow complexion, had on when he went away, a light grey ratteen Coat, brown linen Jacket and Breeches, white Shirt, red spotted silk Handkerchief, an old felt Hat. Whoever will take up and return said Negroes, shall have five dollars reward for each, and all necessary charges, paid by

LEVI BOOTH,
SAMUEL TUDOR.

East-Windsor, June 24, 1783.

Reprint: Connecticut Courant, 07-15-1783.

Connecticut Courant, 09-16-1783.

RUN away from the subscriber last night, a NEGRO LAD, named FRANK, about nineteen years old, a likely well made fellow, rather short—it is supposed he had on a blue broadcloth Coat, but may change it as he took sundry other Coats and small Cloathing with him—he formerly belonged to Mr. Alexander Hunt, and went off in company with a white Boy, about 16 years old, named George Graves.—Whoever will take up said Negro and return him to the subscriber, shall be paid Ten Dollars, and all reasonable charges.
    EBENEZER PLATT. Hartford, September 10, 1783.
    Reprint: Connecticut Courant, 09-23-1783.

Connecticut Courant, 09-23-1783.

RUN away from the Subscriber on Sunday night last, a Negro man named TACK, about 25 years of age, midling stature, likely, active, and well made, was born and brought up in this town, he had with him all his cloaths, among which were a white broad cloath Coat turned up with blue made short, a scarlet cassimer Coat, nankeen Vest and Breeches, blue corduroy Breeches, white Shirt, tow cloth Trowsers, check'd homespun Shirt, an old claret coloured Coat and beaver Hat half worn, he plays well on the Flute and Fife,—and went off in company with a Negro Wench of Mr. Platt's of this town, who carried her cloaths and female child, she is about 40 years old, thick and fleshy and pretends to be his wife. Whoever will take up and bring said Fellow to the Subscriber shall be paid TEN DOLLARS Reward and reasonable Charges.
    THOMAS SEYMOUR.
    Hartford, September 8, 1783.
    *An earlier notice appeared Connecticut Courant, 09-09-1783.

Connecticut Courant, 10-28-1783.

RUN away from the Subscriber, a Negro Man, named JACK, about 22 years of age, of a yellow complexion, long black hair, speaks good English, and a little Dutch; had on when he went away, a red Jacket and blue Coat, a pair of yellow Breeches, was brought up to the farming business, and is a good fidler. Whoever takes up said Negro, and returns him to his master, shall have Eight Dollars reward, and all necessary charges paid, by
    EPHRAIM WHEELER.
    Nine-Partners, (State of N. York) Sept. 16, 1783.

Connecticut Courant, 01-06-1784.

RUN-AWAY from the Subscriber, a Negro servant named ENOCH, had on when he went away from me, a felt Hat; blue great Coat, with a brown velvet cape, buttons under the arms and a flappet with button-holes on the shoulders; a brown Coat, with short folds; a striped linen double breasted Jacket, with a belt; old white cloath Breeches; mixed coloured Stockings; silver Shoe and Knee Buckles. He is about five feet high, thick sett, pretty black, a great whistler, about 23 years old, was born in Norwich. Whoever will take up said Negro and return him to me the Subscriber in Hebron (in Connecticut) or secure him in any goal in this State and give information to me shall TEN DOLLARS REWARD and all charges paid by me,

JORDAN POST, jun.

N.B. All masters of vessels are forbid carrying off, or other persons harbouring said Negro, on penalty of the law. Hebron, December 29, 1783.

Connecticut Courant, 02-17-1784.

RANAWAY from the Subscriber on the 9th instant, a Negro Wench, named CHLOE, about 24 years of age, she talks much and loud, she is supposed to have gone to Boston the metropolis of the Massachusetts Bay. Whoever shall take up said Wench and return her to the Subscriber shall have Ten Dollars Reward and all necessary charges, paid by

THOMAS SEYMOUR.

Hartford, February 14, 1784.

Reprint: Connecticut Courant, 03-02-1784.

Connecticut Courant, 03-16-1784.

Twenty Dollars Reward!

RAN away from the Subscriber in Suffield, on the night of the 19th instant, a Negro man, named GILLAM, 23 years old, about 5 feet 2 inches high, very black; had on a reddish brown Coat; new Boots, much too big for him. Said fellow stole Ten Dollars in money; a silver mounted Pistol, and sundry other articles. Whoever will take up and secure said Negro in any goal in the United States and give information thereof shall receive the above reward of

JOSIAH GRISWOLD. Middletown, February 23, 1784.

Connecticut Courant, 04-20-1784.

Ten Dollars Reward!

RAN away from the Subscriber a Negro man named SIP, about 25 years of age—5 feet 6 or 7 inches high, slender built, drops his under lip, has a heavy loping walk, dances and runs very spry; had on and carried with him a round felt Hat with a yellow lace about the crown, a grey great Coat, a short brown homemade Coat, reddish Vest, one pair of brown cloth Breeches, and a pair of pale blue flannel Do. white yarn Stockings, a pair of square silver Shoes Buckles, carried with him a Fiddle on which he plays poorly, and likewise a small Musket. Whoever will return said Negro or secure him so that the owner may have him again, shall have the above reward and necessary charges.

AZARIAH WRIGHT.

Colchester, April 16, 1784.
Reprint: Connecticut Courant, 04-27-1784.

Connecticut Courant, 05-18-1784.

Ten Dollars Reward!

RUN away from the Subscriber, on the night of the 12th inst, a Negro man, named JUBE, about 34 years old, six feet high, has a large under lip, speaks good English, keeps his knees near together when he walks, runs his shoes on one side, chaws much tobacco, had on and took with him, a dark brown outside jacket and under do. both homespun cloth and lined with black, striped towcloth shirt and trowsers, 1 pair white yarn 1 pair homespun thread and, 1 pair blue yarn stockings, a short nankeen jacket with sleeves, a pair of nankeen breeches, a pair of white woollen do. a dark grey homespun great-coat, two white Holland shirts one ruffled over the hands the other at the bosom, 1 pair of turn'd pumps patched, a pair of plated silver shoe buckles, and a tale caster hatt newly dressed. Whoever will take up and deliver said Negro to his master in Hartford, shall have the above reward and charges paid, by GEORGE SMITH.

Hartford, May 17, 1784.
Reprint: Connecticut Courant, 05-25-1784; 06-01-1784.

Connecticut Courant, 06-22-1784.

RUN away from the Subscriber the 17th instant, a Negro Wench, named SILVA, about 24 years of age, smallish sett, thick and well made, had on and took with her 2 brown Shirts and striped short Gowns. Whoever will take up and secure said Wench and give information to the Subscriber, shall have Five Dollars Reward and charges paid by

ELIJAH HENSDALE.
Farmington, June 19, 1784.

N.B. Said Wench before she run away threw a stone and fractered the skull of her master and otherwise much wounded him.

Reprints: Connecticut Courant, 06-29-1784; 07-06-1784.

Connecticut Courant, 07-13-1784.

Ten Dollars Reward!

RUN-away from the subscriber the 3d instant, a Negro man, named CYRUS, about 22 years of age, near six feet high, well built, speaks good English; had on and took with him a felt hat, a home-made light brown great coat, a straight bodied coat and vest much the same colour, also a dark borwn coat and blue vest, a short red soldiers coat, 2 shirts and 3 pair trowsers made of new tow cloth, 1 pair blue and white woolen stockings, 1 pair blue do.— Whoever will take up said Negro and return him to his master, or give information where he may be found shall have the above reward and all necessary charges paid, by JONATHAN ROOT.

Southington, July 9, 1784.

Reprints: Connecticut Courant, 07-20-1784; 07-27-1784.

Connecticut Courant, 08-17-1784.

RUN away from the subscriber, a Negro or Molatto Girl, named Hannah, but assumes the name of Hannah Watson, had on a callico bonnet, and other thin cloths, midling size, with long black hair, was the property of Thomas Philips of Salisbury; from whom she pretends an emancipation in writing, but 'tis an illegal one. It is supposed she intends to reside in Farmington, or to press on to Rhode-Island where said Philips bought her. Whoever will secure said Girl, so that the subscriber can get her, shall be entitled to Three Dollars reward and reasonable charges, paid on notice where she is secured.

ADONIJAH STRONG.

Salisbury, August 12, 1784.

Connecticut Courant, 10-19-1784.

TWENTY DOLLARS REWARD.

RUN-away from the subscriber living in Redding, on Saturday night last, a Negro Man named CLEMENT, about a midling stature, very black, has a remarkable twilt in his gait as he walks supposed to be occasioned by one leg being shorter than the other; had on and took with him a butternut greatcoat with a white cape, striped blue and white coat and trowsers, a pair homemade corded breeches and jacket. Any person that will take up and secure said Negro, so that the owner can have him, shall the above reward and all reasonable charges paid, by LAZARUS BEAGH.

N.B. Said Negro was seen in Woodbury on Monday evening, and is supposed to have Roered towards Boston state.

Redding, September 30, 1784.

Reprints: Variant notices appear in the Connecticut Courant, 10-05-1784 and 10-12-1784.

Connecticut Courant, 02-08-1785.

RUN away from the subscriber the 30th of January last, a Molatto Fellow, named John Demeratt, commonly goes by the name of Jack, about 22 years of age, five feet and ten inches high, wears very large bushy, curled hair, thick set, well and strong made; had on when he went away a white coat, corduroy vest, white woolen overhalls, a black felt hat, a white shirt almost worn out; he carried with him a blue coat and a new check'd shirt. Whoever will take up and secure said servant, shall have Five Dollars reward and all necessary charges paid, by WILLIAM WADSWORTH.

Hartford, February 9, 1785.

Reprints: Connecticut Courant, 02-15-1785; 02-22-1785.

Connecticut Courant, 05-16-1785.

RUN away from the subscriber the 24th instant, a Negro BOY, named Boat-swain, 16 years of age, large of his age, very black, born in this state, had on and took with him a dark homemade coat, jacket and overhalls, a [mix'd] homemade great coat, an old bever hatt, one check woolen and one stripe linen shirt, a pair new shoes with large [???] buckles. Whoever will take up said Negro and return him to his master, shall receive Four Dollars reward and reasonable charges paid, by EBENEZER PLUMMER.

Glastenbury, April 30, 1785.

Reprint: Connecticut Courant, 05-23-1785. An earlier variant of notice appeared Connecticut Courant, 05-10-1785.

Connecticut Courant, 05-23-1785.

RUN away from the subscriber the night after the 20th of February last, a Negro or Molatto Slave, about five feet five inches high, eighteen years old, wore away a claret coloured coat, cut off at the skirts, corduroy breeches, a pair of old boats, and an old felt hat. Whoever will take up said negro, and return him to the subscriber at New-Hartford, shall have Five Dollars reward, and all necessary charges paid, by STEPHEN CHUBB, jun.

New-Hartford, May 16, 1785.

Reprints: Connecticut Courant, 05-30-1785; 06-06-1785

Connecticut Courant, 07-25-1785.

RUN away from the subscriber in Colchester, on the [17th] inst. a Negro Man, named Quam, about 35 years of age about five feet nine inches high thick set, walks very straight had on when he went away a light coloured plain cloth coat a light coloured camblet jacket, tow cloth trowsers, an old castor hat, striped linen shirt, and several pair of stockings. Whoever will take up said negro and return him to the subscriber, shall have Ten Dollars reward, and all necessary charges paid. JOSEPH TAYLOR.

Colchester, July 10, 1785.

Reprint: Connecticut Courant, 08-08-1785.

Connecticut Courant, 10-31-1785.

On Tuesday evening the 25th instant, ran away from my Tan Works, my Negro Man JACK, aged about 24 years, about 5 feet and half high, marked with a large gash or cross on each cheek, and part of his scalp taken off the back part of his head, he cannot straiten his right little finger.—Whoever will take up said servant and return him to me or confine him in some Jail, shall have all necessary charges paid and be handsomely rewarded

THOMAS DENNY.

Wethersfield, October 31, 1785.

*** Any intelligence about the Negro sent either to Mr. Joseph Webb or me at Wethersfield, will be thankfully acknowledged.

Reprint: Connecticut Courant, 11-07-1785.

Connecticut Courant, 10-31-1785.

NOTICE is hereby given to the creditors to the estate of TABITHA BIG-ELOW, late of Hartford, deceased, that the Hon. Courts of Probate for the district of Hartford has allowed three months from the date for said creditors to exhibit their claims for settlement. The Administrator is ready to receive all claims till the expiration of said time, after which none will be allowed.

JONATH BIGELOW. Adminst'r Hartford, October 28, 1785.

N.B. A Mulatto Servant named JERE, belonging to said estate has lately runaway, one of his legs is shorter than the other. Whoever will inform the Administrator where he may be found shall be reasonably rewarded. All persons are forbid harbouring or concealing said servant.

Reprint: Connecticut Courant, 11-07-1785.

Connecticut Courant, 01-15-1787.

RUN-away from the subscribers, in Fairfield, the night following the third inst. a Negro man called TOM; had on when he went away, a blue coat, a pair of corduroy breeches, about six feet high, well set, his ankles turn in and his feet out. Also, another Negro Man run-away from Capt. Ezekel Hull at the same time, supposed to be in company with the other, his name FRANK, about six feet two inches high, remarkable large hands and feet; had on when he went away a black and white flannel coat, a pair of leather breeches. Whoever will take up said Negroes and secure them so that their masters shall have them again shall have Sixteen Dollars reward and all reasonable charges paid, or Eight Dollars for either of them.

JOHN NICHOLS,
EZEKEL HULL.

Fairfield, Jan. 4, 1787.

Reprint: Connecticut Courant, 01-22-1787.

Connecticut Courant, 09-17-1787.

RUN away from the subscriber, in Greensfarm, Fairfield, a Negro Man, named Amos, about 20 years of age, about five feet and an half high, thick set hair naturally grows very low on his forehead, had on when he went away short coat, with a patch on the elbow, under jacket and new trowsers, both Fustian, white worsted stockings, a new wool hat with a black ribbon and buckle, sometimes plays a fife. Whoever will take up said negro and return him to the subscriber, or secure him so that he may have him again shall have five Dollars reward, and all reasonable charges paid, by

NATHANIEL ADAMS.

Fairfield, August 31, 1787.

N.B. It is supposed he is gone into the state of Massachusetts.

Reprints: Connecticut Courant, 09-24-1787 and 10-01-1787.

Connecticut Courant, 10-01-1787.

RAN away, on Sunday evening, the 26th day of the present month of August, from John Duncan, of Hermitage, in the district of Schenectady, and county of Albany, in the state of New-York, a negro named Caesar, about 36 years of age; a very stout fellow though of middle stature, his legs rather small in proportion—has remarkable large feet—speaks good English. He was born near New-London, in Connecticut, and lived a considerable time with Ralph Isaacs, merchant in New-London: about eight years ago, was sold by said Isaacs, together with his wife, to one Samuel Howe, who brought them to

Claverack, where Mr. Duncan bought them of said Howe. The same Negro lived some years with Seth Austin in Suffield, Connecticut, before he lived with Mr. Isaacs.

It is well known he is gone to, or at least towards, some of the Eastern States, as he was apprehended about 21 miles to the eastward of Albany, the day after he ran-way, and was put in the hands of John W. Schermerhorn, Esq. from whom he made his escape the same afternoon. He is cunning, subtle, plausible fellow, and very capable of deceit: he cannot, with any kind of truth, attest any cause for running away, except his being too kindly treated by his master, from whom he never received any kind of punishment—no, no so much as a single stroke; nevertheless, he robbed Mr. Duncan of sundry articles, at his departure, some of which he left at Mr. Schermerhorn's, when he made his escape from thence.

From these facts it is hoped that no honest man will give him any countenance or employ; but on the contrary, it is requested that he be immediately apprehended and secured in some goal, so that, on notice, he may be sent for by his master, for which the sum of Five Pounds, York currency, in silver or gold, shall be paid to any person who does that service, Ten Pounds if lodged in Albany goal, or Fifteen Pounds of like money, if delivered at Hermitage, by

JOHN DUNCAN.

N.B. He left his wife and three children at Hermitage, and a daughter at Mr. Isaacs's, who, it is said, went with his daughter to Norwich, when she married.

August 30, 1787.

Reprint: Connecticut Courant, 10-08-1787.

Connecticut Courant, 09-15-1788.

TWENTY DOLLARS REWARD.

RAN-way from the subscriber, in the night after the 4th instant, a likely Negro Man, named BEN, about 5 feet 10 inches high, well set, a small scar on his forehead, speaks good English, and some of the Dutch language, and is about 26 years of age. He took with him one homespun bearskin coat, one do. white jacket, one spotted Jean jacket, one Holland Shirt, one tow cloth frock, two pair of tow cloth trowsers, one painted red on the knees, one old wool hat, and two pair of shoes. Whoever will take up and return said Negro to the subscriber, living in the town of Washington, county of Dutchess, State of New-York, shall be paid the above reward and reasonable charges, by

JAMES TALLMADGE.

New-Haven, Aug. 13, 1788.

Reprint: Connecticut Courant, 09-22-1788.

Connecticut Courant, 03-26-1787
Eight Dollars Reward.

RUN away from the subscriber in October last, a negro servant named CUFF, (calls himself Tom) a well built black, about twenty six years of age, five feet ten inches high, country born, speaks good English, has on a short blue coat, with white buttons, was taken last week at Stockbridge, Massachusetts, for theft, and made his escape—he is supposed to be lurking about Salisbury or Canaan. Whoever will apprehend said black and return him to the owner, shall receive the above reward, and reasonable charges paid by,

WILLIAM SEYMOUR.

Hartford, March 23, 1787.
Reprint: Connecticut Courant, 04-02-1787.

Connecticut Courant, 03-24-1788.

RUN away from the Subscriber, on the 12th inst. a negro girl named Simile, about 18 years of age—trim built—very thick lips;—had on a light coloured striped quilt—a brown loose gown—a crimson cloak and a black bonnet. Whoever will bring said negro to the subscriber, shall have Four Dollars reward, and necessary charges paid. ELIZUR TALCOTT, jun'r.

Glastenbury, March 23, 1788.
Reprints: Connecticut Courant, 03-31-1788; 04-07-1788.

Connecticut Courant, 07-14-1788.

Ten Dollars Reward.

RUN-away from the Subscriber on the evening following the 30th of June, a negro man named Oney, about twenty years of age, about five feet eight inches high, very black, has lost the middle finger of his left hand: had on when he went off a butternutt coloured Coat and Vest, coloured tow cloth Trowsers, was barefoot; also an Apprentice, molatto boy named Mint Fagins, about eighteen years of age, five feet eight inches high; had on when he went off a brown sailor Jacket and green Vest, striped tow Shirt and plain tow cloth Trowsers was barefoot; said fellows have once been taken in Hartford, and by violent means made their escape.—Whoever will take up, secure or return said boys to their Masters—shall have the above reward, or five Dollars for either of them, and all reasonable charges paid by

EBENEZER BISHOP and EZRA CLARK.

N.B. All Masters of vessels and others are forbid harbouring, concealing, or carrying off said fellows on penalty of the Law.

Lisbon, June 30, 1788.

Connecticut Courant, 03-30-1789.

RUN away from the subscriber on the 24th instant, an indented Molatto BOY, named Jacob Simbo, aged about nineteen years, tall and slim—wore away one jacket, under vest, and breeches, all of homemade brown cloth, the jacket with two rows of metal buttons, carried with him a fiddle, on which he can play—Whoever will take up and return said BOY to his master, shall have Sixpence Reward. All persons are hereby forbid harbouring him under penalty of the law. WILLIAM MILLER. Glastenbury, March 26, 1789.

Reprints: Connecticut Courant, 04-06-1789; 04-13-1789.

The Connecticut Gazette, 10-17-1761.

RUNAWAY on Monday the 14th Instant September, from Gale Yelverton of Poghkeepse, in Dutchess County, a Negro Man, named Prince, 30 Years old, about 5 Feet 5 Inches high a well built Fellow; had on when he went away, a brown Jacket, tore a little down the back Part, but darned up again; a white Shirt, check'd Trowsers, Light-Colour'd Stockings, white Metal Buckles in his Shoes. Whoever shall take up said Negro, and secure him so that his Master may have him again, shall have FIVE POUNDS Reward, and all necessary Charges paid by me, GALE YELVERTON.

An earlier variant of this notice appeared in the Connecticut Gazette, 10-03-1761; 10-31-1761.

The Connecticut Gazette, 10-24-1761.

NOTICE is hereby given, That there is now in Litchfield Goal, a Molatto Fellow, who calls himself Caesar Sambo, about 5 feet 10 Inches high, speaks good English, well made, and sprightly, and is about 25 Years old: he says he is free, and that he formerly belonged to Capt. Benjamin Green of Greenwich, (Rhode Island.) He was lately taken up in Norfolk, for travelling without a Pass, and by Order of Authority committed. It is suspected, the Fellow has been in Company with a Gang of Negroes, who have lately infested this Part of the Country. His Master, if he has any, may have him, upon paying Charges, and if no Owner appear, he will soon be disposed of in Service to answer the Cost, according to Law.

Litchfield, October 6, 1761

John Newbree, Goaler.

The Connecticut Gazette, 11-07-1761.

RUN-away from the Subscriber's Dwelling House, in Kent, in Litchfield County, on the 27th of October last, his Negro Man TRACE, about 25 Years old, a well set Fellow, middling for Stature, speaks good English, plays on a Fiddle, one of which he carried off with him; had on an old brown Coat, striped woollen Jacket, Leather Breeches, dark grey Stockings, and check'd woollen Shirt. Said Negro was lately owned by Esq. Ransom of Kent, and formerly by Capt. Ross of Dover. Whoever shall take up said Slave, and deliver him to Mr. Josiah Tibbals, or the Subscriber's Wife at said Kent, shall have Forty Shillings L. Money reward, and all necessary Charges paid by,
 Kent, Nov. 2, 1761.
                Nathan Tibbals.
Reprints: The Connecticut Gazette, 11-14-1761; 12-05-1761.

The Connecticut Gazette, 12-05-1761.

RUN away from the subscriber in Wallingford, on the 28th of November last, a Negro Man-servant named Jack, of a middling Stature, is mark'd with the Small-pox, speaks good English, had on when he run away, a red Duffel Coat, blue Jacket without Sleves, Leather Breeches and an old Frock, he has some Scars of the Whip on his Back. Whoever shall take up said Negro, and return him to his said Master or secure him in any of his Majesty's Gaols, shall have Five Dollars Reward and all necessary Charges paid by me David Cook jun.
 Whoever shall apprehend said Runaway, are desired to secure him in Irons.
Reprint: The Connecticut Gazette, 12-12-1761.

Connecticut Journal, 09-29-1769.

September 29, 1769.
 RUN away from the Subscriber, of Beekman's Precinct, in Dutchess County, on Saturday, the 23d Instant, a Negro Man, named Cuff, about five Feet high, about thirty Years old, a thick well set Fellow; he wore a lightish Colour'd Broad Cloth Coat, a Blue Everlasting Vest, with red Lining, and light Thickset Breeches, had with him one Pair of Tow Trowsers, speaks very good English. Said Negro formerly liv'd with one Mr. John Peck, of Wallingford. Whoever shall take up said Runaway, and deliver him to me, shall receive Five Dollars Reward, and all necessary Charges paid by me
              YEREY EMENGH.
Reprint: Connecticut Journal, 10-06-1769.

Connecticut Journal, 05-10-1771.

RUN away last Tuesday Night, a Negro Man named ABEL, about 20 Years old, of a small Stature, talks good English; had on when he went away a Felt Hat, a greenish colour'd Flannel Coat with brown Lining, a white Fustian Jacket something wore, a check'd Linnen Shirt, Sheep's Skin Breeches, and blue Stockings with white at the Tops, and Brass Buckles in his Shoes— Whoever shall take up said Negro, and return him to the Subscriber, or send him Word so that he may have him again, shall have Four Dollars Reward, and all necessary Charges, paid by
GIDEON PLATT, jun.

Milford, May 10, 1771.

Reprint: Connecticut Journal, 05-24-1771.

Connecticut Journal, 05-24-1771.

FIVE DOLLARS REWARD.

RUN-away from the Subscriber the later End of April last, a Negro Man, named DOVER, is a stout well made Fellow, of a yellow Complexion, is about 22 Years old, and about 5 Feet 8 Inches high, had on when he went away a whitish colour'd Coat, a blue Jacket, and Duffil Trowsers.—Whoever shall take up said Negro, & return him to the Subscriber, shall have Five Dollars Reward, and all necessary Charges, paid by NATHANIEL SPERRY.

New-Haven, April 10, 1771.

Connecticut Journal, 05-24-1771.

RUN away last Tuesday Night, a Negro Man named GLASGOW, about 23 Years old, a very stout Fellow, about 6 Feet high; had on when he went away a Castor Hat, a red Duffil Great Coat, Chocolate colour'd strait bodied Ditto. with Breeches of the same Colour, and a red Jacket.—Whoever shall take up and return said Negro to the Subscriber, or send him Word that he may be taken again, shall have Five Dollars Reward, and all necessary Charges, paid by
Milford, May 10 1771.

JOHN TREAT.

Connecticut Journal, 07-26-1771.

Waterbury July 22, 1771.

Run-away from the Subscriber, on the 20th Instant, a Molatto Fellow named BEN, of a Copper Complexion, about 17 Years of Age, well set and sprightly, he has a black bushy Head of Hair, speaks good English and is addicted to swearing—is very large of his Age. Had on when he went away a white Linen Shirt and Trowsers, a stript Linsey Woolsey Jacket with Sleeves; has been used to the Sea, and tis supposed he will endeavour to get on board some Vessel as soon as possible. Any Person that shall take up said Fellow, and return him to his Master or give notice where he is, shall be honorable rewarded, and all necessary Charges paid by ISAAC WOODRUFF.

Connecticut Journal, 08-30-1771.

SIX DOLLARS REWARD.

RUN-way from the subscriber of Waterbury, on the 1st instant, and since on the 9th instant escaped from the subscriber after being taken at Lyme, a Negro man slave named BOSTON, about 35 years of age, being the Negro man that was formerly owned by Ezra Shelden, of Lyme; he is something of a short well built fellow, hath had the small pox, and hath lost one of his fore teeth, he had no cloaths on when he escaped but a pair of short trowsers and check'd linnen shirt, saving a pair of iron handcuffs which he may have got off; he is pretty talkative and flattering, and will tell any story to deceive so as to prevent being secured. Whoever shall take him up is cautioned to take care he don't again escape. And whoever shall take up said Negro and confine him in any of his Majesty's gaols, or secure him so as his master may have him again, shall receive Three Dollars reward, and all necessary charges, paid by me

CALEB HUMASTUN.

Lyme, August 10th, 1771.

N.B. If said Negro shall be taken out of the town of Lyme, by any person and secured as aforesaid, an additional reward of Three Dollars more shall be paid and costs; and if taken in the town of Lyme he or they that take him may deliver him into the custody of said Seldon.

* An earlier variant of this notice appeared in the Connecticut Journal, 08-16-1771; 08-23-1771.

Connecticut Journal, 04-15-1774.

TEN DOLLARS Reward.

RAN-AWAY from the Subscriber of Bedford, in the Province of New York, on Sunday the 10th Instant, two Negro Men, one named Caesar, about 32 Years old, about 6 Feet high, knock-knee'd, has with him a grey Great Coat, two grey Jackets, and a Pair of Leather Breeches. The other named Cuff, about 28 Years old, about 5 Feet 8 Inches high, slim made, is very lively and active, and pretends to be a Sailor; had on a red Great Coat, blue Broadcloth Jacket with Metal Buttons. Swanskin Ditto, blue Duffil Trowsers, and black Breeches. 'Tis supposed they have a forg'd Pass. Whoever shall take up said Negroes, and secure them, or return them to the Subscriber, shall have Ten Dollars Reward for both, or Five Dollars for each, and all reasonable Charges paid by me,

LEWIS M'DONALD.

N.B. Masters of Vessels of Others, are forbid concealing or carrying off said Negroes, as they will answer the same at their Peril.

New-Haven, April 13, 1774.

Reprint: Connecticut Journal, 04-22-1774.

Connecticut Journal, 05-27-1774.

RUN AWAY last Night from the Subscriber, a NEGRO MAN, named TORY, about 30 Years old, about 5 Feet 9 Inches high, this Country born, had on a brown Homespun Coat, (no Lining) old Kersey Jacket, check Shirt; had with him a Tow Shirt, 2 Pair ribbed Stockings black and blue, Trowsers, old felt Hat and new Shoes. It is thought he went away in Company with a Squaw, named Lydia, who had twin female Children about 15 Months old. She was a Native of Farmington. It is thought they are gone towards Stockbridge. Whoever will take up said Negro, and bring him to his Master, or secure him so that he may have him again, shall receive a Reward of Five Dollars, and all reasonable Charges paid by me,

JOHN BLAKISTON.

Branford, May 12, 1774.

*An earlier variant appeared in the Connecticut Journal, 05-17-1774.

Connecticut Journal, 08-05-1774.

New-Haven, July 30, 1774.

LAST Night ranaway from the Subscriber, of the Parish of East-Haven in New Haven, a Molatto Slave named Toney, 22 Years old, about 5 Feet 9 Inches, has a Scar under his Chin, and very large Corns on his Toes; is likely, active, and well made, has short negroish Hair, had on and took with him a dark brown Homespun Coat and Breeches, blue Broadcloth Jacket with Metal Buttons and bound with blue Ferret, red Everlasting Jacket, white linen Shirt, check'd Ditto, Tow Trowsers, Felt Hat with a white loop and Band and white wash'd Metal Button, a Pair of white Linen Stockings, Shoes with Flesh Side out, Steel Buckles, and a red Silk Handkerchief.

Whoever shall take up said Slave, and return him to his Master, or secure him, so that I have him again, shall receive FIVE DOLLARS Reward, and all necessary Charges paid, by JACOB SMITH.

All Persons are cautioned not to harbour or carry off said Toney, as they will answer it at their Peril.

Connecticut Journal, 08-19-1774.

FOUR DOLLARS REWARD.

Ranaway from the Subscriber on the Night of the 12th Instant, a Molatto indented Servant, named POMPEY, he had on and carried with him, an old red Duffil lose Coat, a brown Duroy or Sagathee tight Coat, a blue Jacket with Sleeves, a brown Waist Coat, a White Shirt, an old checkt ditto, a Pair of new Tow Trowsers, a Felt Hat Macaroni cut, with a white Button, &c. He is about 5 Feet high, pretty thick set, has wool Hair, is much addicted to strong Drink, and plays indifferently on the Fiddle. Whoever will take up said Pompey and secure him, or convey him to the Subscriber, shall receive four Dollars Reward, and all necessary Charges paid by John Fowler, junr.

All Masters of Vessels and others are forbid to carry off or conceal said Servant, as they will answer the same at the Peril of the Law.

Milford, August 17th, 1774.

Connecticut Journal, 09-09-1774.

FIVE DOLLARS REWARD.

RANAWAY from the Subscriber on the 28th of August last, a Negro fellow named GUINEA, about 5 Feet 3 or 4 Inches High, and about 41 or 42 Years old, had on when he went away, and carried with him a Brown outside Waistcoat, a Yellow Linnen under Waistcoat Otter colour, and Breeches of the same, a coarse Holland Shirt, one check'd Ditto, a Pair of strip'd Trowsers, one red Ratteen Waistcoat without Sleeves, and Pewter Buttons, one Pair mixt red and blue Stockings, one Felt Hat, and has work'd at the Clother's Trade; and it is tho't he went away with a Molatto Fellow named Larry, who is free, and likely will shew a forg'd Pass. Whoever will take up said Negro, and return him to the Subscriber, shall be entitled to the above Reward of Five Dollars, and all necessary Charges paid, by

HEZEKIAH ORTON. Litchfield, Sept. 5th, 1774.

Connecticut Journal, 09-16-1774.

Man of St. George, August 23d, 1774.

RANAWAY from the Subscriber at the Manor of St. George, on the South Side of Long-Island, opposite of Brook-Haven, a MOLATTO SLAVE, half Negro and half Indian, named DICK, about 5 Feet 8 Inches high, full faced, thick Lips, bushy Hair, is about 23 Years of Age; carried away with him a Bundle of Cloaths that cannot be particularly described, except a red Cloth Jacket, blue Cloth Coat. Also,

Ranaway with him from Col. Nathaniel Woodhull of the same Place, an INDIAN FELLOW, named JOE, about 20 Years of Age, about 5 Feet 6 Inches high. Whoever takes up either of the said Fellows, and secures him or them in any of his Majesty's Gaols, or shall bring one or both of them to their Masters, shall have Twenty Shillings Reward for each if taken up in this Colony, and Five Pounds for each if taken in any other Colony, and all reasonable Charges paid, by

WILLIAM SMITH.

Connecticut Journal, 11-04-1774.

RUN AWAY from the subscriber on the 16th of October last a Negro man named JACK, about 5 feet 3 or 4 inches high, big lips; had on when he went away a blue coat, a green double breasted rateen waistcoat, blue short breeches. Whosoever shall take up and secure him so that his master may have him, shall have One Dollar reward, and all necessary charges paid by me

DAVID SHITTON.

N.B. All persons are forbid harbouring said Negro upon the penalty of the law.

Reprint: Connecticut Journal, 11-11-1774.

Connecticut Journal, 03-08-1775.

RANAWAY from the Subscriber, last night, a Negro slave, named Daniel, about 19 years old, stout and well-made, a little round-shoulder'd, had on a mix'd blue Jacket, red under ditto, checkt woollen shirt, blue & white mix'd checkt breeches, castor hat, about half worn cockt in taste. Whoever shall take up & secure him, or return him to me, shall be reasonably rewarded, and have all necessary charges paid by

MOSES WELLS.

New-Haven, March 8, 1775.

Connecticut Journal, 03-13-1776.

LAST Night strayed from the Subscriber, a Negro GIRL, about 18 Years of Age, a short thickset Wench, had on a checkt flannel Coat and short Gown, and some other Cloaths with her. Whoever will take up said Wench, and secure her in any of the Hon. Congress's Goals, or deliver her to Mr. John Wise, at New Haven, or Rev. John Foot, at New Cheshire, shall be well rewarded for all Cost and Trouble by me,

JOHN FOOT.

New Cheshire, March 12th, 1776.

Reprint: Connecticut Journal, 03-26-1777.

Connecticut Journal, 04-10-1776.

RANAWAY from the Widow Easter Morris, of East-Haven, on or about the 24th of September last, a Negro Man named Jack, about 40 Years old, a short thick set Fellow, about 5 Feet high; had on when he went away two brown Kersey Jackets, blue Breeches, a white tow Shirt, black and white Stockings, a pair of new Shoes, a good Castor Hat; carried away one brown Great Coat, one checkt Holland Shirt, one pair of black knit Breeches, and a pair of pale blue Stockings. Whoever will take up said Negro, and bring him to the Subscriber, or inform where he is, shall have Two Dollars Reward, and all necessary Charges paid by me the Subscriber.

                                                           ESTHER MORRIS.

Connecticut Journal, 11-20-1776.

RAN-away from Josiah Willabie, of Goshen, in Litchfield County, on or about the 19th of October last, a NEGRO MAN, named YORK, (formerly belonged to Colonel Pitkin, of Hartford) he is about 51 Years of Age, and of a middling Stature; had on, as is suppos'd, a pale red Duffil Great Coat, a blue strait bodied Ditto, and an old Pair of Shoes. Whoever shall take up said Negro, and confine him in the nearest Gaol, and send Word to said Willabie, shall have One Dollar Reward, and all necessary Charges paid.

                                                        Nov. 4, 1776 (73)

Connecticut Journal, 12-25-1776.

RAN away from the subscriber in Waterbury, on Sunday evening the 1st of Instant December, a NEGRO MAN named ROBIN, about 27 years old, about 5 feet 5 or 6 inches high, a well set fellow, has had the small-pox; had on or carried with him a pair of new Dearskin breeches, a pair of check'd trowsers, a white Holland shirt, a check'd linen ditto, a woollen ditto, a light brown coat, a brown strait bodied coat, an old brown ditto, an oldish castor hat, supposed to have two or three vests. Whoever shall take up and return said Negro, shall receive Ten Dollars reward, & all necessary charges paid by

    Waterbury, Dec. 2, 1776 (77) ENOS GUNN.

Connecticut Journal, 11-11-1778.

                          TWENTY DOLLARS REWARD.

RUN away from the subscriber, an indented servant mulatto boy, named Obadiah, 16 years of age, about 5 feet 4 or 5 inches high, of a slender make; had on when he went away, a brown linsey woolsey jacket, a tow shirt, an old pair of tow trowsers, a pair of old shoes and stockings, and took with him a rifle sack. 'Tis supposed he went to New-Milford with an intention of inlisting in Col. Meigo's regiment which lay at that place. Whoever will take up and secure said servant, so that his master may have him again, shall receive the above reward, and all other reasonable charges paid by

JOHN GRENELL.

Fairfield, October 22, 1778 (8)

Connecticut Journal, 10-13-1779.

RANAWAY from the subscriber about the 12th of September last, a Negro Man named Charles, about 30 Years old, slender built, speaks broken English; it is supposed he is concealed in this Town by some evil minded Person.—Whoever shall take up said Negro and secure him to the Subscriber, and discover the Person who has conceal'd him, shall be handsomely rewarded, and have all necessary Charges paid. HEZEKIAH JOHNSON.

Wallingford, October 5, 1779.

Said Johnson has for Sale choice West India and New England Rum by the Barrel or less Quanity, Maderia Wine, Rock and Lisbon Salt, Wool Cards by the Dozen or [?]ogle Pair, Barcalona Handkerchiefs, &c.

Reprint: Connecticut Journal, 10-20-1779.

Connecticut Journal, 07-27-1780.

RUN away from the subscriber on the 18th of July, a negro man named Alexander, 36 years old, about six feet six inch high, speaks good English, in a high and polite stile. Had on when he went away, a light colour'd [floore] jacket, striped shirt, and tow trowsers carried with him a blue great coat, with a black velvet collar, trim'd with basket buttons. It is supposed he will attempt to get to Long Island. Whoever will take up and return said negro, shall be [entitled] to one hundred dollars reward, and all necessary charges paid by ELIAS DUNNING.

July 25, Woodbury

Connecticut Journal, 03-15-1781.

RUN away from the subscriber, of Stratford, a NEGRO Man, named JACK, a short thick set fellow much pock broken, with a small spot bald on the crown of his head, had on when run away, a Kersey great coat and a strait bodied coat of the same. Whoever will take up the said Negro and return him to me, shall be generously rewarded by
        EBENEZER HURD.
                                                    Stratford, Feb 28, 1781.

Connecticut Journal, 05-17-1781.

Escaped from his keepers at the route of the widow Tharp, in North-Haven, on the night of the 13th instant, a Negro fellow named Pomp, lately belonging to James Barker, Esq; of Branford, but now enlisted in Col. Meigs's regiment; who, on the 11th instant, wilfully and barbarously murdered the Negro servant of the late Col. Douglass, at the house of Samuel Hitchcock, innholder in North-Haven. The said Negro is six feet high, about 30 years of age, has large eyes, and is well spoken, had on his regimentals when he made his escape, viz black coat, white vest and overhalls; it is supposed he is gone for the camp, but may be lurking somewhere in the country. Whoever will take up the said Negro, secure him that he may be brought to justice, shall be liberally rewarded by me,
                                                    HANNAH DOUGLASS.
                                                    Northford, May 15, 1781.

Connecticut Journal, 07-12-1781.

THIRTY hard dollars REWARD

RUN away from Nathaniel Durkee, jun. and Capt. Nathan Bomford of New Milford, 2 NEGRO Men on Tuesday night. One named BUD, about 21 years old about 5 feet 6 inches high, wore a brown coat home made, and small cut castor hat, two holland shirts, one pair of leather breeches, and sundry other articles.—The other named PETER, about 18 years of age, six feet high, very stocky, had with him a brown homemade coat, a new felt hat, leather breeches, one or two pair of trowsers, two check'd shirts, and sundry other articles—Also a NEGRO woman named NABBY, about 21 years of age, very short and stocky, has a suit of brown, and suit of white linen with her. Said NEGROES are supposed to be in the woods, or concealed by some person nigh the sea shore, with an intent to get to Long-Island. Any person that will take up the said NEGROES, shall have the above reward, or for either of them ten dollars, and necessary expences, by committing them to goal or sending word to,

NATHANIEL DURKEE, jun.

New Milford, June 30th, 1781.
Reprint: Connecticut Journal, 07-26-1781.

Connecticut Journal, 07-26-1781.

TWENTY hard dollars REWARD.

RUN away from the subscriber, two NEGRO Servants, in the night after the 8th instant, named Hampton, and Gad, one is about 30 years of age, about 5 feet 7 inches high: the other about 22 years old, and is near 6 feet high, and walks bout forward, had between them when they went away, two tow-cloth shirts, and one check'd linen shirt, each had on a pair of tow cloth trowsers, and the least of them, a striped linen jacket with sleeves, as also, a light colour'd great coat, it is supposed that they will endeavour to get to Long-Island by way of Horse-Neck, as Gad has serv'd in the State troops upon that station, the least of them is very artful, is heavy [??ed,] has a great appearance of homespun. Whoever takes up said run-aways, and return them to the subscriber, shall receive the above reward, and necessary charges paid by,

JOSEPH JOHNSON,
SIMEON BRISTOL.

New-Haven, July 17, 1781.

Connecticut Journal, 06-20-1782.

RUN away from the subscriber living in Green-Farms Parish, Fairfield, a NEGRO WENCH, named TAMOR, the 10th inst. about 19 years of age, having a child with her about 15 months old, and pregnant with another, nigh her time. Whoever will take up and secure said Negro so that the owner may have her again, shall be generously rewarded and all necessary charges paid, by JOSEPH HIDE.

Green's-Farms, June 12, 1782.
Reprints: Connecticut Journal, 06-27-1782; 07-04-1782

Connecticut Journal, 10-24-1782.

TEN DOLLARS REWARD.

RUN away from the subscriber the 7th inst. a MOLATTO fellow, named DICK, 22 years of age, about 5 feet 2 or 3 inches high, middling thick, pitted with the small pox, walks wide with his knees, pretty surly look: had on when he went away a tow shirt and trowsers, took with him an old check'd shirt and leather breeches, which he may have since put on. Whoever will secure the said fellow so that I may have him again, shall receive the above reward and all reasonable charges paid, by JOB MULFORD.

Stansburgh, (State New-York) Oct. 8, 1782.

N.B. It is likely he will offer to enter on board some vessel to go to sea, or attempt to get within the enemy's lines—All masters of vessels are cautioned against carrying him off; and those who live near the sound, are desired to prevent his going to Long Island.

Reprint: Connecticut Journal, 10-31-1782.

Connecticut Journal, 07-16-1783.

FIFTY DOLLARS REWARD.

RAN away from the subscriber the night following the 7th instant, a likely well built NEGRO MAN, named DERY about 22 years of age, near five feet and a half high, clear black, talks pretty good English; had on when he went away a deep blue coat, brown waistcoat, and brown tow cloth trowsers, with a pair of linen breeches under them, check'd shirt almost worn out, a large brim'd felt hat, almost new, white yarn stockings, thick shoes, large block-tin shoe buckles, his hair turn'd back, went away with a Negro named Pomp, about 23 years of age, thick set, talks broken, is clear black, about 5 ½ feet high, wore chiefly linen clothes. Whoever will take up said Negroes, or find said Negro only, and return him to the subscriber in Glastenbury, or secure him in any public goal, shall receive the above reward from

ELIZUR TRYON.

Glastenbury, July 8, 1783.

Reprints: Connecticut Journal, 07-23-1783; 07-30-1783.

Connecticut Journal, 10-22-1783.

Twenty Dollars Reward.

RUNAWAY from the Subscriber on Thursday the 9th Inst. a NEGRO MAN named SAM, about 24 Years old, but appears by his Countenance to be much older, a tall, stout, well built Fellow, in Colour a dark yellow has a very large Foot, he speaks pretty good English, but with something of the Dutch Accent, which Language he had some little Knowledge of, having been brought up in a Dutch Family on Long-Island; had on an old flap'd Hat, a strip'd blue and white Tow-Cloth Coatee and Vest, a white homespun linen Shirt, a Pair of twill'd Tow-Cloth Trowsers patch'd on the Knees with plain Tow-Cloth, and was bare-foot when he left Home. Whoever will take up said Negro, and secure him, or return him to the Subscriber, shall be entitled to the above Reward, and all necessary Charges. JOSIAH BURR.

New-Haven, October 11th, 1783.

Reprint: Connecticut Journal, 10-29-1783.

Connecticut Journal, 01-28-1784.

Ten Dollars Reward.

RUN AWAY from the Subscriber on the last instant, a NEGRO MAN, named SIM, about twenty years of age, this country born, about 5 feet 6 or 8 inches high, with a large head & long face, his hair turned back, his colour not so black as some, his feet very large, thick set, stout built fellow; had on when he went away, a light butter-nut-coloured coat, striped flannel waste-coat, leather breeches newly mended, a pair of thick shoes, with strings, a pair of blue or sheep's black & white stockings, a new felt hat; he carried away sundry other articles of cloathing in an old kersey table cloth. It is likely he will change his cloathes. Whoever will take up said negro, and return him to the subscriber, or secure him in any public goal, shall receive the above reward, and all necessary charges paid by me STILES CURTISS.

Stratford, January 26, 1784.

Reprints: Connecticut Journal, 02-04-1784; 02-11-1784.

Connecticut Journal, 08-04-1784.

Long-Island, Suffolk County, Smithton, July 24, 1784.

RUNAWAY from the Subscriber, a NEGRO BOY, about fifteen Years old, very witty, an excellent Whistler of any March, mannerly, and speaks good English, his Name is Isaac, but very likely to change it; when he went away had on nothing but a Shirt and Trowsers, being much tarred. Whoever will take up said Boy, so that the Owner may have him, shall be entitled to Fifteen Dollars Reward, and reasonable Charge paid, by JOHN HARTT.

N.B. Whoever may have taken up said Boy, must be very careful or he will get away.

Reprints: Connecticut Journal, 08-18-1784; 08-18-1784.

Connecticut Journal, 12-08-1784.

RAN-AWAY from the Subscriber on Friday last, a NEGRO SERVANT, named JACK, aged 17 Years, 5 Feet 6 Inches high, thick set, Copper coloured; had on a blue Flannel Coat, white Pewter Buttons flowered, light colour'd Linen Vest, white Holland Shirt, blue striped Overalls, brown Linen Stockings, small Felt Hat, light colour'd Flannel Great Coat, plain Pewter Buttons. Whoever will take up said Servant, shall have Five Dollars Reward, and all necessary Charges paid by

MILES MERWIN.

Milford, Dec. 6, 1784.

Masters of Vessels are forbid employing him or carrying him off, as they will answer it at the Peril of the Law.

Connecticut Journal, 04-06-1785.

Stradford, March 2, 1785.

RAN-AWAY from Ebenezer Hurd, a NEGRO MAN, about 30 years old, is short and thick set, has large legs, much pitted with the small-pox, has a bald spot on his head, occasioned by a scald when young; had on and took with him when he went away, a pair of thick sole shoes, two pair of stockings, a pair of red duffil trowsers, a linen jacket, a new strait bodied cloth coloured coat, a great coat half worn, a new woollen checkt shirt, & a new felt hat. Whoever takes up and secures said Negro, so that I have him, shall receive a GUINEA reward, and all necessary charges paid by

EBENEZER HURD.

He stole and took away a small sum of money, and two razors.

All persons are forbid to harbor, or employ said Negro.

Connecticut Journal, 08-10-1785.

Twenty Dollars Reward.

RAN away from the Subscriber, on Wednesday the 13ult. a negro servant woman, about twenty years old, almost white. The wench is a smart likely girl, about five feet five inches high, slim built, speaks but little, has a scar on her right arm which appears to be a scald: was bred on the Island of Barbadoes. In all probability will try to make that place again. All persons are forbid harbouring her, masters of vessels are requested to pay a particular attention, as they will answer it at their peril. JOHN CAPE.

New-York, July 15, 1785.

N.B. All charges paid. We have heard that she had made an acquaintance with a negro man from Eastward.

Reprint: Connecticut Journal, 08-17-1785.

Connecticut Journal, 12-21-1785.

RANAWAY from the subscriber, th[is] morning, a negro man, named GIF[F] about 21 years of age, a stout thick-set fellow, 5 feet 5 or 6 inches high, had on and took with him, a dark brown coat, jacket and overalls, blue shaloon coat, a pair [of] Russia duck overalls, a flopt hat, striped [red] and blue worsted cap, and a small [red] blanket. Whoever will take up, and [re]turn said negro, to the subscriber, shall ha[ve] TWENTY DOLLARS reward. JOHN ROGERS.

New-Haven, Dec. 13, 1785.

Connecticut Journal, 01-11-1786.

Run away from the Subscriber, two Negro MEN, one about 50 years old, of a small size, can read and write, and may forge passes; had on when he went away, a reddish coat and leather breeches. The other of about 18 years old, of a small size, handsome and well built; had on when he went away, a brown coat and leather breeches, with trowsers over them, and a small wool hat. Whoever will take up said Negroes, and secure them in goal (for they are old offenders) so that the owner may have them again, shall be entitled to FIF-TEEN DOLLARS Reward, and reasonable charges paid. JOHN HARTT.
 Huntington, (Long-Island) Jan'y 10, 1786.
 Reprints: Connecticut Journal, 01-18-1786; 01-25-1786.

Connecticut Journal, 05-31-1786
 Ran-away on Saturday Night, being the Night after the 27th Instant, May, from the Subscribers, a Molatto Slave, named ROBIN, about 5 Feet, 2 or 3 Inches high, 18 or 20 Years old, speaks slow and good English; had with a redish Sailor Jacket, black round Hat, a light colour'd long Coat, Corduroy Breeches, white Vest, Holland Shirt, and a Blanket. All Masters of Vessels are warned against shipping him, and all Tenders of Ferries are desired to secure him. Whoever will take up said Fellow, and deliver him to the Sub-scribers, shall have TEN DOLLARS Reward, and all reasonable Charges paid by
          LEMAN STONE & Co.
 Derby, May 29th, 1786.
 Reprint: Connecticut Journal, 06-14-1786.

Connecticut Journal, 08-16-1786.

Ran-away from the Subscriber, on the fifth instant, a negro named STE-PHEN, about twenty-one years old, about six feet high, a stout built fellow, pretty black; carried away with him a pale blue coat, linen shirt and trowsers, a felt hat, a grey coloured great coat, pieced at the bottom. Whoever will take up said fellow and secure him in gaol, so that his master may have him again, shall have TEN DOLLARS reward, and all reasonable charges paid by me
         THOMAS HELME.
 Brook-Haven, Long Island,
 August 7, 1786.
 Reprints: Connecticut Journal, 08-23-1786; 08-30-1786

Connecticut Journal, 09-27-1786.

Five Dollars Reward.

RANAWAY from the Subscriber, on the 17th Instant, at Night, a Negro Man, named Glasgow, about 40 Years of Age, about six Feet high, well built, and very black, the middle Finger of his right Hand crooked, and has Holes in his Ears. Had on, and took with him, a grey Great Coat, a dark brown Surtout, red Vest, dark brown ditto, and striped Linen Trowsers; had a large Pack, in which, among other Articles, was a Fiddle, on which he plays. Whoever will take him up, secure him, or return him to his Master, shall receive the above Reward, and all necessary Charges paid by EBENEZER PLATT.

Milford, September 18, 1786.

Connecticut Journal, 08-29-1787.

RUNAWAY from the Subscriber, the Night after the 27th Instant, a white Man, named ELY HULL, about 2[4] Years old, about 5 Feet 8 or 9 Inches high, and took away with him one Negro Fellow named AARON, about 18 Years old; said Negro is a slim built Fellow, and took with him a grey home made Coat, Jacket and Breeches, and a Butternut coloured Great Coat; the white Man is a slim built Fellow, and has on a white Hat, and took with him a blue home made Coat, & black Shaloon Jacket and Breeches; they also took two or three Pair of new Shoes. Whoever will take up the Negro shall have Five Dollars Reward and all necessary Charges paid, and for the white Man, a reasonable Reward, by

JOSHUA PORTER.

Southington, August 28, 1787.
Reprint: Connecticut Journal, 09-05-1787.

Rhode Island 1758–1789

[VOL. XIII.] THE [NUMB. 653.]

PROVIDENCE GAZETTE; AND COUNTRY JOURNAL:

Containing the freshest ADVICES, Foreign and Domestic.

SATURDAY, JULY 6, 1776.

MR. CARTER,

If you think the following Observations of any Importance in promoting the Welfare of this Country, you may give them a Place in your next Gazette.

MY friends and countrymen, when the tyranny of Britain, and the stoppage of the usual channels of supply, of foreign manufactures, render the highest improvement in those of America absolutely necessary, especially in the articles of clothing, I presume that every honest attempt to promote such an interesting design, must meet with the public approbation; and therefore hope the following thoughts, on the culture and treatment of FLAX, will not be unacceptable, as they are founded on observation and experience in this country, and the treatment of that article in Ireland.

The soil most suitable for growing it is a loom, if to be had, as that is equally secured from the two extremes of drought, and too great a degree of moisture; and, if not lately brought under culture, should be manured, to render it tolerably fertile. Land from whence barley, a crop of Indian corn, or potatoes, were taken the year preceding, is generally found best, probably because of the general usage of dunging in the hole, and the greater ease of rendering it entirely mellow, which is of such great importance in this crop, that it will amply repay the trouble of at least three times plowing, and as frequent harrowing, followed by repeated bushing, to break and pulverize the clods. In a country so greatly infested with worms as this, the first plowing should be as early as the frost will permit, that being exposed to, they may be destroyed by the cold; and probably if it should be plowed before the setting in of the winter frosts, it might effectually destroy these pests: The experiment, however, can be attended with but small expence. I have been credibly informed, that a judicious farmer in Connecticut, when he discovered the worms first begin to eat, has found the scattering of dry ashes plentifully over the flax, at three or four inches high, while the dew is yet on in the morning, an effectual remedy against them. However this may be, I cannot doubt but that it will amply repay him both for his ashes and trouble, in the additional fertility of the land. The amazing destruction of flax, in almost all parts of this country, this very year, will fully justify the minute attention I have here paid to this noxious reptile.

It has been found, by repeated experiments, that seed imported from the southward, not even further than Long-Island, will produce nearly if not quite a double crop, other things being equal. The great importance of having it entirely clean needs not be mentioned; of which, on rich lands, two bushels at least should be sown on an acre, unless your object is principally to raise seed; and if you mean to raise it for very fine cloth, three bushels will not be too much. For several years successively we have been visited with great drought in the month of June, which has greatly diminished the quantity of flax in this part of the country: Would it not be adviseable therefore to begin the sowing as early as there is any prospect of being secured from the frost? Observation this year proves that the flax sowed about the middle of April is generally best, except in land very subject to frost.

After the blossoms are fallen, and the bolls about half grown, pull your flax, observing to put that of equal length together, and bind it in sheaves immediately, of about six or eight inches diameter; and the next day, if convenient, lay it under stagnant clear water, if to be had; be sure to keep it entirely under for eight or ten days, trying a small quantity from the middle of the sheaf, to find when the coat will begin to separate from the stalk. Be sure to take it out to drain before it is sufficiently rotted for dressing, lest it should be over done; when drained, spread it as usual in the country for dew-rotting, which will happen at a season of the year when there will be no danger of long storms to rot it too much, to prevent which there ought to be the utmost care, lest by this means you should lose your labour. Probably, as at that season of the year the dews are commonly heavy, one week of dew-rotting may be too much. As the time of its lying under water is taken from the usage in Ireland, it may be too long for this, which is a hotter climate; this must be guarded against by frequently trying it; but this you can easily remedy by sowing a piece for that purpose; while on the other hand you will have your flax finer, more certainly well rotted, and fit for almost immediate use (which in this time of great scarcity is of no small importance) as well as a much larger quantity from the same ground.

I am aware that many will slight these hints, through a strong attachment to their paternal modes of culture, and a reluctance at trying new methods; but the more speculative judicious farmer will readily admit, that the cultivation of the soil in this country is but in its infancy; and that experience ever was, and ever will be, the only method of perfecting it in any country.

There is already in this town a cambric loom, erected by a patriotic merchant, who well understands the business of weaving it, and wishes to have a quantity of fine flax produced, that the daughters of liberty may be decked with the fine linen of America, manufactured by themselves: But the season is too far advanced to obtain this purpose the present year, except by pulling by itself the finest already grown.

If these hints should induce an abler hand to do this important subject justice, my end will be fully answered. I hope at least, those whose observation or reading will enable them to point out any defects in this piece, and to throw more light on the subject, will be so kind as to transmit authentic accounts thereof to the printer of this paper, that some person of ability and leisure may digest and publish them.

PHILO PATRIÆ.

MR. CARTER,

The following Address, lately published in a neighbouring Colony, may in some Measure serve to illustrate the Wisdom and Justice of the present Test-Act. *By inserting it in your Gazette, you will oblige at least one of your Readers.*

An Address to the Freemen, on the Absurdity and Stupidity of a pretended Neutrality.

"*How long halt ye between two opinions? If the Lord be God, follow him: But if Baal, then follow him.*" Prophet Elijah.

"*Every Principle of Justice and Honor should prompt a Man to use his best Endeavours for the Benefit of any Community of which he is a Member, and of whose Privileges he partakes.*" Dr. Priestly.

"*When Freedom calls, none shall from Danger start,*
"*But take a noble, a decisive Part.*

THAT there is an eternal and infinite difference between *truth* and *falshood*, in speculation, and *right* and *wrong* in practice; and that mankind in general are capable of discerning this difference, and of conforming their words and actions to the *laws of reason*, are principles upon which commerce is carried on, and government founded. Upon these principles, it seems, we justly blame the man that breaks his promise, or neglects to fulfil his contract.

Upon these principles, we can bear to see robbers and murderers punished; and hear of *tories*, those robbers and murderers of millions, being gently tarred and feathered, or despised and neglected by all mankind. Upon these principles, we condemn all pretended *neuters* in a community, as the real enemies of their country. Though in pretence,

" Neuters *are neither true, nor false, good nor evil;*
" *Neither sons of God, nor servants of the devil.*"

But in reality, perhaps, there never was a *neuter*. And indeed no man ought to stand as an idle spectator of injured innocence, oppressed by fraud or violence. For we are all obliged, on pain of eternal damnation, to make use of all lawful endeavours to preserve our own lives and liberties, and the lives and liberties of others. And "*omissions* are ranked by civilians and moralists among the number of *actions*, because they apprehend them as the effect of a *voluntary suspension* of the exercises of our faculties ‡."

So that, it seems, for any man *to omit to do right*, is in this sense *doing wrong*. If a robber and murderer should break into a house, and attempt to rob and murder a man's mother, will any mortal venture to affirm, that her own son has a *right* to stand as an idle spectator, or pretended *neuter*, and suffer his own mother to be robbed and murdered? Or, would it be a sufficient compleat justification, if the son should very modestly and ingeniously confess, that he was afraid, if he interposed, that he should be in danger of losing a *petty post*, which he held under the murderer, *during pleasure?*—— "To attack the constitution of a state (says *Vattel*) and to violate its laws, is a capital crime against society; and if those guilty of it are invested with authority, they add to this crime a perfidious abuse of the power with which they are invested." And I will venture to add, that it seems, that all their advocates, aiders and abetters, are guilty of the same crime, namely, of high-treason against the majesty of the state—and ought to be treated as traitors, and common enemies; though their transgressions must be greater, or less, in proportion to their former obligations. I would likewise add, that all pretended *neuters*, in a state, may be considered as real enemies of the most maligant kind. The pretended neutrals at *Nova-Scotia* confirm this observation.

I would observe once more, that all pretended *neuters*, in a state, are not only real enemies, but gross hypocrites, and as such odious to God, and all good men.

For tamely to suffer ourselves, or our neighbours, to be deprived of happiness, is inconsistent with *reason, truth*, and *justice*. And every pretended *neuter* that appears ready and willing to sacrifice his country, out of complaisance to the arbitrary commands of a *lawless tyrant*, for the sake of some *petty post*, deserves to have his name struck out of the roll of the society of which he was a member, and be treated as a common enemy to the happiness of the community †. The *luke-warm* are mentioned in Revelations as the vilest of mortals, intolerably nauseous, and loathsome. "Because thou art *luke-warm*, and neither *cold* nor *hot*, I will *spew* thee out of my mouth." And indeed the Son of God, "who is the brightness of his Father's glory, and the express image of his person," tells us that "no man can serve two masters," and "he that is not with me is against me."

There is also danger of detection. "*Nemo fictam personam diu sustinere potest.*" "No man can dissemble always," one time or other he will be surprized, and forget himself, and let his mask fall; or, some accident, or rather providence, may make the discovery. For instance here, we need only have recourse to the infamous, hypocritical *Hutchinson* and his letters; a man, in the opinion of the faithful, "just saint enough to play the devil." By which letters also we may discover, who have been fond of complimenting away our rights and privileges, by telling that *tool of tyranny* what he had wrote, to inslave America, "*was the most unanswerable,*" &c. acting as *judge of admiralty*, and greedily condemning and sharing poor men's property, may serve to convince us, that such a pretended *neuter* is rather a lover of himself than his country. "A court partaking in the fruits of its own condemnation is a robber," says the judicious *Burke*; and is contrary to "the spirit of the English constitution, which, diffused through the mighty mass, pervades, feeds, unites, invigorates, vivifies every part of the empire, even down to the minutest member. It is the love of the people, it is their attachment to their government, from the sense of the deep stake they have in such a glorious institution, which gives you your *army* and your *navy*," says Mr. *Burke*. Again I would observe, keeping company with *tories*, and enemies of their country, may likewise serve to discover the man that endeavours to conceal himself.

"*Pares cum paribus facillime congregantur.*"
In English thus,—" Birds of a feather
" Will flock together."

And "can two walk together, except they be agreed?"—" For what fellowship hath righteousness with unrighteousness? And what communion hath light with darkness? Or—he that believeth with an infidel? Or what communion can a son of liberty have with a servile *tory*?

And now, my dear countrymen, as we are all deeply engaged in defence of our civil and religious constitution, I shall venture to advise you, to choose no man into more than one civil office of importance at the same time; nor to continue any men too long in office, lest from dignified *servants*, they become your absolute *masters*, and lord it over you.—Among the Romans the *consuls* were chosen but for one year;

‡ *Vide Burlamaqui's Principles of Law, vol. 1, fol.*

† *Vide Polit. Nat. fol. 230.*

Figure 2.1. Cover page: Providence Gazette, published as The Providence Gazette; And Country Journal, 07-06-1776

Chapter Three

Rhode Island Notices

The American Journal and General Advertiser, 06-09-1781.

Ten Silver Dollars Reward.

RAN-away from the Ship Marquis la Fayette, a Negro Man, named JACK, belonging to Messirs Wells Cooper and Co. of Virginia; he is a low built, well set Fellow, was born in the North of England, speaks after their Manner, his Face is marked with a Number of Scars. Whoever will take up the said Negro, and deliver him to the Captain on board said Ship, or to Mr. John Brown, in Providence, shall receive the above Reward, and all necessary Charges.

Providence, June 9, 1781.

Reprint: The American Journal and General Advertiser, 06-30-1781.

The Newport Mercury, 12-04-1759.

RUN away the 4th of October last, from Joseph Hall, of Wallingford in Connecticut, a Molatto Man Slave, 26 years of Age, middling Stature, brought up among us; of quick and clear Speech, and can read well. When he went away, he had on a pale Duroy Coat with red Lining, one dark brown Flannel Coat, one checked Holland Shirt, one white ditto, and one much worn Flannel ditto; pale blue Stockings, and a white Bed Blanket.

Whoever will take up the said Slave, and bring him Home, or secure him, so that I may have him, shall have Twenty Shillings Lawful Money Reward, and all necessary Charges. JOSEPH HALL.

The Newport Mercury, 04-22-1760.

FIVE DOLLARS Reward.

RUN away on the 22d of May last, from Robert Stanton of Stonington, in the County of New-London, and Colony of Connecticut, a Negro Man, about 25 Years of Age, short and thick, has a large Leg and Lips, his Teeth stand at a Distance before. He can play on a Violin. Had on when he went away, a lightish coloured Broadcloth Coat, with flowered Brass Buttons, a Kersey Jacket, a white Flannel Shirt marked C on the Bosom, and a Pair of Broad-cloth Breeches, with short wide Trowsers over them, and a Felt Hat. Whoever will bring said Runaway to his Master, or secure him in any of His Majesty's Goals, and give Information thereof to the Subscriber, shall have Five Dollars Reward, and all necessary Charges, paid by ROBERT STANTON.

The Newport Mercury, 12-27-1762.

December 9, 1762.

A Negro Man was taken up and committed to his Majesty's Gaol in King's County, in this Colony, who says his Name is Solomon, and that he run away from his Master, Nathaniel Durkee, of Wooderry, in the Colony of Connecticut. The Owner of said Negro is desired to take him away, and pay the Charges.

I. Case, Goal-Keeper.

Reprints: The Newport Mercury, 01-03-1763; 01-10-1763; 01-17-1763; 01-24-1763.

The Newport Mercury, 05-09-1763.

RUN-AWAY from Jonathan Haszard of South-Kingstown, on the Eleventh of this Instant April, a Mustee Boy, about thirteen Years of Age, a thick sett Fellow, his Countenance something hard, with a large Scar on the Top of one of his Feet: He had on a blue Broad Cloth Jacket and Breeches, a pretty good Beaver Hat. Whoever will apprehend said Fellow, and bring him to his said Master, or put him in any of the Goals in said Colony, shall have Thirty Pounds Old Tenor Reward paid by me. JONATHAN HASZARD

42—45

The Newport Mercury, 05-16-1763.

Stonington, May 7, 1763.

Ten Dollars Reward.

RAN-AWAY from his Master (James Richardson, of Stonington, in Connecticut) a Mulatto Servant Man, named Joseph Smith, alias Joseph Mingore. He was last Year at the Havannah with Lieut. Col. Hargill, of Rhode-Island, and passes as a Soldier. He says that he was brought up with Stephen Cottril, of South-Kingstown, in Rhode-Island Government; is about 6 Feet high, about 24 Years of Age, much Pock-broken, talks good English; had on when he run away, two Suits of Broad-Cloth Cloaths, one of which was blue, and the other of a light Colour; a red Waistcoat, a Callico ditto, a Duffil Great Coat, a Pair of Buckskin Breeches, and a Leather Jockey-Hat.—Whoever takes up the said Servant, and returns him to his Master, shall receive TEN DOLLARS Reward, and all necessary Charges paid, by me

JAMES RICHARDSON.

Reprints: The Newport Mercury, 05-23-1763; 05-30-1763; 06-06-1763; 06-20-1763; 07-04-1763; 07-11-1763.

The Newport Mercury, 06-20-1763.

Warwick, June 18, 1763.

RAN-AWAY last Night from his Master, Othniel Gorton, Esq; of Warwick, in the County of Kent, and Coony of Rhode-Island, a Negro Man Servant, named Peter, aged about 18 Years, of a slim Stature, not tall, speaks good English, born in this Country; he has a small Bunch on his Forehead, and another on one of his Wrists; had on when he went away, one old striped Linsey Woolsey Jacket, without Sleeves, one new full Cloth Jacket, of a redish Colour, and an old Beaver Hat: He carried away a new full Cloth Great Coat, of the same Colour as the Jacket; likewise two new Tow Cloth Shirts, and two Pair of new Tow Cloth Trowsers, which were made pretty wide and short: He also took with him one fine white Shirt.—Whosoever shall take up said Negro, and return him to his Master, shall have FIVE DOLLARS Reward, and all necessary Charges paid my me, OTHNEIL GORTON.

Reprints: The Newport Mercury, 07-04-1763; 07-11-1763.

The Newport Mercury, 03-26-1764.

A Negro Man, named JOB, belonging to Stephen Sampson of Plymouth, ran-away from thence the 15th Instant. He is about 25 Years of Age, 5 Feet 8 or 9 Inches high, had on a light colour'd Serge Jacket & Breeches, a blue Pair of Yarn Stockings; a red Baize Shirt; his left Hand and Wrist is very weak; he understands the Blacksmith's Trade. Whoever takes him up, and secure him, or conveys him to Billings Throop of Bristol, shall have 8 Dollars Reward, and all necessary Charges paid.

March 26, 1764.

Reprints: The Newport Mercury, 04-09-1764. This notice was also printed in The Providence Gazette; and Country Journal, 04-07-1764; 04-14-1764; 04-21-1764; 05-05-1764.

The Newport Mercury, 09-10-1764.

On the 20th of August run away from JOHN BANISTER, his Negro Man, Caesar, 35 Years old, a well-set Fellow, stoops forward remarkably when he walks, speaks good English for one of his Colour.—Whoever takes him on Rhode-Island, (where it's probably he lurks) and deliver him to his said Master, shall have TWO DOLARS; off the Island, FOUR DOLLARS, and necessary Charges.

Reprints: The Newport Mercury, 09-17-1764; 09-24-1764; 10-01-1764.

The Newport Mercury, 09-10-1764.

Ran-away from James Greene, of Warwick, on the 12th Instant, two Apprentice Boys, viz. Samuel Clarke, a white Lad, about sixteen Years old, dark brown Hair; had on when he went away, a striped Flannel double-breasted Jacket, long Tow and Linen Trowsers, Felt Hat, and Shoes without Stockings.—John Tobe, a Molatto Boy, about fourteen Years old, resembles an Indian, short and thick, short Neck and thick Shoulders, has a Scar on his Throat, and hath lost one fore Tooth; had on when he went away, a striped Flannel Jacket, a thick cloth colour'd ditto, long Tow and Linen Trowsers, and old Beaver Hat, and Shoes without Stockings; his Hair newly cut off.— Whoever will apprehend said Servants, and secure them in any of his Majesty's Goals, or give Notice to the said James Greene, so that he may have them again, shall have Eight Dollars Reward, and all necessary Charges paid; or if but one of them should be taken, shall have Four Dollars.

JAMES GREENE.

FORTY SHILLINGS REWARD.

The Newport Mercury, 11-04-1765.

ALBANY, September 19, 1765.

RUN-away from the Subscriber, Yesterday, a Mulatto Negro Man, a Spaniard, named JOSEPH; about 25 Years old, a short well made Fellow, speaks broken English, (he went off with a big Spanish Negro belonging to Mr. Bayard of New-York, sent here to sell.) He had on when he went away, a blue Jacket, an old light-coloured Ratteen ditto without Sleeves, and Oznabrigs Shirt, old Leather Breeches, a Pair of black ribb'd Stockings, a Hat bound with Worsted Binding, and a Pair of new Shoes with Brass Buckles.

Whoever takes him up, and secures him in any of his Majesty's Gaols, so that his Master may have him again, shall have the above Reward, and all reasonable Charges, paid by Mr. JOHN ERNEST, Merchant, in New-York, or the Subscriber in Albany. BARENT TEN EYCK.

N.B. All Masters of Vessels and others, are forbid to conceal, harbour, entertain, or carry off the said Servant, as they will answer it at their Peril.

Reprints: The Newport Mercury, 11-11-1765; 11-18-1765; 12-09-1765.

The Newport Mercury, 09-09-1765.

RAN-WAY from his Master, Jonathan Haszard, Esq; of Boston-Neck, in South-Kingstown, on the 16th Instant, a Mustee-Man-Slave, named Ben, twenty Years of Age; he has a remarkable gray Spot of Hair on the back Part of his Head, and several Scars about his Wrist; he is about five Feet eight Inches high; had on when he went away, a Thunder and Lightning Woollen Coat, a double breasted striped flannel Jacket, a Tow Shirt, and Worsted Stockings: He carried off, two Pair of Shoes, one Fair new, and the other old.—He likewise carried off a Bundle of Cloaths, consisting of Tow Shirts, and a Check Shirt, with other Things unknown.—Whoever will apprehend and secure said Mustee Man Slave, so that his Master may have him again, shall receive FOUR DOLLARS Reward, and all necessary Charges paid by

JONATHAN HASZARD.

South-Kingstown, August 17, 1765.

Reprint: The Newport Mercury, 10-07-1765.

The Newport Mercury, Monday, May 19, to Monday, May 26, 1766.

South Hold, on Long-Island, May 12, 1766.

RAN-AWAY from their Masters, (Micah Moore, and Abraham Corey) on Saturday Night last, two Negro Men, one named Prince, about 30 Years of Age, of a middling Stature, well set, one of his upper fore Teeth gone, of an Oliver Complexion; had on when he went away, a light-blue homespun Broad-Cloth Coat; he some Time since belonged to the Rev. Mr. Barber of Groton. The other is 25 Years of Age, 5 Feet 9 Inches high, well set, has lost half of one of his upper fore Teeth, is very black, named Crank; had on when he away, a homespun Broad-Cloth Coat, of a light blue, trimmed with black, and double-breasted, black Everlasting Waistcoat, Leather Breeches, blue ribb'd Yarn Stockings, thin Shoes, with plain Silver Buckles, and a new Castor Hat; speaks good English.—Whoever shall take up said Negroes, or either of them, and secure them, so that their Masters may have them again, shall have a Reward of FIVE DOLLARS for each, and all necessary Charges, paid by me, ABRAHAM COREY.

Reprints: The Newport Mercury, Monday, May 26, to Monday, June 2, 1766; Monday, June 2, to Monday, June 9, 1766; Monday, June 9, to Monday, June 16, 1766.

The Newport Mercury, Monday, May 11, to Monday, May 18, 1767.

Ran-away from the Subscriber, in South-Kingstown, on the 20th of this Instant, April, a Mustee Fellow, a Slave, named Harry, about five Feet ten Inches high, has a bushy Head of Hair; had on when he went away, two Check Flannel Shirts, a Pair of striped Kersey Trowsers, the Stripes running round the Legs. Whoever will secure said Fellow in any of his Majesty's Gaols, or bring him to me, shall FIVE DOLLARS Reward, and all necessary Charges paid.

S. Kingstown, April 23, 1767.

ENOCH HASZARD.

The Newport Mercury, Monday, February 22, to Monday, February 29, 1768.

RAN-AWAY from his Master, PELEG SHEARMAN, a Negro Man named Taff, of a middling Stature, with a larger Guinea Mark on each Cheek; had on a Hat and Cap, a red Watch Coat, a dark coloured Jacket lined with striped Flannel, Oznaburgs Shirt, light coloured Breeches and Trowsers, and Stockings and Shoes.—Whoever will take up said Negro, and bring him to his Master shall have Two Dollars Reward, and necessary Charges paid.

N.B. All Persons are desired not to entertain him.

The Newport Mercury, Monday, August 29, to Monday, September 5, 1768.

Five Dollars Reward.

RAN AWAY from his Master, a thick, well-set Mulatto Fellow, named CATO, about Twenty Years of Age, about Five Feet Two or Three Inches High, had on Shoes and Stockings, Red Breeches, Linen Shirt, & a Striped Flannel Jacket: Said Fellow is left-handed sometimes plays on a Fiddle; has a Scar across one of his Feet, his Hair was long when he went away.

Whosoever apprehends said Fellow, and delivers him to the Subscriber his Master, or secures him in any of Majesty's Jails, and gives Notice thereof, shall have FIVE DOLLARS Reward, and all necessary Charges paid by JONATHAN HASZARD, living on Boston-Neck, in South-Kingstown, in the Colony if Rhode Island.

August 14, 1768. (20)

The Newport Mercury, Monday, July 25, to Monday, August 1, 1768.

RAN away from Thomas Chadwick in Newport, on the 14th day of this instant July, a Negro Man named Quako, a short thickset fellow, had on an Ozenbrigs Frock, a striped Flannel Shirt, a pair of red Duffil Trowsers, pretty much patched, an old hat and black Wig: Whoever will take up said Negroe Man and bring him to the subscriber his Master, shall have 5 Dollars Reward, and all necessary charges paid by THOMAS CHADWICK.

Reprint: Newport Mercury, Monday, August 1, to Monday, August 8, 1768.

The Newport Mercury, Monday, January 23, to Monday, January 30, 1769.

Eight Dollars Reward.

RAN away from the Subscriber in South-Kingstown, on the 7th Instant, a light-coloured Mustee Indented Servant, named CUDJO, but commonly called HUNK, a lusty stout Fellow, about Nineteen Years of Age, near Six Feet high, having a large bushy Head of Hair; had on a white Wollen Jacket, and white Breeches and Stockings: Whoever will apprehend said Fellow, and deliver him to Capt. ROBERT LILLIBRIDGE, jun. at Newport, or send him to any of his Majesty's Jails in this Colony, and give Notice thereof to said Lillibridge, or to the Subscriber, shall have the above Reward, and all necessary Charges, paid by said Lillibridge, or by WILLIAM HULL.

South Kingstown, January 12, 1769.

The Newport Mercury, 06-26-1769.

Ten Dollars Reward

RAN away from the Subscriber, a likely, well built NEGRO MAN, named CUFF, about 26 Years of Age: He has on One of his Legs, and also on One of his Feet, a large SCAR, and stoops very much when he walks, had on when he went away, a pair of Kersey Breeches, Flannel Shirt, and Shoes and Stockings:—Whoever will take up said Negro, and convey him to his Master, or confine him in any of his Majesty's Goals, so that his Master may have him again, shall receive TEN DOLLARS Reward, and have all necessary Charges paid, by JOSEPH CONGDON.

South-Kingstown, March 27, 1769. (63)

Reprint: The Newport Mercury, 08-07-1769.

The Newport Mercury, 10-05-1772.

RAN away from the subscriber, on the 3d instant, a Mulatto man, named PERO, about 30 years of age, of a middle stature, had on, when he went away, a dark mixed coloured broad cloth coat, trim'd with black, a brown cut plush waistcoat, a pair of black knit breeches, a checked shirt, worsted stockings, claf-skin shoes, and silver buckles, a felt hat, had a white Holland shirt, and check'd trowsers with him, his hair cut short on the top of his head, and left longer in his neck and foretop, has a long head, is very talkative, goes leaning forward, and swing his arms very much when he walks: Whoever will take up said runaway, and convey him to his master, or secure him in any of his Majesty's jails, so that his master may have him again, shall have FOUR DOLLARS reward, and all necessary charges, paid by GEORGE BABCOCK.

    N.B. All masters of vessels are hereby forbid carrying off said servant.

    (35) South-Kingstown, Oct. 5th, 1772.

    Reprint: The Newport Mercury, 10-19-1772.

The Newport Mercury, 08-29-1774.

RAN away from the subscriber, the 17th day of this instant, a Mulatto fellow, named DICK, about 23 years of age; about 5 feet, 10 inches high; has on his upper lip a scar, or bunch, occasioned by a kick from a horse, pretty full ey'd and pimpled face.—Had on when he went away, a grey Kersey jacket, white towcloth breeches, white towcloth shirt, and an old felt hat, a linen handkerchief on his neck, and a bandanno handkerchief on his head: Whoever will take up said runaway, so that his master may have him again, shall have a reward of five DOLLARS, and all necessary charges, paid by

    SAMUEL CONGDON. South-Kingstown, Aug. 22, 1774.

    Reprint: The Newport Mercury, 09-05-1774 (Supplement).

The Newport Mercury, 10-31-1774.

SIX DOLLARS REWARD.

RAN away from the subscriber, last night, a Negro man, an indented servant for 6 years, named POMP, a well made fellow, of middling stature, lively and active, about twenty-five years old, speaks quick, and something broken English, can talk some Dutch, has lost the upper joint of his left thumb, the nail turns down partly over the end of the same; carried away with him a home made mix-coloured blue and red coat, lined with blue shalloon, trimmed with yellow metal buttons, cloth-coloured duroy jacket and breeches, two pair of leather-breeches, a new felt-hat laced with yellow tinsel, old ditto not laced, a white shirt, and striped ditto, checked linen trowsers, cloth coloured great coat, much worn, a pair of turn'd pumps, and double soled shoes, silver-plated shoe buckles, and sundry pair of stockings:—Whoever will take up said Negro, and bring him to his master, shall have the above reward, and all necessary charges, paid by the subscriber. All masters of vessels, and other, are forbid carrying off, or harbouring, said Negro, at their peril. SAMUEL BROWN, jun.

Stockbridge, Oct. 9, 1774.

The Newport Mercury, 01-30-1775.

RAN away, on the 4th day of January, 1775, from STEPHEN HASSARD, of South Kingstown, a MUSTEE man slave, named JO; about 20 years old; a thick, short fellow, long hair behind, a little curled, and on the top of his head cut short; his complexion is as light as an Indian, being part Spanish Indian; had on, when he went away, three jackets, his outside jacket and breeches were of mill'd colour, but something faded, his jacket had pewter, and his breeches brass buttons; his middle jacket a very short one, one fore skirt of it torn off, and has been torn down the black seem by wrestling, his under jacket is an old red duffil, much patched and faded; a good felt hat about half-worn, a pair of white yarn stockings, and an old pair shoes:—Whoever will take up said fellow, and secure him in any of his Majesty's gaols, so that his master gets him again, or convey him home, shall have EIGHT DOLLARS reward, and all necessary charges, paid by STEPHEN HASSARD.

Reprint: The Newport Mercury, 02-06-1775.

The Newport Mercury, 08-02-1773.

WHEREAS Ann Gorman, an indented servant girl, (being of a short stature, black ey'd, and very chatty and impudent) has run away from the subscriber, this is to give notice, that whoever harbours or employs said servant, may depend on being prosecuted according to law. She was seen in company with a black girl at Portsmouth, last Friday, who ran away at the same time. The white girl is an excellent spinner and has two years time to serve, which will be sold at a reasonable rate.

(78) JOSEPH BULL.

The Newport Mercury, 08-09-1773.

RAN away from BARZILLAI BECKWITH, of East-Hadam, in the colony of Connecticut, a Mulatto man slave, about thirty-three years of age, about five feet eight inches high, thickset, with curl'd hair, round shouldered; carried away with him, and had on, a coat and breeches of a claret coloured cloth, a green ratteen jacket; one jacket of cotton and linen, of a redish colour, one striped linen shirt on his back, felt hat, short, wide tow-cloth trowsers, a pair of pumps on his feet, but no stockings: Whoever will apprehend said servant, and commit him to his Majesty's gaol, shall have six Spanish mill'd DOL-LARS reward, and all necessary charges, paid by BARZILLAI BECKWITH;

All masters of vessels, and others, are hereby forbid harbouring or carry-ing off said run-away.

Reprints: The Newport Mercury, 08-23-1773.

The Newport Mercury, 12-06-1773.

RAN away from JOHN EARLE, in Dartmouth, on Sunday, the 15th of November inst. a Mustee slave, about 5 feet 4 inches high, thick and well set, 25 years old, having a remarkable scar on one of his cheeks, and another on his right arm, a very fine set of teeth, and true Negro hair; had on a cloth-colour'd double-breasted jacket, and a pair of new leather breeches, and fustian breeches with him, with sundry other articles. Whoever will appre-hend said run-away, and return him to said EARLE, or confine him in any of his Majesty's jails, and give notice thereof, shall receive SIX DOLLARS reward, and all necessary charges, paid by JOHN EARLE, Nov. 29.

Reprint: The Newport Mercury, 12-13-1773.

The Newport Mercury, 02-07-1774.

RAN away from John Wady, of Dartmouth, on the 25th day of October last, a Negro man, named Cesar, alias Hanover, of about 5 feet, 3 inches high, and 24 years, old a very well set fellow, and commonly stout for his size, with broad face and pretty well looking; he has a very large white set of teeth, one of his great toes having been formerly split with an ax, on which is a scar, the whole length of the toe, but can't be discovered, without being closely exam-ined; had on when he went away, a maple colour'd fulled jacket, a striped flannel shirt, and a cotton and linen shirt: Whoever shall take up said Negro, and return him to the subscriber, or confine him in any of his Majesty's jails, and give notice thereof, shall receive six dollars reward, and all necessary charges, paid by JOHN WADY.

Reprints: The Newport Mercury, 02-21-1774; 02-28-1774; 03-07-1774.

The Newport Mercury, 05-30-1774.

RAN away from the subscriber, living South-Kingstown, on the 22d day of May current, a Mulatto servant man, named JACK, about 19 years of age, a slender, straight limb'd fellow, about 5 feet 7 inches high, wears his own hair, very much curled, has a scar on one of his thumbs, occasioned by it being mash'd; had on, when he went off, a white flannel shirt, black knit breeches, tow stockings, a blue and white flannel jacket, a narrow brim'd felt hat, with a wire chain for a band; he carried with him a check'd shirt, a pair of stockings, and a striped linen jacket.—Whoever will apprehend said fellow, and secure him, so that his master may have him again, shall receive FOUR DOLLARS reward, and all necessary charges, paid by (THOMAS GARDNER 21)

Reprint: The Newport Mercury, 06-13-1774 (Supplement)

The Newport Mercury, 09-05-1774.

Westerly, August 31, 1774.

RUN away from the subscriber, on the 13th instant, a molatto boy, about 16 years of age, named GEORGE GREGORY, had on when he went away a new felt hat, flannel jacket, striped with red and blue, tow and linen shirt and trowsers, two pair of each, new shoes, bushy hair, is supposed to have gone to Providence, Bristol or Dartmouth, in order to go a whaling; whoever will take up said boy, and secure him so that his master may have him again, shall have five dollars reward, and all necessary charges, paid by SAMUEL TOMPSON.

N.B. All masters of vessels are forewarned carrying off said servant. (36)
Reprints: The Newport Mercury, 09-12-1774; 09-19-1774.

The Newport Mercury, 09-05-1774.

RAN away from his master, Thomas Chadwick, a Negro man name Quaco, a fellow pretty much bursten, and well known in Newport, he had on when he went away an old striped flannel shirt, patched with linen, narrow trowsers, white breeches under them, and a white jacket without sleeves, is branded on one shoulder with two letters: It is suspected he is gone toward Dartmouth.— All persons are cautioned against secreting, harbouring and carrying off the said run-away, as they would avoid being prosecuted for the same: Any person securing the said Negro and conveying him to his said master, shall have two dollars reward and all necessary charges, paid by THOMAS CHADWICK.

N.B. He stole a blue great-coat when he went off.
Reprint: The Newport Mercury, 09-12-1774.

The Newport Mercury, 11-21-1774.

RAN away from Newport, a few days past, a Mulatto man, named PRIMUS, the property of CORNELIUS HARNET, Esq; of North Carolina; a thick, short, well-set fellow, sometimes wears a wig over his hair, which is thick and short: He formerly belonged to Mr. BENJAMIN BRENTON, in the Neck, and is supposed to be somewhere in Narraganset at present.—Whoev-

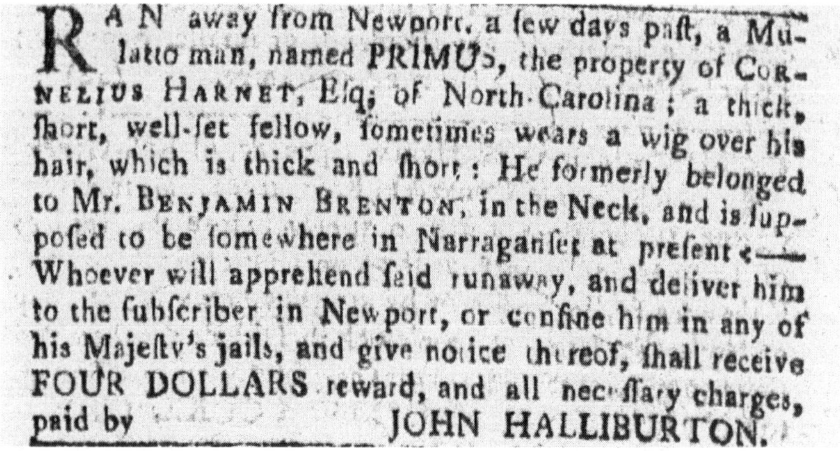

Figure 3.1.   Primus, *Newport Mercury*, November 21, 1774

er will apprehend said runaway, and deliver him to the subscriber in Newport, or confine him in any of his Majesty's jails, and give notice thereof,
shall receive FOUR DOLLARS reward, and all necessary charges, paid by
                                                    JOHN HALLIBURTON.

The Newport Mercury, 04-03-1775.

RAN away on Tuesday last, from the subscriber at Newport, a mulatto man,
named Moses, about 4 feet 7 inches high, a short well set fellow, of a yellow
complexion, with a bushy head of hair, somewhat different from a Negro,
speaks exceeding good English; and had on when he went away, a new felt
hat, and a blue cap, a red duffel great coat, a green ratteen jacket, and a thin
cotton one underneath, a buck skin pair of breeches, a light coloured pair of
worsted stockings, and shoes about one half worn: Whoever will apprehend
said Mulatto, and deliver him to the subscriber, shall have a reward of four
dollars, and all necessary charges, paid by JOHN DENNIS.
    N.B. It is imagined he has directed his course towards Bedford, in Dart-
mouth, and that he has got a pass with, dated last November.
    Newport, March 25, 1775.
    Reprint: The Newport Mercury, 04-10-1775.

The Newport Mercury, 08-14-1775.

RAN away from the subscriber at Nantucket, a Negro fellow named CESAR,
about 17 years of age; had on a cloth coloured outside serge jacket, a green
under jacket, an old pair of brown cotton thickset breeches, he lisps a little,

he is a straight limb'd fellow, slender built, and of a middling stature:— Whoever will apprehend said runaway, and send him to Nantucket, or secure him in any of his Majesty's jails, and give notice to the subscriber, shall have Ten Dollars reward, and all necessary charges paid, by TIMOTHY COFFIN.

N.B. Said Negro understands something of the rope-making business.

NANTUCKET, July 12, 1775.

The Newport Mercury, 05-04-1782.

RAN away, from the subscriber, on the 27th of April last, a Negro man named PERO, about 5 feet 7 inches high, middling well set, was bred in the country, and speaks good English, is a quiet peaceable fellow, looks somewhat sleepy with his eyes, had on when he went away, a white flannel shirt, a pair of light grey broad-cloth breeches, with dark grey waistcoat thereto, a dark grey full-cloth jacket, a striped flannel jacket, grey yarn stocking, old shoes, one cap'd at the toe, a grey kersey full cloth great coat, and a felt hat, it is supposed that he went off with a couple of Mulatto fellows, or at least they looked like such: Whoever will take up said fellow and return him to me, or secure him so that I may get him again, shall have EIGHT DOLLARS reward, and reasonable charges paid, by

JOSEPH RAYNOLDS. Exeter, May 2, 1782.

The Newport Mercury, 02-21-1784.

RAN away from Charles Baujean in Norwich in the State of Connecticut, on the 14th of January last, a Negro Man, named LEANDER, who is a Barber by Trade, speaks both French and English, is about Five Feet Eight Inches high, somewhat pitted with the Small-Pox. Whoever will apprehend said Negro, and secure him in any of the Jails of the United States, and give Notice thereof to said Baujean, or to the Subscriber, at Tiverton, or deliver him to either, shall receive TEN DOLLARS Reward and all necessary Charges, paid by said Baujean or PARDON GRAY.

Toverton, Feb. 13, 1784.

The Newport Mercury, 07-03-1784.

FOUR DOLLARS Reward.

RAN away, from the Subscriber, on Monday the 21st instant, a Mustee Boy, named JONATHAN WHITE, about 15 Years of Age, is a short, thick, well set Fellow, has a Scar on his left Thumb; had on when he went away, white Tow and Linen Shirt and Trowsers, with a Stock round his Neck, two grey Jackets, one with Sleves, the other without, a Felt Hat bound, and a Pair of Shoes, one or both cap'd at the Toe. Whoever will apprehend said Boy, and return him to the Subscriber shall receive the above Reward, and all reasonable Charges paid, by THOMAS TRIPP. Dartmouth, June 24, 1784.

The Newport Mercury, 09-10-1785.

Eight Dollars Reward.

RAN AWAY from the Subscriber on the 21st instant, a Negro Fellow, called JEREMIAH, about 20 Years of Age, about Five Feet 8 Inches high, not very black, well built; had on when he went away a Tow-cloth Shirt and Trowsers, and striped Towcloth Coat, and a large bound Castor Hat, also carried away with him a Towcloth Shirt and a Pair of coperas green Trowsers, Whoever will take said Negro, and deliver him to the Subscriber shall receive the above Reward and all necessary Charges paid, by, JOHN ALMY.

N.B. All Masters of Vessels are forbid carrying him off, and whoever shall attempt to harbour or secrete said Negro may depend upon being prosecuted to the utmost Rigour of the Law. Toverton, August 23, 1785.

Reprint: The Newport Mercury, 09-24-1785.

Newport Herald, 01-22-1789.

NEW YORK, Dec. 15, 1788.

Ten Pounds Reward.

RAN-AWAY on the morning of the 9th inst. from the subscriber, the following Negroes, viz. James Smith, a country born negro: he has a yellow and surly countenance, about 28 years of age, 5 feet 10 or 11 inches high, a very active, stout, well-made fellow, has a crook in one of his legs, occasioned by having it broke. Had on when he left this place, a brown coat, white cloth jacket, and buck-skin breeches; but he may alter his dress as he robbed the house the night before he went away of a light coloured coatee, and sundry other articles,—And also robbed the store of Messieure Sawin in Queen-street, of womens shoes, shirts, and sundry other articles.—The other a wench named Mary, 25 years of age, about 5 feet high, of a yellow complexion and down look; had on and took with her three gowns, one striped cotton, a light chints small figur'd, and a calico, brown cloth cloak, black bonnet, two white petticoats, one blue linsey and one striped short gown, and sundry other articles; they went to Rhode-Island with Jonathan Fairbanks.— Whoever apprehends the said negroes and secure them in any gaols so that they may be brought to justice, shall have the above reward, or Five Pounds for either of them, with reasonable charges, paid by WILLIAM TUNDRAN.

The Providence Gazette, 07-09-1763.

Cranston, July 8, 1763

RAN away from DANIEL FENNER, in Cranston, in the Colony of Rhode-Island, about the 28th of April last, one Sarah Hammet, a likely lusty Mulatto Servant Woman, about 38 Years of Age—She had on when she went away, a dark colour'd Camblet short Wrapper, an old grey Petticoat, very much patch'd, and a brown Camblet Bonnet; she is extremely nice in her Head Attire, which is generally ornamented after the modern Fashion; she affects Politeness, and is very ingenious at Drawing, Embroidering, and almost any Kind of curious Needle-Work, &c. &c.—It is suspected she is gone toward Boston, as she has both Male and Female Acquaintances that Way.— Whoever takes up and secures said Servant, and give Notice thereof to the Subscriber, shall receive Twenty Pounds, Old Tenor, Reward, and have all reasonable Charges paid. DANIEL FENNER.

Reprint: The Providence Gazette, 07-16-1763.

The Providence Gazette, 10-15-1763.

North-Kingstown, October 11, 1763.

RUN away Yesterday, from John Fry, of North-Kingstown, a Negro Man named Elisha, about 21 Years of Age, born in this Country: He is a short thick Fellow, and had on when he went away, a homespun Serge Jacket, a Linen Shirt, a Pair of blue Worsted Stockings, old Shoes, a Worsted Cap, and an old Felt Hat.—Whoever takes up said Negro, and delivers him to his Masters in North-Kingstown, or secures him in any of His Majesty's Goals, so that he may he had again, shall receive FOUR DOLLARS Reward, and have all necessary Charges paid, by JOHN FRY.

N.B. All Masters of Vessels and others, are hereby forwarn'd secreting or carrying off said Fellow, as they will answer it at their Peril.

Reprints: The Providence Gazette, 10-22-1763; 10-29-1763.

The Providence Gazette, 01-31-1767.

Ten DOLLARS Reward.

Hardwick, January 31.

RAN AWAY on the Night of the 27th instant, a Mullatoe Fellow, named Arthur Toby, about 5 Feet 8 Inches high, 20 Year old, and square shouldered, he had on a blue outside Jacket, a red Baize under Jacket, and a Pair of old Deerskin Breeches. He was taken into Custody about Five Days ago, for committing a Rape on a Woman of Credit, he has been guilty of many such Villainies, and has often broke Goal; carried off with him a very likely large

Sorrel Horse, near 14 Hands and a half high, trots and paces. Whoever will apprehend said Villain, so that he may be brought to Justice, shall receive the above Reward, and all necessary Charges paid by BENONI SHUTLEFF.

Reprints: The Providence Gazette, 02-07-1767; 02-14-1767; 03-06-1767.

The Providence Gazette, 12-26-1767.

Three DOLLARS Reward.

RUN away from the subscriber, on the night of the 24th instant, a Mulatto servant man, named Absalom Norton, about fifteen years of age, of a middling stature, with a large bushy head of hair; had on when he went away, a dark cloth-coloured mixed coat, and an old felt hat.—Whoever takes up said fellow, so that his master may have him again, shall receive the above reward, and all necessary charge, paid by me DANIEL CHENEY.

N.B. All masters of vessels are forbid carrying off said servant.

Pomsret, December 25, 1767.

Reprints: The Providence Gazette, 01-02-1768; 02-06-1768; 02-13-1768; 02-20-1768.

The Providence Gazette, 05-14-1768.

RUN away from the Subscriber, on the fourth of this Instant, a Negroe Man Slave, named Sterling, about 24 Years of Age, a likely, well-built Fellow, has had the Small-Pox, and talks bad English; had on, when he went away, a blue strait-bodied Shag Coat, and a Jacket, cuffed with red Shag. Whoever takes up the said Slave, and secures him, so that his Master may have him again, shall have Two Dollars Reward, and all necessary Charges, paid by JOSEPH BUCKLIN.

Providence, May 10, 1768. (27)

Reprints: The Providence Gazette, 05-21-1768; 06-11-1768.

The Providence Gazette, 05-14-1768.

RUN away from the Subscriber, a Negroe Man, named Barrow, about 20 Years of Age, and speaks good English; had on a Flannel Shirt, Leather Breeches, striped Flannel Jacket, black Stockings, and old Shoes. Whoever takes said Negroe, and secures him, so that his Master may have him again, shall have Three Dollars Reward, and reasonable Charges, paid by OBADIAH SPRAGUE.

N.B. All Masters of Vessels are desired not to carry him off. (27)

Reprint: The Providence Gazette, 05-28-1768.

The Providence Gazette, 07-01-1769.

RUN away from on board a Brig lying in the River, a Mulatto Man, named Franciso, of a middle Stature, thick set, speaks broken English; had on a blue Jacket, Sailors Trowsers, and took a small Hat belonging to one of the People. Whoever takes up said Mulatto, and brings him to the Subscriber, shall have Two Dollars Reward, and necessary Charges, paid by JOHN NASH.

N.B. He has a Sore on his right Hand. All Masters of Vessels are forbid to carry him off. (86)

Reprints: The Providence Gazette, 07-15-1769; 07-22-1769; 07-29-1769.

The Providence Gazette, Saturday, November 3, to Saturday, November 10, 1770.

RUN away from his Master, Benjamin Cole, of Warren, on the 6th Instant, a Negro Man Servant, about 19 or 20 Years of Age, a tall slim Fellow, with a large Scar on one Hand: Had on when he went away a Kersey Jacket and Breeches, of a Sheep's Black Colour, blue Stockings, but no Coat. Whoever takes up said Negro, and conveys him to his Master, shall have a handsome Reward, and all Charges, paid by BENJAMIN COLE.

Warren, November 10, 1770

The Providence Gazette, Saturday, January 26, to Saturday, February 2, 1771.

RUN away from the Subscriber, on the 14th Instant, a Mustee Apprentice Boy, named David Jenings, About 16 Years of Age, tall and slim, has a large Head of black Hair, which he wears tyed behind; has a small Scar on his Nose; took with him a good Felt Hat, a fulled Cap, two Pair of Shoes, three Pair of Stockings, two Pair of Breeches, two Pair of Trowsers, two Flannel Shirts, four Jackets, a blue Great-Coat, a strait-bodied brown Coat, and a black Silk Handkerchief. Whoever takes up the said Fellow, and brings him to the Subscriber, shall have a handsome Reward, and all necessary Charges, paid by HANNAH THOMAS.

Reprints: The Providence Gazette, Saturday, February 2, to Saturday, February 9, 1771; Saturday, February 23, to Saturday, March 2, 1771.

The Providence Gazette, Saturday, December 7, to Saturday, December 14, 1771.

RUN away from the Subscriber, on the 10th Instant, a Mulatto Fellow named HARRY; he is about 25 Years of Age, well set, about 5 Feet 10 Inches high, has bushy Hair, cut pretty short on the Top, has a Scar on the Top of his

Head, something like the Letter A, which may be discovered by parting the Hair; speaks good English, and is much addicted to drinking: Had on, when he went away, a striped woollen Shirt, a short blue Sailor Jacket, double-breasted, with one Row of Brass Buttons; a home-spun Bearskin Great-Coat, with Pewter Buttons; an old Pair of Moose-skin Breeches, mixed blue and white Stockings, grey Leggings, and pretty good Shoes. Carried with him a striped woollen Shirt, an old white Holland Ditto, and a Pair of mixed blue and white Stockings. Whoever will take up said Fellow, and bring him to me the Subscriber, shall receive THREE DOLLARS Reward, and necessary Charges, paid by STEPHEN KEYES.

N.B. All Masters of Vessels, and others, are forbid to carry him off, at their Peril.

Pomsret., Dec. 11, 1771.

Reprints: The Providence Gazette, Saturday, December 14, to Saturday, December 21, 1771; Saturday, December 21, to Saturday, December 28, 1771; 01-04-1772.

The Providence Gazette, 05-02-1772.

RAN away from the Subscriber a Mulatto Man, called Dick, about 30 Years of Age, he can read and write, and speaks good English: Had on when he went away a Beaver Hat, somewhat wore, a light coloured homespun Broad cloth Jacket, and a Pair of Wash-Leather Breeches. Whoever takes up said Runaway, and secures him in any of his Majesty's Goals, so that his Master may have him again, shall have Eight Dollars Reward, and all necessary Charges, paid by JOHN BOWEN.

N.B. All Masters of Vessels, and others, are forbid harbouring or carrying off said Runaway.

Reprints: The Providence Gazette, 05-16-1772; 05-23-1772; 05-30-1772.

The Providence Gazette, 05-09-1772.

RAN away from the Subscriber a Mulatto Man, named Moses Perry; he is about 26 Years of Age, 5 Feet 10 Inches high, and very large over the Shoulders; he wears a Felt Hat, or red Cap, a mixed coloured double-breasted Jacket, with Flaps, and a striped Flannel Shirt; reads, writes, and cyphers, and has a Sore on the great Toe of his right Foot. Whoever takes up said Run-away, and brings him to his Master, or secures him in any of his Majesty's Goals, shall have Eight Dollars Reward, and necessary Charges, paid by JOHN PERRY. Tiverton, April 25, 1772.

N.B. All Masters of Vessels, and other, are forbid carrying off or harbouring said Runaway.

Reprints: The Newport Mercury, 05-11-1772; 05-18-1772; 05-25-1772.

The Providence Gazette, 06-20-1772.

RAN away from Mrs. Payson, Widow, in Woodstock, on Monday Night, the eighth of this Instant, a Negro Man Servant, named CAESAR, a Fellow well made, about 5 Feet 8 Inches high, between 50 and 60 Years of Age, his Hair grey, speaks tolerable good English, and sometimes pretends to be free: He formerly lived with Samuel Chandler, Esq; had on and carried away with him the following Cloaths, viz. one Cloth coloured great Coat, three close bodied Coats, viz. one Cloth coloured, one blue, and one mixed coloured red and blue; one Cloth coloured Jacket, two Cloth Jackets without Sleeves, two striped Cotton and Linen Dito, one Pair of Leather Breeches, one Pair new striped Thicken Trowsers, one fine Shirt, three Two Ditto, one striped Ditto, two Flannel Ditto, Stockings, Shoes, &c. Whoever will apprehend said Negro, and bring him with his Cloaths to said Mrs. Payson, in Woodstock, shall have FIVE DOLLARS Reward; or if they will convey him to the Subscriber, in Providence, they shall receive EIGHT DOLLARS Reward, paid by PAUL TEW.

N.B. All Persons are hereby strictly forbid to entertain or employ the above described Negro, as they would avoid being prosecuted with the utmost Rigour of the Law. Providence, June 17, 1772.

Reprints: The Providence Gazette, 06-27-1772; 07-04-1772.

The Providence Gazette, 06-27-1772.

RAN away from his master, in this town, the 25th instant, at nine o'clock in the morning, a young French negro boy, named EUSEBECK; he is about twelve or fourteen years of age, and speaks a little English. Whoever will take up said negro boy, and bring him to his master, at Mrs. Westrand's, shall receive TWO DOLLARS reward from his master.

Providence, June 26, 1772.

Reprint: The Providence Gazette, 07-04-1772.

The Providence Gazette, 03-13-1773.

RUN away from his Master, the Subscriber, the 20th Instant, a Negro Man Servant, named Jack, about 25 Years of Age, 5 Feet 8 Inches high, a straight well-built Fellow, with a Scar upon his Neck, made by a Wound from a Scythe: Had on when he went away a striped Flannel Shirt, Buckskin Breeches, a dark striped Waistcoat, a Butternut-Bark coloured lappelled Jacket, a new grey home-made Bearskin Great Coat, with large Metal Buttons, blue Yarn Stockings, Calfskin turned Pumps, Pinchbeck Buckles, and a Felt Hat.

Whoever will take up said Negroe, and confine him in any of his Majesty's Goals, and give Notice thereof to Theodore Foster, Esq; of Providence, or to the Subscriber, at Preston, in Connecticut, or convey him to either of them, shall have Five Dollars Reward, and all necessary Charges, paid by TIMOTHY LESTER.

Preston, February 23.

Reprint: The Newport Mercury, 03-15-1773.

* Earlier variants of this notice appeared in the Providence Gazette; and Country Journal, 02-27-1773; 03-06-1773.

The Providence Gazette, 08-28-1773.

Woodstock, August 20, 1773.

RAN away from his Master, Barzillai Beckwith, of East-Hadam, in Connecticut, on the 29th of July last, a Mulatto Man Slave, named Syl, alias Sylvanus: He is middling for Height, is well set, but is something round shouldered, and goes a little slooping; he wears his Hair, which curls handsomely, hath a thin Beard, is white for a Mulatto, and of an Indian Look: He had on and took with him a Coat and Breeches of plain Cloth, of a Caret Colour, a green Ratteen Waistcoat, a striped Linen Shirt, short Trowsers, a little Felt Hat, and a Pair of Pumps. Whoever will take up said Runaway, and secure him in any of his Majesty's goal, so that his Master may have him again, shall have Four Dollars Reward, and reasonable Charges, paid by me BARZILLAI BECKWITH.

N.B. All Masters of Vessels, and Owners, are hereby forbid carrying away said Slave, on Pain of incurring the utmost Severity of the Law. He has been travelling with a white Man, who may help him away.

Providence, August 10, 1773.

Reprints: The Providence Gazette, 09-04-1773; 09-25-1773; 10-02-1773.

The Providence Gazette, 10-02-1773.

RUN away from the Subscriber, a Negro Man, named Mingo, a tall Fellow, about 38 Years of Age, has got a Guinea Mark on each Cheek, has lost four upper Teeth, and understands all Sorts of farming Work: had on, and took with him, when he went away, a new Felt Hat, white Fustian Coat, a homespun Kersey Linen Coat and Jacket, a blue and white Flannel Jacket, one Pair of Cloth, and one Pair of knit Breeches, both Cloth coloured; two white Shirts, two Tow Ditto, one Flannel Ditto, two Pair of Trowsers, one Pair of pale blue ribb'd, and one Pair of Linen Stockings; a Pair of Pumps, and a new Silk red and yellow Handkerchief.

Whoever takes up said Runaway, and brings him to his Master, in Johnston, or to Job Smith, in Providence, or secure him in any Goal, so that his Master may have him again, shall have Ten Dollars Reward, and all necessary Charges, paid by JOB HAWKINS. Johnston, September 29.

The Providence Gazette, 10-16-1773.

RUN away from me the Subscriber, of Mendon, on the eleventh Day of October, a Negro Man named Caesar, 20 Years old, of middling Stature, has a Scar near his left Eye about an Inch long, and plays well on the Violin; had on Leather Breeches, a Holland Shirt, a Scarlet Jacket, and a green Coat. Whoever takes up said Negro, and returns him to his Master, or secures him in any of his Majesty's Goals, shall receive Ten Dollars Reward, and all necessary Charges, paid by me, DAVID DANIELS. Mendon, October 15, 1773.
 Reprint: The Providence Gazette, 10-23-1773.

The Providence Gazette, 07-16-1774.

RUN away from his Master, Robert Fish, of Dilon, a Negro Man, named Caesar Rich, about 40 Years of Age; he has one crooked Finger, a Scar on one of his Shoulders, and a sharp full Eye: Had on an old thick Coat, of a redish Colour, and calls himself Doctor and Fortune-Teller. He run away from his said Master at Hopkinton, on the 5 th of July inst. Whoever takes up said Servant, and conveys him to his Master, or secures him, so that he may be had again, shall have Five Dollars Reward, and reasonable Charges, paid by ROBERT FISH.
 Reprint: The Providence Gazette, 07-23-1774.

The Providence Gazette, 05-27-1775.

RUN away from the Subscriber, on the 6th Inst. a Mulatto Man Slave, named Toney, a tall, strait, well-limbed Fellow, of a light Copper Complexion, has Negro Hair, and is about 24 Years of Age: Had on and took with him a blue Ratteen Jacket, a red Duffil under Jacket, with flat Pewter Buttons, black Breeches, a Pair of Nankeen Ditto, a white Shirt, a checked Flannel and Two Ditto, grey Stockings, an old Beaver Hat, with an old Gold Band and Stone Buckle, a checked Silk Handkerchief, and plated Buckles in his Shoes; he is 5 Feet 8 Inches high without Shoes, has worked in a Rope-Walk, and spins a good Thread. Whoever takes up and secures said Slave, so that his Master may have him again, shall have four Dollars Reward, and reasonable Charges, paid by NICHOLAS POWER.

N.B. All Masters of Vessels and others are forbid to carry off said Slave, at their Peril.

The Providence Gazette, 06-10-1775.

RUN away from the Subscriber, on the 4th Instant, a Negro Boy, named Prime, about 14 Years old, and about 4 or 4 and an Half Feet high; had on when he went away a Check Shirt and Trowsers. He has Marks on the inside of his Arms, and on his Back, occasioned by his having been severly whipped in Surrinam. Whoever takes up and secures said Boy, or returns him to his Master, shall have Two Dollars Reward, and all necessary Charges, paid by JOSEPH BROWN. Providence, June 8, 1775.

Reprint: The Providence Gazette, 06-24-1775.

The Providence Gazette, 09-30-1775.

RUN away from the Subscriber, on the 28th Instant, a Negro Man, named Prime, about 5 Feet 8 Inches high, a likely well made Fellow, speaks broken English, and is very black; had on when he went away a Homespun Linsey-woolsey Jacket, remarkably ragged; a red Duffil under Ditto, Ozenbrigs Shirt and Trowsers; he is about 18 Years of Age, and went off without Shoes, Stockings or Hat. Whoever will take up and secure said Negro, so that his Master may have him again, shall have Three Dollars Reward, paid by
JOHN HOPKINS.

Providence, Sept. 3-, 1775.

Reprint: The Providence Gazette, 10-07-1775.

The Providence Gazette, 10-14-1775.

RUN away from the Subscriber, on the Evening of the 1st of October inst. a Negro Man, named Prince, about 34 Years of Age, short and thick set, has a high Forehead, his Toes froze off, speaks plain English. Whoever will take up said Negro, and return him to his Master, at Windham, in Connecticut, shall have Six Dollars Reward, and all necessary Charges, paid by SHU-BAEL ABBE.

Windham, October 11, 1775.

Reprints: The Providence Gazette, 10-21-1775; 11-11-1775.

The Providence Gazette, 03-30-1776.

RUN away from the Subscriber, a Negro Fellow, named Sy, about 5 Feet [?] Inches high, thick set, 25 Years of Age, a yellow Complexion; had on when he went away a thick black and white mixed Jacket and Breeches, Stockings much of the same Colour, a striped blue and white Flannel Jacket, and Check Shirt; he carried with him a mixed black and blue Jacket, a B[lue] Cap, a Felt Hat, and a Fiddle. Whoever takes up said Negro, and secure him, [or] returns him to his Master, shall have F[ive] Dollars Reward, and all necessary Charges, paid by JOSEPH POWERS. Lyme, March 8, 1776.

The Providence Gazette, 10-19-1776.

RUN away from the subscriber, at Bridewater, on the 17th of October, a Negro man, named Bristol, a thick well set fellow, 5 feet 7 inches high, about 40 years of age, speaks broken English; had on when he went away a light coloured thickset coat, an old brown Devonshire kersey waistcoat, dirty buckskin breeches, white or grey yarn stocking, double soled shoes, with strings, and a brown wig or cap. He went off in company with an Indian squaw, about 30 years of age, of a very fair light complexion, named Betty, supposed to be bound towards New-York: Whoever takes up said Negro, and brings him to his master, or secures him in any gaol within the United States, shall have Four Dollars reward, and all necessary charges, paid by
EDWARD HOWARD.

The Providence Gazette, 05-10-1777.

RUN-AWAY from the Subscriber, a Negro Man, named PRINCE, 25 Years of Age, about 5 Feet 8 Inches high, has three Marks on each Temple, made in Guinea; speaks somewhat hoarse: Had on when he went away, a lightish coloured Great-Coat, Jacket and Breeches, much worn, an under Jacket of striped Flannel, and an old Felt Hat. Whoever will take up said Negro, and confine him in any Gaol of the United States, or convey him to his Master, shall have Five Dollars Reward, and all necessary Charges, paid by SAMU-EL GARDNER.
Hopkinton, April 12, 1777.
Reprint: The Providence Gazette, 05-17-1777.

The Providence Gazette, 10-11-1777.

RUN AWAY from John Fenner, of Gloucester, a Negro Man named YOCK-WHY, about 28 Years of Age, 5 Feet 8 Inches high, marked on both Cheeks, from his Temples down: Had on and took with him when he went away, a light Cloth coloured homespun Coat, made plain, with wooden Buttons, Breeches of the same Colour, a blue Serge Jacket, with Buttons of the same Colour, a Pair of good Leather Breeches, a fine Holland Shirt, 1 fine Tow Ditto, 1 coarser Ditto, 1 Pair of new Thread Stockings, 1 Pair of new dark Worsted Ditto, 1 Pair of white ribbed Yarn Ditto, 1 dark Silk Handkerchief, 1

Linen Ditto, 1 good Castor Hat without Loops, 1 Felt Ditto with Loops, a new Pair of Shoes, with Strings, and a Pair of Silver Sleeve Buttons. Whoever will take up and secure said Negro, so that his Master may have him again, shall have Six Dollars Reward, and all reasonable Charges, paid by JOHN FENNER.

N.B. All Masters of Vessels are forbid to carry off said Negro, at their Peril.

The Providence Gazette, 10-25-1777.

RUN AWAY from the Subscriber, a Negro man, named NED, a well-built Fellow, about twenty Years of Age, 5 Feet 10 Inches high, speaks hoarse, and hath a Scar over his right Eye: Had on, when he went away, an old Felt Hat, a thick Kersey Jacket, of a Sheep's Grey, striped Flannel Waistcoat, double-breasted, without Skirts, a Tow and Linen Shirt, a Pair of Russia Drab Breeches, of a brownish Colour, white Yarn Stockings, a Pair of single soaled Shoes, not much worn; he plays on the Fiddle, and carried one with him. Whoever will take up said Fellow, and return him to the Subscriber, or confined him in any of the Gaols in the United States, so that his Master may have him again, shall receive Five Dollars Reward, and all necessary Charges, paid by me, JOHN ROSE.

South-Kingstown, Oct. 20.

Reprint: The Providence Gazette, 11-08-1777.

The Providence Gazette, 10-25-1777.

RUNAWAY from the Subscriber, a large Negro man, 20 Years of Age, about 5 Feet 10 Inches high: Had on and carried with him, homespun Ash coloured Cloth Coat and Breeches, a Wilton Jacket, much worn, a red Duffil Great-Coat, much worn, a Pair of woollen Trowsers, an old black and white checked woollen Shirt, and a good Felt Hat, almost new. Whoever will take up said Negro, and secure him, so that his Master may have him again, shall have Ten Dollars Reward, and all necessary Charges, paid by MATTHEW TALCOTT.

Middletown, Oct. 13, 1777.

Reprint: The Providence Gazette, 11-01-1777.

The Providence Gazette, 07-25-1778.

RUN away from the subscriber, the 29th of June, a Negro fellow, named London, 6 Feet high, well set, and is a barber by trade; took with him a blue coat faced with buff, a nankeen ditto, 3 white shirts, 2 flannel ditto, and several other articles. Whoever takes up and secures said Negro, so that his master may have him again, shall have a handsome reward, and charges, paid by PICKET LATEMORE.

New-London, July 1, 1778.

The Providence Gazette, 08-07-1779.

RAN away from the Subscriber, a Negroe Man, named CATO, about 50 Years of Age, of a middling Stature, speaks broken English, has his Country Marks in his Face; had on when he went away an outside Cloth coloured woollen Jacket, a Linen striped under Jacket, Linen Shirt and Stockings, and a Pair of good Shoes. Whoever shall take up said Negroe, and return him to his Master, in Rehoboth, shall have Twenty Dollars Reward, and all reasonable Charges, paid by me. DANIEL HUNT.

N.B. All Masters of Vessels and others are cautioned against harbouring or concealing said Fellow, as they would avoid the Penalty of the LAW.

Rehoboth, July 23, 1779.

*Earlier variants of this notice appeared in the Providence Gazette; and Country Journal, 07-24-1779; 07-31-1779.

The Providence Gazette, 09-04-1779.

RAN away from the Subscriber, on the 20th Day of June last, a Mulatto Man Servant, called Primus, about 25 Years of Age, a likely well made Fellow, speaks good English; had on, and took with him, when he went away, a Pair of Leather Breeches, almost new, two Pair of Linen Trowsers, two Linen and two Woollen Shirts, three Flannel Waistcoats, two Pair of Hose, one Pair of good Shoes, a new Beaveret Hat, one Irish Linen Shirt, a Suit of green Cloaths, not much worn, and an old Great-Coat; also took with him a considerable Sum of Money. Also ran away the last Evening, a Mustee Apprentice Boy, called Primas Watt, alias Toby, aged about 14 Years; had on when he went away a Linen Shirt, Flannel Waistcoat, a thick homespun Jacket over it, a Pair of Shoes, and a small old Hat, lopped, and pieced round the Brim. If either of them will return to their Master, before taken up, they shall be forgiven their Crimes; but whoever shall take up said Servant, and convey him to his Master at Warwick Neck, in the County of Kent, shall have Twenty Dollars Reward; and whoever shall take up said Apprentice, and return him to said Master, shall have Ten Dollars Reward, and all reasonable Charges, paid by BENJAMIN GREENE.

N.B. All Masters of Vessels, and others, are cautioned against harbouring or concealing said Servant or Apprentice, as they would avoid the Penalty of the Law, in such Cases provided.

Warwick-Neck, September 2, 1779.

Reprints: The Providence Gazette, 09-11-1779; 09-18-1779.

The Providence Gazette, 07-22-1780.

Four Hundred Dollars Reward.

RAN away from the Subscriber, a Negro Man, named Anthony, a likely well-made Fellow, near 6 Feet high, about 23 Years of Age, and has a Scar in his Forehead: Had on a white Blanket Coat, a blue Jacket, and Ozenbrigs Overalls. Whoever will secure the above Negro, and give Notice to his Master, in Providence, so that he may have him again, shall have the above Reward, and all necessary Charges, paid by SILAS TALBOT.

Providence, July 14, 1780.

The Providence Gazette, 04-13-1782.

RAN away from the Subscriber, on the Evening of the 28th of March, a Negro Boy, named Warwick, about 5 Feet 6 Inches high, about 18 Years of Age, has the Guinea Marks on his Forehead, Cheeks and Chin, and Holes through the Sides of his Nose: had on when he went away, a Pair of thick Mooseskin Breeches, white Stockings, woollen Shirt, black and white mixed Coat, white woollen Jacket, Cloth coloured Great-Coat, and an old Beaver Hat, newly dressed; carried with him a striped Linen Coat, a Pair of white Stockings, a Pair of blue and white mixed Ditto, one fine Home-made Shirt, and a white Linen Jacket and Breeches. Whoever will take up said Negro, and deliver him to the Subscriber, or secure him so that he may be had again, shall have Ten Dollars Reward, and all necessary Charges, paid by
EBENEZER CRAFT.

N.B. All Persons are forbid to harbour or carry off said Boy, as they will answer the contrary at the Peril of the Law.

Sturbridge, April 2, 1782.

The Providence Gazette, 05-04-1782.

RAN away from the Subscriber, in the Evening of the 28th ult. A NEGRO FELLOW, named BRISTOL, about 19 Years of Age, about 5 Feet 9 Inches high, rather clumsily made, slow of Speech, walk upright, not over-witted; had on, when he went away, a blue Coat, a Pair of old striped Flannel Trowsers, patched with Cloth of a different Colour, and an old check'd Shirt; carried with him two white Shirts, a white Jacket, white Breeches, and old white Worsted Stockings. Whoever will take up said Fellow, and secure him so that his Master may have him again, shall have Eight Dollars Reward, and all necessary Charges, paid by JOSIAH FINNEY.

N.B. All Masters of Vessels are forbid to carry him off at their Peril.

Bristol, May 3, 1782.
Reprints: The Providence Gazette, 05-11-1782; 05-25-1782; 06-01-1782.

The Providence Gazette, 09-14-1782.

RANAWAY, From the Subscriber, A SHORT well set Negro Man, named TOM, about 26 Years of Age, 5 Feet 7 Inches high, marked with the Small-Pox; had on, when he went away, a striped Tow Shirt, brown Tow Jacket, full'd Cloth Breeches, white Worsted Stockings, his Shoes mended, one round and one square Brass Buckle, an old Felt Hat bound with white; the small Toe of each Foot has been frozen off; took with him two Tow Shirts, and some other Apparel. Whoever will take up said Runaway, and return him, or give Notice to the Subscriber, so that he may have him again, shall receive a Reward of TWENTY SILVER DOLLARS, and all necessary Charges paid by JOHN COOKE.
Tiverton, Sept. 13, 1782.
Reprints: The Providence Gazette and Country Journal, 09-21-1782; 09-28-1782.

The Providence Gazette, 10-19-1782.

RAN AWAY from the Subscriber, on the 10th Instant, a NEGRO MAN, named PERO, about 20 Years of Age, 5 Feet 4 Inches high, speaks good English; had on, when he went away, a Felt Hat, grey Jacket, Leather Breeches, old Stockings, good Shoes and Buckles.—Whoever will take up said Negro, and return him to the Subscriber, or to Slack's Tavern, in Rehoboth, shall receive Three Dollars Reward, and necessary Charges, paid by OABDIAH READ.
N.B. All Masters of Vessels are forbid to carry him off.
Rehoboth, October 18, 1782.
Reprints: The Providence Gazette, 10-26-1782; 11-09-1782.

The Providence Gazette, 04-12-1783.

FORTY DOLLARS Reward.
RAN away from the Subscribers, on the Night of the 7th of April inst. a NEGRO MAN, named Richard, about 5 Feet 10 Inches high, 25 Years of Age, is very much pitted with the Small-Pox; he had on a blue Jacket, dark London brown Breeches, is a Native of Virginia, and speaks good English—has followed the Sea for a Number of Years. He has a Wife in New-York,

and is supposed to be gone that Way.—Whoever will apprehend the above Negro, and return him to the Subscriber, shall receive the above Reward, and all necessary Charges. ALFRED ARNOLD.

Providence, April 11, 1783.

Reprint: The Providence Gazette and Country Journal, 04-26-1783.

The Providence Gazette, 02-22-1783.

Six Dollars Reward.

RAN away from the Subscriber, in the Evening of the 12th Instant, a Negro Man, named Cash, about 21 Years of Age, speaks good English, small of his Age, carried no Cloathing with him except what he had on, which was a checked woollen Shirt, a grey home-made Coat of fulled Cloth, Jacket and Overalls of home-made woollen unfilled Cloth, grey woollen Stockings, and a Felt Hat. Whoever will take up and return said Fellow to the Subscriber, shall receive the above Reward, and all necessary Charges, paid by ISAAC MORGAN.

N.B. All Masters of Vessels and others are forbid carrying off said Fellow, as they would avoid the Penalty of the Law, in that Case made and provided.

Plainfield, Feb. 20, 1783.

Reprints: The Providence Gazette, 03-01-1783; 03-22-1783.

The Providence Gazette, 09-20-1783.

RAN away from his Master, the Subscriber, on Monday last, a Mulatto or Mustee Servant Boy, named Pero, about ten Years of Age, cross-eyed, and has black curled Hair resembling that of a Negro; had on, when he went away, a Shirt and Trowsers of Linen. Whoever will take up said Boy, and return him to his Master, shall be handsomely rewarded, and have all necessary Charges paid, by AMOS ATWELL.

Providence, Sept. 19, 1783.

The Providence Gazette, 10-25-1783.

TEN DOLLARS REWARD.

RAN away from the Subscriber, last Night, a Negro Man, named FREEMAN, about 38 Years of Age, about 5 Feet 6 Inches high, stout and well made; had on a dark great Coat, with Horn Buttons, a grey Kersey Jacket, and took with him a Variety of other Cloathing.—Also a Negro Wench, his Wife, named VENUS, about 32 Years of Age, tall and likely; took with her a red short Cloak, a black Bonnet, a Cloth coloured Worsted Gown, and Plenty of other Cloathing. Whoever will take up and return said NEGROES to their Master, shall have TEN DOLLARS Reward, and all reasonable Charges, paid by SAMUEL TOMKINS.

Cranston, Oct. 24, 1783.

Reprint: The Providence Gazette, 11-01-1783.

The Providence Gazette and Country Journal, 09-11-1784.

RAN away, on the 5th Instant, from Daniel Greene, of Warwick, a Mulatto Fellow, named DAVID, about 18 Years of Age, about 5 Feet high; carried with him a Coat of filled Cloth, of a mixed Colour, red and black, and a Waistcoat of the same; likewise a Cloth coloured Coat, a Pair of dark Breeches, and sundry other Cloathing.

Ran away at the same Time, from John Low, of the same Town, a Negro Fellow, named CAESAR, about 18 Years of Age, about 5 Feet 2 Inches high; had on when he went away a Kersey Jacket and Trowsers; took with him a Snuff coloured Broadcloth Coat, a Pair of dark Corduroy Breeches, and sundry other wearing Apparel.—The above Slaves went off with a Mulatto Fellow, called Toney, about 48 Years of Age.

Whoever will take up the said DAVID and CAESAR, and return them to their Masters, shall have TEN DOLLARS Reward, or FIVE DOLLARS for each, and all necessary Charges, paid by DANIEL GREENE,

JOHN LOW.

Warwick, Sept. 10 1784.

Reprints: The Providence Gazette and Country Journal, 09-18-1784; 09-25-1784.

The Providence Gazette, 04-02-1785.

Stop a Thief and Runaway!

RAN AWAY from the Subscriber, the second of March inst. a Negro Servant Girl, named SILVIA.—She is about 17 Years of Age, about five Feet high, round faced, and has a very flippant Tongue. Had on, when she went away, a Plaid short close Gown, an old brown Camblet short Cloak, and a Petticoat, one Side green, the other black.—Whoever will take up said Runaway, and return her to her Master in Providence, or give Information where she is, shall receive Five Dollars Reward, and all necessary Charges, paid by PETER TAYLOR.

N.B. All Persons are forbid harbouring or carrying off said Servant.

Providence, March 18, 1785.

Reprint: United States Chronicle, 04-07-1785.

* Earlier variant of these notices appeared in the United States Chronicle: Political, Commercial and Historical, 03-17-1785; The Providence Gazette and Country Journal, 03-19-1785; The United States Chronicle: Political, Commercial and Historical, 03-24-1785; The Providence Gazette and Country Journal, 03-26-1785; The United States Chronicle: Political, Commercial and Historical, 03-31-1785.

The Providence Gazette, 05-21-1785.

RAN away from the Subscriber, on Sunday Evening last, a Mulatto Servant LAD, about 17 Years of Age, named Stephen, about five Feet six Inches high, and well grown: Had on, when he went away, a striped Jacket, Frock and Trowsers. Whoever will take up and return said Servant to his Master, shall have Five Dollars Reward, and reasonable Charges, paid by SAMUEL TOMPKINS.
    Cranston, May 20, 1785.
    Reprints: The Providence Gazette, 05-28-1785; 06-04-1785.

The Providence Gazette, 05-12-1787.

Ten Dollars Reward
    RAN AWAY from a Sloop, lying at Clark and Nightingale's Wharff, a NEGRO BOY, about 17 Years of Age; had on, when he went away, a small Felt Hat, with a Twine Thread run round the Brim, and a blue think Jacket, patched with Canvass, a Check Shirt, patched Linen Trowsers, and a Pair of double-soled Shoes; he is about 5 Feet high, a thick set Fellow, has thick Lips, and sometimes smiles when spoken to.—Whoever takes up said Boy, and returns him to NATHAN GREENE, in East-Greenwich, shall have Ten Silver Dollars Reward, and necessary Charges.

CHARLES BRIGGS.
    N.B. He has a forged Pass, in which is inserted the Name of Michael McCarter, and signed Capt. Benedict Smith; his right Name is Thomas Biscoe.
    Providence, May 11, 1787.

The Providence Gazette, 08-25-1787.

RAN away, from the Subscriber, on the 21st of April, a Negro Girl, name CHLOE, about 17 Years of Age; her common Dress, when she went off, was a short striped Cobler, a brownish coloured woollen Shirt; she wore a black Pealong Hat, trimmed with Gauze, and a black Calimanco Cloak; carried away with her a purple and white Calico Gown, one woollen Gown, one checked Apron, a striped Linen Gown, a Worsted Skirt, a striped Tow and

Linen Shirt, 3 or 4 Pair of Stockings, 4 or 5 Neck Handkerchiefs, 1 Pair of Tow and Linen Sheets, and 1 Bolster-Case.—Whoever will take up said Runaway, and return her to her Master, shall receive a Reward of Two Shillings, but no Charges, paid by JOHN WICKES.

N.B. All Persons are strictly forbid harbouring her, on any Pretence whatever.

Warwick, August 21, 1787.

Reprint: The Providence Gazette, 09-01-1787; 09-08-1787.

The Providence Gazette and Country Journal, 09-13-1788.

SIX DOLLARS REWARD.

RAN AWAY, on the Night of Wednesday the third Instant, a Negro Servant, about Twenty Years of Age, a short, thick-set Fellow; he had on, and carried with him, a striped blue and white Linen Coat and Waistcoat, a dark mixed coloured Cloth Great-Coat, and a Waistcoat of the same; two Pair of Trowsers, one white Towcloth and one dark-coloured Flannel. He carried off with him a large dark-brown Dog—his Legs and under his Neck, are of a yellowish Colour. —Whoever will take up said NEGRO, and return him to his Master, shall have Six Dollars Reward, and all necessary Charges, paid by

MOSES BARBER. Hopkinton, Sept. 6, 1788.

Reprint: The Providence Gazette and Country Journal, 09-20-1788; 09-27-1788. This notice was also printed in the United States Chronicle, 09-25-1788.

The Providence Gazette and Country Journal, 08-15-1789.

Five Dollars Reward.

RAN AWAY from the Subscriber; last Night, a small NEGRO MAN, of a yellow Complexion, about 19 or 20 Years of Age, a Servant for Life: Had on, when he went away, brown Tow-Cloth Shirt and Trowsers, a short blue Jacket, Yarn Stockings, and pretty good Pair of Shoes.—Whoever will take up said NEGRO, and return him to his Master, or secure him in any Gaol with this State, shall have FIVE SILVER DOLLARS Reward, and all necessary Charges, paid by WILLIAM HALL, Son of John.

North-Kingstown, July 20, 1789.

* Earlier variants of this notice appeared in the Providence Gazette And Country Journal, 07-25-1789; 08-08-1789.

The United States Chronicle, 06-10-1784.

Ten Dollars Reward.

RAN-AWAY, from the Subscriber, on the Night of Thursday the 3d Instant, a Negro Man, named POMP, born in this Country; had on and took with him a light blue superfine Broadcloth Coat and Waistcoat, lately turned, a Pair of Buff coloured Breeches, white and Check Shirts, worsted Stockings, old Shoes and an old Beaver Hat, newly dressed: He is a short thick Fellow, about 24 Years of Age, is a great Talker, and a little hard of Hearing. Said Negro was detected in Stealing. Whoever will take up and return him to his Master, shall receive the above Reward, and all necessary Charge, paid by DANIEL TILLINGHAST.

Providence, June 10, 1784.

Reprints: The United States Chronicle, 06-17-1784; 06-24-1784.

United States Chronicle, 08-11-1785.

Stop Thief!

Ran-away, from the Subscribers, on the Morning of the 30th of July, a Dutch NEGRO MAN, who calls himself PETER; he is about 5 Feet 4 or 5 Inches high, and between 22 and 26 Years of Age, pretty thick set; had on when he went away, a Pair of striped Flannel Trowsers, patched across the Striped on the Knees, plated Buckles, a very old Hat, with Holes in the Crown, a Tow-Cloth Shirt, and a coarse green Jacket, without Sleeves. Whoever will apprehend said Negro, and deliver him to the Subscribers, shall receive Three Dollars Reward, and all necessary Charges.

POWER and TILLINGHAST.

Providence, August 4, 1785.

The United States Chronicle, 10-13-1785.

RAN-AWAY from the Subscriber on the 5th Instant, an indented Mulatto Boy, about Sixteen Years of Age; —had on when he went off a grey home-spun Jacket, talks remarkably quick.—Whoever will take up and secure said Boy, and convey him to his Master in Sandwich, or send Intelligence thereof, shall receive TEN DOLLARS Reward, and all necessary Charges paid by JOSEPH NYE.

Sandwich, October 5, 1785.

Reprints: The United States Chronicle, 10-20-1785; 10-27-1785.

United States Chronicle, 08-28-1788.

RUN away from the Subscriber, on the Twentieth Instant, an Apprentice Negro Girl, named BARSHABA, aged about Fifteen Years; she has a large bushy Head of Hair, and is of a strong and hardy make;—had on when she went away a Cotton and Wool, purple and yellow coloured Gown.—Whoever will take up said Apprentice, and return her to her Master, shall have One Shilling Reward. JOSEPH BORDEN, jun. Johnston, August 25th, 1788.

N.B. All Persons are forbid harbouring said Runaway on Penalty of the Law.

Reprints: United States Chronicle, 09-04-1788; 09-11-1788; 09-18-1788; 09-25-1788.

The United States Chronicle, 12-06-1787.

A runaway Negro.

RAN-AWAY, from the Subscriber, living in Rehoboth, a NEGRO WOMAN, named PHILLIS, about 34 Years of Age.—Whoever will take up said Negro, and return her to her Master shall receive ONE SHILLING Reward. JOHN IDE.

Rehoboth, December 5, 1787.

Reprints: The United States Chronicle, 12-13-1787; 12-20-1787.

New Hampshire 1757–1789

FRIDAY, FEBRUARY 17. 1758.   NUMB. 72.

New-Hampfhire GAZETTE

Containing the Frefheft Advices   *Foreign and Domeftick.*

Farther ADVICES, brought by the EARL OF HALIFAX PACKET-BOAT, Captain RAND, which arrived at New-York on the 19th of laft Month, VIZ.

LEIPSICK (*a City of Germany, in the Circle of Upper-Saxony, 42 Miles N.W. of Drefden, fubject to the Elector of Saxony, King of Poland*) *October* 26.

THE Prince of Pruffia, who is actually in this City, is fallen fick, in Confequence of the continual Fatigues he has undergone fince the Beginning of the Campaign, which the indefatigable Conftitution of the King his Brother, feems alone capable of enduring; and indeed it is fomewhat inconceiveable how this Monarch can bear them as he does; ever bufy in his Tent and in the Field, ever in Motion, taken up with a thoufand Objects, and looking into every Thing, flying to every Place where his Prefence is neceffary, bidding Defiance to Fortune and her flippery Tricks, and bearing up boldly againft the moft formidable League that ever was formed againft any one Potentate.

LEIPSICK, *Nov.* 11. The Prince of Pruffia, who has been dangeroufly ill, is now in a fair Way of Recovery. At his Royal Highnefs's we have been informed, that the Pruffian Army fpent the Night of the Action on the Field of Battle, and that on the 6th, by Day-Break, his Majefty put himfelf at the Head of all the Cavalry and Huffars he could find, and went in Purfuit of the Enemy, who retreated by the Route of Naumbourgh, came up with them and attacked their Rear, upon which a very fmart Skirmifh enfued. It is faid another Engagement happened the 7th, with a Corps of Auftrian Cavalry, fuppofed to be General Landun's; but there are no exact Accounts of either of thefe Skirmifhes, which probably have given rife to the Report of a fecond Battle.

NAPLES (*one of the greateft Cities in the World, C. of the K. of Naples, in Italy*) *Nov.* 1. As the Troubles of Germany ftill continue, and 'tis impoffible to forfee when or in what Manner they will end, frequent Councils are held at Court, in order to confult upon the prefent Tranquility of Italy.

BERLIN, (*Capital of the King of Pruffia's Dominions, in Germany, on the R. Spree*) *Nov.* 14. Yefterday folemn Thankfgivings, was rendered to the Almighty in all our Churches for the late fignal Succefs vouchfafed to his Majefty's Arms.

It is reported that a Letter has been lately intercepted from Marfhal Ungern de Sternberg, the Swedifh General in Pomerania, wherein he earneftly requefts the French General to fend a Body of Troops to his Affiftance, without which he muft be obliged to ftop the Courfe of his Operations in that Province, and retire under the Cannon of Stralfund, in order, in Cafe of Need, to re-embark with his Army, and thereby to avoid falling into the Dilemma in which that of the Saxons found themfelves laft Year.

—*Nov.* 19. The King has honoured Major General de Seydelitz with the Order of the Black Eagle, in Confideration of his Valour in the late glorious Action.

PETERSBURG (*the Capital of Ruffia, fituate between the Gulph of Finland and the Lake Ladoga*) *Octo.* 15. Winter Quarters are not yet affigned Marfhal Apraxin's Army; on the contrary, it is faid, he is to refume his Operations, and will be reinforced with 20,000 Men.

STOCKHOLM, (*the Capital of Sweden, on an Ifland in Meller Lake,*) *Nov.* 1. As we may from Time hence have Occafion to reinforce our Army in Pomerania, Orders have been given to feveral Regiments to hold themfelves in Readinefs to embark for that Province, and they are already affembling Tranfport-Veffels for that Purpofe. Sir Charles Williams arrived here on the 30th ult. by the Way of Finland.

MADRID, (*Capital of Old Spain*) *Oct.* 25. It is affured, that Application having been made to the King to employ his Mediation to oppofe the prefent Broils, he made Anfwer, that the refpective Claims were fo intricate, that he would not intermeddle in the Affair.

LISBON, (*Capital of the K. of Portugal, fituate on R. Tagus, once a magnificent City, but lately ruined by an Earthquake*) *Oct.* 18. The 10th Inftant, about ten in the Morning we had another ftrong Shock of an Earthquake, which was felt the fame Day and the fame Hour at Alcantara and Viana, a fmall City fituated on the other Side of the Tagus. This Shock was ftill more violent at Evora, being preceeded by a terrible fubterraneous Noife, but happily did no other Damage any where than alarming the Inhabitants.

HAMBURGH, (*a City and Port-Town in Germany*) *Nov.* 11. According to our laft Advices from the Ruffian Army, Part of their Troops have already entered the Dutchy of Courland to take Winter-Quarters, and the reft, except the irregular Troops which were

marching into the Empire, and about 12 or 15,000 Men, who are left in the Environs of Memel, were on their March toward Livonia, fo that there is no Appearance of this Army's Undertaking any Thing, at leaft this Campaign, againft Pruffia. H. Gazette.

ROCHFORT, (*a Port Town of France, in the Pr. of Guienne*) *Nov.* 3. The Court has fent Orders here as well as to Breft, to difarm all the Men of War and Frigates, who were ready to put to Sea on the firft Notice. As we have nothing now to apprehend from the Englifh, the City Gates here and at Rochelle are opened, and every one is returned to his Employment as before.

BREST, (*a Port Town in France*) *Oct.* 20. Juft as M. de Conflans, with his formidable Fleet, was ready to fail, Orders came from Court to difarm all the Ships but four; which, with fome Frigates, are to protect our Trade during the Winter.

The Eagle, of 64 Guns, is fitting out to carry Provifions to Louifbourg.

TOULON, (*in France*) *Oct.* 12. The Marquis de Fermon, Lieut. General, who commands upon the Coaft, is conftantly employed in vifiting the Troops and Batteries, and, by Way of Precaution, all the Batteries upon the Coaft have had an additional Number of Guns and Men fent to them, fo that we have nothing to apprehend from any Expedition of the Englifh, however fecret it may be. In the mean Time, we have upwards of 3000 Men at Work in our Dock-Yards, building new Men of War and Frigates; the fmalleft of the former will be of 60 Guns, and the leaft Frigate of 34. They are affembling in Provence a Body of between 26 and 30,000 Men, for whom Quarters are preparing with the utmoft Difpatch.

—*Oct.* 23. M. de la Clue's fix Ships go To-Morrow to Vignettes, two Leagues from our Road, where they are to wait for a favourable Wind. Their Deftination is no longer a Secret, being bound for St. Domingo.

PARIS, (*in France*) *Nov.* 14. Laft Saturday we received the difagreeable News, that the King of Pruffia had attacked and defeated the Combined Army the 5th of this Month; and that the Lofs of that Army amounted to three Thoufand Men; we wait for a more particular Account of this Affair.

PARIS, (*in France*) *Nov.* 18. The fatal Affair of the 5th of this Month, greatly affects the Court and the Publick. Every Body deplores the Lofs of the Number of brave Officers killed, wounded, or taken Prifoners, on that Day. Nothing can condole them but the Hopes of feeing the Honour of our Arms avenged in fome fignal Manner. All the Officers who had Permiffion to quit the Army, to come to fee their Families, have received Orders to return immediately.

—*Nov.* 19. The Minds of the People are fo deeply affected with the fatal Affair of the 5th Inftant, that even the moft Moderate can fcarce refrain from fpeaking of the Caufes to which this fad Event is attributed.

Prince Soubife feems uncommonly touched with his Misfortune. In his firft Letter to the King he expreffes himfelf in the following Manner, "Sire, I write to you in the utmoft Difpair, your Majefty's " Army is entirely defeated."

Another Shock of an Earthquake, much ftronger than the former one lately mentioned, has been felt in the maritime Parts of Normandy and Britany, which has obliged the Inhabitants again to quit their Habitations.

CONSTANTINOPLE, (*the Metropolis of the Turkifh Empire*) *Oct.* 29. This Morning at Four o'Clock, we were informed, that Sultan Ofman died in the Night; at Break of Day the Cannon of the Port was fired; therefore the News is certainly true. The New Emperor is Sultan Muftapha; and hitherto every Thing has paffed in great Tranquility.

UTRECHT, (*the Capital of the Province of Utrecht, in the United Netherlands, fituated on the Channel of the Old Rhine, 23 Miles S. E. of Amfterdam*) *Nov.* 24. His Pruffian Majefty, who was the 7th at Leipfic, has treated the French Officers who were taken Prifoners in the Battle of the 5th, with the greateft Politenefs, having ordered them to be fupplied with all Neceffaries, invited them to his own Table, and declared to them, that they were at Liberty to retire where they pleafed, upon their Parole of Honour. By a Letter from Cobourg of the 11th, we learn, that Baron Pretlack, one of the General Officers of the Empire, was brought in there dangeroufly wounded: That there were in the fame Town, as alfo at Saalfeldt, feveral other wounded Officers; and that Major General Meyer had paffed thro' that Neighbourhood with a Body of Huffars and Pruffian Dragoons in Purfuit of the French upon their Retreat. Advices from Brunfwick and Halberftadt, fay, that every Thing was in Motion.

The

Figure 3.2. Cover page: New-Hampshire Gazette, 02-17-1758

Chapter Four

New Hampshire Notices

Exeter Journal, 10-13-1778.

Ten Dollars Reward.

RANAWAY from Daniel Tilton of Exeter, on Thursday last, a Negro Servant named Cato, 19 Years old, about five Feet 8 or 9 Inches high, and slim, speaks tolerably plain, had on when he went away, an old Felt Hat, check Linnen Shirt, a pair of coarse strip'd Tow and Linnen Trowsers, a red half thick Waistcoat, and a blue outside jacket very ragged; without either Shoes or Stockings. Whoever will take up said Negro, and convey him to me the Subscriber, shall have the above Reward and all necessary charges paid, by DANIEL TILTON.

Exeter, October 6th, 1778.

Freeman's Journal, 06-01-1776.

RAN AWAY on the evening of the 29th inst. a NEGRO MAN, named Seneca, about five feet eight inches high, 47 years of age; a stout thick sett fellow, talks good English; he carried with him two coats, one red the other blue; one blue pea Jacket; one brown lappell'd, and one strip'd homespun dit. 2 pair leather breeches; 2 pair worsted, and 2 pair yarn stockings; 2 pair shoes; a mill'd cap turn'd up with fur, &c. Whoever will return said Negro, or confine him so that his master may have him again, shall have FOUR DOLLARS reward, and all necessary charges paid by SAMUEL HALL.

Portsmouth, May 31st.

Reprints: The New-Hampshire Gazette, 08-17-1764; 09-07-1764.

Freeman's Journal, 08-17-1776.

Five Dollars Reward.

RAN away from the Subscriber, about the 1st inst. a Negro-Man named Newport, between 30 and 40 years of age, speaks good English, 5 feet 7 inches high, carried with him a Round, homespun Jackett, Leather Breeches, long Trowsers, check'd homespun Shirts, &c. Whoever will convey said Negro to me, or confine him in any Goal in this State, so that I may have him again, shall have Five Dollars Reward, and all necessary paid by

Tilly Haggens.

Berwick August 15, 1776.

Reprints: Freeman's Journal, 08-31-1776; 09-07-1776.

Freeman's Journal, 09-28-1776.

Two Dollars Reward.

RAN away from me the subscriber, the 26th of Aug. last, a Negro man named Cato, about 25 years of age, 5 feet high, speaks good English; carried with him a light-coloured fustian coat, grey homespun breeches, striped woolen shirts, &c. Whoever takes up said negro, and conveys him to me, shall have two dollars reward, and all necessary charges paid by WILLIAM HALEY.

Kittery Sept. 13, 1776

Freeman's Journal, 11-26-1776.

RUN away from York a Negro Man named Caesar, about five feet six Inches high. Had on when he went away a yellowish homespun Coat, blue plush Breeches, a light bound Hat, about forty years of age, speaks very good English—Whoever will take up said Negro and convey him to his Master or secure him and give him Information thereof shall have eight Dollars reward and all necessary Charges paid by Richard Talpey.

York, Nov. 9th, 1776.

N.B. All masters of vessels are caution'd carrying off said Negro as they would avoid the penalty of the Law.

Freeman's Journal, 04-12-1777.

RAN-AWAY from the Subscriber April 1, 1777, a NEGRO MAN named BONE, about five Feet nine Inches high, between 20 and 30 Years of Age, speaks good English;—Had on when he went away, a striped Cotton and Linnen Shirt, two short Waistcoat, inside one white wollen mill'd, the other brown, with claret colour'd Sleeves, Leather Breeches, light blue Yarn Rib

Stockings, & a very narrow brim'd Felt Hat: He has been in the Continental Service 19 Months and it is suspected that he will, if he can, get to the British Troops. Whoever will take up said Negro, and return him or secure him, and give Information to the Subscriber, shall have Eight Dollars Reward, & all necessary Charges paid by

Rochester, April 3, 1777.

JOSEPH KNIGHT.

N.B. All Masters of Vessels are caution'd against carrying off said Negro as they will avoid the Penalty of the LAW.

Freeman's Journal, 11-15-1777.

Two NEGROES, Runaway.

RUNAWAY from JAMES McCOBB, Esq; of GOREHAM Town, the 20th of the last September, two NEGRO MEN Servants, one named Cato, and the other Jack;—Cato about five Feet nine Inches high, speaks good English, and carried with him two Suits of Cloaths; his best Cloaths Flesh Colour'd Cloth with Mohair Buttons; and Silver Buckles in his Shoes; his every Day's Claoths a Check Woolen Shirt, a striped Jacket wove with a Wale; Woolen Trousers Hemlock Colour—Jack about five Feet six Inches high, speaks somewhat broken English, had a Blemish on one of his Eyes; he carried two Suits of Cloaths with him, his best Cloaths was Snuff Colour'd Cloth; Silver Buckles in his Shoes, and a large Gold Lace round his Hat; his every Day Cloaths was a Check Woolen Shirt, Striped Woolen Trousers Hemlock Colour, a Striped Jacket wove with a Wale.—WHOEVER shall take up the said Negroes, and secure them in any Goal in this State, shall have Eight Dollars Reward for each of them, and the Prison Keeper well Rewarded for his Trouble. Direct to me at George Town, in the County of Lincoln.

George Town, Oct 18, 1777. JAMES McCOBB.

P.S. It is thought they will try to get to the British Troops. All Masters of Vessels are caution'd from carrying them off.

Freeman's Journal, 05-12-1778.

Ranaway Saturday the 9th inst. A Negro Man named Caesar, from his Master Sam Wallis of Rye—35 Years of Age—Five Feet and a half high; had on when he went away a blue Kersey Coat, grey homespun Breeches and grey Stockings.—Whoever takes up said Negro and returns him to his Master shall have Twenty Dollars Reward.

The New-Hampshire Gazette, 07-28-1758.

RAN-away the 24th of this Instant July, from his Master Dennis Fernald of Kittery, in the Province of the Massachusetts Bay, a Mulatto Servant named POMP, about 21 Years of Age, five Feet eight Inches high, a stout thick set strait Fellow. He had on when he went away, an old Felt Hat much wore, a Worsted Cap, a checkt Woollen Shirt, blue homespun fly Coat with flat white metal Buttons, a green Frize double-breasted Jacket with Leather Buttons, dark coloured Leather Breeches, blue Stockings, Shoes newly cased at the Toes: He also carried with him a pair of homespun Breeches and a grey Jacket without Sleeves.

Also went away at the same Time a white Girl about 16 Years of Age: she had on a striped cotton and linen Gown, and carried with her a chints Gown and scarlet Cloak, a black Hair Hat, a blue quilted Petticoat. Whoever will take up said Persons, and convey them to the abovesaid Fernald, or otherwise secure them, so that he may have them again, shall have FOUR DOLLARS Reward for both, or Two Dollars for each of them, and necessary Charges paid by Dennis Fernald.

The New-Hampshire Gazette, 06-10-1763.

Deserted from his Master, Samuel Hanson, of Epping, a Negro MAN, about 40 Years of Age, named Adam; a thick Sett Fellow: had on when he went away, a dark color'd Homespun Jacket, Leather Breeches, white Shirt, and blue Stockings.—Whoever will take up said Negro, and convey him to his said Master at Epping, shall be handsomely rewarded.

The New-Hampshire Gazette, 07-15-1763.

RAN-AWAY from their Owners in Black-Point, in Scarborough, Four NEGRO-FELLOWS, with a large WHALE-BOAT, having a large Iron Bolt, with an Eye to it, in her Stem: Two of said Fellows belonging to Timothy Prout, Esq; one of them named Cesar, a subtle, cunning, sly Fellow, shows his fore Teeth considerably, especially when he laughs, about 5 Feet 6 Inches high, well-sett good looking Fellow, something upwards of Forty Years of Age; he had on a fly cloth-color'd Broad-Cloth Coat, a strip't Jacket, cloth-color'd Breeches, very full Pair of Trowsers.—Another NEGRO named Quam, about Thirty Years of Age' a stout, thick Fellow, and very lusty, long Visage, very thick Lips, and lost a Joynt of one of his great Toes; had on a stone-grey Coat and Breeches blueish ribb'd Stockings, full Pair of Trowsers.—Another NEGRO belonging to Mrs. Anna Thompson, named Prince, about 18 Years of Age, about 5 Feet, 8 Inches high, full large Eyes, a

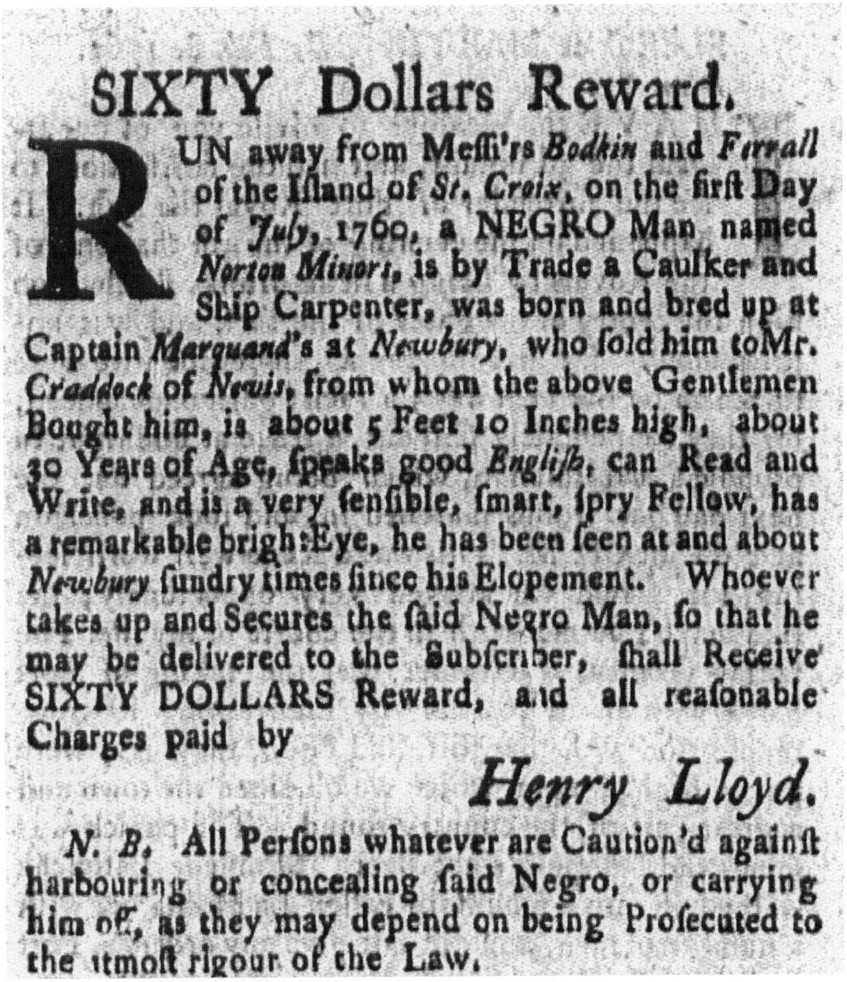

SIXTY Dollars Reward.

RUN away from Meſſ'rs *Bodkin* and *Ferrall* of the Iſland of *St. Croix*, on the firſt Day of *July*, 1760, a NEGRO Man named *Norton Minort*, is by Trade a Caulker and Ship Carpenter, was born and bred up at Captain *Marquand*'s at *Newbury*, who ſold him to Mr. *Craddock* of *Nevis*, from whom the above Gentlemen Bought him, is about 5 Feet 10 Inches high, about 30 Years of Age, ſpeaks good *Engliſh*, can Read and Write, and is a very ſenſible, ſmart, ſpry Fellow, has a remarkable bright Eye, he has been ſeen at and about *Newbury* ſundry times ſince his Elopement. Whoever takes up and Secures the ſaid Negro Man, ſo that he may be delivered to the Subſcriber, ſhall Receive SIXTY DOLLARS Reward, and all reaſonable Charges paid by

Henry Lloyd.

N. B. All Perſons whatever are Caution'd againſt harbouring or concealing ſaid Negro, or carrying him off, as they may depend on being Proſecuted to the utmoſt rigour of the Law.

Figure 4.1.   Norton Minor, New Hampshire Gazette, May 21, 1762

pleasant Countenance; had with him two striped Woolen Jacket, one yellow Thick sett ditto. One Pair Leather Breeches, one Pair Trowsers, one Pair of blue ribb'd, and one Pair light Stockings, 1 check'd Shirt, one green worsted Cap, one red and white cotton ditto.—Another NEGRO, belonging to Mrs. Elizabeth Deering, named Robbin, about 18 Years of Age; a short, thick, likely, well sett Boy, with a cloth-color'd Jacket, one Pair Leather Breeches, one check'd and one white Linnen Shirt, one strip't worsted Cap; WHOEV- ER shall secure the said NEGROES, or bring them to their Owners, shall have TEN DOLLARS Reward for each, and all necessary Charges paid, per Joseph Prout

Scarborough, N. England, July 12. William Thompson,

Elizabeth Deering.

N.B. They Ran away on Wednesday the 6th of this Inst. July, 1763

P.S. All Masters of Vessels and others, are forbid to entertain, conceal, or carry off said Runaways, as they would avoid the Penalty of the Law.

Reprints: The New-Hampshire Gazette, 07-22-1763; 07-29-1763.

The New-Hampshire Gazette, 01-20-1764.

RAN away from his Master Francis Mathes of Durham, about three Weeks ago, a NEGRO MAN, named Adam, about 38 Years of Age; a thick sett Fellow, goes with his Knees very close together:—Had on a light Colour'd round Jacket, with a Striped Jacket underneath Black and White, a Pair of old Snuff colour'd Plush Breeches, and an old Felt Hatt; Whoever shall take up said Runaway and convey him to his Master, or secure him in any of his Majesty's Goals, so that he may be had again shall have TWO DOLLARS Reward, and all necessary Charges paid by me, Francis Mathes.

* Earlier variant of this notices appeared in the New-Hampshire Gazette, 12-30-1763; 12-30-1763.

The New-Hampshire Gazette, 06-01-1764.

RUN away from his Master William Wentworth of Kittery in the County of York a Molatto Man named CATO, He speaks good English, is about 30 years of Age and was brouget up on a Farm, is a streight limb'd Fellow and stammers in his speech, if spoken to suddenly, he wears his Hair and some-times a dark Wig, he is 5 feet 8 inches high, he had on when he went away, an old bearskin Coat, two check Shirts and striped swanskin Westcoat, three pair of Stockings a felt Hatt, whoever will take up the said Runaway, confine or bring him to his Master, shall have SIX DOLLARS Reward, and all necessary charges paid by me, WILLIAM WENTWORTH.

N.B. ALL Masters of Vessels are cautioned against carrying away the said servant, as they would avoid the penalty of the Law in that Case.

Reprint: The New-Hampshire Gazette, 06-08-1764.

The New-Hampshire Gazette, 06-01-1764.

RUN away from Benjamin Fernald of Kittery, in the County of York, the 29th Instant, a Negro Man named ADAM, about 27 Years of Age, a short thick Fellow, about five Feet one Inch or two high, born in New England, speaks good English; He had on when he went away, a blue sea Jacket, gray Stockings, striped woollen Shirt, and frequently wears Wigg: If any Person can, and will apprehend said Runaway, and bring him to the Subscriber, or confine him in any of his Majesty's Goals so as the Subscriber can have him again, shall have SIX DOLLARS Reward. BENJAMIN FERNALD. Kittery May 30th, 1764.

Reprint: The New-Hampshire Gazette, 06-08-1764.

The New-Hampshire Gazette, 07-20-1764.

RAN away on the 7th of this Instant July, from his Master John Merrill of Topsham, in the County of Lincoln, and Province of the Massachusetts Bay, a NEGRO MAN named Adam, about 27 Year Old, and about five Feet and three Inches high; he speaks good English;—had on when he went away, an old narrow brim'd Hat, a yellow Wig, a blue round Tail out-side Jacket, a striped Woollen Shirt, a red under Jacket, brown Breeches, Thicken Trowsers, blue Stockings, a pair of Pumps—Whoever will take up said Runaway, and bring him to said Merrill, or otherways secure him, so that he may have him again, shall have FOUR DOLLARS Reward, and all necessary Charges paid by me, John Merrill.

N.B. All Masters of Vessels and others are hereby cautioned against Entertaining, Concealing or carry off said Runaway.

The New-Hampshire Gazette, 04-25-1766.

RUN away from his Master, John Moody of Newmarket, a NEGRO Man named Neptune, about twenty eight or nine Years of Age—Had on a Home made Coat, the Forepart lin'd with red Shaloon, a green Jacket, a New Pair of Shoes and blue Yarn Stockings;—has lost two of his Toes, and can't move his Under Jaw. If any Person will take up said Run away, and return him to his Master, or secure him, that he may have him again, he shall be allowed for Charges, and be satisfied for his Trouble, by me the Subscriber,

Newmarket, April 21. JOHN MOODY.

* Earlier variants of this notice appeared in the New-Hampshire Gazette, 03-25-1763; 03-31-1763.

New-Hampshire Gazette, 07-25-1766.

FIVE DOLLARS REWARD.

RAN away last Monday Night, from THOMAS WALLINGSFORD, Esq; of Somersworth, a NEGRO MAN, named Primus, about 30 Years of Age; a short thick well set Fellow, he shows considerable of white in his Eyes, has a smooth Face. Had on when he went away, brownish Kersey Coat, metal Button; carried with him several Jackets, Breeches, Trowsers, Shirts, and Stockings, and about Thirty Dollars. Whoever takes up said Servant, and secures him, so that his said Master may have him again, shall receive FIVE DOLLARS Reward, and all necessary Charges paid by me, THOMAS WALLINGSFORD .

N.B. All Masters of Vessels are hereby cautioned not to carry off said Servant, as they would avoid the Penalty of the Law.

July 17.

The New-Hampshire Gazette, 10-10-1766.

RUNAWAY from the Subscriber, in the Night of the 14th Inst.—A Negro Servant man, Named BOSTON, about 20 Years of Age, a stout lusty Fellow; had on when he went away, a brown homespun Coat, lin'd with check'd Worsted, and white Mettal Buttons, likewise a diaper Jacket, Faced with Chince, Worsted Stockings, a Felt Hatt, Speaks broad Scotch.—Whoever shall take up said NEGRO, and convey him to me in Londonderry shall have a Reward of three DOLLARS, and all Charges paid by me, JOSEPH BELL.

N.B. All Masters of Vessels are cautioned against carrying off said Negro, as they would avoid Trouble.

Londonderry, Sept. 11, 1766.

The New-Hampshire Gazette, 06-05-1767.

RUNAWAY from his Master Daniel Rogers, Esq; of Durham, last Saturday, a NEGRO MAN, named Cato, formerly went by the Name of Mingo—He was of a middling Size, well set spry Fellow, born in the Country; about 30 Years of Age—Had on when he went away a blue Ratteen Coat, light colour'd Sarge Jacket, Leather Breeches, and old Bever Hat—He's a great Lyer, and very Cunning—Whoever will take up said Negro, and convey him to his said Master, shall have Five DOLLARS Reward, and necessary charges paid by Daniel Rogers.—

N.B. All Masters of Vessels are forbid carrying off said Servant, as they would avoid the Penalty of the Law.

If he will return immediately he shall be forgiven this Time.—

Reprints: The New-Hampshire Gazette, 06-12-1767; 06-19-1767.

The New-Hampshire Gazette, 07-22-1768.

Thirty Dollars Reward.

RAN AWAY the 17th Instant from Durham, from their Masters Daniel Meserve, Ichabod Chests, and Samuel Demerit, two Negro Men, and a Melatto Man; it is supposed they are all gone together.

The first, which is reckon'd the greatest Rogue , is named Primus, belonging to Daniel Meserve, who formerly belonged to James Gray of Saco Falls; he is a sly Fellow, and very spry, about 21 Years of Age; 5 Feet 10 Inches high.

The other Negro, belonging to Capt. Samuel Demerit, is about 26 Years of Age, a lusty likely well set Fellow, about five Feet and half high; has no particular Mark by which to describe him; he carried away with him, a Gun, and some Ammunition.

The Melatto Fellow, belonging to Ichabod Chests, is about eight or nine and twenty Years of Age, about 5 Feet 10 Inches high, a slim strait Fellow, with long black Hair; the Hair on the top of his head is generally kept close cut—He also took with him a Gun and Ammunition.—Whoever will take up said Servants, and convey them to their said Masters, SHALL HAVE THIRTY DOLLARS REWARDS, or TEN DOLLARS, FOR EITHER OF THEM, & all necessary charges paid.—N.B. ALL Masters of vessels and others are forbid entertaining, concealing, or carrying off said Servants, as they would avoid the Penalty of the Law in that Case made & Provided.

Reprints: The New-Hampshire Gazette, 07-29-1768; 08-05-1768.

* Earlier variants of this notice appeared in the New-Hampshire Gazette, and Historical Chronicle, 06-17-1768.

The New-Hampshire Gazette, 09-09-1768.

RUNAWAY the beginning of last Month from Merrimack, a Negro Man named Exeter, from his Master Samuel Wentworth,—a lusty strong Fellow about 30 Years of Age, a Cooper by Trade—Had on when he went away a Pair of Trowsers, Frock and Shirt—He was born in the Country. Whoever takes up said Negro, so that his Master may have him again, shall be well rewarded. He some Times Lets himself out as a Cooper.

N.B. All Masters of Vessels and others, are hereby forbid Harbouring or carrying off said Servant, as they would avoid the Penalty of the Law, in that Case made and Provided.

The New-Hampshire Gazette, 02-03-1769.

RAN-AWAY from Old-York on Sunday January 29th, 1769, from me the Subscriber, a NEGRO MAN named TONEY, about thirty-six Years of Age, about five Feet and three Inches high. Had on when he went away, a blue German Sarge Coat, a red Cloth Wastecoat, Buff Leather Breeches. Whoever will take up said Run-away, or confine him, shall have FOUR DOLLARS Reward, and all necessary Charges paid by me, EDWARD GROVE.

The New-Hampshire Gazette, 08-09-1771.

Ran away from Eliphalet Hale of Exeter, on Saturday Night last, a Negro Man, named Kelley, about 40 Years old, about 5 Feet 10 Inches high, a stout built Fellow; had on and carried with him, Beaveritt Hatt, a black Wig, a red Cap, a green Coat cuff'd with Red, and a red Coat, a Chince Jacket, one blue Ditto two white Woolen Shirts, one white Linnen Ditto, a Pair of red Plush Breeches, a Pair of Worsted Stockings, one Pair of Yarn Ditto a Pair of Shoes, a pair of Pumps, a Pair of yellow Mettle Shoe and Knee Buckles, a Pair of white short Trowsers: Any Person who will take up said Negro, and bring him to me the Subscriber, at Exeter, or secure him in any of his Majesty's Goals, and give me Notice, shall receive four DOLLARS Reward, and all necessary Charges paid by Eliphalet Hale.

N.B. All Masters of Vessels are cautioned against carrying off said Negro.

Exeter, August 7th 1771.

Reprints: The New-Hampshire Gazette, 08-16-1771; 08-30-1771.

The New-Hampshire Gazette, 05-15-1772.

A RUNAWAY

Ran-Away from Benjamin Little in Hampstead, a NEGRO MAN named Peter, about 5 Feet 7 Inches high, and about 38 Years old, he carried Away with him two Sutes of Cloaths, one of Brown, with bright Buttons, and one Suit of White ditto. And Plays well on a Fiddle: Whoever will take up said Negro Man Peter, and Secure him, so that I shall have him, shall have FOUR DOLLARS Reward and all necessary Charges paid, by me, BENJAMIN LITTLE.

Reprint: The New-Hampshire Gazette, 05-22-1772.

The New-Hampshire Gazette, 10-09-1772.

RAN away from his Master George Berry of Falmouth a NEGRO MAN named Dick, the 11th of last Month, he is about five Feet and a Half high, forty Years old, something Pock-broken, walks with his Toes turned in; he had on a Mous-color'd homespun Coat, lined with green Baize, mohair Buttons, a striped homespun Jacket, and striped Shirt; short Trowsers and blue homespun Stockings; a small felt Hat, and dark color'd Wig, has a Scar on his under Lip—Whoever takes up said Servant, and conveys him to his said Master shall have four Dollars Reward, and all necessary Charges paid by me, George Berry.

Falmouth, Sept. 7, 1772.

The New-Hampshire Gazette, 07-29-1774.

Four Dollars Reward.

RANAWAY from his Master Mark Hunking of Barrington, in New Hampshire, a Negro Servant named Caesar:—Had on when he went away, a striped homespun lapped'd Waistcoat, a Toe Shirt, black Serge Breeches, grey Jacket, a pair of Breeches and Jacket of a black and Hemlock dye, striped Toe Trowsers, black and white Yarn Stockings. He is a strait Limb'd Fellow about 5 Feet nine Inches high, very white Teeth, smiling Countenance; was bro't up to Farming Work.—Whoever shall take up said Runaway, and secure him, so that his Master may have him again, shall have Four Dollars Reward, and all necessary Charges paid by

MARK HUNKING.

N.B. All Master of Vessels and others are forbid carrying him off, as they would avoid the Penalty of the Law. Barrington, July 12, 1774.

The New-Hampshire Gazette, 11-23-1782.

RAN AWAY from his master, Monsieur D' Hiseures, yesterday night, a Negro Man, named Jaseinte, 5 feet 6 inches high, well set; had on a dark color'd jacket, a grey waist-coat, cloth color'd breeches, red cap, and black hat, was 23 year of age.—Whoever takes up said negro, and conveys him to his master in Portsmouth, shall have FOUR DOLLARS reward, and all necessary charges paid, by Mons. D'HISEURES,

(Capt. Commandant reg. of Venois, on board the Auguste)

Portsmouth, Nov. 22, 1782.

The New-Hampshire Gazette, 05-24-1783.

RAN-AWAY from her Mistress the tenth instant, a Negro Girl about 16 years of age, named VILOT, speaks good English, and is of short stature— Whoever will take up said Negro, shall be handsomely rewarded, and all charges paid by me

ELIZABETH SERVICE.

Portsmouth, May 17, 1783.

Reprint: The New-Hampshire Gazette, 05-31-1783.

The New-Hampshire Gazette, 08-12-1785.

Ran-away

From Capt. John Donaldson, on Saturday the 6th instant a NEGRO GIRL, named VIOLET, about 16 years of age, this country born, had a remarkable nub on one of her ears—she carried off considerable clothing mostly new and good. Whoever apprehends the said NEGRO and delivers her to the subscriber, shall receive FOUR DOLLARS reward, and all reasonable expences. ALEXANDER EWEN.

Portsmouth, August 9, 1785.

Reprint: The New-Hampshire Gazette, 08-19-1785.

Appendix

(A copy of Jefferson's argument on Howell's behalf)
Thomas Jefferson, Memorandum
ARGUMENT IN THE CASE OF HOWELL vs. NETHERLAND.

On behalf of the plaintiff it was insisted, 1st. that if he could be detained in servitude by his first master, he could not be aliened. But 2nd. that he could not be detained in servitude.

1. It was observed that the purpose of the act was to punish and deter women from that confusion of species, which the legislature seems to have considered as an evil, and not to oppress their innocent offspring. That accordingly it had made cautious provision for the welfare of the child, by leaving it to the discretion of the church wardens to choose out a proper master; and by directing, that that master should provide for it sufficient food, clothing, and lodging, and should not give immoderate correction. For these purposes the master enters into covenants with the church wardens; and to admit he had a power after this to sell his ward, would be to admit him a power of discharging himself of his covenants. Nor is this objection answered by saying that the covenants of the first master are transferred to the alienee, because he may be insolvent of the damages which should be recovered against him, and indeed they might be of such a nature as could not be atoned for, either to the servant or to society ; such, for instance, would be a corruption of morals either by the wicked precept or example of the master, or of his family. The truth is, the master is bound to the servant for food, raiment, and protection and is not at liberty, by aliening his charge, to put it out of his own power to afford them when wanting. The servant may as well set up a right of withdrawing from his master those personal services which he, in return, is bound to yield him. Again, the same trust which is created by express compact in favor of the first mulatto, is extended by the law to her

issue. The legislature confiding that the choice of a master for the first mulatto, by the church wardens, would be prudent, vest the issue in him also without further act to be done ; and the master, at the time he takes the mother, knowing that her issue also is to be under her servitude on the same conditions, does by accepting her, tacitly undertake to comply with those conditions raised by the law in their favor. These servants bear greater resemblance to apprentices than to slaves. Thus, on the death of the first master, they go to his executor as an apprentice would, and not to his heir as a slave. The master is chosen, in both cases, from an opinion of his peculiar propriety for that charge, and the performances of his duty in both cases is secured by mutual covenants. Now it is well known that an apprentice can not be aliened ; and that, not from any particular provision of the legislature, but from the general nature of the connection and engagements between them : there being, as was before observed, a trust reposed in the diligence and discretion of the master ; and a trust by our law cannot be assigned. It adheres to the person as closely as does his integrity, and he can no more transfer the one than the other to a purchaser. But,

2nd. It was insisted, that the plaintiff, being a mulatto of the third generation, would not be detained in servitude under any law whatever : the grand position now to be proved being that one law had reduced to servitude the first mulatto only, the immediate offspring of a white woman by a negro or mulatto man ; that a second law had extended it to the "children" of that mulatto ; but that no law had yet extended it to her grandchildren, or other issue more remote than this. To prove this, a general statement of these laws was premised. Act of 1705, c. 49 s. 18. "If any woman servant shall have a bastard child, by a negro or mulatto, or if a free Christian white woman shall have such bastard child by a negro or mulatto ; in both the said cases the churchwardens shall bind the said child to be a servant until it shall be of thirty one years of age." In other parts of the act, it is declared who shall be slaves, and what a manumission of them ; from sect. 34 to 39. are regulations solely relative to slaves, among which is sect. 36. "Baptism of slaves doth not exempt them from bondage ; and all children shall be bond or free according to the condition of their mothers and the particular directions of this act."

Act. 1723. c. 4. s. 22. "Where any female mulatto, or Indian, by law obliged to serve till the age of thirty or thirty one years shall, during the time of her servitude, have any child born of her body, every such child shall serve the master or mistress of such mulatto or Indian, until it shall attain the same age, the mother of such child was obliged, by law, to serve unto."

In 1748, the Assembly revising and digesting the whole body of our acts of Assembly, in act 14. s. 4. incorporate the clauses before cited, without any addition or alteration. And in 1753, c. 2. s. 4. 13, the law of 1748, is re-enacted with some new matter which does not affect the present question.

Now it is plain the plaintiff does not come within the description of the act of 1705, s. 18 ; that only reducing to servitude "the child of a white woman by a negro or mulatto man." This was the predicament of the plaintiff's grandmother. I suppose it will not be pretended that the mother being a servant, the child would be a servant also under the law of nature, without any particular provision in the act. Under the law of nature, all men are born free, every one comes into the world with a right to his own person, which includes the liberty of moving and using it at his own will. This is what is called personal liberty, and is given him by the author of nature, because necessary for his own sustenance. The reducing the mother to servitude was a violation of the law of nature : surely then the same law cannot prescribe a continuance of the violation to her issue, and that too without end, for if it extends to any, it must to every degree of descendants. Puff. b. 6. c. 3. s. 4. 9. supports this doctrine. For having proved that servitude to be rightful, must be founded on either compact, or capture in war, he proceeds to shew that the children of the latter only follow the condition of the mother : for which he gives this reason, that the person and labor of the mother in a condition of perfect slavery, (as he supposes to be that of the captive in war) being the property of the master, it is impossible she should maintain it but with her master's goods ; by which he supposes a debt contracted from the infant to the master. But he says in cases of servitude founded on contract, "The food of the future issue is contained or implied in their own maintenance, which their master owes them as a just debt ; and consequently their children are not involved in a necessity of slavery." This is the nature of the servitude introduced by the act of 1705, the master deriving his title to the service of the mother, entirely from the contract entered into with the churchwardens. That the bondage of the mother does not under the law of nature, infer that of her issue, as included in her, is further obvious from this consideration, that by the same reason, the bondage of the father would infer that of his issue; for he may with equal, and some anatomists say with greater reason, be said to include all his posterity. But this very law admits there is no such descent of condition from father to child, when it imposes servitude on the child of a slave, which would have been unnecessary, if the condition had descended of course. Again, if it be a law of nature that the child shall follow the condition of the parent, it would introduce a very perplexing dilemma; as where the one parent is free and the other a slave. Here the child is to be a slave says this law by inheritance of the father's bondage : but it is also to be free, says the same law by inheritance of its mother's freedom. This contradiction proves it to be no law of nature.

But the 36th section of the act will perhaps be cited as entailing the condition of the mother on the child, where it says, that "children shall be bond or free according to the condition of the mother, and the particular direction of this act." Now that the word "bond" in this clause relates to "slaves" only, I am justified in asserting, not only from common parlance, but also from its sense in other parts of this very act. And that on the other hand it considers those who were to be free after a temporary servitude, as described under the word "free." In this very section, 36, it says, "baptism of slaves does not exempt them from bondage." Here then in the very sentence now under consideration, the word bondage is used to express perpetual slavery ; and we cannot conceive they meant to use it in two different senses in the same sentence. So in clause nineteen of the same act, it says, "to prevent that abominable mixture of white men or women with negroes or mulattoes, whatever white man or woman being free, shall intermarry with a negro or mulatto, &c. shall be committed to prison, &c." Now unless the act means to include white servants and apprentices under the denomination of "freemen," then a white servant or apprentice may intermarry with a negro or mulatto. But this is making the act miss of its purpose, which was "to prevent the abominable mixture of white men or women with negroes or mulattoes." But to put it out of dispute, the next clause (twenty) says that "if any minister shall, notwithstanding, presume to marry a white man or woman with a negro or mulatto," he shall incur such a penalty. Here then the prohibition is extended to whites in general, without saying "free whites" as the former clause did. But these two clauses are plainly co-extensive ; and consequently the word "free" in the nineteenth, was intended to include the temporary white servants taken in by the twentieth clause, under the general appellation of "white men or women." So that this act where it speaks of bondmen, means those who are "perpetual slaves," and where of "freemen," those who are to be free after a temporary servitude, as well as those who are so now. Indeed to suppose, where the act says, " the children of a bondwoman shall be bond," that it means " the children of a temporary servant shall be, temporary servants," would infer too much : for it would make temporary servants of the children of white servant women, or of white apprentice women, which yet was never pretended. The conclusion I draw from this, is, that since the temporary service of a white woman does not take from her the appellation of a freewoman, in the sense of this act, and her children under this very clause are free, as being the children of a free woman, neither does the temporary servitude of a mulatto exclude her from the same appellation, and her children also shall be free under this clause, as the children of a free woman. So that the meaning of this clause is, that children shall be slaves, where slavery was the condition of the mother; and free, where freedom either immediate or remote, was her condition : excepting only the instance of the mulatto bastard, which this act makes a servant, though the mother was free. This is the case alluded to by the last words of the clause, "according to the particular direction of this act." Because in this case, the act had made a temporary servant of the child, though the mother was not so.

Then comes the act of 1723, directing that where any female mulatto or Indian, by law obliged to serve till thirty or thirty one, shall have a child during her servitude, such child shall serve the same master to the same age. This act does itself prove that the child was not obliged to serve under the former law of 1705, which had imposed servitude on the mother ; and consequently that the clause "children shall be bond or free, according to the condition of the mother," affected the children of slaves only. For wherefore else was this law made ? If the children of a mulatto held in temporary servitude were to follow the condition of the mother, and be temporary servants under the law of 1705, that of 1723 was wholly unnecessary. But on the contrary, when we find an Assembly within eighteen years after the law of 1705, had been passed, the one half of whom would probably be the same members who had passed that law, when we see these people I say, enacting expressly that the children should be temporary servants, it is a strong proof the makers of the first law had not intended they should be so. *Expositio contemporanea est optima*, is a maxim in our law, because such exposition is supposed to be taken from the makers of the law themselves, who best knew their own intention; and it is doubly conclusive, where the makers themselves pass a new act to testify their intention. So that I hold it certain, the act of 1705, did not extend to the children of the first mulatto, or that of 1723, would not have been made.

That the act of 1723, did not extend to the plaintiff, is apparent from its words. "Where any female mulatto by law obliged to serve till thirty one (that is, the plaintiff's grandmother) shall during the time of her servitude, have a child born of her body (that is, the plaintiff's mother) such a child shall serve till thirty one." This act describes the plaintiff's mother then as the subject on which to operate. The common sense of mankind would surely spare me the trouble of proving the word "child" does not include the grandchild, great-grandchild, great-great-grandchild, &c. *in infinitum*. Or if that would not, the act itself precludes me, by declaring it meant only a "child born of her body." So that as the law of 1705, has made a servant of the first mulatto, that of 1723, extends it to her children.

The act of 1748, is the next in course. At this time all our acts were revised and digested, and sent in one volume to receive his Majesty's approbation. These two laws being found to be on the same subject, were then incorporated without any alteration. This however, could not affect their meaning, which is still to be sought after by considering the component acts in their separate state. At any rate it cannot affect the condition of the plaintiff, who was born in 1742, which was six years before it was made. The same may be said of the law of 1753, which is copied from 1748, with only the addition of some new matter, foreign to the present question. So that on the laws of 1705, and 1723, alone, it is to be determined ; with respect to which I have endeavored to shew ;

That the first of them subjected to servitude, the first mulatto only.

That this did not, under the law of nature, affect the liberty of the children,

Because, under that law we are all born free.

Because, the servitude of the mother was founded on compact, which implies maintenance of her children, so as to have them under no obligation to the master.

And because, this descent of condition from parent to child, would introduce a contradiction where the one parent is free, and the other in servitude.

That as little are they affected by the words of the act, "children shall be bond or free, according to the condition of the mother."

Because that act uses the word "bond," so as to shew it means thereby those only who are perpetual slaves, and by the word "free" those who are entitled to freedom in *praesenti* or in *futuro*; and consequently calling the mother "free," says her children shall be "free."

Because it would make servants of the children of white servants or apprentices, which nobody will say is right.

And because the passing the act of 1723, to subject the child to servitude, shews it was not subject to that state under the old law.

And lastly, that the act of 1723, affects only "children of such mulattoes," as when that law was made were obliged to serve till thirty-one ; which takes in the plaintiff's mother who was of the second generation, but does not extend to himself who is of the third.

So that the position at first laid down is now proven, that the act of 1705, makes servants of the first mulatto, that of 1723, attends it to her children, but that it remains for some future legislature, if any shall be found wicked enough, to extend it to the grandchildren and other issue more remote, to the *"nati natorum et qui nascentur abillis."*

Source

Paul Leicester Ford, comp. and ed., *The Writings of Thomas Jefferson* (New York, G. P. Putnam's Sons, 1892), 1: 373–381.

Glossary

This glossary is an introduction to the references to clothing fashions and local vernacular that appear in the runaway advertisements. Over time and space, spelling varies. The definitions are drawn from several sources: Billy G. Smith and Richard Wotowitcz, *Blacks Who Stole Themselves: Advertisement for Runaways in the Pennsylvania Gazette, 1728–1790*, Philadelphia: University of Pennsylvania Press, 1989, 179–183; Graham Russell Hodges and Alan Edward Brown, *Pretends to Be Press: Runaway Slave Advertisements from Colonial and Revolutionary New York and New Jersey*, New York: Garland Publishing, Inc., 1994, 329–334; Linda Baumgarten, *What Clothes Reveal: The Language of Clothing in Colonial and Federal America*, New Haven: Yale University Press, 2002; and, the *Oxford English Dictionary*.

Baize: A coarse woolen material with a long nap.
Beaver: The fur of the rodent, used generally in making hats. Can also refer to a heavy woolen cloth like beaver fur.
Binding: A protective covering for the raw edges of fabric.
Bodycoat: A dress coat that was worn relatively close to the body.
Brazier: An individual who manufactures and repairs objects in brass.
Brevet: A rank in the army, without the appropriate pay.
Brig: A vessel with two masts square-rigged like a ship's fore- and main-masts, but also carrying a lower fore-and-aft sail with a graff and boom.
Brigantine: A small craft rigged for sailing and rowing, speedier and more maneuverable than larger vessels.
Broadcloth: A fine, plain-woven black cloth used primarily in men's clothing.

Buckskin: Leather made from a buck's skin; may also refer to a thick smooth cotton or woolen cloth.

By trade: A servant who has received training in a particular skill.

Calicoe (calico): A coarse cotton cloth used in a variety of eighteenth-century clothing.

Callimanco: A glazed linen fabric showing a pattern on one side only; described by some writers as a fashionable woolen material with a fine gloss.

Camblet (camlet): Originally an attractive, expensive fabric from the Far East, the name later referred to imitations fashioned from different materials. The raw materials for this cloth ranged from camel hair, silk, and velvet to blends of wool and silk.

Cassimir: A thin, twilled woolen cloth used for making men's clothes. From Kashmir, India.

Castor: The binomial nomenclature for the North American beaver is *Castor canadensis.* Castor referred to a hat made of the fur of this animal or imitating the genuine article. As rabbit fur and other substitutes were employed in hat manufacture, the term *castor* came to be used to distinguish such models from true beaver hats.

Chemise: An undergarment usually made of linen or similar fabric and worn by women.

Chintz: Cotton printed in several colors.

Chitterling: A frill on the breast of a shirt. Such a frill resembled the mesentery which connects the intestine to the abdominal cavity.

Clocks: Expensive stocking were embroidered in this manner on stocking side with silk thread.

Cloth coloured: Of a drab color.

Coating: Any material used to make coats.

Cooper: The manufacturer of barrels, tubs, pails, piggins, and other containers.

Crape: A thin, transparent, gauzelike fabric, plain woven, without any twill, of highly twisted raw silk or other staple, and mechanically embossed, so as to have a crisped or minutely wrinkled surface.

Cravat: Apparel worn around the neck, primarily by males.

Cue (queue): An eighteenth-century hairstyle in which hair hung down behind the head; the hair might be either one's own or a wig.

Damascus: A fabric woven in elaborate patterns of silk, wool, or linen.

Dimity: A fine ribbed cotton fabric made first in Damietta, used throughout the period.

Dowlas: A coarse sort of hefty linen employed in the fabrication of shirts and smocks.

Drugget: Used primarily in work clothes, this woolen stuff might also consist of wool and silk or wool and linen mixtures.

Duck: A strong linen fabric without a twill.

Duffel (duffels): A coarse woolen cloth having a thick nap or frieze; used to produce jackets and coats.

Duroy: A variety of coarse woolen cloth formerly produced in the west of England—but not synonymous with corduroy.

Everlasting: A sturdy woolen material used in clothing, including ladies' shoes.

Fearnothing (fearnought, dreadnought): A heavy woolen material often used during harsh weather abroad vessels at sea as protective outer wear.

Felt: A fabric made of wool and hair.

Ferret: A narrow ribbon or tape of cotton or silk; used mainly for binding, such as buttonholes.

Firkin (freize): A thick and warm woolen cloth in use since the fourteenth-century.

French Negro: A black servant born or raised in either a French colony or among the French.

Frock: A long gown with loose sleeves.

Fustian: A species of cloth, originally made at Fusht on the Nile, used for jackets and doublets as early as the fifteenth-century. It has a warp of linen thread and a weft of thick cotton.

Fuzee: An American variant of fusee, a large-headed match for lighting a fire in the wind.

Gad: A cut on the ear of cattle or a slave as a sign of ownership.

Gaol (sometimes spelled Goal): Variant spelling of jail.

Garlix: A sort of linen fabric originally from Gorlitz, Silesia.

Gelding: A castrated animal, particularly a horse.

Gilt: Usually specified a metal which covered an object and gave the appearance of gold.

Gingham: A kind of cotton or linen cloth, woven of dyed yarn, often in stripes, checks, and other patterns.

Great-coat (greatcoat): A topcoat or large, heavy overcoat worn as added protection from the cold.

Half joe: Slang for a Portuguese coin, the Johannes.

Halfthick: A sort of coarse cloth.

Heckling: The splitting and separating of flax and hemp fibers.

Hempen: Referring to material or cloth made of hemp.

High Dutch: An eighteenth-century term for German.

Hodden: The coarse woolen cloth produced by country weavers on hand looms.

Holland: A linen fabric named after the Netherlands' province of Holland from which it originated.

Homespun: Any cloth made of homespun yarn, also including coarse material of loose weave meant to imitate homemade cloth.

Hostler: An individual attending to horses at an inn; a stableman, a groom.

Hundred: A division of a county in the British-American colonies or provinces of Virginia, Maryland, Delaware, and Pennsylvania, still existing in the state of Delaware, for example Red Lion Hundred.

Instant (Inst.): The current calendar month.

Jockey cap: A cap with a peaked from and round crown, usually decorated with a ribbon around the crown.

Joseph: A lady's riding habit buttoned down the front. When worn open this garment was popularly called a "flying Josie."

Kersey: A coarse woolen cloth, often ribbed, which originated in Yorkshire, England.

Last: Shoemakers used these wooden or metal forms shaped like a human foot to produce and restore shoes for their clients.

Leggins (leggings): A pair of extra out coverings (usually of leather or cloth), used as a protection for the legs in inclement weather, and commonly reaching from the ankle to the knee, but sometimes higher.

Linsey Woolsey (lincey): A coarse woolen stuff first made at Linsey in Suffolk, England and very popular in the colonies.

Logwood: An Indian tree, producing a substance used in dyeing.

Low Dutch: Referred to the Germans along the sea coast and the northern and northwestern flatlands, including the Netherlands and Flanders.

Lugs: Ear lobes; wattles.

Maccaroni: A nickname for a London fop, satirically based on a pretentious craving for the Italian dish. Refers to hair or hats shaped like the noodle.

Manchester velvet: A fine cotton used in making dresses.

Match-cloth: A coarsely woven wool often traded by Europeans to Native Americans.

Matchcoat: A type of robe prominent among Native Americans, initially consisting of fur skins and later of match-cloth.

Molatto (mulatto): The offspring of a Negro and a European. Eighteenth-century Americans freely called any person of mixed blood a mulatto if he or she resembled one.

Mustee: A person of mixed ancestry. Vernacular for molatto.

Nankeen: A sort of cotton material, initially manufactured in Nanking from a yellow variety of cotton.

Nap: Initially describing the projecting fibers found on fabric surfaces, the term subsequently described the purposeful raising of the short fibers on the surface of a textile followed by trimming and smoothing.

Napt: Any surface that has a nap.

Negro Dutch: A dialect composed of Dutch and a variety of African tongues.

Nicanees (niccanee): A kind of piece goods formerly imported from India.

N.B.: The abbreviation for *nota bene*, which means to mark well and pay particular attention to that which follows.

Ozenbrig (oznaburg, oznabrig): A coarse linen made in Hanover and named for a province of that name. The commonest material purchased for slave clothing.

Papaw or popaw: A vernacular term for African captives taken from the Slave Coast, specifically the kingdom of Dahomey.

Pea jacket: A stout, short overcoat of coarse woolen cloth, now commonly worn by sailors.

Penniston: A coarse woolen stuff made in England.

Periwig: An artificial head of hair or part of one; worn formerly by women and then by men as a fashionable headdress.

Pettycoat: A woman or girl's skirted undergarment hanging from the waist or shoulders. Worn universally and made of every sort of material.

Piece of Eight: The Spanish peso of eight *reals*.

Pinchbeck: A piece of cheap jewelry.

Pistoles: Spanish gold coins often used in the specie-poor American colonies. One pistole was equal to slightly more than one Pennsylvania pound during the middle decades of the eighteenth-century.

Plaited hair: Hair that has been braided.

Plush: A cloth comprised of silk, cotton, wool, and other materials, alone or in some combination, with a nap longer and softer than velvet.

Pock-fretten: "Fret" refers to a wearing away or a decayed spot. Thus, "pock-fretten" described the presence of scars resulting from a bout with smallpox.

Pomatum: An unguent used mainly for hair dressing; pomade.

Pothook: A hook over a hearth for hanging a pot.

Pothooks: An iron shackle with protruding prongs.

Prunella: A light-weight stuff used for clergyman's gowns usually a dark color.

Pumps: A shoe with a thin sole and low heel, oftern worn by seamen as part of their shoregoing finery.

Ratteen: A thick, twilled woolen cloth, generally friezed or with a curled nap.

Russet: A twilled woolen stuff like baize, common in the colonies.

Russia duck: A fine, imported bleached linen used for summer clothing.

Saggathy (sagathy): A woolen stuff.

Sartout (surtout): A man's greatcoat or large overcoat.

Sawyer: A worker who cuts logs into structural timbers and boards or firewood.

Schooner: A small, sea-going fore-and-aft rigged vessel, originally with only two masts.

Scutching: The beating of flax stalks necessary to separate the straw in preparation for hackling. Hemp, cotton, and silk were treated in a similar fashion.

Scythe: An agricultural implement for mowing grass or other crops, having a long, thin, curving blade fastened at an angle with the handle and wielded with both hands in a long sweeping stroke.

Serge: A durable twilled woolen cloth, sometimes blended with silk.

Shag: A heavy woolen cloth with a long nap.

Shalloon: A woolen fabric not unlike modern challis and made in Chalons, France.

Shallop (shalloop): 1. A large, heavy boat, fitted with one or more masts and carrying fore-and-aft or lug sails and sometimes furnished with guns; a sloop. 2. A boat propelled by oars or by a sail, for use in shallow waters or as a means of effecting communication between, or landings from, vessels of a large size; a dinghy.

Sheeting: A heavy fabric comprised of cotton or linen, such as is used for bed linen.

Shift: Underclothing made of cotton, linen, or other fabric.

Sloop: 1a. A small, one-masted, fore-and-aft rigged vessel, differing from a cutter in having a jib-stay and standing bowsprit. 1b. A relatively small ship-of-war, carrying guns on the upper deck only. 2. [obs.] A large open boat; a long boat.

Snuff colour: The color of snuff, that is, a brownish color.

Sorrel: Of a bright chestnut color; reddish-brown.

Spanish Negro: A black servant born or raised in either a Spanish colony or among the Spanish.

Squaw: A Native American woman or wife.

Stroud: A coarse blanket cloth. From Stroud, in Gloucestershire, England.

Stuff: Woven material, especially wool, used to manufacture clothing.

Surtout: A man's greatcoat or large overcoat.

Swanskin: A fine, thick, fleece-like fabric; a kind of flannel.

Thickset: A material possessing a close-grained nap.

Thrumb'd: To make or cover with thrums, the unwoven end of a warp-thread, or the whole of such ends, left when the finished web is cut away.

Ticklenburg (ticklenburgs): For Tecklenburg, from a town and county of this name is Westphalia, noted for its manufacture of linen; a kind of coarse linen cloth.

Tow: The short fibers of flax or hemp which are separated from the longer ones through heckling.

Ultimo: The last or previous month.

Waistcoat: An underjacket or a vest.

Waiting-man: One who waited or attended on an employer or official; a personal servant.

Watch-coat: A stout coat or cloak worn in inclement weather.

Wen: A lump or protuberance of the body; a knot, bunch, wart.

Wherry: 1. A light rowing boat used chiefly on rivers to carry passengers and goods. 2. A large boat of the barge kind.

Whitney: A heavy coarse stuff used for coats, cloaks, and petticoats.

Subject Index

Name Index

About the Author

Antonio T. Bly is assistant professor of history at Appalachian State University in Boone, North Carolina. He received his Ph.D. from the College of William and Mary. His research explores the interplay between African American Studies and the history of the book in America. Currently, he is working on a study about African American culture and resistance in colonial New England.